Energy and
Environmental Balance

Pergamon Policy Studies on Energy and Environment

Cappon   Health and the Environment
Constans   Marine Sources of Energy
De Volpi   Proliferation, Plutonium and Policy
Goodman & Love   Biomass Energy Projects
Goodman & Love   Geothermal Energy Projects
King, Cleveland & Streatfield   Bioresources for Development

Related Titles

Barney   The Global 2000 Report to the President of the U.S.
Fazzolare & Smith   Changing Energy Use Futures
McVeigh   Sun Power
Myers   The Sinking Ark
Starr & Ritterbush   Science, Technology and the Human Prospect
Taylor & Yokell   Yellowcake
*United Nations Centre for Natural Resources, Energy and
    Transport*   State Petroleum Enterprises in Developing Countries

PERGAMON POLICY STUDIES ON ENERGY AND ENVIRONMENT

Energy and Environmental Balance

Earl Finbar Murphy

Pergamon Press
NEW YORK • OXFORD • TORONTO • SYDNEY • FRANKFURT • PARIS

333.7
M97e

Pergamon Press Offices:

U.S.A.   Pergamon Press Inc., Maxwell House, Fairview Park, Elmsford, New York 10523, U.S.A.

U.K.   Pergamon Press Ltd., Headington Hill Hall, Oxford OX3 0BW, England

CANADA   Pergamon of Canada Ltd., 150 Consumers Road, Willowdale, Ontario M2J 1P9, Canada

AUSTRALIA   Pergamon Press (Aust) Pty. Ltd., P.O. Box 544, Potts Point, NSW 2011, Australia

FRANCE   Pergamon Press SARL, 24 rue des Ecoles, 75240 Paris, Cedex 05, France

FEDERAL REPUBLIC   Pergamon Press GmbH, 6242 Kronberg/Taunus,
OF GERMANY   Pferdstrasse 1, Federal Republic of Germany

Library of Congress Cataloging in Publication Data

Murphy, Earl Finbar, 1928-
  Energy and environmental balance.

  (Pergamon policy studies)
  Includes bibliographical references and index.
  1. Energy consumption. 2. Energy policy.
3. Environmental policy. I. Title.
HD9502.A2M87   301.31   79-22202
ISBN 0-08-025082-3

Printed in the United States of America

Contents

Acknowledgments   vii

Chapter

1   THE COMPETITION BETWEEN ENERGY AND
     ENVIRONMENTAL DEMAND   1

2   THE SOCIAL ORIGINS OF ENERGY DEMAND   17

3   URBAN-INDUSTRIAL RESPONSES TO HIGH-
     ENERGY DEMAND   35

4   THE ENVIRONMENTAL COST OF MODERN
     URBAN GROWTH   56

5   URBAN INSTABILITY AND ENVIRONMENTAL
     BALANCE   73

6   HIGH-ENERGY, URBAN SPRAWL, AND THE
     LAND ENVIRONMENT   91

7   GOVERNMENT'S RESPONSIBILITY FOR THE
     LAND ENVIRONMENT   108

8   CHANGING ENVIRONMENTAL VIEWS UNDER
     HIGH ENERGY GROWTH   130

9   THE INSEPARABILITY OF ENERGY AND
     ENVIRONMENTAL DECISIONS   152

10   INTEGRATING FUTURE ENERGY AND
     ENVIRONMENTAL ACTIONS   175

vi   CONTENTS

Notes   203

Index   273

About the Author   281

Acknowledgments

When the creation of a work takes years, the author owes debts to many. I am grateful to the late Dr. Samuel Polsky, co-director, Institute of Law and the Health Sciences, Temple University, and the late Dr. C.A. Doxiadis and the Athens Center of Ekistics. At the Ohio State University, I have had the rare privilege of teaching both in the School of Natural Resources, College of Agriculture, and the School of Architecture, College of Engineering, as well as at my regular post in the College of Law. I must thank the staffs of the libraries at the Ohio State University, most particularly the staff of the Law Library at the Ohio State University. I could not have produced this book without the assistance of the typing and reproduction staff at the Ohio State University College of Law.

During the decade of the 1970s, I have had the enriching experience of being a member of the American Bar Association's Special Committees on Environmental Law and Energy Law and the Advisory Committee on Industrial Siting. Working with the members and staffs, and on the projects, of these committees has instructed me, as also has my membership on the Executive Council of the World Society for Ekistics. I have learned a great deal from the operation of state government in Ohio both as chairman of the Ohio Environmental Board of Review and as a participant at meetings sponsored by various state departments, most especially the Ohio Department of Natural Resources.

And, finally, I thank my wife, Joanne Wharton Murphy, whose help has been essential, and dedicate this book to her.

1
The Competition Between Energy and Environmental Demand

THE PERMANENT NEED FOR MAKING HARD CHOICES

The issues of energy supply, growth demand, environmental response, capital and labor availability, inflation, and the equity of public welfare are growing in their urgencies throughout the world. All these problems can be dealt with by way of the political and economic processes to various degrees. Priorities can be reassigned. Demands can be cut back. Greater reliance upon labor can produce an alternative so that less reliance will be made on traditional investment capital, now lamentably described as being in "short" supply.(1) What cannot be done in any of these situations is the previously easy way of open-ended growth for every demand presented.

Experience with recurring oil crises has offered evidence that very little in the economy is price resistant. This does not mean that matters must be turned over to the market's disposal or to the consumer of goods and services who casts a ballot in the form of a purchase-price paid. Even were a pure market management system for society opted for, the act of making the market-favorable decision would be political. Vastly significant political changes would be required in order to create a structure within which such market-determinable decisions could be made.

It is doubtful that the twentieth century will witness this kind of dramatic change. Other practices have become increasingly established since the end of the nineteenth century in the movement away from reliance on the market. Law and politics have become too significant in reaching decisions on the allocation of resources, finances, and energy to be easily abandoned. Law and politics are affected by the market. Some of their powers could be delegated to the market. Nevertheless, law and politics are not going to be subordinated to the authority of the market in determining priorities.

Thus hard choices about competing demands must be made in the remainder of this century. Neither environmental activists nor those concerned with energy conservation are confused about the hard choices awaiting them. But they want all competitors for resources, capital, and energy to understand that the harshness of such choices is not to be borne only by those wanting conservation for environmental renewability and in energy conversion.(2)

Those who believe environmental renewability is threatened by the demands for rising energy conversion, growth in materials' exploitation, and the sprawl of urban usage over space cannot ignore the current and developing condition of the renewing environment. They insist that human society cannot survive without the existence of viable systems for renewability within the environment. Harmony is very desirable, they agree, between humanity and nature, although harmony cannot be purchased at the expense of nature's capacity to renew air, water, and the biomass for the sake of growth.

From the beginning, urban-industrial demand was cast as open-ended, undifferentiated, and without boundaries for whatever achievements were to be sought. As human numbers and human expectations have alike expanded, the finite character of the renewing environment has come to the fore.

Long before demand has exhausted the raw materials needed for energy conversion or industrial production, such demand will surpass the ability of air, water, and the biomass to serve as sinks for heat, toxic substances, and other matters. This limitation in nature will continue in an accelerating crisis through the rest of this century until either a crisis climax or a humanly arranged resolution has been reached. More than capital shortage, more than the inadequacy of energy supply, nature is growth's ultimate limit.

The competitive crunch for capital and the escalating price for fossil fuels result directly from the inescapable fact that nothing taken from nature is free, whatever its immediate profitability on cash flow charts. Economics and technology may claim that extracted materials were free in their inchoate and unsevered states, or that receiving bodies are able to freely take on wastes. But in terms of nature's finiteness in nonrenewable resources and the limitations that prevail in the operation of life-support systems, no such freedom exists. When urban-industrial demand is imposed upon the renewing environment, the costs come high – first, to nature in the ecological sense; second, in terms of cash costs to society itself.(3)

Conceivably existing social forms will produce behavioral changes which will permit an indefinitely long relationship between demand and the renewing environment.(4) This automatically peaceable future does not appear to be in prospect. Existing social forms can alleviate environmental and energy crises. Yet the intensification in demand traditionally made upon the renewing environment is continuing. Whatever ultimate happiness may lie concealed in events, the current scene points to a worsening of the world's environmental conditions.

The rising demands of urban industrial society, the capital inadequacies present within society to accommodate all demands, and the growing inability of the renewing environment to maintain its systems under these burdens make this clear. The renewing environment requires assistance from those who impose their demands and simultaneously complain of higher prices, capital shortfall, and energy shortages. Growth in energy supplies and affluence can come only within the renewable limits of the environment. To all but the insatiable, the limits remain wide relative to urban-industrial demand.

THE HISTORIC COMMITMENT OF URBAN-INDUSTRIAL SOCIETY

During the eighteenth century in northwestern Europe, societal attitudes toward energy and production changed. As a result, basic social structure correspondingly changed. Urban life and industrial activity had begun their rise to dominance: urban-industrial society had been formed.

The new form of society emphasized the growth of the city, the processing of all that was transmutable into commodities for trade, and the dominance of science and technology in accomplishing the most routine social functions. The impact upon the renewing environment was massive. Nature became another resource for satisfying the demands of an urban-industrial society whose foresight could perceive no limit – nor any need for a limit – to growth.

The impact of pre-industrial demand structures was slight compared to the impact of urban-industrial demand to the environment in the last two hundred years. This change alone has rendered obsolete much experience accumulated under earlier social forms. The impact upon the renewing environment of a high-energy demand structure has proven most unlike the effect of social forms which either were low in energy conversion or in demand for the production of goods and the provision of services.

The extent and the depth of the difference in impact was slowly realized. Discarding past experience as no longer relevant to changed conditions is culturally difficult. Even revolutionary upheavals in urban-industrial society have not always illuminated the absolute difference this society bears to its traditional predecessors.

At the end of the eighteenth century, for example, social theorists were still invoking classical Greece and Rome as models capable of imitation in the future. The American Revolution had occurred and the French Revolution was in full swing, yet these political events had not clarified the situation for theorists and observers. Although the Industrial Revolution had been in process for at least a couple of generations, few could see that it had made Greece and Rome incompatible societal models for the oncoming nineteenth century.

One contemporary critic, however, did grasp the change the Industrial Revolution introduced – a change that separated the past from the future like a chasm opening in a plain. This observer, the Abbe Sieyes, a wily politician whose superior ability to perceive social change may have contributed to his survival, declared to the Estates-General on September 7, 1789:

> Modern European peoples resemble ancient people very little. The foremost question for us is one of commerce, agriculture, manufacture etc. The desire for wealth has turned all the states of Europe into a vast workship; and they dream of little more than production and consumption as constituting happiness. Also, today's political systems are based exclusively upon work; the productive faculties of men are everything. . .(5)

This solitary declaration exposed the inadequacy of the opposing conventional view. As Jean Jaures, the historian of the French Revolution, was to note early in the twentieth century, the Abbe Sieyes was the only philosopher of the Enlightenment who understood the power of surgent industrialism.(6) That power had already made the previously independent sectors of traditional society obsolete. Traditional social forms could only be overwhelmed when the new industrial system imposed its demands for production and consumption.

Social institutions offer a seeming stability of form which fosters the belief that all goes on as it did before. The ideas, demands, and functions composing urban-industrial society have been no exception to this belief. Despite the rushing change thereby introduced and despite the fragmentation of both traditional society and the renewing environment under the impact, the belief remains that urban-industrial society is merely an extension of the social forms preceding the Industrial Revolution. The Abbe Sieyes insight fully noted that such was not the case.

The Industrial Revolution had not merely increased both the supply and the demand for energy. Important as it was to have moved northwestern Europe into a high-energy situation by the introduction of steam motive-power, the shifting of values was to be far more influential on future events. As Abbe Sieyes observed, production and consumption became the dominant operative factor. Consequently a judgmental test for society itself was created whose measure for success or failure lay in the growth or decline of production and consumption. Thereafter people existed solely as producers and consumers, not because they had inherent value in themselves. Demands upon nature as a source of raw materials and energy, as well as a sink for wastes, accelerated in quantity and intensified in their qualitative impact.

Abbe Sieyes chose the word jouissance to describe "happiness" under these changed conditions, a term in law that could mean "interest payable." Under the conditions of rising urban-industrial demand and capital generation, this was of far more significance than a definition of mere unallocated delight. Happiness in the future began to have an inherent cash-and-carry quality.

Abbe Sieyes was concerned with the long-range effect this shift in values would have on human society and traditional morality. His concern was valid. So far, the shift in values has fragmented nature and processed everything into an homogenized production and consumption system. The refusal to recognize the seriousness of the situation by large sectors of the social leadership today is comparable to the conduct of the contemporaries of the Abbe Sieyes, who clung to Greece and Rome for their ideas.(7)

Whether widely noted, the shift in values had occurred before the eighteenth century closed. People had become units primarily for production and consumption. When the great political upheavals of the twentieth century broke out, it was not to Greece and Rome that their leaders turned for ideas. By then, the demands of urban-industrial society had become too well accepted. It was the vestiges of traditional society which had to be cleared away to allow those demands to be better serviced. Nothing in nature was allowed to block the meeting of these expectations.

Society had made its now historic commitment to growth. At no time since the late eighteenth century has any level of energy conversion been seen as more than a transitory stage to another greater surge in the supply of energy. No limits have been set for urban expansion, the exploitation of materials, the accumulation of capital, or the consumption of goods and services.

As the Abbe Sieyes foresaw, no one desires to give up on the promises of open-ended growth. And perhaps in theory that is a "democratic" right. Yet society cannot continue using nature as a free good to supply commodities and as a sink for wastes. Harm to nature will no longer be a cost which can be foregone in the satisfaction of rising urban-industrial demand.(8)

FRAGMENTATION AS PREPARATION FOR URBAN-INDUSTRIAL GROWTH

After more than two centuries of growth, urban-industrial demand promises to massively increase the burdens on nature before the end of this century. In the words of George Simmel, self-interest is the urban-industrial system's only objective measurable achievement. All elements within the system are thereby reckoned as mere numbers whose elements are indifferent in themselves.(9) Such rationality has had a profoundly fragmentizing effect upon systemic relationships.

But this fragmentation was necessary to stimulate growth. In order to measure items of interest, it has been easiest to isolate them from their surroundings. The emphasis upon production and consumption has broken up existing social and biological unities, thus isolating them from their environment.

And demands must be imposed to sustain urban-industrial society and those aspiring to make their societies a part of it. Both production and consumption must increase. Neither social forms nor natural relationships are immune to the demands to produce and consume. All obstacles to continued growth have been swept aside. Raw materials are needed as resources. Air, water, and the biomass are needed to receive wastes. In order to fulfill these needs, all the elements have been isolated from such larger unities as the biosphere and the hydrologic cycle.

Thus fragmentation is an essential preliminary to processing nature into and through an economy which emphasizes how fast and how large production and consumption can grow. Resistant unities have been blended into artificial units. These units acquire their identity and values exclusively in terms of production and consumption rather than through any relationships present in nature. The universe has been reformed to meet infinitely expanding growth demands.

The ability of the life-support systems in nature to withstand such reformation may prove most defeating to the longevity of a social system engaged in processing what is renewable within the environment. The evidence is accumulating that such an ability is lacking. The systems for environmental renewability ultimately cannot withstand a process that fragments and homogenizes their established relationships into units measurable by a rationality that is indifferent to the consequences within those long-existing relationships.(10)

Among the demands urban-industrial society has imposed upon the renewing environment are those for rising energy supplies. It has been a comprehensive, infinitely expansive demand not previously known. The result is a widespread, usually unstated and unchallenged assumption that there must always be energy abundantly available, regardless of the effect upon the environment's capacity for self-renewal.

When steam power was almost choked off at inception by the consumption of the forests, the recourse was to coal. Coal's combustible properties had been known in western Europe since the ninth century A.D., but the heat it could then give was insignificant compared to what it could produce in the age of steam. When the use of steam power threatened the growth of urban-industrial demand, because of the impaction resulting from steam-power's need to concentrate energy sources and usages alike, freedom for more growth was found in the internal combustion engine fired by refined oil. The whole countryside of urban-industrial society was thereby opened up to urban sprawl and industrial expansion. And now that energy growth is threatened by possible limitations in all fossil fuels, society appears ready to risk nuclear power as an important source of future energy growth.

Energy growth seems fundamental to society today. The ambition to command energy cascades to meet any possible human demand is worldwide. There appear few dreams for the future that do not include enough energy to meet the most transient human whim. Modern Utopias, other than a handful opting for deliberately low-level energy demand as their cultural base, assume an almost infinite energy budget.

But one can assert that the proposed Utopias are no more extravagant than the existing energy calls of society. In the history of life, homo faber the high energy user is of relative insignificance. But in that brief interval, the drafts on the energy stores have been huge. The drafts in the twentieth century in comparison with all other centuries particularly have been of massive proportions. The anticipated energy drafts in the near future are projected to be greater still.

Is such increase in available energy necessary to sustain the quality of life that urban-industrial society has come to expect? Many say no,(11) but this is still not the dominant opinion. The common expectation for the twenty-first century and beyond can scarcely find the language to describe future energy drafts.

In addition to abundance, a growth-insistent society wants energy supplied cheaply relative to other economic costs. Indeed, what has often delayed the acceptance of a new means of energy supply has been that it initially appeared more expensive than energy conversion processes already used. When proposed new means of supplying energy show themselves capable of providing energy more cheaply than previously employed methods, general acceptance has been won. Once the determination of cheapness and, hence, abundance is reached, there is indifference to the effects the new method may impose upon nature or the costs that may be diverted from human budgets to the systemic operation of the renewing environment.(12)

One can argue cogently that all societies demand cheap energy and, resultantly, also demand the social structures that produced such culturally defined "cheap energy." On a per capita basis, the use of energy in sixteenth-century Europe was enormous. And most of that energy went up the chimney in a wasteful technology for heating and cooking that sustained the contemporary quality of life.

Sixteenth-century Europeans worried little about energy or its sources, leaving such concerns to their eighteenth century successors at the beginning of the Industrial Revolution. And what makes concern over energy in the late twentieth century still more acute? It is the relatively greater consequence of a demand that enormously increases the conversion of energy and the release of its unwanted by-products in a brief historic span.

A multitude of relationships exist in nature. High demand for energy conversion breaks up these relationships into discrete and often unsustainable fragments. Sadly, this breaking up of natural relationships in the renewing environment is an incidental side-effect of purposes ever more unconcerned with nature.

The giant oil tankers, for example, are used to cheaply deliver a fuel essential to an economy that oil helped create. Only a brief span of days must be spent by these mammouth vessels in the stormy waters off the tip of South Africa. The economies of the voyage, therefore, insist upon a cheap construction that refuses to account for the perils inherent in that brief portion of the trip. Instead, the ships are built for the smoother seas in which they spend so much more time. This allows for a cheaper price for the delivered oil and most of the ships successfully make it. Those who do not, however, find their graves in the water off Africa's southern cape.

The tragedy to nature lies in the fact that these waters are among the most important for sustaining what riches the oceans possess. The damage to the marine world is simply peripheral to the urban-industrial interest – so peripheral that little is being done to correct the situation. Nature's relationships are disregarded or broken up for a cheaper energy source.(13)

Ignoring these natural relationships has immediate payoffs in return on capital investment. Most managers of economic enterprises or political institutions prefer not to absorb the costs of avoiding or redressing harm to the renewing environment. It seems simpler to pass the costs on to nature and to treat items drawn from nature as if they were parts rolling down an assembly line. As acts of simplification, these do achieve a certain success. All traditional modes of life, because of that success, have been replaced with new relationships capable of changing the expectations of humanity.(14)

This success has its price, however. The price has been the fragmentation of too much of the renewing environment needed for replenishing resources vital for the planet's life-support systems. A major redress in behavior is now required in the urban-industrial demand structure that may find it impossible to change its fragmenting conduct. If that should prove true, then the consequences of such inability will have to be faced: either a continuing harm to nature until nature loses all sufficient renewability, or investing to counteract the harm economic demands impose.

In a high demand, high-energy society, the options are as stark as these. Either change the demands or assume their costs – or watch society and the renewing environment together come to human catastrophe. But then, as claimed by the economist Joseph Schumpeter, does not every society actually plan for its own general liquidation?(15) If so, catastrophe will be hard to avoid for our society, too.

THE BURDEN OF HIGH-ENERGY DEMAND IN A FRAGMENTED ENVIRONMENT

None would deny that steam power furthered the Industrial Revolution and that the gasoline engine in the private car opened up the growth of cities so that they could spread over the land. But if changes other than these had not been wrought, human consciousness might still be able to ignore the impact of higher energy demands upon nature. These changes were not, however, the only ones.

Energy cascades are now routinely part of all future planning. Even large industrial nations are calm about the planned expansion of their energy supplies by hundreds of percent over the rest of this century. The technology to make such growth possible is present and every effort is being made to achieve energy conversions at that projected pace.(16) And yet where is the reflection upon the ability of the renewing environment to encompass such growth?

The supply, the flow, and the return of energy are part of a continuing process in nature. This is most evident for biological energy. Life forms draw energy from other levels of the life system in the form of calories, expend these calories on their own life needs, and return that energy to the system at the end of the life cycle. In the paleolithic past, much of this living energy became fossilized in the form of coal, oil, and gas. Without human intervention, this energy was no longer part of the biocycle. The same is true for the energy contained within the various elements. This energy did not affect life activity until science released it through splitting atoms. It is energy which would not be converted except for human intervention.(17)

The active energy cycle affecting life systems has in the past two centuries – most particularly within the present century – gone through enormous increases. Energy conversion, with which life forms traditionally had to cope, was suddenly increased by the burning of the paleolithic wealth of coal, oil, and gas and by the employment of radioactive fission. Never before had the increase in energy levels happened so briefly, or brought forth such a surge of newly available energy, or emitted so many and so complex by-products. These last were by-products called waste only in terms of the processes emitting them. But to natural systems, these wastes either had to become an integral part of natural systems, or had to be their destroyers.

Unlike nature, humanity does not operate on a unified energy budget. Society does not regard its energy demands, its output of energy, and its disposal of energy by-products as part of a single, interlocked system. The demand for energy in modern high-energy cultures has an autonomous quality about it, as if meeting that demand can be done without regard for either where the raw materials for energy conversion originate, or where the unused portions of those materials will go. What is not used is merely waste. And as waste, this is seen as without value, to be dumped heedlessly into the sink of nature.

Total energy budgets in urban-industrial society have been infrequently tried and, when tried, have been unsuccessful.(18) In temperate zones, great sums are expended to generate heat. Simultaneously in other energy activities, heat is a waste product to be dissipated at great expense. To bring the two needs together, where each would relieve the other, is not easy because of the seasonal fluctuations in head needs. Also, when the two are kept as separate operations, each seems cheaper. But in nature they are not independent of each other. However convenient for human technology and economics it may be to keep them segregated, in the larger world of natural relationships they are brought together – and the renewing environment absorbs the costs.

This continued separate treatment of different parts of the energy system is reinforced by the manner in which the environmental aspects of energy conversion have been handled. Protection of the renewing environment has too rarely meant considering changing methods of production or altering the patterns of energy demand. Instead, environmental problems have been handled as if they constituted a separate industry unrelated to the processes that created them. Whole new technologies have been precipitated whose justification lies in getting rid of something – such as heat – which in a unified energy approach would not be a waste product.(19)

This is not peculiar to energy conversion in urban-industrial society. But because high energy demand is so important, the fragmented treatment of the energy budget generates crises as well as power. An across-the-board threat either to energy growth, or energy prices capable of being accommodated within the consumption patterns, or the maintenance of a stable energy supply leads to chaos in the high-energy demand structure. But nearly as threatening is the need to quickly absorb all the costs imposed upon nature by the acceleration in energy conversion.

There is little likelihood that urban-industrial demand can create serendipitously a unified energy budget.(20) But the relation between energy conversion and its environment can be regarded as an interconnected spectrum, rather than as a series of unrelated boxes. The fragmenting of the energy budget and the environment are parts of the same process. This system, which has spread over the globe since the beginning of the Industrial Revolution, breaks natural unities into discrete units valuable to the newly developing economy, regardless of their worth in the larger scheme of an environment capable of self-renewal.

To go against this conventional patterning, and to seek unifying ways of coping with the urban-industrial impact upon natural systems, has been most uncommon. Energy conversion still soars on a worldwide basis. Urban sprawl continues. The exploitation of resources within the renewing environment maintains its attitude of indifference to nature's ability to sustain it.

But the duty to make changes in this system presses stronger than ever. When serious people insist that reliance upon OPEC oil will produce a declining dollar, that neither natural gas nor nuclear power will permit much increase in energy conversion, that ever intensive exploration will provide no more than five million daily barrels of domestic American oil by the late 1980s, and still insist that the real energy crunch will not occur until the century's end, some effort at a change in energy patterns impends.(21) Otherwise, the totality may suddenly become far less than the sum of its parts, for the element of viability will have been deducted.

ENERGY DEMAND AND URBAN GROWTH

Since the end of the eighteenth century, the increase in energy supply has perhaps had its greatest social and environmental effect in the size and manner of urban growth. In turn, the city which developed reacted upon the growth in energy demand so as to strengthen the open-ended and undifferentiated aspects of energy growth. Initially the Industrial Revolution called into being numerous new towns, the famed "black cities" of coal smoke, tenements, and burgeoning capital formation. Because of the power source – the steam engine or the water wheel – these were compacted cities, with high levels of population concentration and close construction. With the coming of the gasoline engine for the car and electricity for transmission lines, city growth in this century has been of a very different sort from either the traditional city of pre-industrial times or the city dependent upon steam power.

Part of the reason why such a high energy demand current exists is the kind of urban growth that has been intensifying throughout the present century. The nominative term best suited to describe the contemporary situation is the combination of the two words "urban" and "industrial." The operations and actions summed up in the term "urban-industrial" include the accelerating demand, the high-energy levels and, ultimately, the never-faltering growth in energy cascades.   Taken together, all this has become the fundament for the future social organization and exploitation of nature.

Urban growth has progressed so far from historical examples that the word "city" is now obsolete. Words like megalopolis, conurbation, slurb, and metropolitan district have been invented to name the urban developments best identified from aerial photographs. Even this effort cannot tell the whole story of how the urban mode has engulfed society and most of nature. But what is urban is not merely a matter of gridiron streets and localized population densities. There simply is more to the current omnipresence in nature of urban demands than the spreading of a slurb through what were rural woods and fields.(22)

The urban mode in a high-energy situation imposes costs upon the environment because of the demands to process everything in nature into the service of urban growth. Indeed, these demands are commonly called "needs" or "requirements"; and, while a rigorous person could insist such terms are false, the conditions for the continuance of the urban mode as it now exists set the limits of discourse. For such a mode of existence, high demands for growth truly are needs.(23)

The present urban mode reaches into areas not covered by urban structures. It determines the dependence of the relatively open exurban areas upon such energy dependent supplies as fertilizers and motor-driven agricultural machinery. It exposes the wilderness and raw regions to the high-energy demands of a recreation industry. The most seemingly remote corners have carried to them the demand for growth in energy and the processing of the renewing environment.(24)

Urban growth, in this respect, is becoming more like a computer model and less like the biological relationships in nature. The identification of separate purposes has become more significant than finding any commonality they may possess. Humanity and the renewing environment are both open systems. But in an open-ended demand structure, there are more seeming advantages in their artificial unitization than in stressing their unities. It should not be surprising if nature soon reacts in humanly disadvantageous ways.(25)

The seeming advantage of fragmented urban growth is that it conceals the general costs it imposes. In so doing, it makes certain segregated units successful while dooming others to what appears to be a self-selected failure. An appearance results in which events apparently operate according to externally ordained rules determinative of success or failure for each segregated unit. Those who think the market produces these results automatically also believe the results to be the inevitable consequence of the way "ballots" are cast through acquiring or spending money.

Nothing is automatic, however, about what is happening. The process is indeed external to the conditions of these segregated units. Individually, these units lack control over their own abilities to attain success or fend off failure as these terms are defined by the urban-industrial demand structure. The process, though, is not exotic to that demand structure nor imposed upon an unwilling society.(26)

Most people today live in the artificial environment of urban sprawl. For them, nature is an abstract and remote concept not felt as part of an immediate experience.(27) As the urban sprawl engulfs previously rural areas, this reinforces the remoteness and sense of abstraction nature holds for urban people. The segregation conceals from the urban residents the highly arbitrary test of what constitutes success or failure in the modern megalopolis.

In consequence, as the cities have exploded, it seems obvious that the slurbs are the place for wise fiscal investment while the inner city is not. The urban edges have seemed free of pollution while the congested avenues of expansion have not. And the result has been the conferring of surrogate wisdom upon an allegedly "free-market" in cash and ideas. But, in truth, has it ever been a "free" market on the issue of urban sprawl?

What accounts for all the apparent automatic successes? Government subsidies through tax breaks and mortgage. Subsidized highway construction and the supply of city services to thinly populated urban verges. Cheap energy rates for decades for electricity and natural gas and the regulation of the prices for many petroleum products. Each of these has been part of the governmental contribution to urban sprawl. None is easy for government to give up, as the reaction to President Carter's relatively modest oil deregulation program in 1979 revealed.

And in the presence of so many apparently automatic successes, why have the equally self-evident, automatic failures occurred? Why have there occurred in the United States the bankruptcy of mass transit, the dependence of the economy on increasingly remote energy sources, the decay of the inner city, the strain upon local government with its ever-enlarging responsibilities and its failure to expand fiscal resources to discharge them? Certainly government has played a large role in accomplishing many of these negative results. Steadily, as the segregated successes and failures have been accumulated under conditions of fragmented urban growth, the benefits have been siphoned off onto individuals, small groups, or local titles. And the costs have been left to nature or the general fund to handle.(28)

Now the social costs, once concealed by the fragmented character of urban growth, are being widely revealed. The segregated city, which first imposed social costs and then hid them for so long, is now a barrier for any mobilization to unifying action. Once revealed, the costs of fragmentation can no longer be shuffled off upon receiving bodies in the land, air, water or the biomass. Both benefits and costs must be brought into a relationship that is evident to the urban-industrial demand structure as well as to unthinking ecosystems.

Among the first victims of the undifferentiated impact of growth in energy conversion and urban expansion has been urban government itself. This has been especially true in democratic societies where urban government has stood in the frontline, receiving the blows of demand for growth and of the renewing environment's inability to viably respond to that demand. The failure of urban government, therefore, has been of the greatest importance to those who care about the impact of energy and urban-industrialized growth upon the renewing environment.(29)

The increase in energy demand and the expansion of urban forms over the landscape have changed the operations of renewing environmental systems. All the current indicators point in the direction of an enormous worldwide increase of both kinds of growth. The renewing environment can only receive still greater impact from them and exhibit further deterioration in its ability to be renewed.

Neither law, nor government, nor market operations can continue to intensify either this impact or the inability to respond in nature. What has been developing since the advent of the Industrial Revolution must now be reversed. And the time to act is now.

URBAN-INDUSTRIAL GROWTH AND THE LAND RESOURCE

Nature reacts to humanity's deliberately autistic demands with an interrelated reaction productive of all sorts of surprises. Just to view the notoriously fragmenting way urban growth has used — and continues to use — open land shows the source of these surprises. Neither the market nor government has acted as if these events concerned their functions.

Instead, they have furthered ribbon development and all the enthusiastic paving programs that have converted green fields into parking lots, highways, and drainage aprons. Trifling heed has been paid to how runoff would be thereby accelerated, how pollutants coming from storm-water drainage would be increased, and how the recharge of water tables would be cut off. The power of green cover to absorb air pollution has been exchanged for non-absorbent concrete. The renewing environment on the land has been treated as discrete items that could be segregated for individuated profit without a chance at unhappy consequences.(30)

Those elements in the landscape which urban-industrial society takes for granted are actually at the center of ecosystemic activity. The rivers, the drainage basins, the forest systems, the air sheds are the central structures of the renewing environment, and relate to each other in a larger natural unity. They do not react well to fragmentation caused by political jurisdictions or the growth demandant society. The land resource is treated in this way only at the greatest peril.(31)

Across the land, run-off water flows to replenish streams and to recharge aquifers. The land creates baffles that strain the pollutants produced both by nature and human activity from streams and aquifers. On the land much of the biomass exists. It is contained in both the soil and the ground cover, and absorbs the waste of other systems, recycling it as the resource of renewing systems. Out of the land resource, artisans can create landscape, scenery, the imagery of recreating nature according to human terms. There can be a remodelling of the land by humanity that would be endless in time and infinite in choices.(32)

There are many such possibilities for using the land resource to satisfy demand – if there is a fundamental realization that land is not in infinite supply and that the natural systems relating to it are far more important than the human demand for their fragmentation. Some means must be found for providing unified responses to demands with full understanding of their fragmenting impact.

Whatever human devices are used, none alone will assist the renewing environment. Each will require the social decision to direct urban growth in relation to the consumption of the land resource. The amount of energy to be converted will have to be determined, as well as how much open space is to be covered with construction and what the pace of population relocation will be. The facilities to handle the by-products of demand cannot be treated as afterthoughts, much less totally neglected as is now so often the case.(33)

The relationship between demand and the land resource up to this point has been one of infinite expansion of demand and the increasingly limited characteristics of the land. Denying the interconnectedness of all the natural systems composing the land resource has guaranteed the most serious consequences to the forces of environmental renewability. Society has preferred to resort to high-energy acquisitions and manipu-lations in order to veil any recognition of this interconnectedness. Instead, society has hoped that accumulating energy cascades could support the modern dedication to permanent growth in production and consumption.(34) The result has been a wasting and spoilage of the land resource that is almost irremediable.

It would be pleasant to predict that improvement will come when the demand upon the land resource is reduced. That is most unlikely. Society shows every indication on a world scale of desiring to continue urban expansion, materials exploitation, increasing energy conversion, and enlarging both production and consumption. Moderating demands will not likely create a balance.

What is more likely will be an attempt to induce an increase in the renewing environment's capacity to respond to these demands. This will mean actions in addition to slowing down the processing and consump-tion of the land resource. Once a significant portion of the resources of urban-industrial society have been assigned to conserve renewing systems, the fragmenting of nature that has occurred over the past two centuries will moderate instead of continuing to intensify.(35) Once institutionalized in government bureaucracy, private corporation, and the operations of politics and the marketplace, the self-renewing aspects of the land resource will require support. And the investments in this support will have to be large.(36)

But once a unified consideration is given to urban-industrial demand, the impact of that demand upon the land resource, and the cost of preventing that demand from further impairing the capacity for renewal of the environment, the costs will provide a conduit for regenerating the life-sustaining forces which until now have been merely fragmented and shortsightedly exploited.(37) And when all this has been done, then perhaps there will be a balance between the demands for growth and the ability of nature to respond to that demand.

URBAN-INDUSTRIAL VALUES AND THE RENEWING ENVIRONMENT

Human action has the capacity to interfere with even such cosmic natural systems as the major phases of the hydrologic cycle. But the supreme fact humanity must remember, despite this power, is that renewing systems are continuously seeking homeostasis. Whatever the catastrophes involved, there will be a final balance. It may mean the system will operate for ends quite different than those previously served. It may mean that human institutions dependent upon a different systemic operation will perish. It may even mean that the final balance will have the appearance of death to a human observer. But, cosmically, systems will balance; and urban-industrial society, however inconvenient it may find this to be, must accept such a tendency in nature.(38)

Where humanity looms largest in nature, consequently, is precisely the point where nature is necessary for both human survival and the flourishing of human culture. But if the biologic consequence to humanity from nature seems remote, they ignore what occurs in nature's systems. The relationship to nature of human technology may be perceived cognitively; but even when perceived, there seems little immediate incentive to treat the life-support systems in nature with other than cavalier disregard.(39)

The renewing systems, which are part of life or needed for the support of life, are the most vulnerable to human intervention. Even though the larger universe would outlast the extinction of life-support systems in nature, thereby asserting what was truly independent in nature from the effect of human action, the parts most necessary to support humanity and culture can be fatally affected through the demands imposed by urban-industrial society. Indifference or opposition to the manner in which nature services living and renewing systems have been a too common element in the formation and imposition of urban-industrial demands. The values of that demand put little or no premium on what is necessary for all life processes in the culture's servicing of open-ended growth in production and consumption.(40)

What occurs in the renewing environment is not the result of thought or preconception. It will be up to urban-industrial society, therefore, to provide the thinking and the planning for this correlative relationship. This means that the institutions of urban-industrial society must accept responsibility for the interrelationships between its demands and nature; the attempt at approximating a unified energy budget; and the recognition of nature's finiteness when compared to the infinity of the human imagination.

In a decision-making process so reconstituted, values can be deduced for planning the environmental future of humanity. If planning is to be more than extrapolating the present — thereby intensifying every problem patent or latent from the present to the future — there has to be a reselection of values by which the planner or manager can behave differently.(41)

Through this decision making for change, society can develop the different values that would allow a massive demand-structure to keep operating within a sustained renewing environment. Planning and management could then internalize the costs urban-industrial demands impose upon renewing natural systems. Only then could projects be identified and foregone because they impose costs too heavy to be borne either by nature or the urban-industrial economy.(42)

Perhaps the limits of growth are not as severe as some have foreseen. Limits in nature, though, do exist, whereas present societal values put no limits on the demands which may be made upon nature. But the environment, of which humanity is a part, is a series of interconnections and finite capacities. A value system that has little regard for these inherent limitations or for the consequences of interrupting long-established connections is headed for grave difficulties.

Up until now, many of the so-called environmental reforms have been tactical defenses set up by urban-industrial society. They have themselves been fragmenting in their effects upon the renewing environment. They were the resort of a demand structure acting under severe criticism yet unwilling to change. There is still a widespread refusal to concede that urban-industrial demand cannot go on processing the renewing environment without recognizing any limits.

But the crises relative to energy cascades and the renewing environment are accelerating to a complex series of climaxes. The planners and managers of this society's economy and polity have yet to effectively encourage a shift to values that are supportive, rather than destructive, of nature's life-support systems. In the not very long run, there will be no more important activity for these people to undertake.(43)

2 The Social Origins of Energy Demand

THE HISTORIC RISE IN ENERGY CONVERSION

The term "energy crisis" became a cliche in the 1970s, first in 1973 and again in 1979. Fuel prices rose abruptly and cut-backs in allocation of fuels, such as oil and natural gas, became common in a way that appeared sudden to most people. The apparent rapidity of the onset of an energy crisis led many to the easy conclusion that it had been quite recently formed. The "crisis" was simply a problem not commonly perceived until after 1970, since the energy crisis had long preceded its "discovery."

The origins of the energy crisis in the late twentieth century are quite old. The Industrial Revolution accelerated humanity toward that crisis. The energy innovations of the twentieth century, by exploding the city over the landscape and markedly intensifying energy demands, advanced the date of the crisis.

To examine the growth in world energy demand, modern history since 1700 can be divided into three segments. These successive stages are the decades from 1700 to 1860, the near century from 1860 to 1958, and the years since 1958. In each segment, the growth in the economic and technical applications of energy have been huge compared to previous energy growth. What is important in each segment is that the time of the demand for energy expansion has been shortening while the relative increase in energy use has been growing much larger.

The growth in energy use had been made possible after the post-1700 introduction of the steam engine, initially run on wood or charcoal and later on coal. The Age of Enlightenment had vague perceptions that steam had begun a process that had to enormously increase available energy, although it could not yet realize the impact this would have on society and nature. By 1830 in northwestern Europe, however, even the most routine minds were aware that there was energy in an abundance that had never been hitherto dreamed possible.

Yet great as the 1700 – 1860 period was for energy growth, one can almost ignore it. Practically, it is not 1700 which can fruitfully be taken as the best base line for energy growth. Rather, 1860 is the realistic base line for purposes of measuring forward until 1958.

In doing so, the observer will note an average annual rate of 3¼ percent increase per year in world energy production between 1860 and 1958. In some of those years, the growth level reached rates as high as six percent annually, but other years saw what appeared to be almost stagnation in the growth of energy. The result is that when the overall comparison is made for this period, there emerges a steady growth rate of 3¼ percent per year for the entire world.(1)

By itself (assuming there had been no growth after 1958), this growth in available energy had not been inconsequential. It had multiplied the base line of 1860 by just under 375 percent. Compared to previous history, this energy increment must be considered enormous for so brief a time span.

Extended over a century, however, it seemed to have an even more important significance for planners. The annual growth rate of 3¼ percent was an indicator of stability. It gave evidence of the possibility of safe future predictions of the energy demands of urban-industrial society. On a planetary basis, it seemed to indicate further that there would be a smooth transition in energy growth rates from the lower ones of traditional society to the high urban-industrial energy rates.

So acute a resource economist as Harold J. Barnett, observing these past energy growth patterns, was impressed by the statistical appearance of stability and smooth transition from low energy use patterns. This was further buttressed by a consistent falling (at the rate of one percent per year compounded) of the total BTU requirement in the United States in the four decades from 1910 to 1950. Looking at these statistics, Barnett concluded that in 1965 there would be no greater energy requirements for motive power than had existed in 1947, and that total energy requirements would be only about thirty percent greater.(2)

On the basis of the evidence available at the middle of the twentieth century concerning energy growth patterns over the previous century, the logic underlying this conclusion was excellent. It should have accurately predicted the future of energy demand during the remainder of the twentieth century. Unfortunately for the comfort of planners, this was not the case.

Instead a sharp break occurred in this comforting pattern. The break began to manifest itself in 1958. A previously unprecedented rise in energy production began and continued through the 1960s. The statistics prior to 1958 had given a false indication of stability.   Just as accelerating energy growth had to be accepted as an accomplished fact by every early nineteenth century man of affairs, so must intense and open-ended growth on a global scale be reckoned with by late twentieth century planners.

In the United States from 1960 to 1970, residential and commercial uses of energy consumption increased by one hundred forty percent, industrial uses by thirty-seven percent, and all power consumption by fifty percent. This produced a relative shift in the users of energy consumption in the United States so that industrial power sales in the same decade dropped from fifty percent of the total to forty-one percent. The increase in the decade of the 1960s was presaged by the fact that, from 1921 to 1971, all United States energy consumption rose fourteen hundred percent.(3)

No continent is without examples of national experiences concerning huge increases in energy demand and supply. The global energy picture in the 1970s shows little sign of slackening in the pace of growth in energy demand. This has been true despite the rise in the price of oil and natural gas. In country after country, the growth in energy demand could be monotonously documented. The most dramatic rates of increase come from the regions that were most laggard until well on into the twentieth century. But as these regions came into the course of urban-industrial civilization, there were simultaneous rises in population, energy demand, and industrial expectations.(4)

Indeed, there appears to be a symbiotic relationship in these region's early stages between the growth of population and the growth in energy demand. At the later stages of development – although population expansion has a tendency to drop in its rate of increase compared to energy growth – the latter then takes on a similar double-bind characteristic in the increment of material expectations. The cause-and-effect in energy and material demands rocks back and forth between the two.

The relationship between energy use and gross national product is more complex. Common sense indicates that since energy is so pervasive, movements in energy conversion ought to be in unison with overall GNP figures. Common sense in this case, however, is wrong.

Historically, the United States has only intermittantly shown a unison between energy and GNP statistics. This history breaks into two parts: From 1880 to 1910 there were persistent increases in the input of energy per unit of GNP (and this was probably also true for a long time prior to 1880); since 1920, however, the record tends to a persistent decline in the rate of energy to GNP.(5)

As an urban-industrial economy grows, it needs less energy per unit of GNP to sustain the GNP growth. In the early stages of an urban-industrial economy's growth, greater infusions of energy per unit are required. The growth experience of the People's Republic of China seems to illustrate this. From 1949 to 1974, energy consumption there grew more rapidly than GNP. As the economist Vaclav Smil said, "Energy consumption and economic wealth must be very closely linked, the latter being in fact the result of the former."(6)

The importance of this difference between the early and the late developers of urban-industrial economies in their comparative demands for energy per unit of GNP would be hard to over-estimate today. It is a situation frought with high risk. At the very time energy costs are soaring, energy demand is accelerating throughout the world.(7)

When examining the figures for the percentages of growth in energy demand for the urban-industrial late-comers, the initial base lines may seem of modest proportions. This also has often been true of population figures and is almost entirely true for industrial production. Yet one ought not to be misled by this initial modesty.

The increases have grown so large, year by year, that, aggregately, they are major factors in swelling the world energy budget, population, and industrial production. Where energy production is concerned, such places as Ghana, Brazil, China, and the Balkans, which in 1910 were almost negligible in their energy demands, are now individually significant. Together, such places have become important components in accelerating world energy demands.

People today are so tied to energy cascades that if the world's population of the late 1960s doubled by the year 2000, the energy production, in terms of current expectations, should expect to increase five-fold. Expectations can be denied by events. Such a symbiosis between energy demand and material expectations, however, is not surprising in a world where the per capita utilization of raw materials went from an average of fifty tons per year in 1880 to over three hundred tons per year in 1970.(8) Countries both rich and poor in urban-industrial terms are increasing their demand for energy, their exploitation of materials, and their impact upon the environment.(9)

The United States perhaps best illustrates the trend toward increased growth in all these matters. As one of the older urban-industrial societies, its history is worth close examination. And that history reveals that in the twentieth century, dramatic per capita increases in energy usage and materials exploitation occurred in the United States.

In 1900 the United States was a basic agricultural and manufacturing economy. By 1970 it was described as a "mature service-oriented economy." This means that, although the United States was an urban-industrial society in 1900, there had been great intensification in urban-industrial demand in the seven subsequent decades. Thus in terms of constant 1967 dollars, the demand for energy materials had increased by a factor of about seven and the demand for physical structure materials by a factor of nearly five.(10) The experience of the United States in this regard has proven to be merely a preview of what most of the rest of the world is now experiencing, perhaps particularly the areas that had previously adhered closest to traditional ways.

Any world-wide energy projections for the rest of this century must run the risk of flowing right off the graph paper. The base line in the year 1860, from which the comparison for modern times began and which looked so useful as a point of comparison as recently as 1950, will appear irrelevant and trivial by the year 2000. 1860 will be a date as meaningless to 2000 as 1700 was to 1860 and as primitive as the year 1000 appeared to Voltaire.

But still the risk could be quite different. Amory Lovins rejects predicting the future in any way other than writing alternative scenarios. For him, "The energy problem is intimately related to all the great issues of our day, and is arguably only a symptom of deeper social disorders that the energy strategist cannot safely ignore."(11) And by

2000, a much more modest sum of energy usages than traditional practice would predict may be established.

THE IMPACT ON CULTURE OF ENERGY CASCADES

Despite recent challenges, the dominant contemporary conviction remains that a high-energy usage level is necessary. Urban-industrial production and consumption are dependent first upon creating high-energy demand and then upon stepping up the growth in energy supply. To make this change-over possible and, preferably, swift, traditional social ways must be willingly given up and new forms of social organization adopted.

The creation of energy cascades inevitably must also produce breaks in cultural practice. Previously unknown quantities of energy cannot be introduced into a culture and not change the culture in a way that cuts it off from traditions. To think otherwise is to miss the intimate connection between the mores of human societies and the energy sources of those societies.

In the merging conurbations of urban-industrial society, cutting off energy for more than a few hours would produce chaos. It would be a chaos made worse by the inability of the energy suppliers to cope with such a crisis, which would be tightly confined in time and space. Indeed, maybe no existing units in the present social structure are capable of dealing with an abrupt and total cut-off of the supply of energy in time to prevent disastrous social losses.(12)

This is not to say that nothing could compel a reduction in the demand for energy growth. If the accelerating pace in the increase of energy supply were to falter, particularly if it did so gradually, the economy could respond. But this lag in the growth of the energy supply would mean a lag in the economy. Expectations as to what material resources the society could obtain would have to be altered. The whole social structure would then have to begin accommodating to the reduction in the growth of energy supply.

Humanity, of course, does not "produce" energy. Human effort does, however, release or expedite the flow of energy. Yet whatever descriptive terms are used, the existence of energy cascades constitutes a life-support system for the current demand structure.

The dependency upon high-energy supply extends far beyond the immediate heavy manufacturing processes or urban services. Such dependency exists even in apparently remote and autonomous agricultural regions. One can hope enough viability would remain in the individual human being and in the social group to respond with a substantial level of survival if suddenly faced with a stoppage of the energy supplies at the level which has been available for less than a century of humanity's history.

The brittle quality of what appears to be urban-industrial abundance ought not to be allowed to mask the ultimate character of that issue. It is true that brittle materials can be both strong and lasting. But when they break, it is not uncommon for them to shatter.

THE IMPACT OF DIFFERING SOURCES
OF ENERGY SUPPLY

The current crisis in the relationship between energy and the environment had its origins nearly three centuries ago. In those three centuries, the emerging high energy culture has experienced intense spasms
that seemed to foreshadow an inevitable break in the rising energy
curves. The intensity of each crisis was presaged by the steady growth
in available energy which had begun in 1698 with the Savery steam
engine. It was almost a toy; and it required about as much energy as it
produced, which is not unusual with technical innovations. But it was
the beginning of a fossil-fueled, urban-industrial society.

It was also the start of a fossil-fueled recurrent crisis wherein
energy demand pressed hard upon supply. And even when the energy
supply exceeded the demand, a sort of Parkinson's law came into
operation. The demand was expanded to equal the supply. Eventually,
the feeding of an energy demand, which required accelerating expansion, produced calls for energy that continuously threatened to be
ahead of the growth in energy supply.

When in the late eighteenth century, the shortage of trees to make
charcoal seemed to mark an end to energy growth, coal became the
energy-producer. When steam seemed to have reached the end of its
capacity to maximize the utility of direct power, electricity appeared
as a means of greatly increasing energy flow. When the steam generators seemed to have impacted society to the breaking point, the
gasoline engine was invented to expand the locations of economic
activity. Each time a break seemed imminent, a way around it to a still
larger energy cascade was found.

The value of electrical energy was greater than expressed in
Michael Faraday's quip to Gladstone, then the Chancellor of the
Exchequer: "Someday it will produce something you can tax." Electricity, of course, has amply proven Faraday a social prophet. Both
directly and indirectly electricity has brought masses of taxable qualities into being. But electricity and the automotive engine could do what
steam had been unable to do: free human beings from having to locate
near the source of the energy.

No longer did energy have to be concentrated at a few sites. Energy
could be distributed without restriction. The necessity for the direct
application of steam and the power of the early water wheel and the
windmill to production had been their chief shortcoming.

The inability of the steam engine to free the location of economic
activity created a crisis at the end of the nineteenth century that
threatened a break in the growth of material resource exploitation.
The concentration of economic activity became so intense in the urban-
industrial centers of the 1880s that collapse seemed imminent. The
simultaneous arrival in usuable forms of electricity and automotive
power at the close of the nineteenth century relieved these concentrations and resolved the crisis.(13)

True, electricity was generated by steam engines and water wheels. But the web of the transmission lines could spread power out over the countryside. The gasoline engine, once roads were built to accommodate it, even more dramatically resolved the crisis of energy impaction. The need for a real concentration had been reduced.

Technological innovations had appeared which the urban-industrial society's demand structure could seize upon for the salvation of continued growth. An energy-induced disaster had been averted. As the social commentator Harper Leech said: "If energy had not been made distributable, the concentrated and complex mechanism of steam-powered urban civilization would eventually have collapsed, perhaps in violence, when it imposed too great a strain upon man."(14)

This might be described as a "temporary" solution. But as a technical answer to a crisis generated by a social demand for energy cascades, it worked for nearly a century. This had been an energy crisis brought on by the consequences of what was then a recent change in energy production. How much longer society could have stood the strain of such concentration was never tested. Technological innovation resolved the crisis – at least for a time.

Now, in the last quarter of the twentieth century, this technical resolution, based upon hydrocarbon fuel sources for both electricity and automotive power, seems to be breaking up. Just as technological innovation provided a "temporary" solution at the close of the nineteenth century, most people anticipate that technological innovation will prove equally available at the close of the twentieth century.

One does not have to be a philosopher in order to question any solution, even one that lasts a century, that intensifies the basic conflicts compelling the initial solution. Electricity and automotive power have brought an intensification to the demand for high energy. Victorian society had been threatened by reliance on a power demanding concentration of economic activity at the site of power production. Late twentieth century society is threatened both by the outpouring of energy cascades into the renewing environment and by the impending inability to keep those cascades flowing in the increasing volume which has now become traditional.

A dozen generations have passed since 1700. During that time, an increasingly intimate relationship has developed between social structure and energy supply. Barring a vision more often associated with prophecy than with foresight, the expected human action in the face of energy crisis has been – and likely will be – to turn to technology for heightening the energy cascades.

Just as our generation cannot be sure that the Victorians produced a worse crisis than the one the Victorians were solving, we cannot be positive that new technological "fixes" for greater power will not create a worse future situation than the one we are now struggling with. What is certain is that any doubts in the wisdom of increasing the energy cascades probably will be stilled. The quick solution turned to will be the promise of more – and hence cheaper – energy.(15)

THE ABSOLUTE DEPENDENCE OF URBAN-INDUSTRIAL
SOCIETY ON HIGH-ENERGY

The rise in energy demand and supply since 1700, taken in conjunction with the increasing cultural receptivity to changing the energy sources, created the present energy crisis. It has been a long time in coming but its arrival has been inevitable. Yet few have willingly perceived that energy crises are recurrent phenomena in this demand-structure. Such crises are a result both of the pitch of demand and the manner in which the demand has been responded to in organizing the supply of energy.

Henry Carey in the mid-nineteenth century and Frederick Soddy in the early twentieth century were among the first to perceive the absolute dependence of society upon energy. Carey has been called the "Father of American Economics," while Soddy, a physicist turned economist, had an approach similar to that of any pioneer in a discipline. Consequently, both were accused, perhaps justly, of being dogmatic on the subject of the economy's dependence on the energy supply. Yet, given the relationship today between high-energy levels and the apparent affluence of urban-industrial society, one can conclude that their dogmas were based upon a large measure of truth.(16)

Carey insisted that energy models were the patterns for law and ethics. As a result, energy had to be more important in regard to law and ethics in a high-energy flow condition compared to a low-energy demand situation. He was among the very first to see the levels of energy use dividing the world. On the one side were England, western Europe, and the United States, with a long established and rapidly growing high-energy level in the first part of the nineteenth century. On the other side stood the rest of the world with a traditional, low demand for applied energy.(17)

It was Henry Carey's claim that this dichotomy would divide the world on the basis of energy demand. Given the importance of energy, all that ultimately could equalize the two halves once more would be the location of energy resources among the low energy users, which would be vital to those with a high-energy demand. Failing that, however, Carey saw the world by the end of the first third of the nineteenth century as permanently divided between those who were well along with their growth in energy demand and those who were not.(18)

By the 1870s, Carey was even more certain that energy and its flow was the dominant consideration for world economic activity. Years before Edison had lit the first light bulb or Alexander Graham Bell had heard the Emperor of Brazil say of the telephone, "The damned thing talks," Carey was discussing the future exclusively in terms of electricity. He saw it as intensifying the cultural values of urban-industrial society and pushing along in expectable progression the growth in the energy supply.

For Carey, as later for Frederick Soddy, energy was related to an inherent quality in human society that, if not biological, was so socially primordial that the first humans had the first experience of an energy crisis. They regarded energy crises as being precisely that old. However, once a culture converts its social structure so that it may respond only to high-energy demand, the depth of any energy crisis of low-energy cultures has to be seen as relatively less significant insofar as the survival of the low energy culture is concerned.

Philosophically it would not be without justification to perceive both the individual and society as energy. The individual is a bundle of energy as well as a transmitter of energy. Society is a series of networks connecting the individual work function with materials and other sources of energy other than the individual's. In this sense, therefore, Henry Carey and Frederick Soddy were right in their dogmas: Everything in human society is energy.(19)

The material universe is stored energy. The human being is kinetic energy. Human institutions are the processes that release, distribute, and employ both current and stored energy. The totality of energy in the sun, the tides, the wind, biological processes, and tensile reactions is not calculable. The history of the human race could be said to run in precise accord with the extent, at each moment in time, to which energy has been made available for humanity to control for their own purposes. Even now in the late twentieth century, when humanity speaks so casually of mastering energy and of having energy cascades at increasing disposal, only a fragment of the total energy in the world has been put under any sort of human control. This also is a part of the current energy crisis.(20)

Advocates of high energy demand are quick to point out that low energy cultures requiring an augmentation of energy, either to provide an elite with leisure or to support energy systems that are inefficient in delivery of energy units, do so by augmenting energy in the form of either slavery or some other institution of enforced labor.(21) With the movement to higher energy levels since 1700, the need to turn to the enforced labor of human beings in order to increase the energy supply has decreased. As Isaac Asimov has observed, "With steam, electricity, and radio beams to do our work for us, there was no longer the need for the comparatively weak and fumbling human muscle. . . ."(22)

The issue, however, is not the inferiority of low-energy to high-energy systems under all conditions. Rather, the issue is to what extent urban-industrial society and the renewing environment can maintain a viable relationship relative to energy. The effort must be made to absorb the demands posed by dramatic changes in energy sources. The switch from fossil fuel to renewable energy sources will not remove all the environmental consequences of such demand.

The cost of sharp and apparently open-ended rises in the curves of energy demand and supply must be calculated. The recurringly severe crises these human insistences created in the renewing environment must be first recognized and then accommodated. And herein lies the heart of the crisis.(23)

THE COMPARATIVE ENVIRONMENTAL EFFECTS OF
STORED AND CURRENT ENERGY

The past great revolution in energy supply was the movement from current energy to stored energy sources. The next energy revolution may well reverse the process. But even now the first energy revolution is easily overlooked. As a result, its importance is slighted, which may have the effect of slowing the technology that ought to be preparing a reversal from stored, exhaustible energy sources to ones that are renewable.(24)

When humanity moved from what the life processes provided in the form of firewood, grass, animals, and human muscle, to fossil fuels, humanity moved to a larger share of what the sun, photosynthesis, and the decay processes can store for energy use. Society thereby freed itself from an energy supply that, under then prevailing techniques, was limited both by the time required for the renewal of life processes and by whatever was currently available in their operations. By moving to stored energy sources, people became capable of drawing, in any one year, upon milennia of solar energy's interaction with life activities, moving into what has been called a "paleozoic prosperity."(25)

However, this change also brought into harsh emphasis the other consequence of this action. Humanity had made themselves reliant upon a limited energy source which released into the atmosphere, the water, and the life processes all the life elements that were formerly confined. With the abundance of energy drawn from stored energy sources, there also came an abundance of problems concerning humanity's relationship with the natural environment.

Just as people in one century could convert the energy that had been stored over millions of years in the fossil fuels, so would they thereby release, in that same brief time frame, all the elements stored over those millions of years which had not been transformed into economically usable energy. It underscores the comment of the environmental lawyer Peter Junger, "The problem of energy resource allocation underlies almost all environmental problems, pollution being almost invariably a function of energy consumption or production. . . ."(26) Recently, this has been phrased with an instructive difference: ". . .problems of scarce energy, clean environment, and price inflation are inseparable."(27)

Still, heavy as the drafts upon stored energy sources have been, simply changing to current energy sources may not sufficiently relieve those burdens. Proponents of reliance on solar power by means of biomass conversion may be putting too much emphasis upon the feasibility of the technology.(28) Tree and crop production can be drafted into the current energy demand with confidence in their processes of natural renewal if right techniques of conservation apply.

These renewable sources, however, will contribute to the same energy cascades as energy from stored sources. Whether energy comes from stored fossil fuels or from current biomass conversion, impact upon renewing environmental systems will occur. Simply switching from stored to current energy sources – even if this proves both a technological and economical option for prompt action – may not be sufficient. Challenging the accelerating force of the energy cascades themselves may prove necessary in order to protect the renewing capacities of the environment. Challenging, rather than accommodating, demands for growth in the energy supply may be the common future reaction.

CHANGING VIEWS ON THE ENERGY SUPPLY

Classically energy was always in short supply because only currently renewable energy was technologically available. The result of this in the classic economics of the ancient Greeks, as expressed by Aristotle, was a consciousness of a high value in conserving energy.(29) This did not, however, prevent the Greek merchants from deforesting the hillsides for ships. Erosion, desiccation, and probably increased temperatures resulted; but so did the profit to the Greek ship-owners. Plato regretted the cutting of the forests, but knew why the trees were cut. He regarded the act as short-sighted, producing an immediate, fleeting profit that guaranteed a long-term harm.(30)

Yet the ancient Greeks would have generally agreed that resources were finite. They considered the energy supply limited, and thought that both resources and energy should be conserved. There was no view in the ancient world of boundless energy cascades and limitless resources in nature for human exploitation.

When energy began cascading forth after 1860, escalating in quantity upon the already high level that had accumulated since 1700, general attitudes changed. What had been a paucity of energy in practical terms of a supply available at any single moment to meet a human demand had become an apparent cornucopia. Human conditions had been changed, it seemed, from needing to conserve to possessing a superabundance of energy. Humanity suddenly believed themselves free to develop expectations of wealth, unconstrained action, and opportunity for unlimited growth.

Only now is this promise seen as a contract unenforcible against nature into the infinite future. Limitations on the relationship between energy and environment have appeared. Yet whatever limitations lie in the future, the past performance for mankind under this open-ended promise has proved to be materially substantial for very large numbers.

Howard Odum has clarified this fact by comparing the energy-usages of primitive and urban-industrial social orders. The present organization of society is the product of the subsidy provided by the fossil fuels. Rediscovering independently the arguments made a hundred years before him by Henry Cary, Odum says: "To survive and maintain a competitive position, a system must draw the maximum power budget possible in a situation and process this budget in works that reinforce future stability."(31)

In order to free humanity from the uncontrolled play of natural forces, energy was directed into human social organization. The larger a culture's energy supply, the more energy it will have available for social organization. The immediate result is that there arises both more demand and an increased supply of energy.

To follow Howard Odum's thumbnail history of humanity, primitive human social orders had such a decentralized power control that little or no energy could be put into social organization. This left the individual human being to be oppressed by whatever natural forces had substantial power budgets compared to human society. The individual, of course, was freed from the burden of human social organization, yet the price for that freedom was to remain outside of any major energy flow. Simple individual systems could never have taken advantage of the energy cascades flowing out of the exploitation of the fossil fuels.(32)

For an ecologist like Odum, unless humanity closes the circuit, the outflow of energy released through these drafts upon fossil fuels and fissioned materials constitutes disaster in the making. It is through the management of energy demand and supply that humanity has a chance to assume responsibility both for the operation of human systems and the impact of energy cascades upon natural systems. Odum really believes that the very increase in energy efficiency, which occurs as the number of units in the social organization increases, makes the closing of the circuit nearly inevitable.(33)

If Howard Odum should be right, perhaps the solution to the present energy crisis is now in the process of being worked out at a cultural level, which need not include conscious, comprehensive planning. Society may be in the process of responding more fully to the consequences of change in social attitudes to energy supply. Still, happy as that outcome would be, the evidence seems much stronger for a needed conscious human effort to change the present impact of energy on the renewing environment. The time for re-establishing a viable energy-environmental balance grows very short.(34)

ENERGY DEMANDS RELATIVE TO SOCIAL ORGANIZATION

Power increases responded to demand and the demand for energy is a product of social organization. There is a symbiotic relationship between the demand for and the growth of the energy supply, so that the one does not exist without the other. The growth of the energy supply is not an independent variable to which social structure responds. As Kenneth Arrow has said, "Power isn't the whole of civilization, anyway; it's not the whole of our economy."(35)

The present demand for energy results from generational changes which have led to the formation of these current demand patterns and projections. Then, too, the increase in the quantity of energy available imposes the duty upon social structure and natural systems to absorb it. Energy demand serves as its own generator. Demand is not pre-existent.

In the case of energy, one has to realize that the appetite grows in the feeding, especially when the appetite is cheaply and easily fed.

Urban-industrial society has praised the opportunity returns that a high-energy culture makes possible. But high-energy cultures also increase the opportunity costs as well as the returns. Opportunity costs are the values foregone and the burdens imposed in order to obtain the favored returns. In a situation where energy demand and supply are reacting back and forth upon each other in a manner that has little or no regard for any consequence except the growth in available energy, everything else becomes an opportunity cost.

One cannot deny that opportunity costs were certainly present in traditional low-energy societies, from the hunting economy to the commercial glories of the trading cities of Italy in the Renaissance. But the urban-industrial demand-structure has had options open to it which before had not been present. It has produced a focus upon, and an increase of, opportunity costs as the flow of energy going through the social system has been enlarged.(36)

A high-energy culture makes demands on established values to such an extent, and in so brief an instant, that they are inconceivable to a low-energy culture. For this reason from the viewpoint of a high energy culture, everything that precedes it, from hunting societies through urban-commercial civilization, can be lumped under the term "traditional." In fact, so great is the difference between high- and low-energy cultures, that the solutions painfully worked out by the low-energy cultures for the assistance of social structure become problems once energy has begun its relentless increase in the succeeding high-energy social conditions.

This shift in the energy demand and supply on the one hand and society's, as well as nature's, adjustment to it, on the other, produces revolutionary change in social relationships and in the connection humanity has with natural systems. Fred Cottrell, a political theorist concerned with the interconnection between energy levels and social values, has pointed out that the traditional equilibrium in society, to which all high-energy cultures look back with nostalgia, was integral to the earlier low-energy cultures. This equilibrium may not be attainable again.(37)

The settlement of claims on the sources of energy had been worked out over long periods of time. Such lengthy time frames have not been available to high-energy culture. The result in low-energy cultures, however, was stable only partly as a result of the slow process of negotiating the claims for energy. The other reason was that the recurrence of energy seemed unresponsive to human tampering skills.

The belief that energy was only very limitedly under human control gave a routine, day-to-day meaning to such terms as balanced and stable social and environmental relationships. The memory of this stability can now be cherished in the flux of high energy cultures.

People in high-energy cultures have been compelled to recognize that they live in a culture in which change has become common, equilibrium rare, and adjustment slow. Adjustment, indeed, has perhaps been slowest of all when the culture became most casual about the commonness of change and the rarity of equilibrium. This consequence appears paradoxical, but that is not the case. What, after all, is adjustment?

In itself, social adjustment is the establishment of an equilibrium among relationships within society as well as between society's demands and the renewing environment. It may be ephemeral; it may be a stage in an on-going process. Yet adjustment is meant to express a moment of tranquillity within the society, and the individuals composing that society, because the essentials of a settlement have become known, familiar, and, for at least a time, fixed. When everything connected with the demand and the supply of energy produces flux and instability, it is highly unlikely that a high-energy demand structure will self generate a tranquil, long-lasting adjustment.(38)

THE ENERGY BUDGET IN THE RENEWING ENVIRONMENT

This ascendency of flux and instability in high energy situations is due, in large part anyway, to a refusal to see energy in terms of environmental consequences as well as social demand. It is symbolized by the refusal to recognize the relationship between a calory of energy coming from food and a kilowatt stemming originally from fossil fuel or atomic fission. This refusal obscures both the existence of real energy deficits and the consequences that the recurring energy crises impose upon human values and the environment. The economics of energy may be disaggregated, but nature operates on an integrated energy budget.

In the complexities of a high-energy demand-structure, merely discovering whether or not there is a point at which output exceeds input of energy requires a major effort. And when it has been discovered, as in the case of modern agricultural methods, it is nearly impossible to get anyone to see the presence of a problem.(39) Even determining which operation has an energy surplus and which has an energy deficit is a task most often postponed until some ecologic, economic, or social crisis compels attention.(40)

There are such interlocking systems in nature that the energy output of one is the energy input of another. What is common to all living organisms in nature is the inability of any of them to live off the product of their own wastes. Modern social organization treats each human demand for energy as if it were an independent variable, unrelated to any other energy demand. This has induced a blindness that the complexities of a high energy system allow to flourish for far longer periods of time than is possible in low-energy cultures. But in the long run, the price for not dealing with energy deficits in a high-energy culture will be no different than such failure in a low-energy one: the demise of the culture.

Energy is basic to achieving all values in all societies. From the beginning of humanity, energy has been a necessary part of the cost of achieving all values. As Fred Cottrell long ago noted, in the traditional, low-energy cultures, in which energy costs seem to be fixed or to vary only slightly over long periods of time, these fixed costs represent a core that has the normal values of the culture statistically distributed around it. When the costs of energy begin to vary, the traditional norm upon which the values have been distributed is lost. At that moment, social structure, which Cottrell describes tersely as "the expectancies of repeated choice," has to undergo responsive change so as to reallocate values around the new norms which changed costs have created.(41)

The crisis aspect to all this is that in the situation of energy cascades, the period of adjustment time is insignificant compared to what it traditionally was before modern culture moved into a high-energy phase. The energy budget for the renewing environment becomes skewed. The product of this skewing from the swiftness of events are changes that can scarcely be expected to occur with unconscious ease. A conscious process of painful adjustment to the harshly imposed consequences in the renewing environment is not to be avoided.(42)

THE SOCIAL PREFERENCE FOR HIGH-ENERGY USAGES

The world has been dedicated to a high-energy culture. This dedication has established a preference to risk the greatest environmental danger. Whether this preference for high energy includes a willingness to socially absorb environmental costs remains doubtful.(43)

The human bias for high-energy levels has been increasing in intensity, although a break may now impend. Whatever causes cultures to make new commitments has caused culture after culture in the past three centuries to accept the value of energy cascades. Leaders of societies have been willing to take on the costs inherent in the maintenance of engines powered by coal, oil, natural gas, and atomic fission. They have created high demands for higher speeds, higher energy outputs, and the thrusting upward of all mechanical production levels.

The issue has never been whether or not the enormous historic spurt in energy demand and supply should have occurred. Rather, the convulsions since 1700 have centered on how the demanded accelerating energy growth could be divided, and how widely its effectiveness could be spread throughout the social structure. The new high-energy usages, with their multiplying effects, have been released for the use of larger and larger masses of human beings.

The result of the struggles over whether and how energy benefits are to be extended to larger social groups has been the identification in the popular mind of the goodness of having more energy. More electricity, more machinery, more power, greater weight, the lesser use of human muscle, increased movement to urban centers, and the growth in both choices of employment and the chance at leisure are each seen as highly esteemed popular values whose costs seem clearly worthwhile. The justification for the world-wide political upheavals of the two centuries since the American Revolution has been the electrification of the countryside, the provision of employment in the urban-industrial economy, and the extension over the land of motor and air routes.

Most reforms suggested in contemporary urban-industrial society seem to demand high-energy levels. Each social improvement seems to require energy in almost limitless quantities in order to service the aggregate of human demands. Although some of these demands may scarcely rise to the dignity of whims, they are being made. And by what market-determined, urban-industrial norm should they not prevail?

The movement of an economy from primary to tertiary or quaternary economic activity could increase the demand for energy even more.(44) High-energy demand is intimately connected with the rise of the importance of service industries. Although consumption of energy per unit of the Gross National Product rises during an output-structure and declines with the growth of a broad service component on the economy, the very condition making this possible guarantees enormous total growth. An energy-intensive leisure economy, such as the quaternary economy of Herman Kahn, could even return to a rise of energy consumption per unit of GNP.(45) In the popular mind, at any event, the anticipation of high energy on demand has acquired nearly the same moral quality as the affluence to be expected from urban-industrial society.(46)

In the movement from a low-energy culture, it is not easy to distinguish purely technical innovation from the responses of social structure. The converters of energy, as Fred Cottrell has seen, are deep within a social matrix in which it is tough to separate out technical operations from actions primarily arising from changes occurring in social organizations.(47) An excellent example of an attitude toward energy that sees its abundant use as the way to affluence can be found in a social commentator of the 1930s, Harper Leech.

Writing in the midst of the Depression, Leech insisted that the basic capital inherited by urban-industrial society had been fossil fuel. Only by hugely increasing its expenditure could the pace of affluence be restored. Units of energy had to be made so cheap that there could be no value in preserving existing structures. The original units of energy which had gone into their construction would have lost scarcity value in relation to the rapid cheapening of the cost of energy conversion. Staring at the wrecking of buildings in Manhattan, he could only praise the "electric shovels remorselessly tearing into and breaking up costly marble slabs and pillars. It seemed ruthless and Philistine waste. It was true economy. . .(48)

For Leech, the only fact to seize upon was the value of steadily and drastically lowering the cost of each unit of energy. The possibility that rare materials might not exist at a later date – or the workmanship to form them – was insignificant. The important datum, as Leech's contemporary Virgil Jordan claimed, was that energy be universally available, distributable without limit, and that the supply be open-endedly increased. If all that could be done, humanity would be guaranteed plenty and would have a stable future forever because people would be "self-sufficient."

Contrary to Barry Commoner's argument in the 1970s, Virgil Jordan happily argued that such abundantly supplied energy would produce a synthetic chemistry which would replace all natural substances as the source of manufactured goods.(49) Perhaps the final idea this inimitable school of thought offered on the value of energy was summarized by Harper Leech himself: "The cost of killing a Chinaman will rise in proportion to the increase in the kilowatt of energy used in China...There is no other means of social uplift."(50)

The years since 1932, when these words of Harper Leech and Virgil Jordan were published, have proven their words both prophetic and erroneous. How prophetic? Energy was cheaply abundant for decades although events since 1973 have obscured this experience. Materials after World War II were increasingly treated as throw-aways and synthetics have steadily encroached upon natural commodities.

Jordan and Leech seem only to have made two errors: The passage of events has not produced stability either for the social structure or for humanity's relations with nature. Whatever they meant by their mysterious term "self-sufficiency," has not been obtained by either the increase in or the cheapening of energy units. Of course, not everyone agreed with Leech and Jordan even in their own time. As their contemporary C.C. Furnas observed, "We live by digging into the storehouses laid down a hundred million years ago." Like Giacomo Luigi Ciamician, the early twentieth century authority on fuel, he too saw there were growth limits to what the Italian had described as "the neurotic age of coal." Far from talking about increasing the burning of coal or natural gas in such a way as to increase its supply and make it so cheap that demand would soar, Furnas urged that there was a need to begin a search for other energy sources, and recommended the sun as one possible source. He found the accelerated world dependence upon coal, oil, and natural gas folly. The ultimate social price, he believed, would be too high in comparison with the intermediate benefits.(51)

Furnas, so far, has not been prophetic and does not even match Leech's and Jordan's fulfilled prophecies. Urban-industrial demand has preferred to see only the benefits of burning hydrocarbons and nuclear fission. The insistence remains that the future costs of such actions, if any, are in the far future, while the benefits are now and seem to be substantial.

Viewing with self-satisfaction the worldwide rising energy curves has been the easier course. To think about the costs which these upward curves are causing has not been popular. The journalist John Chamberlain sarcastically described the differences in such energy-use points of view:

> . . .under the prod of the energy crisis two contending philosophies met head on. The newer belief, that nothing be dared without endless. . .public confrontations between 'friends of the earth' and those crasser souls who want the 'earth to do something for our creature comforts' went against the grain of 350 years of 'let's-get-on-with-it'.(52)

Such an outlook is simply a recent expression of a fairly old view. Chamberlain did not miss it by much when he mentioned 350 years of "getting-on-with-it." In that period, those who have looked critically at energy-conversion growth curves have been considered either as irrelevant aesthetes, anachronistic aristocrats, nostalgic reactionaries of the Luddite persuasion, or advocates of an asceticism not congenial to an age dreaming of experimental cities wherein one could sample alternate lifestyles.

However, regardless of these viewpoints, alternative possibilities to current behavior patterns concerning energy do exist and may become necessities. The quadrupling on all prices produced a world recession in the mid-1970s. The further abrupt increase in 1979 of those already elevated prices threatened at least equal economic distress. More disruptive energy actions could produce still larger economic and social crises.(53) In the presence of these very real possibilities, no one concerned about the relationship between human demand and the environment need be embarrassed into silence. The precarious condition of social organization under present and projected energy conditions in urban-industrial society, and the numerous efforts to organize institutions capable of coping with that precariousness, have obviated any such embarrassed silence.

3 Urban-Industrial Responses to High-Energy Demand

THE POLITICIAN'S ROLE IN HIGH-ENERGY CONDITIONS

In high-energy cultures, the importance of the state greatly increases. The pressure high-energy demand puts on the state for across-the-board intervention grows. What has been described as a "politics of integration" comes into operation, working in a manner that could unify what has been disruptive.(1)

It becomes the duty of the state apparatus in high-energy cultures to intervene constantly. This intervention is meant to prevent the social community from becoming the focal point of fierce conflicts over the energy supply. It is also intended to provide support for the sustaining environment. If the state were not to intervene, the on-going acceleration in energy demand would be fatally interrupted.

The machinery of high-energy conversion and use cannot tolerate interruptions. A high-energy culture demands a flexible response by society and the environment which insures no resistance to the changes that result from rising flows of energy. Powerful bureaucratic structures are created to serve as directors and mediators. Individuals, social structures, and the renewing environment are compelled to alter their conduct as a part of the process.(2)

The pressure in the political arena has been building steadily as the energy crisis has deepened. Fred Cottrell sensitively noticed this in the 1950's. By this date, urban-industrial society had committed itself to low-priced energy, regardless of other social costs. The modern politician can no longer be "a referee in a game with well-established rules," as might have been true in the traditional past. Instead, the high-energy politician is compelled to be intensely sensitive in order to succeed. Political success is measured by an ability to perceive the emergence of new norms, to articulate them, to implement them, and to apply sanctions against those who would resist them.(3)

Politicians in the world have failed to do all the sensitive things Cottrell said they would have to do and this has made them a kind of litmus paper for the severity of the energy crisis. As they turn blue and the crisis deepens, it becomes obvious that they have not been able to make the selections necessary from these norms in conflict around them. The result has been a sharpening in the conflict between and within nations.(4)

Much attention has been concentrated upon the location of so much of the world's known oil reserves under the land of Arab states. But one should not overlook the fact that forty-nine percent of the remaining known energy resources of the United States exist within six states with only three percent of the nation's population. Those small numbers are protected by a federal structure whose importance is summarized by Governor Richard Lamm of Colorado: "We believe the states should control their own destinies and not be run over and dictated to by the United States government."(5)

As this indicates, the political choices are narrowing on how to resolve the conflicts inevitable in cultures demanding energy cascades. In the brooding presence of the break-up of traditional social norms and the battle arrays of conflicting forces within society, all the technical problems appear small compared to the political ones.(6)

THE DEPENDENCE OF ENERGY TECHNOLOGY ON SOCIAL DEMAND

The technical problems are not inherently small in themselves. One must remember, however, that their existence is largely a function of the operation of high-energy social organizations. Plenty of these vast technical problems exist.

There are currently insufficient supplies of oil and natural gas for the economies of many parts of the world. Refining facilities and deep or off-shore ports for unloading are lacking. Heavy demands are being put upon coal. The production of electricity is being outpaced by the demand for its supply.(7)

Crises in energy supply and in increasing the energy conversion rate were not common until the early 1970s in the advanced urban-industrial societies. Only those societies moving from low- to high-energy cultures were thought subject to energy supply crises. Persons who said these crises could occur in high-energy cultures were treated as cranks or as premature alarmists because of the rarity of system breakdowns.

The abrupt events of 1973 affected attitudes markedly. Natural gas valves were shut off. Gasoline stations were closed down. Industrial assembly lines were stopped. Energy supply no longer appeared secure. The easy relationship between energy demand and the increase in energy conversion was revealed as far more precarious than individuals in charge had suspected.

The technical problems had proven to be a function of social demand. The 1977 American fuel crisis with the natural gas supply and the 1978 fuel crisis with coal-generated electricity reinforced this experience, and a still greater reinforcer was the 1979 international oil crisis, with its simultaneous impact upon economic recession and inflation.

Each of the technical crises in the current energy situation is the result of social decisions. Refinery capacity in the United States serves as an example. It takes about sixteen years to put a new oil refinery "on line." Refinery capacity in the United States has been expanded only slightly since 1960, despite soaring rises in the demand for refined crude oil. In the 1970s, oil companies withdrew plans to build new refineries in the United States for a variety of fiscal reasons.(8) This could only increase the dependence upon imported refined oil.

Under these conditions, it would seem to require little prescience to foresee problems in the supply of distillate fuel oil for heating or refined oil for all other purposes. Greater dependence upon foreign petroleum supplies could only worsen the balance of payments difficulties of any nation. To talk about "independence" in the energy situation by the early 1980s, or to argue the United States should obtain "independence" through the liquefaction and gasification of shales and coal, seems almost irrelevant once one perceives the decision about refinery capacity in this country that has been made over the fifteen years after 1960.(9)

"Solutions" concerning crises in energy conversion rates are for the benefit of the next generation. If past architects of energy use had been at all concerned about an energy crisis in the 1970s, they would not have set a rate for natural gas in the 1950s so low as to deter continued exploration. The industry, which continuously cast a dark eye at the long-term future of its production under such a rate structure, would not have pressed its sales of natural gas knowing that these buyers would suffer grave cutbacks years later. The social decisions of a previous generation have created the current so-called technical problems.

The same will be true for the energy conversion processes of the future. Fast breeder reactors or fusion reactors, the draining off of energy from fast moving ions in an energy field, high-energy bulk storage batteries for peaking purposes, and all the hypothetical processes of solar power production will each depend upon current social decisions concerning investment and diversion of capital. They will not begin to be felt in the energy markets until the current generation make their move in terms of social organization.(10)

There exists throughout the world today, as the result of social decisions going back to 1700, an urban-industrial society resting upon the promise of an abundance of raw energy. This society was not designed to work under conditions of scarce energy supplies. It should not be surprising, therefore, that official projections for energy show huge increases by the end of the century. It is all part of the social commitment that energy supplies should be cheap, ample, and subject to open-ended increase.(11)

THE FRAGMENTARY CHARACTER OF ENERGY GROWTH

Fragmentary energy decisions have composed the common course of action. Nothing illustrates their fragmenting character better than the federal interstate highway program in the United States in the years after 1956.

The launching of the interstate system was an almost obdurate refusal to see the interrelatedness of all energy decisions. Putting aside the impact that program had upon mass transit and urban life, and giving attention solely to what was done by the concrete ribbons themselves, one can only be bemused by the program's disregard for energy. The conditions of American refinery capacity, the future of domestic oil production, and the possibility of a dependence on foreign oil were all non-existent issues. The prospect that any problems might develop in relation to these was treated with as much indifference in 1956 as were the problems of air pollution or inefficiency in fuel consumption of the average American motor car.

The reason for this persistent myopia is the embedding of energy conversion in a social matrix that does not differentiate technical operations from those with a social character.(12) Even when the natural gas industry insisted that price setting by market forces would raise natural gas production, the Federal Power Commission was equally insistent that natural gas production in the United States had both peaked and entered an indefinite decline.(13) What the technical truth may be is still caught up in the social action.(14)

Whatever the situation in low-energy cultures, social action and technology meld under the pressure of high-energy cultures. It can scarcely be otherwise. Over a century ago, Henry Carey claimed that "men like Watt and Stephenson, Morse and Henry, Liebig, Faraday. . .(are those) to whom the world stands most of all indebted for the wonderful growth of wealth and power that marks the period in which we live."(15) There is scant evidence the situation has since changed so far as the social indebtedness to high-energy levels is concerned.

Indeed, the discoveries of a man like Faraday are sources of ideas for still further inventions that will increase the world's conversion of available energy for industry and urban growth. There is no indication that ideas mentioned by Carey have yet approached their fullest development for increasing the energy supply.(16)

The ease with which social and technological action has been melded has been aided by the fragmenting character of the pressure for increased energy cascades. Little effort has been expended in establishing even the appearance of unity. There exists a close, across-the-board bond holding together the meld of technology and social action in a high-energy culture. For this reason, the intervention of the state is sought to provide the missing unifying action. Just as the energy cascades are themselves the product of technology and preceding or concurrent social decisions, so also is the call for state intervention.

THE PRESSURE TOWARD ENERGY CONSERVATION

One of the decisions of a most ambiguous character is whether or not to reduce the amount of energy used to meet urban-industrial demand. In 1972 the United States Office of Emergency Planning claimed that the use of existing technology by itself could reduce energy demand in the United States by five to ten percent per year. Within ten years, through the replacement of inefficient equipment and energy-saving design, the energy demand could thereby be reduced by the equivalent of 77.3 million barrels of crude oil each year. The crucial phrase here was "energy-saving design." Significant changes in transportation, building construction, and recycling would be required on the basis of presently existing technology.(17)

If such actions should ever be taken, it is obvious that alterations more than merely technical will have taken place in American life. The present social structure has produced the current energy usage which has caused political and economic leaders to think in terms of simply increasing the energy cascades. Major social action will be needed to induce those same leaders to think in terms of improving the efficiency of energy use and obviating the need for such massive energy conversion increases as are projected over the next generation.

It is the contrary insistence on conserving energy, both directly and also indirectly through the conservation of materials, that makes R. Buckminster Fuller so unusual. His "dymaxion" principles insist on gaining the maximum production from the application of energy. His emphasis is upon the minimal investment of energy so that in production there would be a constantly increasing performance in relation to the quantity of energy being used. In his New England manner, Buckminster Fuller has called this "doing more with less." He is particularly concerned with using contemporary energy sources efficiently in terms of the unit of energy converted from each unit of fuel.(18)

In world terms, comparing production of and consumption by the various kinds of engines used, Buckminster Fuller claims that energy conversion from energy's fuel sources is only about six to eight percent. At its best, the efficiency of conversion does not run above twenty percent in any part of the world. Efficiency is quite low in the gasoline-powered automobile, which is twelve percent in terms of energy produced in relation to fuel input. Steam railroad buffs should note that the steam locomotive is only seven percent efficient. From these lows in efficiency, the rate goes to thirty percent for the gas engine, forty percent for the steam turbine, eighty percent for the hydro-electric turbine.(19)

These comparative figures show that power sources are not interchangeable for different uses. They cannot be taken to show, therefore, that the gasoline engine should or could be given up for the hydro-electric turbine. In the latter case, perhaps the need for landscape to store water would offset the efficiency of energy delivery. Nothing is to be viewed in isolation by anyone who perceives the essential unity of nature in its responses to human demand.(20)

What is important to remember from Buckminster Fuller's insistence on "doing more with less" in the energy field is that humanity has insisted for decades upon a technology which does little with a lot. The economies of automotive and electrical power in terms of technologic efficiency in energy delivery and application represent social indifference to technical inefficiency. Employing such energy converters, social decisions were made that caused these technical inefficiencies to be economic successes in that they produced human employment and amenities. By avoiding the recognition of the larger costs, these "profits" could be very real.(21)

The conversion of energy at low levels of efficiency is worldwide. Technology could reduce the current energy usage levels. The inefficiencies in energy conversion could be eliminated, both in the manner by which energy is supplied and the way in which demand is formed for that energy supply.

Public apathy to inefficient conversions of energy has long been typical. The social organization has favored measures that keep nature's unified energy budget disguised by a fragmenting human use of energy. That same social organization has insisted upon shunting costs onto nature or to layers of the social structure that cannot resist the redirection.

Through this process, the units of energy have been made to appear cheap. The sharply rising curves of demand and consumption are seen only as beneficial. Costs that may outweigh the benefits are not perceived.

As a result, government, despite the call upon it to mediate all disputes and to maintain the growth of urban-industrial demand, is most reluctant to reduce the expansion of energy conversion. To do so would reallocate wealth and produce conflicts, which politicians in high-energy cultures strive to avoid. A widespread conviction must exist that social change is necessary if the intervention of government is to be successful. Absent such a conviction, the current patterns of energy use will continue on their crisis course.(22)

ENERGY DEMAND AND PRICE

Energy costs determine both the initial increase in demand and the frugality with which that demand is serviced.(23) Any policy of cheap energy supply represents three simultaneous social decisions. These decisions will tend to increase energy use regardless of the efficiency of energy conversion, try to step-up the demand for cheaper energy, and attempt to conceal all the costs that a socially pre-determined "cheapness" prefers not to consider.(24)

In Carey's early statistics, evidence is strong for both such a social policy and for this kind of connection between energy cost and demand. In 1826, for example, when anthracite cost as much as $10 per ton, the use of coal was six tons per one thousand persons. In 1846, when the price was $4.00 per ton, the use was one hundred twenty-five tons per one thousand persons.(25)

The major source of energy for any age – coal in Carey's time, oil today – is never totally price-resistant. Carey, however, was able to claim that once an economy had become dependent upon high-energy levels and the demand had hardened around particular energy sources, high prices did not tend to lessen the demand. By themselves, higher prices would not return the demand to anything like previous low-energy levels.(26)

Henry Carey's voice from the nineteenth century can participate in the late twentieth century debate on lowering demand for any energy source by sharply increasing its price. The rate of increase in demand, rather than any absolute reduction in the demand, may be reduced. What was true for Carey's anthracite is far more true for the energy sources vital to today's economy.(27)

In a high-energy economy, the likeliest expectation from sharply higher prices is a reduction in the rate of increase. This is the form resistance prefers to take to the spiraling costs. The dependence on energy denies the option to give up the high levels of energy use or even to reduce them. Only a major social decision accepting severe economic dislocations, amounting to substantial reallocations of wealth within the social structure of the world economy, would allow such sacrifice of energy. Before this will be done, many other recourses will have been tried.(28)

The function of government is closely interwoven with these operations of energy in the economy, and government has been doing its best in high-energy societies to keep energy supplies ample, cheap, and expanding. In the United States, natural gas in interstate sales was kept underpriced for a generation in relation to the price it could command in the market. In the 1970s, "old" domestic oil was kept underpriced relative to the market price set by the OPEC cartel. This, combined with retail price control, held down the real increase in the price of gasoline, so that in the 1970s American consumption could grow with the simultaneous national increase in the use of such gasoline-guzzlers as vans, recreation vehicles, and heavy cars.(29) It seems to have been an unstated American governmental policy to price the most heavily demanded forms of energy below their true marginal value. As Walter Mead said, ". . .the primary problems of energy are best understood in a long-lost discipline called 'political economy.' "(30)

Given its dependence on energy urban-industrial society resists lowering its levels of energy usage or demand. There are other preferences. One is for rationing and price control. This is opted for even though the economy's functioning will be skewed in a way difficult to correct. Hard to control (if not outright uncontrollable) inefficiencies, both technical and economic, inevitably are produced. Another preference is an acceptance of higher prices, although higher prices may mean the serious imbalancing of severe cost-push inflation and other social and economic malaise. The choices, then, are fairly limited within a high-energy system.

When a policy of cheap energy exists, energy is often produced in a manner that wastes the resource providing the fuel. Also under such a policy, much of the energy produced would be allowed to spill out as a waste product. With this policy, there is little reason (other than a vague altruism) for conservation of natural resources involved in energy supply and application. Under such a policy, energy is used in quantities and for projects marked by a seriously inefficient conversion of the energy in the industrial process.(31)

THE CONCEPT OF THE TOTAL ENERGY BUDGET

Trying to keep cheap energy under conditions of high-energy usage may have indefinitely delayed the chances technology offers to set up total energy systems. It is partly for this reason that the limited experiments in total energy budgets have failed. Such budgets may reflect the unity existing in nature, but often enough they do not represent any economic advantage. Total energy proponents are compelled to fight the forces favoring the fragmenting, processing, and homogenizing of the environment for the benefit of rising growth curves in production and consumption. Apart from their technical difficulties, they find themselves negated by tax structures, regulations, and technical operations favoring a fragmented energy system. Those who do not find individual profit from a total energy system will not favor it.

Proponents of total energy budgets claim that it is possible "to convert 70 to 80 percent of the potential energy of the fuel supplied into usable energy forms such as electricity, heat, and air conditioning." They compare this claimed potential most unfavorably to the fact that "the average public utility generates only electricity and operates in the 25-30% efficiency range, thereby wasting about 70% of the basic fuel resource."(32)

Normally, heat is rejected into water or the atmosphere. It is produced in the process of generating energy so that it becomes a pollutant rather than a valuable commodity. But heat is a valuable resource in space heating, although in the present fragmented energy situation it can bear no relationship to this wasted by-product. If heat and water could be brought together, humanity would move nearer to a total energy budget with a unifying, rather than a fragmenting, character.

"More with less" needs to be done. Currently each desirable energy commodity is produced independently of the others. Energy is used that produces heat only as a waste. The heat must be expensively disposed of by pollution control devices, rather than used to heat space and warm water. The advocates of total energy systems, aware of the demands imposed simply by the fragmenting of the energy budget, are dismayed by the current non-integrated national energy policy.

The practice continues in the way the present energy crisis is being handled. The production of basic fuel resources is simply to be increased through more exploration, the exploitation of hitherto exotic sources, and conservation of individual energy sources. The result is simply to provide more resources to be fed into the present fragmented systems.

The shift to such a total energy system, or to anything approximating it, is not likely to occur soon. The comparative values assigned to energy and materials in the present economic system do not represent a trend in that direction. As J. Harris Ward has said, the use of energy has "increased geometrically as the ox and the mule have been replaced by wood, coal, oil, gas, and uranium in an ever-increasing supply of energy units. . . .Neither the minds nor the data are available today to tell us. . .the growth rate of total energy use."(33) The contemporary pressures in nature and society are such that most people today cannot believe that they must ever think in terms of a total energy budget.

Total energy systems are presently technologically complex. They require a high degree of skilled maintenance. The market is not conditioned to respond to the full range of their production. In high-priced labor markets, they are fairly labor-intensive, at least at this stage of their technical development. The result is that most contemporary energy planners can see no fiscal savings in moving from fragmentary to total energy systems.(34)

The larger issue of the environment and the on-going energy supply is hardly considered by much present-day reasoning. Instead, solutions generally are sought through the increase of the available fuel supply. Technical problems become overwhelming, blocking the formation of a total energy budget to deal with the energy demands of urban-industrial society.(35)

THE "CHEAPNESS" OF THE GASOLINE
AUTOMOTIVE ENGINE

The gasoline engine is the prime example of the acceptance of a technology once it was socially concluded that gasoline was a cheap energy source. Oil is the very foundation of energy use as industrial society approaches the end of the twentieth century. A substantial part of the oil is used to supply the gasoline and diesel engines of cars and trucks (and the gasoline and kerosene powered engines of aircraft) with fuel. The emergence of the private motorcar as a major source of transportation in the world was made possible by the social decision to make the energy for it cheaply available and to pass the resultant costs off upon nature.(36)

The existence of high external costs connected with the internal combustion engine were quite evident from the beginning. The production of noise, air pollution, and dominance of the roadway were immediately observed. The 1875 Viennese police report of the Marcus Kraftwagen, the first auto driven by a gasoline-powered internal combustion engine, states that it "developed gigantic smoke clouds, smelled badly, and frightened the pedestrians in the greatest proportions."(37)

Since 1875, the smoke clouds have been made largely invisible. The odor either has been removed or we have learned to think it pleasant.

The noise has been individually muted and has become generally acceptable. Pedestrians, through familiarity, have lost their fears. Fearlessly, they compete for space with the auto, even though they are in far greater peril today than were the Viennese who took fright at an experimental version roaming the streets under the personal protection of the Crown Prince Rudolph.

Yet even though the substantial side-effects were early known, the gasoline car was encouraged to take a dominant position by 1900. It has maintained that dominance ever since. Indeed, so strong was its dominant position that in the years from 1900 to 1930, when steam and electric cars sought to compete, their manufacturers had to produce vehicles imitative of the entire appearance of their gasoline-powered rivals.

During 1900 to 1930, no one asked, why was the gasoline car so much cheaper and desirable? In those days, steam and electric cars had competitive advantages not possessed by the gasoline car: quiet ride, smooth torque, no gears, no clutch, and the ability to survive long miles of hard road usage without rapid obsolescence.(38)

Yet in the twentieth century, these autos never seriously rivaled the gasoline car. The latter had instant start, high speed, and by comparison a cheap initial cost. These advantages were purchased at the expense of the atmosphere, high urban noise levels, higher maintenance costs, and quicker replacement needs. Some would claim that these costs add to the additional expense of a more rapid urban decay.

But during the rise to dominance of the gasoline car few people paused to consider what precisely was making it so relatively "cheap." Under the impact of the demands of the gasoline engine, not only did the use of oil increase, but the percentage of a barrel of crude oil refined into gasoline rose. In 1880 in the United States, it was 10.3 percent; by 1923 it was 42.1 percent; and from 1923 through 1968 it drifted steadily upward to about forty-five percent. Since 1968, for a variety of reasons, the demand for gasoline has increased absolutely in the United States.(39)

Prior to 1979, many were quick to suggest that something like pricing "regular" gasoline at one dollar per gallon would go a long way to solving the immediate crisis. In 1979 they pushed their maxima far higher. As an idea, it has simplicity. It should have effectiveness.

But each major reduction in the consumption of oil risks a concomitant dislocation of high-energy use in urban-industrial society.(40) Present demand structures have been predicated on plentiful, cheap energy, especially for automotive fuel. Should the decision be made to abruptly cut oil consumption in the United States by about ten million barrels daily to bring consumption within domestic production, chaos would result. The fact that over one fourth of the fuel resources consumed in 1970-75 in the United States was used for transportation would alone guarantee that chaos.(41)

The United States is without an effective mass transit system for the last quarter of the twentieth century. For nearly half a century, the United States has encouraged suburban development at the expense of concentrated city living. These facts have had the effect of transferring a large portion of the earnings of lower-income persons to transportation. If a major reduction in the availability of gasoline should occur, however, a perhaps more disrupting loss, because abrupt and concentrated, would fall upon the middle class. High fuel costs would affect investments in suburban, and especially exurban, land as well as deeply interrupting the current organization of American urban life.

This is not to deny that these long-run effects from fuel shortages might not be good for urban-industrial society. The Organization on Economic and Community Development's massive January 1975 report on the future of oil consumption made this point very well.(42) All of the following could well be to the general social good: forcing the mass departure from heavy, powerful, fuel-demanding cars; forcing an economic preference for mass transit; forcing a return on economic grounds to the central city in lieu of encouraging the spread of slurbs across the countryside; forcing a reduction in the growth of the mobile home, second home, camper, and off-road vehicle industries with the resultant protection of open space and wilderness. Many might consider these results as making three-dollars-a-gallon gasoline worth the price.

But it was obvious to those who had considered the consequences that such a major reduction in an important energy source would not occur without considerable economic, social and political disruptions. According to many environmentalists, the disruption is badly needed. Perhaps nothing else than such a dramatic transfer of income can accomplish this necessary disruption. But as Bette Davis declaimed at the end of All About Eve, "Fasten your seat belts everybody – we're in for a very rough ride!"

When gasoline was less than two bits to the gallon, during the American retail gasoline price wars in the early 1970s, cars that got six miles to the gallon in city traffic, or less than four miles to the gallon while pulling a camper, could be love objects. When the gasoline price performed multiplying feats, love tended to cool. A price "elasticity" for gasoline was discovered temporarily in 1973-74. This was an event that the paid celebrators of romance in the public relations industry had told Americans was not possible between them and their automobiles. But the public accommodated. One may legitimately wonder at what price gasoline demand in the United States would be restricted.(43)

Sometime in the 1920s at the latest, an important social decision was made in the high-energy American culture. It was not to be made in Europe and Japan until the late 1950s. In each instance, the social decision was made in the sort of unarticulated manner of such basic decisions. The message was clear. Energy would be cheap; energy would be abundant; and energy would not be used frugally.

The result of this decision first effected gasoline for the private car. Later, under a political impetus reflective of the social decision, it was extended to electric power, natural gas, and coal. Some of the cheapness, as in hydro-electric power and strip-mined coal, came from passing the cost along to the environment in the form of massive land uses. Other sources of energy were subsidized at the expense of the general taxpayer. As for the rest, present enjoyments were purchased at the price of postponed crises.

But the advent of the postponed crises came in the mid-1970s. The power of postponement had already been much diminished. Different attitudes, perforce, had begun to surface concerning energy, even though only minority opinion. What has been called the "cheap energy binge" seemed to be coming to an end.(44) And events in 1979 revealed the long-maintained "cheap" price of gasoline to be the social creation it had always been.

REDUCING THE CONSUMPTION OF OIL-DERIVED ENERGY

The energy crisis in the 1970s was in part the result of political action by some major oil-producing states. The urban-industrial economies dependent on this oil had several responses available. One was to simply allow the historically forecasted pattern to continue. This proved very popular among many people for a long while.

Another response was to increase domestic exploration of potential oil sources on land or under waters within their effective control. North Sea oil and gas is one example of this option. Mexican oil discoveries are another. But this kind of response is not available to many economies.(45)

Another recourse was to hope to greatly increase the amount of oil extracted from shale and coal. This assumed the technology existed and the ability of nature to withstand the pressure such strip-mining would impose. Whatever the assumption about nature, technology has yet to economically produce oil from such sources even under oil prices that had advanced astronomically.

There are other institutional devices that would permit economies without oil supplies to reduce imports. The apparently most democratic is the rationing of oil and gasoline. This would impose a governmental control on the rate of increase in demand and might even halt the increase in demand of legally priced oil. Aside from the fall-out effect this might have on the auto industry and those tertiary industries dependent on a population doing its shopping on wheels, there would arise the problem of the black-market. This market would siphon off oil from legal markets and act to reallocate wealth, which would likely further the separation of social classes.

Rationing is a system that produces little revenue for the government. It imposes costs because it demands an enforcing bureaucracy. Such public servants would thus contribute to anticipated deficits in the national budgets which in the late 1970s acquired proportions huge in comparison with the past.(46)

Another institutional recourse might be called the creation of a "white market." This would markedly raise the price of gasoline either by a tax on imports, or on production, or at the pump. However accomplished, the bulk of the cost increase would be passed through to the ultimate consumer. This too would reallocate wealth in the manner of the black market. The difference here is that the government would be provided with a substantial revenue and would need little additional bureaucracy — always assuming the government does not choose to raise oil costs by simply allowing the suppliers to greatly increase prices without an accompanying taxation. But should there be additional revenue, the government would have a means to readjust the regressive reallocation of wealth which had occurred through higher oil prices. This is the recurring American political debate.

There are, of course, other institutional devices for reducing oil consumption. One would be closing all limited access routes in metropolitan regions to any vehicles except trucks and vehicles carrying two or more passengers. Another would be curtailing allocations of fuel to certain uses, though this too raises the demand for a black market. Cheap mass transit on a subsidy basis, accompanied by punitive charges on car parking, could be rapidly developed. Another device is to impose taxes related to horsepower and/or car weight to drive off the road the heavier gasoline users. Unfortunately, many of these recourses have a long-term significance that, at best, would not begin to be felt in the economy until well into the decade of the 1980s.

The American auto industry is being compelled, both by direct governmental fiat and by indirect economic pressure, to do what environmentalists say it has needed to since at least 1960: to reduce the size and weight of their cars and the power of the engines within them. Even the American auto industry had itself agreed by 1975 that it could reduce auto gasoline mileage by forty percent by 1980. The American auto buyer in the 1970s seemingly detested what this meant in auto size, but the United States EPA had long been saying such mileage was easily possible. Indeed, the United States EPA had claimed gasoline mileage could be reduced by sixty percent by 1985 while meeting all emission requirements simultaneously.(47)

Unless the form of automotive power is changed, as it would be if electric cars or cars powered by hydrogen or alcohol replace those fueled by gasoline, these problems will remain for the foreseeable future. Switching to these other fuels would provide other problems, of course. These non-gasoline burning cars do produce pollution which, in turn, imposes costs upon society and nature. Under high-energy demand there is no easy way out. The society that insists upon cheap, abundant energy is in conflict with either energy conservation or energy economy.

Many of the current energy eaters, of which the automobile is only one example, could never have become so significant in our society if they had been compelled from the beginning to absorb within their own production and consumption processes all of the costs they were imposing on society and nature. In fact, even now that they are well established — the automobile as an example — the total internalization of those costs within their processes is not a possibility. Barry Commoner is not wrong when he doubts that cost specificity and subsequent cost internalization are any joint panacea.(48)

Insistence in the United States upon a policy of cheap energy has brought about the present situation for both good and ill. What can produce a reordering of priorities and a different sort of subordination? In the 1970s decisions in the United States seemed only to be a direct function of the oil pricing policies of the OPEC states. Even then, in conformity with the fragmentary approach to energy making urban-industrial society, the major reaction has been one of grudging cut-backs in increased petroleum use. Going beyond that, in a comprehensive way, is not yet an idea whose time has come.

COMMONLY CONSIDERED ALTERNATIVE ENERGY SOURCES

The existing international energy situation places the control over price and quantity of a substantial source of energy in the hands of a few producers. Those who use oil as a major energy source must consider alternatives. The extraction of oil and gas from shale and coal and the increase in atomic power are among the commonly alleged alternatives.

At a time when the daily use of oil has languished but little, despite the actions of the oil-exporting states, national decisions to increase energy supplies from other sources are not surprising. When both the total demand and reliance on the oil exporters seem intent on growing monthly, this is expectable. Here, in fact, is the crisis in a high-energy culture.

Economically, so far as oil or gas production from a synthetic source is concerned, the higher the price per barrel of oil or per thousand cubic feet of gas, the better stands the chance of shale as a competitive source of oil. Costs previously have been a problem for the competitiveness of American energy sources other than oil, natural gas, or coal. The worst possible conditions for the development of alternative energy sources would be for OPEC to cut prices back to where they had been at the beginning of the 1970s. All alternative inquiries would go by the board and the world would return to its cheap energy spree until again faced with an oil crisis. The next crisis, however, would likely be the result of the absolute shortage of the mineral itself.(49)

The ecologic costs of extracting oil from shale or coal have never caused policymakers to back off from the decision to take oil from those sources. If oil is not taken from shale or coal, the reason will be that it can be acquired at cheaper prices elsewhere. The decision to refrain will not be due to any harm which extracting oil from strip-mined shale or coal would bring to the environment.

The governors of the six Rocky Mountain states, where most of the shale, coal, and uranium wealth of the United States lies, can say they will not allow stripping if the environment is thereby affected adversely. They can argue that their people must have an economically beneficial trade-off for the loss of soil, water, and air. Aside from the wisdom of even this much accommodation, one must not overlook what Joseph Sax has pointed out. Well over half of the nation's fuel sources are on publicly owned land and the federal property clause in the United

States Constitution needs no state's approval for what occurs in a federal enclave.(50) Politics can alter that. But in law, the power of the federal government is very strong. The United States federal government is still oriented, wherever possible, to the continuing pursuit of cheap, expanding energy policies.

The United States Department of the Interior in its 1973 report on western shale exploitation certainly did not minimize the cost to the environment of the American West. Partly because economic risks predominated, the Department recommended initial, prototype programs. The Department wanted to see if harm could be kept within the limits foreseen by its experts before the full extractions were begun.(51)

The "bearable" harm foreseen by the Department consisted of profound ground disturbances in an arid climate where surface restoration is at best difficult. The Department recommended that the only way to dispose of the debris accumulated in the breaking process would be to fill up canyons with it – presuming that canyons are waiting, unused by nature, to be used for this purpose. Such activity would cause a reduction in ground water and a disturbance in surface water flows. There would be a deterioration of air quality because of the temperatures of nine hundred degrees F. needed to free the organic material from the rock, plus the dust and by-products driven off in the refraction. The "virtual disappearance" of certain wild species in the mining areas, and the impact of an increasing population to work the mines in these arid regions do not seem major concerns beside the other anticipated problems.

What made the environmental risks seem worthwhile were the estimates that the shale held trillions of barrels of oil. An emerging technology supposedly would be capable of extracting hundreds of billions of barrels from these trillions. More modestly, people had been talking of a daily production of one million barrels by 1988, but experiments have not yet succeeded on a large scale. For reasons unrelated to the environment, shale oil and gas development are still among the "emergent" technologies, despite congressional enthusiasm for "synfuels".

Under conditions of high-energy demand there will always be popular sympathy for seeking energy from shale, stripped coal, or atomic fission in order to assure the flow and increase of the energy cascades.(52) No responsible person, though, can turn away from contemplating the environmental problems that the very success of such programs entails. These are initially problems of mass. To exploit the fuel for this kind of energy means getting coal and rock out of the ground, increasingly from deeper layers, and disposing of large residues whose quantity and condition often make reclamation difficult.(53)

Such extraction systems are also demandant of water, which is often irretrievably consumed or contaminated in the removal process. The run-off and surface streams so important to the arid regions, where so much of this material is located, would be required in large measure to meet all the needs of this extractive usage. The location of these minerals in dry mountainous regions lacking living soil makes land restoration far more difficult.(54)

Regeneration comes much more slowly in arid rather than in humid zones. Some say that land restoration on arid land is impossible; and that the blasted appearance left by the run-off and the subsequent erosion that follows occasional torrential rains are inevitabilities. The exploitation of the minerals in the Rocky Mountains by stripping may simply mean the sacrifice of the land and the life on it for the supply of energy elsewhere in the United States and the world.(55)

Assuming the pessimists are wrong, land restoration in arid regions is bound to be expensive. The tendency, of course, will be to shuffle these costs off on the environment. Every mineral extractor has tried and, traditionally, was allowed to do this. Given the dependency of the present high-energy culture upon ample, cheap energy, one cannot be sanguine.(56)

Government will not be under pressure to take a strong stand to either preserve or restore the environment, to restrain environmentally oppressive extractive processes, or to increase already high prices by forcing an internalization of the costs of environmental restoration.(57) In a high-energy situation, the pressures for maintaining the energy flow are the most immediate.

This is what lies behind the insistence that, as other power sources languish, their place will be amply supplied by the growth in atomic energy power plants – through the fission process initially, later by the breeder reactor and by the fusion process at some later, hard to specify, date.(58) This has been asserted, although in 1973 the old United States Atomic Energy Commission, upon the recommendation of their safety experts, ordered certain plants to reduce power levels up to twenty-five percent. The dispute, intensified by cost-imposing actions in 1979 of the Nuclear Regulatory Commission, remains as to the economics of nuclear generation of electric power. Furthermore, as- sertions of reliability have been made in light of the fact that the 600,000 gallons of high level radioactive waste from reprocessing fuels used in 1973 in the operation of nuclear plants was expected to reach over sixty million gallons by 2000.(59)

Quite apart from accidents that may cause leakage, the life of these substances is calculated in hundreds of years. Nothing must be allowed to disturb their storage or to end the surveillance of these storage units. It is a technician's concept that the surveillance and storage of radioactive waste could be confidently planned over several hundreds of years.

Perhaps the very fragility of the system may make humanity hesitant to do anything which would risk the release of so much malign force. The same reluctance, on a shorter term, would have to hold for the social dangers that could break the water service to a nuclear plant that keeps it cool, or disrupt the operations which keep all but small (though still lethal) amounts of radioactivity from escaping, or that would allow a take-over of the plant by some group intent on holding a government up for a variety of ransoms.

There is no need to frighten oneself with the chance at major nuclear accidents since each one of these might be averted by pre-planned mechanisms for dealing with breakdowns coming from within the system's technology. But one ought not be sanguine about the economic problems of nuclear power. Long before the Three-Mile Island incident in 1979, the economist Carolyn Brancato pointed out the high rates of unscheduled unavailability of nuclear electric generating units in comparison to coal-powered units. She also noted nuclear plants were difficult, slow, and costly to repair, imposing the burden of power purchase from the outage. She could have been writing the internal cost scenario for the owners of all types of nuclear plants unexpectedly closed by the aftermath of what happened at Three-Mile Island.(60) There seem to be occasions when having a nuclear power plant is costlier than delays in getting one built.(61)

Society may be well along the road to making itself liable for hostage through the greater building of nuclear power stations. All the costs and risks present in nuclear power may be worth undertaking in order to maintain the growth in energy cascades. They are, however, not small risks: steady small leakages of radioactivity; an atomic accident or a failure in some control mechanism; danger from earth-quake or storm; the existence of zealots desirous of punishing society or of bringing it to their dictated terms; the likelihood that a stable social structure cannot be maintained forever just to monitor radioactive wastes, and the burden of capital investment and hard-to-predict maintenance costs.(62)

The gains from atomic power, therefore, would − indeed, will − be accompanied by grave environmental and social risks. The same is true for energy to be taken from shale and a stepped up stripping of coal. The question is whether such urban-industrial demand for more energy is worth all the evident risks.(63)

CONSIDERING THE ENVIRONMENTAL RISKS OF HIGHER ENERGY DEMAND

One must first recognize that there seems no condition, however affluent, representing saturation in urban-industrial society. The reason for this, pointed out by Irving Fisher as long ago as 1906, is humanity's disconcern with goods or even with energy. Humanity is concerned with service and the flow of services in time.(64) For this reason, demand is without an absolute limit in the human imagination and must find its restraint in ways external to that human imagination.

A materialist, without environmental sensitivity, might well ask questions having environmental concern under the conditions of open-ended rises in demand. For example, how long, at the projected rate of consumption, are sources for hydrocarbons likely to last? How large an acreage or how much water do various forms of energy production require from the land surface, including the acreage needed for fuel extraction and waste disposal as well as the site of the power plant?(65)

What are the risks of leaks, accidents, and storage seeps in nuclear plants and the factories which clean the rods for reuse? How much release of heat from any source – solar, tidal, or combusted – can the atmosphere handle?(66)

There are many other questions of like import. They are all equally materialist and do not require environmental sensitivity. Perhaps a few examples of them will suffice.

Why is it wiser to permit the advertising of more energy sales or to charge lower rates for greater energy consumption? Why is it good to introduce into the market even more energy-requiring mechanical aids instead of pursuing a contrary policy that would reward low energy users and savers and that would set priorities in terms of a demand for something other than electric toothbrushes and cocktail shakers? Why, in short, is the belief in cheap energy – a cheapness that has to be subsidized at the expense of the environment, of the balance between humanity and nature, and of human health itself – somehow a better public policy than one that would charge into the cost of that energy the amounts in cash that it takes to restore, clean up, or solve the injuries caused by its production?

These are questions a non-environmentally concerned materialist might set down in a list on the basis that the answers could be important in the urban-industrial future. But the questions set out above require no anti-materialist bias. One might believe in using energy cascades from a wide range of fuel sources and still want answers to those questions.

The changes precipitated since 1700 by the growth in energy conversion are irreversible. Still one could question the stability of the foundations upon which the present accelerating energy growth rests. A reasonable mind could question as well the sufficiency of the system to maintain indefinitely such a pattern. To think basic alterations in goals, procedures, or sources might be required could be the thinking of a coldly materialistic, as well as a compassionately environmental, mind.

Suppose goals were to be changed. What should they be in terms of low-energy demand? With enough electric power, as Ralph Borsodi noted nearly half a century ago, population could be returned to rural areas and an economy, combining comfortable subsistence farming with home manufacturing processes, could be set up to replace the concentrated city.(67) Massive concentrations of energy would be needed to produce other energy savings in this kind of social shift.

Another type of society, exactly contrary to Borsodi's, was proposed by the late C. A. Doxiades. His society would concentrate people in urban centers in order to leave the countryside scantly populated. By concentrating energy conversion, there could be an overall reduction in energy generation.(68)

But whether such reforms are right or wrong, they require environmentally a balance of human demand with the limited scope of the renewing environment. Whatever the reform, there must be a conscious articulation of current conditions. Then there must be the recognition of what might be done in relation to such conditions.

A shift to lower energy demands could occur serendipitously. If the pace of the energy growth curves slowed because the available hydro-carbons slowly declined, and if the rate of growth in alternative power sources were unable to make up the slack, society might then make adjustments, imperceptible as they were being made, to accommodate the lag in anticipated energy growth with spaced out decision.

This is not likely, however. Urban-industrial society is committed to trying to maintain the pace of energy growth. The next thirty years are not likely to see in either capitalist or socialist countries willingly made goal-changing decisions to subject energy growth to limitations imposed by low-energy values. Unwillingly made? That could be a different story, particularly in the shorter time frames for most economic and technical decisions.

COPING WITH A CONTINUING HIGH-ENERGY DEMAND

The environmental movement is considered by many as the plaything of the upper-middle class even though the poor are more vulnerable to energy crises and environmental destruction.(69) Business generally considers environmentalists as obstructionists rather than receiving their criticisms as frequently having both environmental validity and the offer of profit opportunities. In brief, the environmental movement is viewed as either a diversion or a burden. Too rarely is it taken as being something central to society.

Present policies will not moderate the energy crisis. The "solutions" for the energy crisis at the end of the 1970s were more of what had produced the crisis: remove production limits in the field; relax restrictions, use fuels risky to public health; exploit fuel origins located in ecologically fragile polar, coastal, and estuarine zones; and take minerals from the bed of the high seas regardless of sharply rising pollution levels, especially in the areas of confluence. While pursuing these actions, the intention is to do as little as possible to moderate the intensity of demand for more oil, gasoline, natural gas, coal, and electric power, and do nothing at all to unify the conversion, distribu-tion, or use of the energy involved. This was the prevailing current policy for the dawn of the 1980s and does not approximate a way out of an energy crisis.

To respond to "demands" like these, there can be no fixed points to which technology is compelled to react in any automatic, unquestioning way. Technology is not the automoton many have depicted. Like the "demand" to which it is applied, it too is humanly devised and subject to social control. The dominating truth here is that all these operations are cultural. Being cultural, they are highly mutable.

Early in the 1970s, the Sierra Club recommended reduction in energy consumption.(70) This would have required a change in social patterns. Decision-makers of the time believed that there was no immediate crisis in energy sources or any absolute limit in the atmosphere's function as a waste receiving body that would compel such a change. Thus no absolute reduction in energy consumption occurred. Any reductions in the rate of expanding energy use in the 1970s were brief and were imposed by OPEC rather than by any wish to hold back energy demands. There was little effective action to reduce energy demand nor much belief in the severity of any impending crisis.(71)

The greater harm done by high-energy usage is not to human beings. Humanity in totality has had the benefits as well as the costs of the historic means of supplying more energy. The greater harm, which has been little offset by benefits, has been suffered by the environment from which people ultimately draw sustenance: in the air and waters warmed by the heat put out as waste in the energy conversion process, in the pine forests browned by the oxides of nitrogen, in the food chains disrupted by oil spills and the steady seeping discharge of oil additives such as lead or polychlorinated bi-phenyls, in the land taken for highways and grid corridors, and in other ways tedious for humans to list but important for nature to feel as invasions.

In the long run, these insidious consequences of human action will cause changes that probably will enforce the sort of absolute limits that are feared but which are not yet imposed. Change initiated in energy use could help. Socially and technically, an integrated energy system drawing on renewable energy sources would multiply the present amounts of energy in such a fashion that neither heat, nor particulates, nor gases would be released in anything like their present amounts.(72)

This planet is far from a saturation level in its ability to absorb energy. Greater energy conversion can bring about material improvement for larger numbers of humanity than heretofore have known comfort. The ability of the planet to support life does not have to be discounted in obtaining the enjoyment of further amenity.

But such a transition cannot come about through reliance on the historic, fragmentary energy converters. Most particularly, such a transition cannot be brought into existence by an overlay of shale or coal liquefaction and gasification or atomic-fission nuclear stations meant to produce electricity and waste heat in mutual disregard. The larger environment in which humanity must live cannot withstand such mistreatment on an ever more common worldwide basis.

Environmentally assimilable energy systems are for the future. There will be one or more transitional generations involved in keeping civilization going until those newer energy systems can be drawn upon. These transitional generations will not want to reduce their high-energy demands. It is doubtful if the firmest leadership could induce them to do more than adopt procedures for reducing growth "needs" in energy conversion.

The changes required are not just technical. They are social. Society itself rather than isolated technologists or experts must carry through the change-over to energy conservation and integration. Specific actions can reduce the pace of growth in energy demand. Taxation could adjust the price of energy sources so that their prices internalize the costs imposed upon the environment. Subsidization of open-ended growth would cease. Should this price oppress the poor, relief could be supplied in the form of free mass transit or in limited amounts of fuel at subsidized prices. A price policy such as this makes far more sense than the tradition of low rates for heavy users or a highway fund concentrated upon interstate expansion to facilitate the high-speed movement of powerful low mileage, single-occupant cars.

When the choice is made to shift to a unified energy system, one hopes it could be done by a gradual transition. None of the energy still being produced in the traditional ways would be wasted. As the shift occurred, the needed technical changes would begin to come on line.

The shift, however, may be neither gradual nor peaceful. Urban-industrial society is perilously dependent on petroleum as a primary resource. The abrupt price actions of OPEC repeatedly demonstrated in the 1970s the fragility of the world's existing energy system.

Yet the decision-makers cling to a petroleum energy source, or to some simulacrum of it. They opt for nuclear power and for making liquids from synthetic sources that would behave just like petroleum. The costs involved are so great that one may well wonder with Amory Lovins and Barry Commoner (73) where the capital will be found to pay the higher prices for oil and other fossil fuels, to build and maintain nuclear power plants and waste disposal and fuel recycling facilities, to initiate synthetic fuel extracting and refining operations, and to develop renewable energy sources.

Until a different social decision is made, technology can only serve the malaise of the present methods for converting, distributing and employing energy. In terms of the present projections based upon current historic practices, energy uses and energy sources in urban-industrial society cannot do otherwise than continue to run in perilous tandem. And anyone might wonder if it is possible to go all ways at once in the pursuit of every kind of energy system and to simultaneously exploit and protect the renewing environment.

The problem with all crises, in social systems as well as in individual physiology, is that anything which throws the mechanisms off their interconnected paces can be fatal. Such interruption ought to be "temporary," yes. If what is interrupted does not resume, however, what ought to have been temporary has the permanency of death. The inducements are strong for undertaking the movement to renewable energy sources and a unified energy system. The costs will be less than what the tradition in energy use has imposed since 1700. And the costs will be far below what the present acceleration forebodes.

4 The Environmental Cost of Modern Urban Growth

HIGH-ENERGY'S WELCOME TO URBAN EXPANSION

In the high-energy societies of the twentieth century the city has sprawled into the countryside. The expansion of city forms – streets, lots, stores – becomes a destroyer of open space, an abuser of the land resource, and a threat to the viability of the natural environment. One wonders if any people will be left to be called rural or if the words urban, suburban, and exurban will describe the whole population.

To many, the automobile and the previously cheap, abundant energy of the twentieth century are alone to blame. They reason that if, somehow, a low-energy society could be substituted, all would be well. These persons welcomed the energy crisis of the 1970s, with its vertically rising energy costs.

Horst Siebert of Hamburg's Die Welt was amused when he said of America, that it "can still not get free of the idea that gasoline, fuel oil, natural gas, and coal must be cheap."(1) Mr. Siebert would be more justified if he extended his irony to every high-energy society as does the social theologian Ivan Illich, who proposes a maximum speed of twenty five miles per hour on all transit. By so doing, the transformation of country existences into city-forms could not continue to occur.

As Illich himself has observed, the use of speedy transit goes back well over a century to the beginnings of the railroad. This commuter service rapidly increased passenger mileage in western countries ninety times by the 1850s.(2) The nineteenth century thereby introduced urban expansion as a public good.

Certainly H. G. Wells, in previewing the twentieth century for his 1901 audience, had no qualms in describing a future of suburban living. He simply gloated over houses being scattered across the country. Each of these houses was to be occupied with independent young couples happily isolated from traditional cross-generational, cross-class settlements.(3)

H. G. Wells felt no nostalgia for the crowded city which nineteenth century energy forms had so concentrated in area. After all, every cultural attribute of city living would be available in the continuous strip-cities Mr. Wells happily predicted would typify the twentieth century. His young couples would have their intellectual lives sustained by a home that would become the direct receiver of culture in the future. Film and phonograph already existed; he was confident technology would offer improved cultural vehicles in the future. Eventually the old institutions mediating culture — theater, opera, the concert hall — would no longer be needed in the flow from creator to audience. Culturally, as well as economically, urban-industrial society was ready for the extended city.

Wells' contemporary readers may have smiled in disbelief. But there is no report that anyone was in an uproar at his predictions of scattered housing, new highways, private autocars for common use, and a city-country interface that would be impossible to separate. Public alarm over H. G. Wells in his youth seems to have been confined to his manners at country houses on long weekends and his doubts about God. His predictions on the growth of the city, the submergence of the old rural life, and the movement away from the urban core were hailed as potentially good news.

How could Wells' Victorian readers, who considered the future, not think his predictions for the best? Where could the harm be in reducing the populations in the city core, or taking away from farm families their churlish isolation, or creating the conditions for young middle-class people to live in unharrassed, pleasant gardens among others of their kind? Where was anything wrong in having individuals speeded in private cars over the paved surfaces of great highways built exclusively for moving that traffic rapidly from self-chosen point to point?

The Garden City of Ebenezer Howard, with its houses spaced through flowering yards and stretching over swards of country, was the Edwardian response to the Tudor challenge of St. Thomas More. In Utopia there had been vistas of what a perfect city would be like: humanity would live continuously in a green and open environment, unconfined by the limitations of the old city. Little regard for what this meant to open space was paid by exponents of "green country town living" as the standard for everyone.

The prospects the new twentieth century would offer seemed too wonderful to worry about the possible effects of covering the green earth with concrete or depopulating the city centers. The diurnal movement of vast numbers of commuters in and out of the city and the elimination of any distinction between city and country were simply not regarded as evils.

When persons by the millions through credit and mobility were enabled to leave the central city for the suburbs, then the visions of St. Thomas More and Ebenezer Howard became reality.(4) Only in the late twentieth century did such a transmutation become perceived as something fearful. It has been a fear closely related to the crisis in cheap energy abundance.

LOW ENERGY'S OPPOSITION TO URBAN EXPANSION

Societies fear urban growth, as well as its sprawl into the countryside, when controllable drafts of cheap, abundant energy are not available. This condition defines a low-energy society. An examination of the attitudes in western Europe in the transition from low energy to high energy availability from the sixteenth through the eighteenth centuries illustrates the hostility of low-energy societies to urban growth. The fears of these societies arose from a lack of expectation of cheap, abundant energy that became the basic indicator of later urban-industrial society.

Until the sixteenth century, expansion in the economy had not yet created a challenge. But the 16th century experienced both the discovery of America, with its surge of gold that ended the protracted European deflation, and the coming of the Commercial Revolution, with its reversal of the adverse European balance of trade. European cities began to grow rapidly in both population and geographical size.(5) The greater prosperity was mostly welcomed, except for the expansion of urban life produced by these dramatically changed economic conditions.

Perhaps fear of the city lay in its attraction to the peasants, or beliefs that cities were unhealthful, immoral and turbulent sinks. A wish to preserve the traditional relations between city and country, so that the country would remain the dominating element, predominated. The city was seen as a burden on the productivity of the country, a drain on energy, and a burden to nature. For example, in 1549 Henry II issued a royal ordinance limiting the size of Paris for the following mix of reasons:

> First, that by enlarging the city, the air would be rendered unwholesome. Second, that cleaning the streets would prove a great additional labour. Third, that adding to the number of inhabitants would raise the price of provision, of labour, and of manufactures. Fourth, that ground would be covered with buildings instead of corn, which might hazard a scarcity. Fifth, that the country would be depopulated by the desire that people have to resort to the capital. And, lastly, that the difference of governing such numbers would be an encouragement to robbery and murder.(6)

No twentieth century individual, concerned over the loss of valuable crop land in California to the Los Angeles subculture, or urban crime, or funding municipal services, or loss of open space, could fail to touch on these same points. Few late twentieth century persons would laugh at this statement, however much the early twentieth century would have found it a subject solely for humor.

The sixteenth century hostility toward urban growth was not an attitude confined to the French court. In 1602 Elizabeth I prohibited any new buildings within three miles of London. She justified her action by saying:

That foreseeing the great and manifold inconveniences and mischiefs which daily grow, and are more likely to increase, in the city and suburbs of London, by confluence of people to inhabit the same; not only by reason that such multitudes can hardly be governed, to serve God and obey her Majesty, without constituting an addition of new officers, and enlarging their authority; but also can hardly be provided of food and other necessaries at a reasonable price; and finally, that as such multitudes of people, many of them poor who must live by begging or worse means, are heaped up together, and in a sort smothered with many children and servants in one house or small tenement; it must needs follow, if any plague or other universal sickness come amongst them, that it would presently spread through the whole city and confines, and also into all parts of the realm.(7)

The Queen was reacting to London's expansion on the south bank of the Thames. Its marshy ground, its roistering conglomerate of bear pits, theaters, and prentices, and its quickly flung-up tenements did not help the image of urban growth. Both James I in 1624 and Charles I in 1630 issued proclamations against building on new foundations.

The English builders were under greater compulsion than the French to spread out the city in the seventeenth century. Relying mostly on timber and wattles, rather than stone, their structures were incapable of bearing the weight of the stone the French used. Although the smaller, lower, lighter London buildings were much cheaper to construct than the higher, heavier French city buildings, they required more city space. Not until the late seventeenth century did the builders of such new additions as Downing Street switch to brick. The growing scarcity of timber and a prosperity that scorned thatch and wattle for city buildings impelled the speculative English builder to compete with the French in erecting the more substantial sort of city structure.

One ought not conclude that London grew in area after the sixteenth century while Paris did not. Despite the tendency of the Parisians to build a more compact city with higher buildings, Paris in the mid-1770s under the young Louis XVI and Marie Antoinette was much different in area to the city Catherine de Medici's husband had attempted to confine in 1549.

Paris had the same number of people in the 1770s as 200 years before, but the city occupied three times the area. Perhaps the royal policy to limit population growth in Paris had succeeded. If so, it had been at the price of letting the city expand over its formerly rural environs.(8) Despite official opposition and technical practices favoring urban concentration, Paris, like London, had greatly extended its geographical area in 225 years.(9)

What happened in both Paris and London, under the influence of a widening prosperity, had been a lowering of residential densities. Both people and urban planners, in centuries when disposable energy supplies increased along with the demand for more energy, desired more living space. Following the Great Fire of London in 1666, the rebuilt city had been far less crowded and more spaciously constructed than its predecessor.

Despite the terrible crowding that later occurred in the industrial towns, the initial demand of urban populations had been for lower urban densities. Centuries later, the demand was renewed when expansive high-energy forms became available. It was impossible to give city dwellers more space for living and not encroach upon the land of the city environs. Royal fears and prohibitions were of little avail. As the economy became industrial, and the energy supply increased, these encroachments came more quickly and extensively. Wholly new views arose as to what were suitable population densities. These changed the efforts of government to another direction. Government was compelled to accept the reality of the city's growth in both population and built-up area.

CHANGING ATTITUDES CONCERNING URBAN EXPANSION BETWEEN LOW- AND HIGH-ENERGY

Any close examination of the period after the mid-eighteenth century would reveal a decided change in attitudes toward city growth in both population and area. During this time in western Europe and much of the Americas, urban-industrial growth was increasingly sprawling and magnetic. The burgeoning energy supply was clearing the ways blocking city growth.

Opponents of city growth by the late eighteenth century were regarded as eccentrics. Only the Scottish philosopher Lord Kames, who was too late for Elizabethan restrictions and too early for the Garden City, could propose a London limited to a population of one hundred thousand. He thought the numbers above that that figure should be distributed among nine new towns whose sites had been selected as "the most advantageous for trade, or for manufacturers." As early as 1774, the English New Town movement had an advocate.

The magnetic quality of cities such as London and Paris left Lord Kames as unimpressed as they would have the most ardent return-to-the-land devotee. No city-limiter in the late twentieth century could say more than, "Zealously disputing about the extent of. . .capitals. . .to me. . .appears like one glorying in the king's evil."(10)

Lord Kames, after all, could still extol the alternative virtues of rural life. In eighteenth century England, reform in agricultural practices to increase domestic crop production had kept pace with industrialization. It was not until much later that industrialization would leave English agriculture limping behind. When that happened, the claim could not easily be made that rural life offered anything like the alternative that had been available in Lord Kames' day.

As the social tides roll the people off the land into the cities, the city converts agriculture into an exurban resource for satisfying urban-industrial demand. In situations where there is high energy demand, a concurrent growth in city and industry will both stimulate that demand and utilize the energy converted. Only in situations of low-energy supply has control of city size not been a problem.

Interestingly, sixteenth century city growth became a subject of legislation in countries like France and England. For these states, it was not just a matter of planning cities with more amenities, which well describes the Italian urban planning of the fifteenth century.(11) Instead, the concern was to limit the expansion of the city into the countryside and hold down the size of city populations.

Only when the late eighteenth century seemed at last to guarantee enough energy to allow all these occurrences with impunity, did society lose sight of them as "problems." Fairly quickly, growth was converted into apparently pure opportunities and did not emerge again as a problem until the late twentieth century. All the costs inherent in the opportunities had first to suffer accumulation before urban sprawl could be seen in a larger perspective.

Conditions of energy supply have played the dominant historic role in urban growth for more than four centuries. Urban population growth and urban land sprawl could simply not be all benefit. But those who made it possible to move from low to high applied energy uses expectedly emphasized only the benefits. Paying for many of the costs had to come later.

THE IMPORTANCE OF HIGH-ENERGY TRANSIT FOR URBAN EXPANSION

Low-energy forms of transit had kept the cities small in area prior to the middle of the nineteenth century. The city growth, feared by French and English monarchs for Paris and London in the sixteenth through the eighteenth centuries, is ludicrously small in retrospect, mocking the attempted restrictions. Shank's mare and the horse were the sole means of locomotion until after 1825. Their limitations kept the ambit of the city relatively small.

Reliance upon animal power for urban movement excited Lord Kames about what could be done with the enormous amounts of dung accumulating in the growing cities. The late eighteenth century was a period of great energy growth; cities were responding to it, as was industry; and yet the horse remained the means of moving the newly increased quantities of goods around the city. The dung was excreted too far from the fields to be carried there because of the expense. The truck-gardens in the suburbs were disappearing to land speculators and Lord Kames saw the dung piling up over the city.(12)

In the early decades of the Industrial Revolution animal power in the cities produced too little energy at too high a cost in terms of the demands of the emerging high-energy culture. Horses were not feasible for long city distances. The digestive needs of the creatures, both their feeding and the removal of their droppings, made it difficult to employ as many as the growing economy needed. The same was true for the extensive stabling needed to house them and the grooms and ostlers needed to care for them.

The new methods of high-energy transit in the nineteenth century tended steadily in the direction of lifting the restrictions of animal power on urban transit needs. The steam engine on rails that became so popular after 1830, and the electric tram car that was rapidly adopted after 1890, made the expansion of the city possible in a way commensurate with the other increases in energy conversion occurring throughout the nineteenth century.

The only reason not to use the word "explosive" to describe urban growth in the nineteenth century through the new forms of transit is that it seems so small compared to what electricity and the automobile were to make possible in the twentieth century. But to those who had experienced the compressing effects of dependence on human and animal muscles in the burgeoning energy situations of the late eighteenth and early nineteenth centuries, the transit changes were a glorious energy release.

The growth of Boston between 1850 and the century's end is illustration enough. In 1850 Boston extended only two miles from City Hall. Few could have predicted, on the experience of the previous two centuries, that Boston would do more than continue to slowly accrete in size. Yet by 1887, the horse cars had quadrupled the area of dense settlement over the 1850 figure. When the electric tram appeared after 1890, the radius of its service thrust out the settled area another two miles and quickly brought into the inner Boston metropolitan zone other towns that the steam railroad had been unable to associate so closely with Boston.(13)

All of this was a response of the urban transit system to the demands of high energy. Although it produced a growth in the economic and social city of Boston, no accompanying growth occurred in the political city. Already the horse car, the train, and the electric trolley had started what the auto was to intensify enormously. This was the expansion of the area of intense urban settlement without the simultaneous creation of a single metropolitan unit to govern or give coherence to what was being grown over the landscape. By the turn of the twentieth century urban sprawl was well on the way.

The city under conditions of high-energy usage and availability tends to encompass all of nature. The city-without-end epitomizes urban-industrial society. Urban-industrial society is led to adopt a narrow rationalizing view that processes nature into units of production and consumption. Only urban-industrial demand has importance.

As the urban planner Robert Moses told a 1973 suburban garden club, "Summer cottages are winterized, winter boarding houses become year-round condominiums. . .Spuds, ducks, corn, cabbage, lettuce, tomatoes and suchlike are unfortunately on the way out."(14) Moses is as responsible as any person for what metropolitan New York became in the half century of his greatest public activity between 1917 and 1968. His actions relative to transportation guaranteed his impact. In this casual remark lies all the optimism, as well as the confidence, that the twentieth century had in the rightness of expanding urban movement and of taking the country out of the countryside. Only lately has the confidence in such action begun to wane.

AGRICULTURE AS A PART OF URBAN-INDUSTRIAL DEMAND

The metropolis under conditions of high-energy usage has been called "the epitome of industrialism," imposing a routine insistent on continuously narrower bases for human decision. As the educator Theodore von Laue claims, this is inevitable since, for both technology and the larger society, "the premium lies on dependability and certainty."(15) Humanity is compelled thereby to control both nature and itself in order for the metropolis to respond to the high-energy demands within it.

Each controlling act is a part of the web of urban-industrial demand that is seen as finally imposing order on a previously natural or traditionally irrational scene. Making agriculture a part of the assembly process is a necessity. This permits an increase in the city's consumption of the previously open or remote countryside, through the thrust of highways out from the city with their encumbrance of traffic jams. By providing the means of supplying, distributing, and further increasing the demands for more energy, more goods, more services, and more urban growth, urban-industrial demand converts nature to a resource to supply growth.(16)

Under high-energy pressures, rural life disappears and urban existences become dominant. Why should this not occur, given the burdens increasing capital demand imposes upon the country? Increasingly, crops must be cash earners and the rural production must be tied to the growth in urban-industrial demand.

The United States, with its unrestrained application of high-energy to agriculture, has produced the bulk of the world's food surpluses. Its agro-business complex pays homage, but no dues, to the idol of the family farm. Even the subsidy program operates to make that adored object – the family farm – an item in agricultural museums.

Less than one-third of the 2½ million farms in the United States produce 85% of the food grown in the country. In 1790 the family farm, beside feeding itself, raised enough food for one-twentieth of another person. In 1973, each farmer raised enough food to support 54 people. In 1830 it took 255 minutes to produce one bushel of wheat in the harvesting process. In 1973 on large, dry-land farm units it took one-half minute per bushel.(17) Since then, American agriculture has increased statistically still further.

The place, however, for the partaker of rural life has nearly disappeared. When "American agriculture, including the vast agribusiness complex, is capitalized at about $400 billion a year, and is the single largest industry in the United States," one can expect the greatest service the traditional dweller could render would be to move to town.(18)

Ironically, the United States, the nation with the longest urban-industrial experience, has much of its power for international bargaining in the late twentieth century residing in its agricultural production. This, however, is no paradox. The subsistence and marginal market farmer has been steadily eliminated in the United States since the agricultural depression of the early 1920s. Few in the city may have been aware of it, but between 1940 and 1974 there occurred "a great revolution in the size of (agricultural) equipment, whether measured in horse power, width of cut, numbers of rows planted, output per hour or whatever measure one chooses. . .lead(ing) to great changes in the production potential of well-managed, highly productive farms."(19) In brief, in those years the farm in the United States became an industrial facility. Crop production had become the organic equivalent of a machine-plant assembly-line.

The United States has shown that by moving the people off the land and industrializing agriculture, the concentrated application of energy will produce a food surplus. All of the American social structure has been drawn into high-energy usages. The rural migrants to the cities, as well as the rural poor who stay behind, have only high-energy images with which to identify. Motown sound, electronic country music, and the exploits of Evel Knievel are none of them low-energy symbols.

It is not that Americans have such high production per acre compared to some labor intensive agricultural systems or that mechanization more efficiently replaces the kinetic energy for making calories. On a total energy budget the American calorie production is not so impressive.(20) The fragmented energy budget, in which the energy costs of fuel and fertilizer can be substantially concealed, makes agriculture a congruent part of urban-industrial demand.

Barry Commoner argues that level of energy invested should be reduced to no more than the amount of energy extracted from the investment. Although he applies this to the energy spent for obtaining energy from fuels, he includes agriculture as well. It is his desire to reduce the hostage to petroleum in which urban-industrial agriculture is held.(21)

Those who disagree say the disaggregated character of energy makes a total energy budget impossible. They agree that a more integrated energy budget might be more rational than the existing fragmented one. Using the waste of one process as heat, or power, or fuel is often technically feasible. Institutions that make such uses economically unreasonable ought to be modified. But that is the smallest part of it. The dispersed levels of energy in the environment, such as solar, tidal and wind power, must be focused in order to be available for many human uses, especially at-command services. Consequently, it is not practical to speak of a total energy budget balancing input with output.(22)

Furthermore, urban-industrial agricultural technology is capital intensive. The use of labor has steadily diminished and a larger labor component would be economically hard, if not socially impossible, to re-establish. Fragmentation that separates consideration of the energy invested from what is subsequently converted stems from the changes wrought in agriculture since the late nineteenth century by urban-industrial energy practices.

The hoe cultivators of Asia may produce more per acre than mechanized agriculture, but there must be great numbers of them to do so. American industry has swept this sort of consumer off the field and freed the resulting production for the urban market. If no-till planting prevails, even the image of the well-tended field will pass, with the plow and furrow alike as antique a memory as fodder in the shock or gleaners in the fields. The fields will be covered instead with grass, through which the tiller will have thrust its seed. Biocides to hold down the grass, or new breeds of low ground cover, will take the place of plowing, altering the demand of mechanized agriculture for energy even as energy output is calorically increased. Still, the change will not necessarily represent a lowering in energy investments.

Over the decades, steady and dramatic rises in agrarian productivity have marked the American economy. Increases of such scope can scarcely be extrapolated into the future, but increases there will be. The population of the American metropolis in part derived from the clearance of people from the land. This clearance has made large agricultural production an industrial possibility. The urban-industrial demands have been interacting ones.(23)

Conditions of high-energy demand cannot afford to ignore the agricultural sector or fail to bring it within the scope of industrial activity. To leave large portions of the population to low energy usages in the countryside, while urban energy usages soar, is to leave a potential for crisis in a high-energy society. If the population of America had remained in 1975 as rural as it had been in 1920, the social condition would be hard to conceive. Putting nostalgia to one side, it is exceedingly doubtful if the resulting scene would be peaceful.

This is in the realm of the problematic. However, some theorists seem unwilling to consider what the world would be like if Americans had stayed down on the farm rather than going to the city. The presence of current urban problems often produces a false nostalgia about the past.

Americans see a mix of cities in the late twentieth century. Serious people claim they can deal with air pollution by penetrating the inversion layers with high stacks having giant pumps to suck the better air down to earth. Their chief criticisms of the proposal are that the pumps would cost too much money, require too much energy, and be a hazard to air traffic. Americans see suburbs building separate sewer systems for storm and sanitary purposes when both of them produce an outflow requiring, minimally, sedimentation control — and undoubtedly a great deal more treatment — if the receiving water bodies would be salvaged.(24)

Modern Americans are aware of the menace inherent in these proposals and events. They think, always nostalgically, that something less urban would have been preferable. But once the nostalgic has been seen as a false glow, a quite different reasoning concludes that greater misfortune may have been avoided when a large bloc of low-energy culture was not left in the countryside. An urban American in no way can learn about low-energy rural life simply by building a second home in the country.

In a high-energy demand situation, the pressure is massive to integrate all levels of society into the dominant demand and supply patterns. The stability of urban-industrial society is endangered if it leaves large blocs of the population within the low-energy demanding confines of traditional social structure or views any part of nature, including open land itself, as other than a resource to be used in serving high-energy demand. This means that both nature and low energy social forms must be processed into the high-energy demand structure.

Both technology and institutional concepts have been mobilized to assist in this change. Networks have been provided to simultaneously move people to urban centers and extend over the landscape. A desire for growth in energy conversion and in urban expansion still persists.

For still too many decision-makers, it is as if energy and open land were infinite in supply or that the costs of their expansion were easily bearable to the renewing environment. For both land and energy, this will not be so. The pressure upon nature and the social costs of continued unconstrained energy growth and urban sprawl are forcing crises upon late twentieth century urban-industrial society.

THE COSTS TO THE ENVIRONMENT OF FRAGMENTING URBAN EXPANSION

Where there is dedication to a policy of cheap and abundant energy, maintenance of anything other than the rate of energy growth is not a forte. Keeping up the condition of the capital that has accumulated in the form of buildings, machinery, and institutions seems of secondary importance to sustaining the flow of services within the economy that set the demand for the growth.(25) There will always be a voice to urge the allowance of deterioration of the urban environment: ". . .the best national policy would be to allow this obsolescence to continue, and allow further deterioration of the older parts of the older cities."(26)

These advocates argue that such decay would drop center city population to the lowest possible level. At some point the decay would reach a level some private investor would consider profitable, or the blasted condition of the city center would make improvement a low public expenditure. As a piece of special pleading, this may seem reasonable. It has, however, the consequent shortcoming pointed out by the late Dr. Margaret Mead in her testimony before a subcommittee of the Senate Committee on Labor and Public Welfare. Such disregard of what she considered the human and natural elements has already slid America into "a pit of deterioration, corruption, apathy, indifference, and outright brutality towards the weak, the sick, the young, and the poor."(27)

Not only energy uses have been fragmented to better conceal costs and put forward isolated appearances of profit. The societal organization of the urban sprawl itself has done the same. In the urbanized land zones under high-energy conditions, there are the decadent cores of the old traditional cities where the poor and those who have dropped out of the bottom of society reside. But there are also the suburbs for the young, nuclear middle-class families, the retirement communities for the elderly, and the apartment complexes for the "swinging singles." Increasingly in such a society, in order to better organize individuals as units for production – and more importantly to advance the amount of consumption – the metropolis is fragmented and, simultaneously, expanded according to age, class or any other market-relatable category that is profitable to some entrepreneur.

Taking the word segregation in its broadest sense and applying it to social divisions of age and marital status as well as race and class, the social pressures under the high-energy conditions of urban-industrial demand point strongly in the direction of the segregated city. More profits are earned by encouraging divisions than in discouraging them. The need to continuously replicate increases the demand for greater production and consumption through the conversion of more energy, the exploitation of more natural resources, and the increase in material goods. The cost to the natural environment is inescapably great.(28)

Nature is in no way separated from humanity, however much society has sought alienation from nature and social segregation along such human choices as class, race, status, age, and so forth. All of this social segregation demands space, energy, and materials which must be supplied from nature. If the environment is partially defined by human activity on the one side and the natural condition upon the other, it is impossible not to perceive the massive burdens social segregation imposes upon nature. In such a situation, a fragmented base of activity too often appears efficient in terms of costs and benefits – only the benefits appear because the costs are swept into obscurity.(29) Urban-industrial society plainly has been most reluctant to recognize the costs to nature of the socially segregated city that seems so profitable.

The viability of both the central city and the suburb are at risk. The poor, the old, and the sick are isolated within the traditional city. The suburbs must sustain the services for the scattered slurb. The gentrification movement of single, young professionals back into the central city has not been enough of a change. The burden of segregation through sprawl will impose such costs that it is prophetic to say "there will be no cities."(30)

Perhaps, no long-run problems will occur from the continued decay of the central cities and the expansion of the suburbs. At some point the decay of the central city and the pleonectic growth of the growing suburbs will produce a crosspoint on some entrepreneurial chart. At that moment, speculating investors will cease pushing expansion into vacant exurban land and transfer investment to reassembling vacated central blocks for new ventures.(31)

The gentrification movement may be the fulcrum for levering change, or the fulcrum may be energy costs or energy unavailability, however determined. One can well wonder if either the central city, the suburbs, the environment, or the general society can sustain the costs of such an economic process while working it out. The worsening atmospheric conditions and the decision to ease energy problems through the burning of high sulfur coal and oil, give substantially negative evidence that the environment can sustain the costs.

THE CONTINUING RISE IN THE COSTS
OF URBAN EXPANSION

In every part of the world where urban-industrial demand has developed, the fiscal expenses of the metropolis have risen sharply. Scott Buchanan has claimed, "History doesn't show that cities have ever had good governments. . .But now we have to have them."(32) There has been no adequate response if this is truly an imperative. The city continues to expand, to be fragmented, to impose demands upon the renewing environment, and to raise up costs which threaten bankruptcy to the entirety of the enterprise.

Yet despite the fiscal expenses and the costs to nature incurred, the modern urban sprawl falls short of even the very modest demands for the "ideal" city of a man like C. Northcote Parkinson. What does he say a center of human activity needs? He says it is "human affection" and that this is expressed in "a continual process of maintenance, improvement, and repair." When that process stops, affection for the city is at an end. Death then ensues.(33)

Sadly, it has been a long time since affection was asserted for the metropolis. In the United States, the decline can be traced in just this century from O. Henry to Damon Runyon to Jimmy Breslin. And if literature is an inadequate source for seeing a decline in a sense of affection for a place, one need only consider Parkinson's test for affection: "a continual process of maintenance, improvement, and repair."

Jacques-Henri-Auguste Greber, the pioneer French urbaniste who drew the first designs for Philadelphia's axial focus, the Franklin Parkway, defined city planning similarly to Parkinson if the city is to provide a high quality of urban life. City planning, according to Greber, is "the art of ensuring a physical setting that will provide happiness for the greatest number possible."(34) When there has to be a constant pounding upward of the rates of energy conversion, land consumption, and capital expenditure, how can a city be held in affection or be a setting for happiness?

Everything currently has become a resource for growth in production and consumption. Like the resources found in streams, forests, and the atmosphere, the urban land and neighborhood are a part of the flow that feeds the growth of demand prevalent in high-energy culture.(35) On a fragmented budget, where profit is isolated from cost, it is the fragmenting urban expansion that generates the greater profit because it requires the greater amount of energy, investment, and resources. And under such pressure, costs can only continue to rise – grossly.

Yet the urban-industrial demand structure chose urban sprawl as the preferred growth model. As the Canadian planner Alexander Leman has said, "Only in the last hundred and fifty years or so (have) small slow-moving urban systems...grown first into large cities and metropolises."If such an urban system were to work for any purpose other than increasing energy growth, it would require what he calls a "synthesis." The failure to make that effort produces the megalopolis "where you have the vast urban sprawl of asphalt and no identity, no focus, no points of reference, no sense of community"(36) – in short, the urban sprawl that insatiably demands energy and exploits nature.

Segregation in urban sprawl is most clearly revealed in the construction patterns of the central cities and suburbs which make up the conurbations spreading around the coasts and along the great lakes and rivers of the interior. New constructions called "towns" go up, or old established towns are lost in metropolitan growth. The suburban "town" governments are increasing who want the tax rates from an industry they have declared clean by passing a zoning ordinance but who do not want the workers from the industry living in the "town."

Zoning and building codes are drafted to determine how best to limit local population in line with predetermined income levels. Tax rates are set to maximally favor the residents of each sealed-in jurisdiction. Services are calculated to pass off as many burdens as possible on surrounding "towns" in the urban zone.

An antiseptic industry is always welcome. A cozy situation is produced by the municipality having control of that particular situation. Conditions are a good deal less cozy for municipalities where the not-so-clean industry drifts, nor for those expected to provide the residences and public services for the workers in every kind of industry. Interestingly enough, the municipalities where the unclean industries are located are often expected simultaneously to be the municipalities where the workers can live.

For the more fortunate residents of the megalopolis, the suburban or exurban "town" can be a very pleasant experience. The local government becomes a means of providing a town that is really a country club. Tax revenues provide the parks, pools, tennis courts, club houses, and other amenities the small, predetermined number of inhabitants desire. Public education and health services have the high gloss of a luxury patina in these delightful enclaves.

In brief, megalopolis grows and grows in area, population, wealth, debt, and in the problems that are the unwanted consequences of the growth. The customary efforts to shuffle off the costs on the renewing environment have failed. The costs are now in the process of revealing themselves and identifying their interrelationships. A unified treatment of the high-energy and growth demands of urban-industrial society becomes an increasingly evident necessity.

ARE THERE ENVIRONMENTAL LIMITS TO URBAN REGIONS?

No city can ever be mere space. It must be, instead, a socio-cultural structure. Today, as in the past, "the relevant system for the study of urbanism has increased to regional or national scale."(37) The city has been converting itself not into metropolis as the end of urban life but into megalopolis or ecumenopolis: the city is now a synonym for the living space of the planet.(38)

Resistance to this change has been strong, not being confined to savorers of nostalgia or celebrants of high energy. In 1935 the National Resources Committee of the United States, a body so comparatively forward-looking as to have been stifled by its contemporary American opposition, refused to see the city as central to regional planning. In an economy that was increasingly both urban and industrial, the Committee did not see urban growth as the basic point of departure for planning.

The Committee's reasons were not trivial. In lieu of the city, they insisted that planning must concentrate on "the broader aspects of resources, economic patterns, and regional interests." To them there was something called the "total region." But the city was to make regional planning "an expanded form of city planning." As Christopher Tunnard said over three decades after the Committee's ill-fated demise, "this was just what was needed."(39)

Urbanized form is the dominant characteristic of megalopolis. Sprawl is not described as "urbanized" in any casual sense. The urbanization of the countryside is one of the costs the city imposes upon nature. To ignore the urban dominance also ignores the resulting distortions.

Environmental planning cannot avoid concentrating on the role of urban growth, industrial demands, and the mobile energy operations. They are the products of decisions for unconstrained growth. These decisions have been dominant and their impacts have intensified in recent decades. The problems of urban growth and its environmental surroundings have been all mixed up from the beginning of high-energy conditions. Environmental concern is incapable of serious application without this recognition.(40)

Although evidence of urban sprawl, fragmentation, and environmental pressure is easily marshalled in the United States, the American economy is not the world's only generator of high-energy levels. Europeans and Asians often dismiss urban decay and urban sprawl as unrelated to their own difficulties. Without denying the cultural differences in each country, there is a growing similarity among cities in the urban-industrial world.

Mitchell Gordon, an urban journalist, observed some time ago that the cities of the world would look more and more like Los Angeles as time passed. He saw the resemblance as the result of the automobile and its increasing ubiquitousness, rather than closer communications. Because it requires space in which to move and to be parked, the auto imposed upon cities the inevitable burden of looking alike. When a visitor looks at the new skyline of Paris with its rim of high-rises, one perceives a similarity to Sunset Boulevard or the Skyline Drive that owes more to the automobile than to architectural innovation.   The auto's widespread adoption had to bring sprawl and congestion in its wake.(41)

The paralysis of streets and highways, occurring despite all the money spent and all the open space or urban neighborhood paved over with concrete, is not an exclusively American phenomenon. The Italian autostrada appeared in the 1920s, the German autobahn in the 1930s, and the American interstate system – modeled upon these lauded forerunners – only in the 1950s. Los Angeles is surely in the process of trying to be the model for the world city of the future, but it has had quite a large share of non-American exemplars. The auto has tended to shape the course of urban sprawl and the face of nature over which that sprawl has moved.

The auto puts a primary limit on the scope of any particular urban region. But the auto is only one important form of high-energy transport.   The jet airplane is another. Its increasing social and economic importance proves that all the world has become a suburb for increasing numbers of people.

Business and intellectual leadership in the urban-industrial demand structure operates in the full time-space continuum. For them, time is primarily future time, while geographical space is merely the site where they act out the dramas of their futurebound existences. Significantly, these leaders also provide the social image toward which the others in the society aim their aspirations for energy, goods, and space. Through these means, the impact of their jetting is magnified.

The elite under high-energy conditions, whatever their personal predelictions, must be physically mobile. This mobility for the elite is integral to the high-energy demand structure's need to maintain the pace of accelerating growth. A sedentary, immobile, socially satisfied elite could not serve this purpose and would have to be reconstituted in such a way as to stimulate mobility.(42) A high-energy situation wants maximum mobility which is welcomed by those profiting from the rising use of energy. Behind the fear of some, and the welcome offered by others, lies a difference in reward and risk.(43)

Under high-energy conditions the surge of growth has been the greatest force. Given this pressure, the rate of energy conversion must also increase. The rate of consumption must rise, as must the rate in the growth of cities. And all this must accelerate. If there are limits in the resources to supply energy, goods, or land for urban growth, the limits are to be minimized, disregarded, or considered a distant problem. The inability to truly "consume" anything is similarly seen as a more or less minor problem.

The contribution of workers solving isolated problems often does little more than feed the continuing unstabilizing operations within the urban-industrial demand structure. Failing some effort at synthesis that does not itself contribute to growth, the question, Are there environmental limits to urban regions?, has one answer: No. Environmental limits, short of catastrophe, will come only when humanity determines the extent they will allow high-energy, urban-industrial demand to reach.

5 Urban Instability and Environmental Balance

THE NECESSITY OF SPRAWL IN CONTEMPORARY URBAN GROWTH

In the 19th century, Fourier and John Muir criticized societies dedicated to the permanent open-ended growth of production and consumption. This means continuing urban growth, rising energy demand, and constantly increasing exploitation of such resources as forests, wildlife, and open space. High-energy conditions have recognized no need to foresee any sort of limit to urban-industrial growth. Growth's benefits have been concentrated upon, and not growth's larger costs to the environment.

An urban-industrial society must continuously provide motivations for ever-increasing consumption and production. In this situation, a near total commitment to physical mobility and consumptive lifestyles becomes a social necessity. Consequently, nature is viewed as only another series of individuated units awaiting processing. The result in this society is a "commonality in the overall goals of the society" for growth and a confining of divergent views to means rather than ends.(1)

The existing urban sprawl, whatever individual names are given to portions of it – New York, London, Rome – is not free from the impact of the world market. That market, "without notice or qualm," will alter demand in complete disregard of any grave wounds the change inflicts on any local economic structures. The local economy, upon which urban-industrial growth impacts, is supposed to absorb the loss and to draw within its central core "what is often dramatized as the 'awfulness'."(2)

Under present conditions, whatever the "awfulness" in the inner cities, there is no likelihood that the outer growth of the urban marches will cease. Inflated building costs and a rise from lower to far higher interest rates may slow the coverage of open space with urban forms; but they will not stop it.(3) As the editors of the magazine Ekistics have said about urban settlements,

All indications point to an era of megalopolitan growth before the world can – hopefully – steady itself at a new level of several times its present population, i.e., ecumenopolis. A handful of new countermagnet cities of half a million are likely to make no more impact upon this rapid urban expansion than the early garden cities exerted upon the square miles of inter-war suburban sprawl.(4)

In the coming decades, world population will continue burgeoning. People will be increasingly drawn to the cities and the cities will steadily push themselves out over the countryside. The social structure will advance into the full development of urban-industrial demands and the consequences of those demands.

These demands will impose a sharp limitation on remaining open space as well as massive drafts on the living and renewing environment. Air and water quality and wildlife will come under the gravest threat. Further attenuation of locational identification will occur. Both mass mobility and the transit jams incident to mass movement over the great distances of low density urban sprawl will multiply. Technology will only serve to expedite this process.

Henry Ford, when not denouncing history as bunk, once said, "We shall solve the city problem by leaving the city."(5) Though bunk it may be, history shows this to be precisely what urban-industrial society has sought to do. Under plentiful energy conditions, the city, or its successor megalopolis, simply proved able to run faster than even Mr. Ford's automobiles.

When the would-be escapers from the city arrive at their rural destination, they find urban forms all around them. There is no haven for urban-dwellers from urban forms. They are like those who flee the plague for they carry the disease themselves and find only new regions to infect. Indeed, before a haven is preselected by the urban-dweller seeking refuge, it is already too far advanced into urban sprawl to be a safe destination. Ford's promise that we can solve city problems by fleeing them is false.

IS ANARCHY A CHOICE FOR THE HIGH-ENERGY CITY?

Unless there are significant changes, the urban-industrial future will be the "spread city."(6) Call it urban region, megalopolis, conurbation, slurb, or whatever, it can be projected as a low-density, formless mass. The demands for high-energy growth and the concealments of a fragmented energy budget are pushing the city out over the land.

Although in such a situation the value of open space ought to be of the kind that the decision first to be made should be where not to build, no one can expect that to happen – barring a sudden shift in awareness. Open space should be claimed by urban-industrial society as one of its more valuable resources.(7)

But how often is the value of open space to the urban-industrial economy itself fully recognized? Too often the use of open space is still left to anarchic decisions in the United States. Perhaps the word "anarchy", used in its popular meaning of a general condition of confused disorder, is misleading. Certainly the "anarchy" in the misuse of open space in the United States is not the result of the absence of government. American government is abundantly present in the confusion regarding open space.

The governmental forms in the United States have permitted, indeed abetted, the social and economic pressures for urban sprawl and the wasteful consumption of open space. In other countries, under the influence of cheap and seemingly forever available energy sources, this kind of expansion also occurred, but not to the same extent: either land was in absolute short supply (as in Holland), or social prejudice preferred the central city for the elites and the suburbs for the poor (as in much of Latin America), or land use was tightly controlled (as in Sweden).

The sort of "anarchy" in land use under the expansion of American cities extends beyond the municipal limits. It can be experienced within those limits themselves – and with equally as much governmental participation in the "anarchy". Japan has rather stood the problems of land use on its head by reversing the American practice. Order for them exists in the countryside while "anarchy" prevails in the use of land within the city. This reversal may produce better results for energy use, environmental protection, and control of growth.

Japanese land use in the countryside, both traditionally and presently, is strictly controlled. The Japanese city is "the only place where an impetuous, anarchical, instinctive life – such as everybody needs for part of the time – is possible."(8) The immediate environment, based on Japanese urban experience, need not be a designed environment but may be a happening.

This is beneficial, however, only as long as it is an alternative to an overall conscious design or the abiding remains of the natural condition prior to human activity. Since the latter situation has been swept away by the advanced, high-energy cultures, only a consciously adopted or traditionally inherited design for land is a real possibility. Without such a design, there is no meaningful option other than "anarchy" as the land is covered by urban growth.

Even those arguing that anarchical city life may be helpful would not allow fragmented urban forms to spread over the landscape. A "free-for-all" in the countryside is destructive, even if the same "free-for-all" in the city might be a creative matrix.(9)

What must never be forgotten is that disorder in the use of land in urban-industrial society, whether in the central city or the countryside undergoing urbanization, is a major consequence of governmental action. Urban sprawl has been only an apparent anarchy, but government has been very much present. Since 1960 costs for public services by local and state governments to the extended urban forms have skyrocketed. In a time in which competition for capital is severe, action that scatters costs across the landscape may seem to accomplish more in the provision of goods and services. It is not anarchy, even so.

Urban sprawl is rarely, if ever, an accident. Nor is the condition of the inner city something that happened independently of governmental action. In a fully developed urban-industrial society, such events do not occur under conditions of true anarchy.

Urban sprawl is only one example of energy-expending operations meant to hike the benefits returned to some landowners. Urban expansion of any sort would not permit true anarchy.(10) The high-energy city is too dependent on the mobilization of all the forces of governments, society, and the environment if its condition of preferred growth is to be sustained.

THE HUMAN INVENTION OF THE LANDSCAPE

Landscape is a highly artificial construct. There never was a Golden Age in which humanity lived in a landscape lacking human imprint. Landscape is a social invention in which stasis between humanity and nature is impossible.

Except in the periods in which trade is nearly extinct, urban markets have largely or entirely determined the use of land. The long-planned order in the rural and wild lands of urban-industrial countries, such as Japan and England, marks the contrast to their cities. This landscaping on the macro-scale of nations has been no accident.

The biologist C. H. Waddington pointed out, "The landscape of Britain. . .was entirely invented in the eighteenth century. . .The whole thing is as artificial as a city." He further states that all productive environments are "man-made," or profoundly "man-altered."(11) Every major civilization conceptually inherits a landscape from the days of the compact city. It has become an inheritance of little worth, however, in a time when compact cities have become the rotting cores of an urban sprawl engulfing the inherited landscape.(12)

The economies of the compact cities no longer exist. Whatever changes occur in transportation or governmental structure, these economies will not exist again. As long as spatial distribution of population imposes the burden of expensive delivery upon such services as health care, education, parks, or other services for the public good, the spreading city must impose high costs.(13)

Urban growth patterns have spread along the networks of transportation. This dependence on networks for the lines of growth, and the fragmented course followed by the planning of each line in the network, imposes the conditions of urban sprawl. Without an integrated, comprehensive plan for the networks — roadways, sewers, water lines, power grids, gas mains — general urban growth cannot be contained. As long as each network is built according to its own growth plan, confusion will result when it is all put together and called "urban sprawl."(14)

Is urban sprawl and the inability to demarcate urban land from countryside the necessary landscape created by urban-industrial society? It seems so at this point in history. Landscape expresses the basic cultural forces of each society. Spanish, Russian, or Chinese human activities made their own distinctive, different, but quite humanly contrived "natural" landscape. An artificial product covers the land everywhere outside their cities.

The city, even when most separated from its surroundings, cannot exist apart from the humanly contrived environs. Not until the twentieth century, however, did energy modes allow urban forms to spread casually over the countryside, obliterating the previous order. At best, only a few attractive fragments replaced the old landscape.

As Siegfried Giedion has noted in his overview of urban growth, humanity in the environment has always been, and doubtless always will be, "in continual danger of losing their equilibrium." The balance will always be swinging between the burdens imposed by the human imagination and nature's ability to respond to those demands. Maybe this balance will be kept narrow by small adjustments, what Giedion calls "man in equipoise"; but nothing exists to set any natural limits to the range of the swinging of this balance.(15) Only catastrophic breaks set the limits of humanity's equilibrium with nature.

From the beginning of any sort of urban location, this ever-shifting balance marked the relationship between land control and city growth. Historically, city markets determined the extent of human grading, cutting, or eroding of the land. The influence might be as slight as a market for wool that put a pastoral burden on land whose exhaustion was sped by that inducement, or as massive as the urban sprawl of the twentieth century.

The point is that there has never been a fixed, strongly-balanced relationship between humanity and empty space – space devoid of intense human activity has never existed. The pounding growth of megalopolis makes the attainment of such a relationship, if not more difficult, at least something requiring careful forethought. The rising costs of energy may impose a counterfoil to urban sprawl, compelling urban growth to return to a concentrated form of location, or may at least decelerate the speed of the rush to more urban sprawl.(16) What will not occur is some automatic return to a happy balance.

While bureaucracies can be built to incorporate all energies into seemingly rational acts, the increasing threat to the delicate mechanisms of both high-energy supplies and the renewing environment is revealed. Just as humanity invented the landscapes they have known, so will they have to invent those of the future. If they are to be viable, these cannot be the fragmented scenes of recent urban expansion.

THE NEED TO INTEGRATE THE ACTS OF
URBAN GROWTH

Planners and doers are being forced to investigate motives, to dissect results and insist that their plans and actions constantly react to whatever is happening immediately around them. Along with high-energy conditions an attitude that the present lacks a significant past and the future will automatically solve all present problems has developed. The practical person can say, "I'm busy doing what has to be done right now" – and feel fully justified.

This single-mindedness characterized the decision makers who opted for railroads in the 1840s, electric trolleys in the 1890s, gasoline-powered autos in the 1920s, superhighways in the 1950s, and nuclear power plants in the 1970s. Each decision set in motion both predicted and unpredicted demands and effects on growth in the economy. The results accelerated and intensified the institutional needs of urban-industrial society for increased energy supplies, capital investment, and growth in the production, provision, and consumption of goods and services. Instability in society, the economy, and the environment thereby became integral parts of the whole demand structure.

The current need for each of these actions has always been acutely expressed. There never seemed to be time or need for doubt or investigation. People and goods had to be moved, cities had to grow, and energy had to be supplied. Everything else had to accommodate at whatever risk of increasing destabilization and chronic structural instability.

In each generation of urban-industrial society, the ingenuity of technological inventiveness has been put to immediate and isolated tasks. Even under the consciousness raising effect of the movements for environmental protection and energy conservation, the issue is seldom articulated in the form of whether there should be more power or if the renewing environment should not be required to contribute still more to increasing this power. Rather, the issue has been framed, as how much the renewing environment can be drawn upon and how more energy might be converted from some source in order to satisfy as broad a spectrum as possible of public opinion.

As each isolated task has been performed successfully, the industrial process has flourished, the city has grown into the urban region, and the balance between humanity and nature has been more delicately weighted. As Andrew Lipinsky of the Institute for the Future said, "We have over complicated society to the point where nobody knows how it runs. The captain is on the bridge, but he can't find the rudder."(17)

It is no wonder that residents of the urban sprawl should be fearful, feel alienated, and perceive themselves as gravely threatened. They have ample reasons for these emotional states. The source for their apprehension is the instability instituted by the limitless demands for energy and the need to reach a balance between urban-industrial growth and the renewing environment.(18)

The urban masses receive from their leaders only assurance of more of the same. Increasingly, the popular conviction is that "the present world has grown over our heads and. . .no one can speak of it with certitude and authority."(19) Only a minority may consciously hold this view, questioning the soundness of current high-energy demands. But they add the instability of their convictions to a system whose balance is already seriously aswing.

If psychosocial fears in urban-industrial society exist to this extent, some might call it captious to worry about the swallowing of open space. Open space, however, is an example of the adverse general consequence of fragmented and often isolated demands for open-ended urban growth. Open space is also essential to natural ecosystems.

Yet open space most definitely performs urban work. It is truly not vacant, unused space. Only when a narrowly rationalized decision distorts open space into mere units of consumption for immediate cash return does it appear vacant. Even a nature reserve, which cannot be used directly for recreation, is important for education and scientific inquiry in a situation where the urban form has engulfed the earth.(20)

As Boris Pushkarev and Christopher Tunnard noted long ago open space in an urbanized environment defines four functions: production, protection, ornament, and recreation.(21) An open space, which confers privacy, insulation from noise, or a sense of spaciousness or scale, becomes an entity to be used and felt in a social and political sense. Open space can give shape to urban forms as they extend over the countryside. Merely dedicating land as forever open does not mean it has in any way been economically sterilized so as to lose its ability to produce income or other fiscal returns for the urban economy.(22)

Yet open space performs more important functions for natural ecosystems. It can assist bird migrations or supply phages for consuming city gases. It may be a breeding ground for the food supply of wildlife, a spot where small creatures, from chipmunks to raccoons or possums, can safely forage. But at the same time all this is being done for nature, the open space also serves human fiscal purposes. It can define or separate human activity, provide vistas for structures otherwise jammed in upon themselves, and eliminate the sense of oppression unbroken slurb commonly imposes.(23)

Colin Buchanan, the English traffic planner who has been criticized as inappropriately favoring the automobile and its highways, has nevertheless been one of the strongest advocates of open space in urbanized areas. When wiped out by the auto, open space becomes an urban life necessity rather than an amenity or a matter of ornamental aesthetics. Little scope remains for treating open space as a variable whose presence or absence would be determined by how much people were willing to pay to have it or how willing they were to substitute dangerous or noisy land uses for a relatively natural open space. As Colin Buchanan insists, environment cannot "be dismissed as a trivial frill which can easily be dispensed with. It is a matter of acting in the public interest and laying down standards. . . ."(24)

Because of the dispersed energy forms of high-energy culture, open space is a rapidly consumed resource. Using it up contributes to the high cost of urban slurb for both the environment and the social structure. Its abuse contributes to the omnipresent instability of urban-industrial society. Many will remain indifferent to the dangers present in the nonintegrative decisions common to open space. Their greatest happiness may be an apartment located at a freeway access point in return for the convenience of being able to whip immediately onto a limited access highway. But the willingness of some to accept such a trade-off does not mean that the larger social decision-making system can prefer decisions of so isolated a character. The survival of the natural ecosystems cannot tolerate a consumption that destroys as much as it utilizes.(25)

Whatever the human capacity to respond under pressure or the ability of natural ecosystems to accommodate to the invasion, integrative actions are required to direct urban growth. It is no longer sufficient to do what "must" be done today unless future consequences are presently projected.

THE EFFECT OF NOT BUDGETING ALL THE COSTS OF URBAN EXPANSION

The impact of urban regimes on the renewing environment has been severe because the forces profiting from urban growth have not been compelled to account for or internalize (much less to absorb in their profits) the costs which they impose upon the environment. Instead, they have been free to pass on the burden of their growth costs to the air mantle, waterways, estuaries and oceans, and biomass. These have been considered common property resources, not individually owned despite a vague assertion of sovereignty by the state or nation.

In the past, the assertion of sovereign superiority was especially vague and feeble in market economies. Even when more vigorously asserted today, it rarely means to protect much of nature. It is, instead, to guarantee to the asserting public entity a claim to some part of whatever profits may accrue from exploitation.

The practice of considering the air, water, and biomass as free goods, effectively open to taking by any exploiter willing to reduce them to personal dominion or use them as waste sinks, has channeled the full pressure of the market system onto the land. Although land can be held in specific title, these other resources – to this legal moment – cannot. Consequently, the urban direction for outward growth has had to consider only the fiscal costs of land. Urban expansion has had to give, until recently, no heed to the common property of air and water.(26)

Urban governments have been reluctant to bring environmental costs within a unified budget. Even when they might have wanted to take up some of those costs, the fragmented condition of urban government has made it nearly impossible to do so. When a local authority seeks to bring a stream or an air shed under public management, these relatively small units can be salvaged only by treating the larger aspects of the ecumene – the oceans, the continental air mass – as free goods to be used as sinks for draw-down or dispersed waste.

A localized action may salvage River A by diverting sewage from it to River B or directly to the ocean. Action may clear the air in Valley C, if stacks are built so high that the gases can be blown out of the valley elsewhere. Each of these actions may have the minimal value of establishing some resource specificity and asserting a meaningful public title for River A or the air in Valley C.

These are each significant steps in a fragmented system. But within that fragmented system they compel an unstated assumption that there are free goods existing elsewhere in the ocean or in the atmosphere that can serve as the great receivers of effluent and emissions. The harm done to other similarly situated local venues and the general ecumene has not been capable of a comprehensive consideration.(27)

Unfortunately, when larger actions are funneled from a central governmental source to local units, the same failure to see the larger effects of such actions occurs. Often only a "crude national equity" that is costly and ineffective is obtained. Federal funding often reinforces the intensity of the effects of fragmentation.(28)

Needed at the national level are jurisdictions that would budget for all the costs of urban expansion.(29) These would bring together the whole range of residuals' management in relation to air, water, and land covering an area where economic relationships are interleaved. Integrating environmental and energy budgets on large regional bases are the least that national policy should attempt.(30)

A metropolitan regional authority for residuals' management in which trade-offs could be made among gaseous, liquid, and solid wastes, would be better than the presently fragmented local responsibility or some single set of necessarily crude national standards. This would be the first step toward an effective national budget comprehensively tying together the larger regions in environmental control. In this way, the assimilative capacities of air, water, land, and biomass in definable regions could be first determined and then served, with the limits being drawn in terms of local economic relationships and the natural phenomena of valleys, air sheds, aquifers, and similar physical participants in the planet's life-support systems.

There is a physical, hence an ecological, interdependence of residuals; and this, in turn, is consonant with the economic activity of any region. However, the natural character of water basins and air sheds rarely corresponds with the reach of economic activities, for these latter have created a market basis for the formation of a region. Rivers and hills, which form and define river basins and air sheds, have not been central points for regional organization. Instead, they have been political boundaries or commercial barriers.

Transportation patterns, land use, tax rates, air quality, availability of credit – each of these, and more – must be considered in drawing up a budget of costs and benefits. The network of matters to be considered must be cast with sufficient range so that the full possibilities of trade-offs can occur. Otherwise, the broad megalopolitan need concerning the urban environment cannot be dealt with effectively.

Presently in the late twentieth century, there is only conflict. The fragmented budget tries to shuffle the burden of competing political subdivisions and zones of economic activity onto the ecumenical relations of renewing systems. Neither the current energy supply system nor the condition of the environment can easily accommodate to these demands.

THE ENVIRONMENTAL COSTS OF THE EXPLOSION
OF HIGH-ENERGY DEMAND

Matters between human activity and the renewing environment are becoming more interlocked. Even the earth and much of its solar system have become intertwined to a degree that not even speculative philosophers might have found credible a few generations ago. But as all these relationships have locked into place and as the cities have sought identification with the whole landscape, urban-industrial demand itself has sought fragmentation, the isolation of discrete units, and the sense of a controller's comfortable remoteness.

With the demand for consumption that urban-industrial society confers, people seek to extract more from nature. A mass demand is created for homes in the mountains or at the seashore. For those of lesser means, the demand is created for mobile homes or highways complete with motor-accessible parks. Every effort is made to emphasize the cordons of separation, because in this separation lies the source of still greater demands.

As the segregating environmental uses increase, the chance at independent subsistence is lost. The energy-supply system under conditions of high growth puts all at risk even if it should only temporarily break down. Isolating demands intensify even as the need grows for constant rational social decisions to maintain the minimum relations for urban-industrial society. The world has been turned into a single interdependent ecumene.

Ironically, the city, having incorporated so much of nature, has become for human exploitation a resource no different than "natural resources." The consequences are the same. Every source of instability, whether from unintended human decisions or designed human activity, that disrupts the ability of the renewing environment to sustain its renewability, is aimed at the ability of urban life to maintain itself.

The cultural thrust in the high-energy situation has been toward urban explosion. The urban region has developed an unstable form by social choice. This form denies or conceals interdependence, the interactive energy budget in nature, and ultimate human reliance on nature. This form exalts the units of production and consumption and reduces the environment to a mere reinforcement of the process. There is an indifference, and often a hostility, to consider constraints present in the renewing environment within which human activity must find a place. A wall of indifference surrounds those who want only their demands promptly and amply served by society and nature.

Jacques Cousteau, the oceanographer, has long lamented the condition of the oceans, the universal sinks of urban-industrial activity. He sees a particularly bad situation as in the several zones of confluence where the waters of the various seas form gigantic mixing areas. He has even predicted the doom of the oceans and the subsequent doom of much of the life on the planet.(31)

Given such conditions, it is hard to understand what the Wall Street Journal describes as the dominant reaction in the world. What is it? It is boredom.(32) Not shock. Not curiosity. Just boredom.

With boredom predominant, how can there be any rescue? If the public builds a global "wall of indifference" to the destruction of the oceans, then the public had better hope that Cousteau is wrong beyond peradventure. Everyone wants the "riches" of the oceans, but no one wants to assume any of the costs of exploiting those riches. No one wants any protective restrictions.

There will always be people who argue that the present way – whatever it may be – is best, and that it should not be changed. They will charge that change would be very destructive to the present state of well-being, even if that state of well-being is the sort praised by Dr. Pangloss.(33)

But this is a time when the well-being is being seen as the result of excluding costs from the calculation. The consequences of that exclusion are beginning to force themselves upon the profit sides of some ledgers in the fragmented social accounting system. Hence, it is not wise to listen only to the ones who want to "leave-it-be." Those who want to begin to put it all together are entitled to attention, too.

With the explosion of high-energy demand, one cannot turn urban instability into stability, resolve the ill-effects of fragmentation and save the natural environment.(34) This explosion of resource uses must be transformed into a realization of the environmental costs imposed. The renewing environment has its limitation in terms of its own renewability. The size of the demands ultimately will depend more on these limitations than upon the continued "explosion" of human desire.

THE NEED TO RECOGNIZE THE SIZE OF
ENVIRONMENTAL COSTS

Now, the varying intensities of resource use and energy demand must be recognized. Government has both reflected and stimulated the social decisions that have set the limits for trade-offs between high-energy demand and environmental systems. But government must change its ways and begin to formulate the costs those demands impose and meet them – or prevent their imposition.

Presently, the failure of certain interrelationships prevent government from functioning as anything other than an agent of the most fragmenting high-energy demands. The demands made upon air, water, land, and the biomass represent physical and ecological linkages. The goods and services government supplies in relation to the environment either reinforce the demands or assist the natural systems to absorb them. Government does not, however, provide any collective choice of alternatives.(35)

As just one example, the discussion on the treatment of residuals does not include the alternatives of their disposal in gaseous, liquid, or solid form; or the adoption of quasi-closed systems; or turning the waste into primary-market products. Instead, only one alternative, or at most a few, are considered. Until at least the full range of potential alternatives is identified, it is bootless to talk of the use of market mechanisms for equating marginal costs with marginal willingness to pay. The models are just too restricted.(36)

In the absence of governmental ability to determine the limits of constraint and the allowances for trade-offs, calculations of willingness to pay are impossible. Only if the full range of interrelationships is brought under single management, can the marginal market operations have some chance to function in a way protective of the environment.(37) Otherwise no chance exists for economic and social stability or for the creation of a maintainable urban environment.(38)

This is underscored by the austere predictions of the planner C. A. Doxiades:

> When we realize that the average urban area is going to have twenty or thirty times more people and a hundred times more machines, and that difficulties grow much faster than the forces causing them, we must understand that this new frame is going to be inhuman in dimensions.(39)

Unless something is done now to bring the situation into a scale of human comprehension, government resources themselves may totally collapse.

Some argue, possibly taking their cue from Spengler and Ortega y Gasset, that the city masses have known so many actual or threatened calamities in the twentieth century, as a matter of daily routine, that "the common awareness of the emergency character of the times" has been dulled.(40) Industrial development and urban sprawl have broken the traditional community bonds that served as cues for danger, anesthetizing humanity. Urban populations have spilled over the countryside like mercury tipped out of a plate. Such views raise all sorts of horrendous possibilities in the delicately balanced urban environment. Still, such dramatic views of danger may be wiser than sticking to the business-as-usual pattern of a little reform here and there.(41)

It is a common experience to hear the arguments of the incremental reformers who want to improve urban conditions and enhance the state of the renewing environment. Nor are their ideas without merit if we are to accept the present situation as basically unchangeable. Incremental reformers become unhelpful, though, when basic changes are just what is needed.

According to some reformers, the only changes needed are incremental. Some coalescence of political power may have value, but a great concentration is unnecessary. Communications all around, as well as up and down, should be improved and, as a result, everything will be much better. "The general interest of the spread city" is not "necessarily damaged by a fragmented decision environment." Indeed, for some this is a positive good. Fragmenting government "guarantees that policies for the area will be the sum of the individual policies of the jurisdictions which exist within it, plus whatever policy imposition is made by the state or encouraged by the federal government."(42) On this basis, one wonders why anyone should express dissatisfaction with the present way urban government operates. One would wonder, that is, if there was not the accumulated evidence of experience in the twentieth century.

The incremental reformers do not see "breakdown and emergency" or "outright failure of law and order" as the permanent condition of urban government in fragmented, high-energy conditions. Consequently, they can favorably describe both the incremental operations of current rates of change in urban government and the remoteness of urban politics from the needed goods and services. They can, given their conviction that crisis is an infrequent event, concede that power centers at the urban level often operate without knowledge of each other and that intraurban conflicts are resolved at the lowest common denominator of assent among the segregated participating units. They see how urban interbureaucratic negotiating often successfully confines state and federal interjection to individual substantive concerns rather than the general concerns of the urban region. They recognize that region-wide urban problems are rarely resolved because there is no arena in which to resolve them. Because urban crisis is a sometime thing, these are flyspecks on the full-blown fruit of the urban environment.(43)

If basic changes are coming, arrangements improving the service of the present fragmented mechanisms should still be made. But it is very hard to grasp why incremental change and ubiquitous "improved communications" should be all that is needed to cope with hugely growing environmental costs. In an urban political process which seems to provide public goods and services only as it is necessary to avert the breakdown of the urban environment, drastic externally imposed changes are occurring or immanently impend.

The costs imposed by urban demands are for long-life capital, long amortization of credit, and long-term capital improvement programs at a time when capital and credit are objects of lively competition. Complicating matters further, these capital calls are involved with environmental linkages that affect wide ranges of space and time. Under the impact of an inflation fueled by rising costs of energy and environmental protection, the built-in institutional diseconomies of urban organization are exposed in all their oppressiveness.(44)

Urban government under high-energy conditions has rarely been good government, although it could often produce isolated instances of amenability.   Urban sprawl, however, has produced something that human institutions cannot control. Continued bad government under these conditions can be fatal — and not just the subject of another moralizing novel on the corruption of politics. Without an effective authority controlling urban expansion, what is still the common property of air, water, and the biomass will continue to be treated primarily as free goods.

Barry Commoner ought to have made it abundantly clear that ecologically nothing exists with the freedom of autarchy in nature — including human beings. Everything living or renewing in nature is part of an ecosystem. To treat parts of one natural system as isolated units without regard for their renewal is to risk rubbing them right out of the chain of being.(45)

It may be inevitable for humanity to regard every living creature or renewing force in nature as a resource for human use. The human creature scarcely is capable of any different outlook, being mostly anthropocentric in both conduct and theory. But human exploiters must keep in mind that each one of these "resources" is part of a natural system in "which demand is liable to outrun the supply."(46)

Every one of the alleged "resources" in nature is limited compared to the potential of human demand. The greater the economic and social importance the "resource" has for that demand, the more pressed its limits will be by it. It is not unreasonable that institutions for regulating demand or assisting the restorative powers of nature ought to be at the top of the agenda for late twentieth century action.(47)

SEEKING COMPREHENSIVE PROTECTION FOR A BALANCED ENVIRONMENT

Persistently, urban government's failures mount while discontent grows. Criticism settles on the inability of political institutions to respond to citizen demands for more effective government for the urban environment. The worried urban-dweller wants protection in routine life and maintenance of the rational, non-violent conduct essential to the urban industrial economy. The perceptive urban resident wants the surging needs of the outward bound urban sprawl and the decay of the central city effectively treated.

The citizen with these concerns rarely thinks the cause for the perceived malaise to be economic pressure for segregation and urban sprawl. This common obtuseness occurs because these pressures may benefit the individual. Not unsurprisingly the cry goes up from citizens such as these for a different institutional solution rather than a change in the way urban-industrial demands are basically formulated.(48)

In the present segregation resulting from urban sprawl, there is scarcely any authority with the capacity, or even the mission, of bringing together all the urban problems for handling. Urgent, even non-negotiable, demands for change are made. But it matters not if they are made when the situation remains so badly fragmented that paralysis must pervade the instrumentalities of urban power.   These instrumentalities, after all, have been meant to further, not to control, the present condition of urban sprawl.

Fragmented local governments do, however, perform some functions efficiently. They are the functions the current beneficiaries of high-energy demand most want accomplished. The existing governmental practices succeed in pushing the city outward and compressing the decay within the core, or redirecting it elsewhere within the limits of the old city. Current practices do not compel internalization of the costs for air and water quality, the consumption of open space, or the demands upon the biomass.

The larger governmental units have avoided their own failures by substantially avoiding responsibility. They have participated fully in the environmental fragmentation. Central government has thrust down upon local governments the burden of duties better discharged by state or federal governments. It is no accident that the federal government in the United States often declines taking jurisdiction away from states, even though statutes allow it when the states have failed in their obligations.

Until very lately, the problems of the environment have been avoided by government and the private economy alike. The common attitude treated nature as a free good. When recognition of these problems was forced on the general public attention, much of the response was to thrust the responsibility down upon the splintered local units of government. Putting the responsibility at the scattered urban level does the least to produce change because it is there that the drives for fragmentation, privatization, and individuation within urban sprawl have been the rawest. For example, the negative action of zoning mostly reinforces the drive for urban sprawl and "planning might as well be non-existent where planning agencies are too profuse."(49)

Urban governments, as presently constituted, are the least likely to emphasize legal responsibility for the environment. Government whether local, state or federal can do little as long as the demand remains for a fragmented situation. That is why transferring the responsibilities from local to larger governmental units will also fail. Decisions emphasizing the unity in nature and the reactive inter-relationships between human demand and renewing environmental systems must first be made.(50)

Given the urban sprawl that explodes continuously because its beneficiaries seek an individuation of profits imposing as few social burdens as possible, it would be unusual if a demand for comprehensive regional urban government was generated in the near future.(51) Although all levels of government could coordinate, many of the existing social impulses oppose effective regional urban government. Unfortunately, the problems surrounding those impulses are not confined to the fragmented units within urban sprawl.

The need to find a balance between urban-industrial demand and the renewing environment grows continuously more acute. The inhuman city of A Clockwork Orange is far closer to reality than incremental change can head off. When C. A. Doxiadis claims that Ecumenopolis, the world-engulfing city of the fairly-near future, should be built in cells of 50,000 people, in units 2,000 by 2,000 yards so that a ten-minute walk is sufficient to cross each unit, he ought not to be dismissed as having come up with a population statistic out of Plato's Republic.(52)

Plato's intuition may have been wrong. Doxiadis may have misassembled his huge quantities of data. But the present urban sprawl is so inefficient, cramping, and consuming of land, air, and water, that the burden of proof should shift to those who assert that present urban operations are working well. There seems little evidence that planning of future urban areas is not on the inhuman scale of even the current urban sprawl. Too much faith is being placed in the little incremental changes in urban government as the way to a future city of human scale.

Considering the urbanized land as a natural resource, far more is going to be needed to produce the social decision for unified energy use and an interrelatedness between human demand and natural systems. Government is a part of that creative process. The power of any urban region is too slight in itself to alone control what must be put under control. Only the organization of the urbanized land and the suppression of urban sprawl will guarantee the long-term existence of the high-energy demand-structure.(53)

The sort of urban sprawl, for example, that Eleanor Clark describes as true for modern Rome in the mid-1970s must be stopped. The old city, as she paints the scene, is,

> . . .bounded more or less by the Aurelian walls, set. . .in a howling wilderness of new apartment complexes, dotted here and there with oases for the very rich. That wilderness of instant slums, pushing out farther every day like some malign vegetation disguised in steel and stucco, would have broken Saint Jerome's spirit in a night. Instant fortunes have been made and are being made on them. . .and they have made the word abusivo – illegal, against building regulations – one of the commonest in the language and edilizia, for the building industry, about the dirtiest. The section called Maglinana, all fields until the middle Sixties, has. . .buildings below the level of the Tiber and subject to floods,. . .but Maglinana seems to be no worse than others in matters of water, electricity, sewage, and shoddy engineering.(54)

In one brief paragraph she catches the basic fragmentation of urban sprawl. Profits are isolated from costs. The costs are pushed onto nature or the social structure. The countryside is covered with an urban form incapable of healthy growth. The new Rome that spreads out into the countryside could be any urban sprawl in any high-energy culture that refuses to take a comprehensive view. There are no piazzas in this Rome, no fountains, no parks, no benches for the old or playgrounds for the young.

As Eleanor Clark so wisely sees, these are "houses built in contempt for human life." As a result, they "have got to be crime-breeders, working in favor of the bad ones who are always with us but who in vecchia Roma have never quite ruled the roost." Her remark could apply to urban wasteland after urban wasteland in the United States and elsewhere. The whole urban environment is at risk.

But Eleanor Clark's account goes beyond lament. It sees the failure of government. Building codes are not subject to abusivo without governmental connivance. The lack of piazzas, parks, and playgrounds, as well as the location of housing on a flood plain that is ill-served by sewerage, she lays directly at the door of the municipal authorities.

Under the impact of a fragmented growth that disguises costs and isolates profits from them, government will operate neither as a constraint nor a directing force.

Local urban government, whether in Rome or the suburban United States, is just another institution for intensifying and spreading urban sprawl. The higher governmental levels are more interested in aiding the construction industry and helping expand urban sprawl, through financing public goods and services, than they are in compelling the local urban governments to constrain or channel that sprawl, much less to interdict it. When Eleanor Clark says that modern Rome "is strained, but not damned or utterly bereft by a long shot," she could be speaking hopefully of every megalopolis being pounded outward over the countryside by those setting the demands for high energy.

Of course, government can act as a preserver of open space. It can protect air and water quality. It can assure the existence of human space in the city of the future that inevitably will spread over the whole earth. Government can do all this, if anyone wants government to so act.

Yet people seem content to see ecumenopolis rapidly forming and are indifferent about providing it with a responsible, comprehensive, and integrating government. Due to this attitude, all proposals to limit city population or city areas have failed since the advent of high-energy cascades.

What has been heralded since St. Thomas More in the sixteenth century is the pulsing growth toward ecumenopolis. Perhaps even Heliopolis, the city of the solar system, has been presaged. Already the first touches have been put to the building of Heliopolis, with the junk left flying in interstellar space or lying on the moon, and sky-lab fallen back to earth. The first impact of this great city, Heliopolis, is the problem of the disposal of residuals, just as if it were, say, Newark, New Jersey.

Humanity insists on the movement from urban sprawl, to an urbanized planet, to a city of the sun, all the time refusing to face the need for a unified energy budget or an interrelatedness between human demand and renewing environmental systems. Until humanity ceases to see these as unrelated fragments, it is pointless to consider bureaucratic schemes for limiting urban population or area.(55)

Our natural resources in the future must include urbanized parts of the globe. Just as the moor is a result of human deforestation in northern England, or the present landscapes in much of Asia, Europe, and the Americas the consequence of past human activities, so modern urbanization is now a part of the natural landscape. People are a part of nature and their artifacts, if they exist long enough, become a part of nature as well. Whatever potential may be concealed in this, these artifacts alone do not spell fatality. Only when these artifacts rip out necessary links in some food chain, or prevent groundwater from renewing itself in acquifers, or poison the atmosphere beyond its gross ability for self-cleaning, does the relationship become fatal.

Urban sprawl is a human artifact. This artifact has become a part of nature by the constraints it has placed on natural systems – demands increasingly difficult to accommodate. Urban demands need not be disruptive to the renewing and living environment, but open-ended demands – for more energy, more goods, and more land – can only be disruptive to nature, perhaps fatally.

Yet the city, even as it now exists, is a natural resource, as important to human survival as the land itself. As Eleanor Clark says, the city is strained but it is not bereft of a chance at survival. But if urban sprawl is not stopped and if humanity does not control its own high-energy demand patterns that sprawl intensifies, then the urban condition will become more and more inhuman as well as more and more burdensome to nature. At some point in that process, strain will turn to fracture. When that occurs, there will not even be talk of what might have been.

6 High-Energy, Urban Sprawl, and the Land Environment

THE GOVERNMENT'S ROLE IN URBAN SPRAWL

Under conditions of high energy use and urban growth, land is one of the natural resources drawn into the consumption process. Rarely has an effective decision been made to limit or precisely channel that change in land uses. The result is the devouring of open space by urban sprawl.

A commonplace for American journalists is a statement that says, "Land-hungry developers ranging up and down the East Coast have backed the remaining unspoiled, rural areas into a tenuous corner."(1) This is true for the American eastern coast, as well as for many other of the world's urban regions — if one understands what is meant by "corner." Open, unchanged acreage still exists in even the most urbanized regions. Open space is diminishing in quantity, however, and its quality for survival is under severe threat.(2) The total amount of land is limited, with the limitations sharpest where the land supply is most subject to urban pressures.

Every year, despite inflation and recurring recessions, more open space is turned into some sort of urban form. Demands range from intense construction coverage to a low density spread that may be the most destructive. Keeping together sufficiently large parcels of open space to be appreciated as areas uncluttered by urban form is a near-impossible task, given urban-industrial demand's illimitable capacity to break up such assemblages.

How open is the "open space" beneath high voltage power lines? How valuable is the "open space" so casually called "waste land" in so many urban-industrial zones? Simply preventing the erection of a building does not guarantee the protection of open space or prevent the misuse of the land resource.

The urban resident's choice of location within the urban sprawl is a function, in substantial part, of the energy available in the culture. The greater the energy available, the wider the range of choice for someone in an advantaged class position. While both western Europe and the United States, for instance, enjoy high-energy conditions, the western European in 1970 used 35 percent as much energy as the resident of the United States. Probably little changes in this comparison occurred during the 1970s.(3)

The range in energy-demanding – hence land consuming – life styles is more limited for the western European than for the American. But considering comparative land consumption, the gap may be closing in how land is used residentially. In the 1960s in the United States, land costs were about fifteen percent of the sale price of a detached single-family residence. By the late 1970s, they were approaching thirty percent of the sale price – and that sale price by 1979 had doubled the national price median. Furthermore, it appeared the share of land costs was heading for forty percent of a still larger sale price. Should this continue in the United States, Americans, like Europeans, would require great personal wealth or some official position to enjoy the land opportunities that middle-class Americans took for granted between 1945 and 1979.(4)

The largest burden of the costs imposed by the provision of a wide range of high-energy demanding options has been sustained, first, by the natural environment and, second, by the general fund of the public fisc. It is most advantageous for those pushing maximum urban sprawl that the resultant costs be assigned to nature as a free good or passed off onto the general fund.

Much is made about the value of "private" choice under high-energy conditions. Very little is said, however, about the extent to which public expenditure makes these private choices possible. The segregated, privatized, suburban bourgeoisie are a publicly-subsidized product, despite their high share of the tax payments providing such subsidies.

Choice under such high-energy conditions is socially conditioned, done often directly by government. At other times, commercial enterprise contributes directly, but its contribution is possible on a wide scale because of the indirect governmental support.

Government builds bridges and limited access highways to replace ferries and old roads. Such actions make economical assembly-line auto production. Government helps locate shopping complexes according to highway proximity rather than the immediately adjacent presence of high population densities. Government provides the public order and ease of communications which, in turn, make possible a national market and easily available consumer credit, so that the demand for goods and services can more easily be met. Even the reliance of the urban-industrial economy upon continuous growth in gross national requirements is substantially a function of governmentally supported expenditure.(5)

Under high-energy conditions, open-ended and undirected growth seems essential. Consequently, even heavy social and environmental costs must be borne in order to make the "private" demands serviceable. The system of constant growth depends on the perpetual enlargement of these "private" demands. Assertions of choice are simply functions of the larger social forms within which "private" demand is formulated.

Larger actions by the public treasury are, therefore, absolute necessities and not accidental political extravagances. Without them, the present form of sprawling urban land use would be impossible. Too much of that present use is predicated upon "private" impulse being promptly met. The multitude is stimulated to form demands, which are socially determined to be both transient and ever-renewed. Under such operations, the masking of costs so that all actions appear to be freely attainable becomes a kind of governmental ideal. If demand could be freely met, the immediate response to impulse demands for energy, goods, and land would provide only benefits. Transaction costs would be nonexistent.(6)

Sadly, though, the costs always exist and their concealment becomes harder all the time. Investments are constantly being made to better serve physical mobility and the satisfaction of impulse demands. Although they are meant to confer only benefits, they inevitably impose costs. Because the costs are often unforeseen, unprovided for, and have their very existence denied, they are skewed in their results and perhaps heavier than they would be if openly admitted and planned for.(7)

The first bridge spanning the Delaware, connecting Philadelphia with Camden, showed this within the first five years of its opening. As slight as this event was compared to the introduction of the gasoline engine or electricity, its cost impact was deep and widespread – and totally unexpected. To consider the adverse consequences, as well as the benefits, of this one action, so small in world terms, is to realize with awe the significance of major experiences such as the introduction of the gasoline engine and electricity.

On the Delaware prior to the mid-1920s, all traffic between Philadelphia and Camden crossed by ferry. Two separate communities, divided by the river and only vaguely tied together by the ferries and the rail service, developed. Each could maintain its own culture and economic life while appreciating the importance of the other. However, in this mutual appreciation lay the basis for the belief that a bridge would greatly benefit both through the interchange of commerce.

With the planning of the Sesquicentennial Celebration of American Independence in 1926, the Ben Franklin Bridge was opened. In the succeeding half-century, it (and its companion bridges) brought a huge interchange of traffic flow between southeastern Pennsylvania and southern New Jersey. In so doing, the demand for land on the Jersey side hugely increased to accommodate the urban sprawl of Philadelphia, particularly to accommodate the flight of the middle class from both Philadelphia and Camden. Due to that movement, profits accrued to many individuals, corporations, and municipalities. In brief, benefits there have been in plenty.

More than benefits, however, have resulted. Within a few years of the opening of the Ben Franklin Bridge, rapid decay overtook both the parts of Philadelphia and Camden that were adjacent to the bridge approaches. On the Philadelphia side, Franklin Square went into a deep slide. Previously the neighborhood had been an end by the river, a goal of activity. After the bridge opened, the square became merely a conduit for traffic passing through. The local Philadelphia novelist, John T. McIntyre expressed what happened very well:

> I never knew why all the prosperity had gone out of this neighborhood until one night when I sat on a bench in the square. I was looking toward the river. I saw the bridge. I couldn't see anything else. I tried, mind you, but I couldn't do it. Every other thing was flattened down; every other thing was withering away and almost done. There wasn't anything much but the bridge; and even the corpses of things that had been it was pulling into its mouth, sucking them in like a sluice sucks water, and hurrying them away to places on the other side of the river that it used to be we'd never heard of.(8)

The decision to build the Ben Franklin Bridge dramatically, if unintentionally, shifted populations, lowering activity in areas near the bridge approaches and raising it elsewhere. Anyone who has read John Keats' description of the south Jersey suburban dormitory communities in the 1950s,(9) or had the courage to walk through Camden in the daylight looking for Walt Whitman's home, can testify to the shift that has produced costs as well as benefits.

When the Ben Franklin Bridge was opened in 1926, its promoters did not realize the consequences of shifting economic activity from a concentrated traditional urban center to dispersed locations on previously vacant ground. Leif Bruneau has observed that such a shift in economic activity requires "a broader perspective including, besides environment, also transport, labour, market policy, and economic growth."(10) Given the lack of this perspective with regard to bridging the Delaware, the grim consequences were inevitable.

Inability or refusal to face the consequences of governmental actions remains common. This is especially true of the impact of moving activities previously concentrated in the city core to open space. When nothing is done along the lines of what Bruneau considers a requirement, urban sprawl results. Growth is handled fragmentarily and the impact of the expansion crunches up the natural environment.(11)

Emrys Jones, a Welsh planner, has compared the growth of London to "the bursting of a wen."(12) It has been a wen that burst beneath the skin, spreading the content in streaks to every part of the body of urban sprawl. Or to be less metaphorical, extending the population of London along networks throughout southeastern England.

Urban-industrial society is more than streets and structures. It is an attitude that views open space as a series of vacancies to be filled by the active urban intellect. When this attitude operates at its worst, it reorganizes the open space of the countryside into the modern urban region – which is to say urban sprawl.(13) Urban-industrial society does not neglect open space. It does far worse than that: it holds open space in contempt.

THE URBAN REGION'S DOMINANCE,
SPRAWL OR NO SPRAWL

There is a refusal to see that the problems of the city core are also the problems of the urban region. This is true not only today, but applied to the city in ancient times. A unity has existed between the city and its hinterland or region from the time the city emerges into history.

The dominant fact for the ancient city, the polis which has given its name to all subsequent city forms in languages borrowing from the Greek, was the unity between the city and the countryside around the city. It was not an invention of the Greeks. Such unity was already known to city-builders in western Asia who preceded the Greeks by thousands of years and to whom the Greeks were deeply indebted for ideas concerning urban planning.

But the Greeks had a self-conscious awareness of the city's indebtedness to its region and a broader definition of what constituted the region. Before Socrates, Athens had become dependent upon the arrival of the grain ships from the Black Sea, drawing on all the resources beyond the barbaric Borysthenes; and the later Athenian Empire knew it could not survive without those shipments.(14)

The Romans in their most ancient stage – when the tribes were the most important constitutional element – recognized certain areas as civitates, even before a town had grown up within those limits. Later, when the cities did appear, they were the centers of these regions. When the authority of the Roman Empire broke down, church authorities were compelled to model their ecclesiastical control upon the civitates.

The organization of the countryside into administrative areas probably preceded the founding of any city. Certainly it seems to have preceded the incorporation of the fully formed city. The corpus of the region was a prerequisite for the existence of the city core. Historically, the relationship between city and region was not so much one of the city growing out into the region. Rather, it was a matter of concentration, a pressing in of the influences for trade and power to create the city.(15)

The importance of all this ancient history for the later twentieth century megalopolitan situation lies both in the difference and in the similarities. Urban growth under high-energy conditions has seized upon the ancient relationship of a city to its supporting region, and filled the open space of the region with urban forms. The region has become a projection of the demands of promoters of certain urban forms and not a discrete non-urban existence upon which the ancient drew for enrichment.

Urban growth seeks identification with all that it touches. The promoters of that growth seek to confer a reason for existence upon nature itself by way of urban sprawl. The vitality of even ancient urban demand was not prepared to be confined within the city walls. Since the Industrial Revolution, the ability of the city to impose urban form across the land has become a reality.

Urban aggression upon the land is intensified by the assumptions which arise under conditions of high-energy demand. These assumptions posit a schism between where the urban dweller works and resides. This alone requires the high-energy city to fill its region.(16)

When urban sprawl is observed from the air, it almost seems as if urban growth were seeking to devour all open space and natural systems. The suburbs extend over hitherto open space and the old city core becomes inaccessible for most of the population in the urban sprawl. The need for a core, indeed, is taken away. Market rivals appear in the midst of the urban sprawl as nucleic points of contact between the suburbs of other metropoli.

Traditionally, whether one thinks of ancient examples or early twentieth century ones, the reason for a city's existence was its core, where industry and exchange were concentratedly carried on. If it had been a very old city when high-energy culture began its greater growth in the nineteenth century, the original center might be by-passed for a new matrix of industrial and commercial activity. But this new matrix was equally a point of intense concentration.(17)

However, when urban sprawl became dominant in the twentieth century, the suburbs destroyed the bases for the earlier urban cores. The only image left in the mind of the average resident of urban sprawl is that "downtown" is now everywhere. Sprawl tries to make the whole urban region what only "downtown" was in other times.

Everywhere cannot be "downtown", of course. But "everywhere" can have scattered through it the functions formerly served by a downtown area, thinly dispersed. In the absence of a comprehensive view, the functions of the city center are everywhere and yet found nowhere in particular. When that occurs, the old city center will be a meadow and round the so-called rim will be a congested jam of traffic supporting what undoubtedly will still be regarded as the need for urban growth. To promoters of urban sprawl, the word "enough" has no meaning when applied to urban expansion.(18)

An intimate relationship exists between a city and the open space of its region. Urban sprawl destroys that relationship. Anciently, this relationship can be traced to the pre-Hippodamian urban planners of classical Greece. More than a passing similarity exists between the deliberately created cities of the Greek colonists from the eighth to the fifth century B.C. and the planned American cities beginning in 1682 with William Penn's "green country town" at Philadelphia. The continuity of Greek and Roman thought on urban life constituted a real conceptual presence well into the nineteenth century; and only the bursting forth of the energy cascades in the twentieth century enabled urban developers to forget this ancient heritage.(19)

There are many historical parallels between the ancient Greek world of city planning and building and the modern American interactions between a region and its urban growth. Some of it, such as the grid-iron street plan, may be conscious imitation. Much of it, however, results from social and economic interactions similar in their operations.

The ancient Greeks were not perfect either. Like late twentieth century American planners of urban renewal, they were capable of imposing a plan on an existing urban structure that totally ignored everything which preceded the imposition of the new plan. As in the case of American urban renewal, the ancient Greeks superimposed later plans as if they had been conquerors from an alien culture come to carve their preferences in the yielding flesh of the conquered.

C. A. Doxiadis has resolutely drawn the similarities between these disregardful acts of planners separated both by thousands of years in time and a cultural barrier. Commenting on the archeological findings, Doxiadis states that when we find "two patterns superimposed, the later one ignoring the earlier one, (this) remind(s) me of what we do today to our cities by superimposing highways, ignoring what happens within the city itself. We are in the paleolithic stage of development of cities."(20)

The late twentieth century city will subordinate everything to satisfying — or vainly trying to satisfy — high-energy demands. Besides this primary task, the protection of open space or such "lungs" as parks provide seem small matters. But the drive for development at the sacrifice of other choices is not new. Marion Clawson has said of the modern city: "Development has been a major driving force of ideology of the American society and spirit, from the earliest colonial days to the present."(21)

The experience has not been basically different in the case of the twentieth century high-energy American city. The difference that does exist lies in urban growth having swallowed up the hinterland. The energy cascades available in the twentieth century permitted the failure to direct development away from sprawl into land-sparing structures.(22)

The American city, from the beginning of the high-energy impact upon urban life, moved boldly into its surrounding region. That influence had to be markedly different from the pressure exerted by a city under conditions of low-energy usages. Substantial as the commercial and handicraft wealth of the ancient cities was, even their potential pales beside the power of a high-energy city to spread itself. Unlike their ancient predecessors, modern urban forms have the capacity to totally consume the entire landscape.(23)

THE COMPOSITION OF URBAN REGIONS

What relationships compose the system of an urban region? Peter House, an environmental planner, says there are five, four of which are physical aspects of the environment. They are natural systems insofar as they are perceived as natural resources, humanly made physical structures, internal connectors or networks for transportation communication, and technology. House's final component is what he calls "persona," the concept of the personality of an area summarized by such descriptive terms as character, ethos, culture or style.(24)

The dominance both of human activity and of urban forms in this concept is plain. High-energy experience makes the city coterminous with the concept of region so that the distinctions, be they natural or traditional, are eliminated. What is not urban is suburban or exurban.

The private automobile has made this possible. H. G. Wells, writing in the last year of the nineteenth century, pointed out that this was already the way of the future. His predictions were uncannily accurate. He foresaw new forms of transport that would "bring with them. . .the distinct promise of a centrifugal application that may be finally equal to the complete reduction of our present congestions." At the opening edge of the twentieth century, Wells looked about him and made his predictions for the next hundred years: the dispersed city and urban sprawl were what he predicted.(25)

By the year 2000, "the vast stretch of country from Washington to Albany will all be 'available' to the active citizen of New York and Philadelphia," with the metropolitan aggregates for such urban regions as New York and Chicago reaching forty million persons each.(26) Wells refused to accede to the then current view that cities grew like a puff ball being inflated. Instead, he saw the expansion as an explosion, bursting out the furthest where resistance was weakest.

Frankly, for H. G. Wells even before the nineteenth century had died, the words city and town smacked of the obsolete. But whatever was the case in 1900, he claimed the late twentieth century would "call these coming town provinces 'urban regions' ".(27) He did not suggest the terms "urban sprawl" or "slurb."

These would be regions given over to profits isolated from processes of destabilization and encouragement of growing instability. As H. G. Wells told his contemporaries in 1900, any attempt on their part to organize government on the city-county dichotomy, wherein the city was different from its region, was doomed to failure. What he proposed, instead, was planning for the rapidly approaching changes. He wanted to come to grips with what he called "the practical revolution in topography that the new means of transit involve."

Already in 1900 Wells could speak confidently of ". . .the great urban region that is developing between Chicago and the Atlantic and which will lie mainly. . .south of the St. Lawrence."(28) Megalopolis was already in the process of being born before the twentieth century had begun. The congested cities produced by the nineteenth century need for concentrated power generation had found the way to disperse urban forms over the land.

In 1900, Wells could not help mixing his tenses. He saw the future. More interestingly still, he alone also saw that the future was already embodied in his present.

There might be a sort of sadness in this general ignorance in 1900 if there were not the greater sadness of the ignorance of later leadership right down to the present. The persons who have made opinion in the years since 1900 were often prepared to see H. G. Wells as the prophet of the twenty first century or, with his War of the Worlds, of the twenty fifth century. What they could not admit was his being simply an accurate reporter of the late nineteenth and early twentieth century conditions.

Wells most certainly was a reporter of current events. Every one of his "prophetic" ideas he already could see in existence in 1900. His insight lay in realizing that there were no reasons why existent concepts and institutions would not develop more intensely and spread their influence in ever widening zones. When Wells was being most the mere describer of his own age, he was being most conceived as the seer of the distant future. This is the sadness in his "forecasts."

The inability of the present to see what is happening is just as great. People talk about the urban explosion without perceiving that it is more than simply a movement of people and urban forms outward from the city.(29) The environmental statesman, Governor Richard Lamm, insists that this explosion is also a process of displosion and implosion within the urban sprawl.

Displosion, as Lamm explains it, "is the uneasy jamming of ethnic groups thrown together into small areas of urban space, dealing with each other in situations of continual tension." Implosion, on the other hand, is the distributional problem between rural and urban areas which leads to the diseconomies of scale in cities as they exceed 200,000 in population and disperse those numbers thinly over a wide land area that is thereby vaguely urbanized. More than the explosion of urban growth has led Governor Lamm to insist that the spatial distribution, which is a necessary part of urban growth in a high-energy culture, requires a limitation of growth in certain areas even as growth is encouraged in others.(30)

Ironically, this is seen as a no-growth policy by many, whereas it is simply an effort to accomplish in the late twentieth century what H. G. Wells called a necessity in 1900: coming to grips with the practical revolution in topography that produces the dispersed city, or what is now called urban sprawl. Terms such as displosion and implosion are simply modern social-science terms for what Wells called the "process of segregating various types of people" – that is, the composition of the urban region.

Governor Lamm, like H. G. Wells before him, is not prophesying the future. Instead he is describing the present. He is criticizing an urban operation that fragments the social structure and the natural environment so that it may digest the consumed pieces. And Lamm also offers alternatives.

Such ideas should not have been visionary in 1900. Definitely they should be the stuff of routine pragmatism now. Under high-energy conditions, open space and the renewing environment cannot continue to be casually fragmented for piecemeal coverage by urban forms.(31) There just are not enough appropriate resources for such an approach.

WHAT MAY DIRECT EXPANSION FROM THE URBAN
FRINGE TO THE URBAN CORE

Commonly, only the benefits of urban-industrial growth have been perceived. Land values have tended to reflect this, frequently falling in traditional city cores and rising in the suburban and exurban areas. In the process, a great deal of wreckage has been strewn about the urban environment. For many urban leaders, planning has meant no more than figuring out how to step round the piles.(32)

But recently some voices have expressed dismay at the undifferentiated consumption of both the core city and open space. As long ago as 1972 a reviewer in Urban Land trenchantly, if prematurely, said,

> a few years ago, industrial development was viewed not only as a boost to an area's economy, but was also expected to perform a host of other minor miracles. Today, with the near universal concern for enhancing the 'quality of life', industrial development is discussed as though it represented the antithesis of happiness. . .(and) might appear at first thought to (require) a eulogy for the passing era of the Industrial Age.(33)

The statement goes too far, of course. No one has yet exchanged his Rolls-Royce for twenty years' supply of bus tokens.(34) But the reviewer's irony represents an industry reaction that would not have existed to any degree prior to 1970.

Public attitude has changed, and the public is no longer satisfied by an additive to diesel fuel that changes the harsh odor to a scent like lavender talcum powder — which was done by the San Diego Transit Corporation.(35) Perfumes and deodorants are inadequate responses from the managers of the urban-industrial demand structure. Once growth is perceived as having high costs in addition to its benefits, provision must be made for dealing with those costs.

Factors are at work, however, that may redirect economic interests from open space to the city core. After 1945, United States' policies for cheap energy, whether speaking calorically of food or in terms of kilowatts or horsepower derived from oil, affected cities in two ways: they provided every inducement to blow the city out over the rural spaces, and served to diminish the value of the traditional urban cores. Should energy, in the forms of food and fuel for power, attain a permanent pattern of higher costs and scarcer supply than those marking the years between 1945 and 1973 (the year world oil prices quadrupled), then the urban growth forms common in those three decades would change profoundly.(36)

Kenneth E. F. Watt and his group, who have studied land use and energy flow, express this view. Even in the low cost energy years after 1945, a high correlation existed between the price of farmland at the suburban edge and the degree of urban sprawl. When the price was low, as around Tulsa, each person added to the urban population in those years caused one acre of farmland to be converted to urban use. On the other hand, in areas of high cost for open space, such as Long Island and the San Francisco Bay region, such population increases caused only a small fraction of an acre of open space to be covered by some urban form.(37)

Watt and his associates compare the perimeter of land around an area of urban growth to a belt which will be loose when energy prices are low and tight when they are high.(38) Prices for future food and fuel will be so high compared to the 1945-73 period, that open land adjacent to urban growth zones will rise sharply in price.(39) As a result the forces pushing urban forms out over exurban open space will decrease and activity will tend to concentrate nearer the urban core.

Most Americans reject this scenario. As Charles Rutenberg of the United States Homes Corporation has said, "Average urban citizens are tired of hearing about programs to rebuild our cities in the future."(40) And why are they tired?

Because "average urban citizens" have decided that they do not want to live in the central portions of the traditional city. They are quite willing to turn that central area over to high rise office buildings, parking lots, and blight. They personally want to keep pushing out into previously open space in order to live in suburban and exurban developments.

The desire may have been conditioned by the experience of the years after 1945, but the desire still exists. As a folk-song commercial in the late 1970s for an exurban development 30 miles from a midwestern American city articulated the average urban citizen's desires, "With my loved ones all around me, far far away in the Hideaway Hills."

Whether this desire can be sustained in practice in any time frame extending much beyond 1980 remains questionable. But American political pressures indicate an effort, at least, will be made.

THE PATTERN OF URBAN SPRAWL

Cheaply available energy in large amounts has made urban sprawl possible. The United States – and only to a little lesser extent England and western Europe – have been involved since 1950 in a process of continuous urbanization of open space. The suburbs are everywhere, with the wealthier leading the way to convert open space into urban land and to abandon the central areas. Between 1945 and 1973, energy costs in real terms declined.(41) On this fragmented energy budget, it was individually profitable to consume open space in this manner. After 1973 it was no longer so simple; but the desire to try remained.

The brilliant theorizing of Brian Berry describes the continuing suburbanization of the United States. As the floods of urban dwellers have moved their residences out over the open land, new growth centers have emerged within America's megalopolitan regions, occurring at the zones of confluence where the radiating waves of growth intersect from the interacting networks of extending metropoli. Berry's description of what has taken – and is still taking – place for urban growth in the United States is worth thoughtful consideration, particularly in the likelihood that the sharp rise in the cost of energy will continue.(42)

As Brian Berry has pointed out, the high-income sectors of the urban population have been the ones moving away from the core areas with increasing speed. In the remote environments of hills, lakes, and forests, those having the wealth to buy the leisure are siting their homes. The less affluent of the urban population aspire to this as their ideal. The environmental movement itself has made open space attractive as a lure. The wealthy can immediately directly experience such living. The less wealthy must settle for imitations in the form of town house projects where the woods once were or condominium second homes paid for out of rentals to transients 11 months out of every 12.

With the energy cascades, the movement of urban growth inevitably followed the networks of communication and power. This would be true whether energy were cheaply or expensively provided. The higher income leisure class leads in the opening of the rural landscape to urban forms. Their higher degree of mobility eventually brings together each outgoing wave of growth from separate metropoli until they meet in what had been previously open space.

An area of overlap thereby eventually appears. Each of these becomes a common zone of confluence wherein further new growth opportunities are concentrated. These nuclei threaten the older cities with extinction, unless energy can be redirected toward the city core.

How can it be otherwise? These nuclei have the least poverty. Populations are growing faster than anywhere around them, while the educational levels and employment rates are the highest in the urban region. Conversely, in the old city centers and in the periphery between the zones of confluence in urban growth, exist the lowest incomes, lowest educational levels, highest unemployment, greatest poverty, and population decline.(43) The suburban and exurban nuclei in the zones of confluence between expanding metropoli shine like bright oases in the urban sprawl.

For Brian Berry these are as near to centers of spontaneous growth that the United States has. This is due in part to the inability of the expanding metropoli to define peripheries. This inability occurs because spontaneous growth simply reflects the segregation and fragmentation of energy budgets, profits from costs, and demand from environmental response. These "spontaneous" nuclei constitute part of a national scene in which rhythmic gradients of income, plunging more sharply in the cores than in the nonconfluent metropolitan peripheries, shade each into the other.(44)

This "spontaneity" has created a core of wealth as an oasis in the urban sprawl. This core causes a gradient reversal for the national income scene, creating a magnet that draws activity away from the old core metropoli which generated the wealth – and still largely continues to generate it. The nuclei call for more pushing of activity into open space. They are "the places where the greatest opportunities for shaping future growth into more desirable forms are now concentrated."(45)

Emerging from a study of these nuclei is the conviction that the bulk of the planning community accepts them as inevitable. Planning today consists more of shaping this kind of growth rather than trying to turn back development from the urban periphery to the urban core. Although the infrastructure of urban facilities exists in the more central urban areas and environmental demand is less than when open space is consumed, the planners do not regard themselves free to consider radical change.

Concentrating growth within the core city has the disadvantage of internalizing too many of the costs within the central city growth projects. When the urban growth occurs on the open land at the urban periphery, costs become easier to conceal. Where planning and building occur on open ground, everything seems easier. Planners prefer to channel the urban explosion over open space rather than directing it onto the already wasted urban spaces of the central city.

Every level of population in a high-energy demand situation has physical mobility relatively far greater than would be true in a low-energy situation. By design, all the urban growth institutions further this sort of expansion. Realtors, credit institutions, the construction industry, and too many planners can pass on costs to the environment and the general fund, even as this activity also enables them to isolate and pocket their private profits. In a physically mobile society, profit can be made through processing the environment into small consumption units. This pattern conserves neither energy nor the environment.(46)

THE DEMAND FOR OPEN SPACE UNDER HIGH-ENERGY CONDITIONS

The stronger social forces, which steadily pound on, encourage expanding urban-industrial growth and the flow of the energy cascades. They produce perpetual mobility for some, distant and frequent movement for many more, and an urban sprawl into the open spaces around the city. The hope persists that someplace there will be a cool forest and a rippling brook where relief flows for urban problems.

It is a vain dream. The problems of the urban region are just as severely posed in the suburbs and the exurbs as ever they were in the core city of the more congested urban past. Only the intensity seems to be absent. And because that is a function of isolating costs from benefits, even that semblance of lower intensity is false.

The value of open space, both to the renewing environment and human social structure, has been persistently subordinated to demands for urban growth. Under the pressure of growing energy cascades, a dedication to increasing production and consumption of all kinds, in an undifferentiated manner, simultaneously occurs.(47) The bulk of the investments can be expected to be made for these purposes. Servicing these kinds of demands had become the dominant urban-industrial purpose. A good deal of talk is thrown about concerning the provision of leisure in relation to demands for open space. But that is only a mask to cover the generation of additional demands for a leisure industry.

Jean Barraud has denounced the "civilization of the leisured," which supposedly describes the later twentieth century, as another guise for demand. The false prophets of futuristic societies, with their requirement of energy cascades, and the present sellers of open space invented it. A deliberate confusion results between the concept of leisure and the activities of the seekers for indicia they have been conditioned to think represent "leisure."(48)

A fragmented energy budget and high-energy demand do not lack justifications for such a treatment of leisure. Andre Fontaine, for example, has an initially unhappy reaction over an autostrada being built through Naples. The autostrada carries high-powered cars with affluent riders to vacations on the beaches south of Naples. But Fontaine's second reaction concludes that this allocation of investment is justified by the economic need to draw money-spenders into a zone of anemic economic action in order to revitalize it.(49)

And how would conditions be changed? By getting money spent where its effect must be greater by a thrust in the direction of urban-industrial development. According to Fontaine, spending the money on the housing, hospitals, and schools in Naples would be a stagnant economic practice, merely ameliorative social relief, while spreading urban forms over the countryside is an investment in movement from traditional agrarian life to something on a far higher energy level.

Indeed, the result of a contrary plan which has succeeded in preserving open space, either in a natural or agrarian state, is often paradoxical. Although the action is directly meant only to preserve open space, what often occurs is the creation indirectly of a potentially high later value. By singling out certain land from the general sprawl, an opportunity has been created for either a subsequent commercial developer or, what is often far more dangerous, a public construction project looking for "cheap" open land – "cheap" because the land is in public title.

Let us assume that a planner has separated out a tract of ground so that it may remain a natural wood, or pasture, or crop land. Meanwhile urban construction, in greater or lesser density, proceeds all around this preserved tract of open space. As this occurs, the surrounding land rises steadily in value. The open space, because it is not built upon, keeps the value it initially had, or the value rises slightly.

This is a spurious low value. The open land confers the bulk of its value upon the surrounding, built-up areas rather than to space restricted to openness. Consequently, this open land, whether in public or private title, commands a comparatively low market price, which is the result of governmental mandate. If government should lift the restriction on using the land only for open space, its market price would rise precipitously.

The now unrestricted open land might not rise so high in price as that commanded by the surrounding land when the built-up areas still had the advantage of an openness that now is about to be lost. Instead, the turn has come for the surrounding land, having been fully developed as urban form, to confer its own external benefit upon the open space whose restriction has been lifted. Urban services, resulting from the earlier development, will shed their refulgence on the newly freed acreage, driving up its price further.

The open-space planner Philippe Saint Marc sees here the origins of great fortunes and the possibility to create states within states.(50) First, a clever planner provides an oasis of open space in what will be developed urban sprawl. Urban development then takes place, absorbing all the costs of furnishing urban facilities and enjoying the price benefit of the nearby mandated open space. The developers then sell off the developed tracts, including in the price both the cost of the urban facilities and the advantage of the commanded open space. Following this, they induce the government to release the restrictions on the open space.

The developers in this way receive from the unrestricted acreage the externally conferred benefit of the previously provided urban facilities. If privately held while restricted, the developers have the advantage of an initial low price and taxes paid on a low assessment during the years of restriction, while the government can justify selling it at a low price while restricted and then conferring on the buyers the benefit of lifting the restrictions.

Such cleverness confers the benefit of the restricted land on the developers of the unrestricted adjoining neighborhood until such time as they can pass on their costs and what will prove to be the illusionary value of being near open space to their buyers. At that point the lifting of the restriction will send the value of the now unrestricted land soaring.

Clearly, planners with such power are operating a state within a state. They cannot be unaware of either the benefits they confer upon certain urban developers or the costs they are imposing upon the larger urban system or the environment. Many find the simplicity of the relationships in such elementary planning hard to grasp – especially politicians when alleged defects are pointed out in the way the scheme operates.

As budget protectors and guardians of the public fisc, politicians want to use formerly restricted space in public title for public construction.   Space kept open by an earlier planning decision is cheaper to use than to condemn and raze structures on already built-up land. No owners and tenants need be ousted. It is tempting to use restricted open space rather than exercising eminent domain on a developed city block; and scarcely a municipality in the world is not deprived of capital for improving urban amenities.(51)

Consider the open green space of a city park adjoining a busy hospital that needs an addition for emergency services. The park was initially created because the ground was subject to flooding. No one questions the need for a hospital addition. Many, however, do regret the loss of the park space because, in terms of current development, it is locally irreplaceable.

Because those who regret the loss of the park may take action to block its destruction, the government moves fast. The trees are cut, the ground laid open with excavations, and nothing of the park is left to preserve except raw, open land. The government's budget has been protected, the park advocates can only mobilize to protect any green space left in the locality.(52)

Such public "saving" through the use of open space could be matched innumerable times in every built-up area in the world. If previous urban operations have preserved any open space, the attraction of such "cheap" sites will attract either commercial developers or government agencies — or both. The "cheapness" is a gift from the past. Like the "gifts" of nature, it is not a costless item to be expended, even if the narrow judgments of real-estate appraisers might lead in that direction.

Open space is never "cheaply" available for construction regardless of whether that construction is for profit or to save public expenditures. At the very least, high fiscal values are attached to such land. Why else would private developers so often cast a covetous eye upon it? Why else would government agencies see it as the preferred site for their construction projects?

The questions offer their own answers. Where urban sprawl consumes open space, the land that has been preserved from that sprawl will more often than not ultimately acquire a higher value. Through preservation by the state additional profit has become possible.

True, this may not occur if urban sprawl has rendered it derelict. Land for which no use can be found, because of adjoining uses or broken character, acquires little value by merely being open space.

Barring that final catastrophe, however, preserved open space has a tendency to rise in market value under conditions of urban sprawl, once the restrictions have been removed. Planners and governments unable to perceive that likelihood are even less likely to anticipate the ecologic significance of the preserved open space. To be so blinkered is to see nothing of ultimate importance.(53)

Planning in urban-industrial society is for growth and not for preservation, whether the object to be preserved is open space, natural systems, or a stable social structure. No common effort to tie together the various interrelated demands has occurred. In the current fragmented, undifferentiated, high-energy situation, too little effort has been made to make those demands responsive to natural systems.

Until a comprehensive view of ecologic interrelationships is adopted by planners, no change in the conduct toward open space and the urban environment is possible. Without that decision, even radical political differences will fail to produce sufficient action. For this reason buildings have been spilling over the landscape in every part of the world under the impact of high-energy demands.

Blending, adapting, conforming with the environment all cost money that must be charged ultimately to growth projects. Failing to do this focuses only on isolable benefits. Invariably such action shuffles costs onto particular competitors, the general fund of taxpayers, or nature. Attempts like these have tempted planners — whether in democratic, authoritarian, or socialist states – to opt for fragmented exploitative actions for urban-industrial society and its structure of high-energy demand.(54)

This has been true even in countries with strong central planning, tight building controls, and publically owned construction outfits. It has not been a practice confined to countries with the custom of anarchic development. All these countries have exhibited an indifference to equilibrium. Only the benefits of urban sprawl to the fiscal economy have mattered.(55)

The classic pattern of urban sprawl is marked by indifference to the natural environment by the developers. Only as sprawl confers a "free" external benefit, fragments the environment into profitable consumption units, and standardizes all activity so as to accelerate the service of high-energy demands is urban growth recognized as having social and environmental effects. Such an attitude will not be subjected voluntarily to any code of conduct embodying ecological guidelines, and mandatory rules will be evaded more enthusiastically than they will be performed.(56)

The social decision for processing the environment has become so well established under high-energy conditions (as well as among those aspiring to high-energy status) that individual restraint, in any event, can only create oases in the midst of urban sprawl. By regarding the environment as a "free" external benefit, individuated profits from isolated benefits can be accumulated. The fact that general losses from interrelated costs are also accumulating is not seriously considered by those enjoying the profits and benefits.

National planning and socialist ideology do not necessarily change this. To do so, they too would have to comprehensively act in accordance with a realization of the interrelatedness between human demand and natural response. A perception that urban forms cannot be undifferentiatedly loaded onto the landscape, without working that landscape's destruction, does not seem to come easily to any sort of growth enthusiast.

Ordered land use means that a planner understands the interrelationship between natural land conditions and human use. The advantages of individuated benefits cause too many planners to deny the interrelatedness of human demand and natural response. Ordered land use means the planner must grasp the limitations of action that do not destroy the values existing prior to the imposition of urban forms.

In high-energy situations, planners may think they bring affluence by ignoring these realities. Unfortunately, no bright prospect exists for this kind of ordered land use. But urban sprawl is not a necessary correlate of urban growth, however much experience may have made it seem so. Planning under conditions of high-energy demand will always have to be done with full consideration for growth. Planning need not accept as inevitable still more urban sprawl.

7 Government's Responsibility for the Land Environment

THE CONTRIBUTION OF THE NATIONAL GOVERNMENT
TO URBAN SPRAWL

There is a sarcastic Senator in the United States named Daniel Patrick Moynihan, who is often wisest when being most sarcastic. Asked if the United States had a national urban growth policy, he quickly said yes. His exact words were, "We have long had a national urban growth policy familiar under the more modest guise of the Federal Highway Program."(1)

Senator Moynihan was being too modest. He might have added other federal bureaucratic structures, such as the Federal Housing Authority. Mortgage insurance requirements in the first thirty years of its existance were a guarantee that American cities would explode outward and the middle-class would have high inducement to leave the old traditional cities. As early as 1922, the Department of Commerce ensured the same pattern with a model zoning ordinance for suburban development seemingly designed to favor urban sprawl.

In brief, for over half a century, considerable federal planning of land use in the United States has affected both formerly urban and rural land. A helping federal hand has worked consistently to increase elimination of rural and the expansion of urban land. The "sprawl, maldistribution, and environmental deterioration," which someone like Governor Richard Lamm laments, have not been happenstance.(2) They have not been the result of such paper tigers as the impotence of government to regulate, or the self-interest of local communities, or the anarchy of capitalism. They have been the result of much federal planning activity.(3)

Matters have not been left to the local communities nor to anarchic capitalism. Regulations at the federal level have not been impotent. The national land planning of the United States government, at least into the late 1970s, has favored urban sprawl, high energy demand, and

108

processing of the environment. These decisions have been national, not local.

What have the federal programs been? Enumerating a few illustrates the goals to which the United States government gave its commitment. First of all, farm programs have been designed to remove the farmer from the land who raised crops for subsistence and not for market. Farm families like these were transferred to the center city. Additionally, mortgage insurance programs created home ownership of detached suburban tract houses which could never have been built if open space had not been made "cheaply" available. After the Flood Control Act of 1936, individuals were encouraged to build in the flood plains, an encouragement not muted until after 1968 and after decades of expensive adverse experience. The federal interstate highway and urban renewal programs that began blasting cities and urban populations after the mid-1950s contributed importantly to the decline of the inner city and the growth of urban sprawl.(4)

The list of such federal action favoring urban sprawl could go on. It hardly marks either the impotency of federal regulation, or the ascendency of selfish local government, or the operation of anarchic capitalism.

Local and private personalities may have been stimulators of federal action on a particular project. But this ought not to disguise the overall, impersonal, quite routine commitment the United States government has made over the past half century to the growth in energy demand, the consumption of natural resources, and the encouragement of urban sprawl. This is a fact too often lost to sight by the full spectrum of American political opinion.

GOVERNMENT'S CONTRIBUTION TO SHAPING THE LANDSCAPE

What must not be lost to sight is that every landscape that is not purely wilderness is humanly designed; and government plays a large part in that design. The English Architectural Review in the early 1950s examined the sprawling interurban fringes, the regions through which the rolling waves of metropolitan growth were passing. The magazine's conclusions might be considered prescient of events that are still transpiring.(5)

First of all, they discovered that the population in the fringes was large, although the density was low, even compared to traditional inner suburbs. Secondly, the movement outward involved families rather than single persons. In addition, these moving families did not want to be renters but rather owners of real property, although ownership was essentially of an equity resting upon a small down payment, flat-rate monthly payments, and a long mortgage term. The most interesting aspect of these movements to the fringe was their mass-character. What the Review was seeing in the early 1950s was the advance guard of the future population of urban sprawl.

The Review then noted that these people were very dependent upon existing urban service centers for specialized needs and tended to commute long distances for both work and shopping. The fringes were not quick to duplicate city services until commuting to the old sites became too difficult. Political boundaries became meaningless and urban forms were imposed without regard for the survival of agriculture.

The early fringe dwellers rarely had sewerage, public water supply, or other customary urban services. Yet despite the lack of such services, land values were already increasing rapidly. Land values sometimes were locally depressed when these fringe areas allowed extensive land uses not tolerated by the residents of the older suburbs, such as track-car racing, junk yards, and outdoor movies that required large quantities of open space and imposed external costs upon even larger quantities of land. In short, the fringes were a mess. But the mess boded high profitability for many, whatever the environmental and social costs.

This description, to the critical, underscores that the growing urban regions in the early 1950s needed over-all, precommitted, ecologically sound land use plans, with planners having both veto-power and positive command functions. Really, such plans had been needed in the United States since the mid-1930s when efforts of the National Resource Committee to plan outward urban development were aborted.(6)

The 1974 proposal of the International Union for the Conservation of Nature and Natural Resources, indicates that an ecologically sound land use plan is still needed for high-energy urban situations. The Union, like the National Resources Committee four decades earlier, was still talking in terms of voluntarism. Comprehensive, positive, mandated land use planning has been needed in high-energy situations since at least the 1920s. Yet, by the 1970s, very little such planning had been realized.(7)

As urban growth continues, the prosperous create their oases of affluence. Luxurious suburban and exurban shopping centers are a part of this development. Meanwhile others must be perceived as only relatively less prosperous in comparison with the upper and upper-middle class persons whose goals provide the growth images for the urban fringes.

Still, they are less prosperous, and must seek less accessible, expensive, or desirable areas with less chance of an appreciation in land value. Suburban industry will locate in these portions of urban sprawl and among them a place will be found for such cultural artifacts as gravel pits and drag strips.

The one demand common to this sprawling development beyond the fringe is energy. And the bulk of that energy can only be made available through extensive reinforcing governmental action that ends in shaping the landscape.(8)

Every class able to grasp some portion of this governmental assistance has moved large numbers of its members into open space that was "cheap." These shifts provided amenities not available at any comparable price within the more congested central city. It has been, however, the governmental infrastructure which made these actions so "cheap" on an individuated basis. Every level of government has participated in providing the publically funded underpinnings for urban sprawl in exurban open space.

In this situation there is no true chaos since chaos is not something rather carefully created. Neither is there anarchy, since nearly everything has occurred as a result of governmental authority, either through financing, or by licensing, or by providing such services as highways, water mains, sewers, or the credit for them. It is the larger social action that treats open space adjacent to expanding cities as a natural resource to be used as "freely" as possible.(9)

LOCATION THEORY AND INTEGRATED LAND USE IN URBAN REGIONS

Often in land use planning today, the value of an equilibrium between the land market and open space is not recognized. Where there is a social preference to split profit from cost, the overall higher worth of equilibrium finds the means of expression difficult. Simply put, land equilibrium is very hard to maintain under undifferentiated demand. A fragmented energy budget and uncorrelated urban-industrial growth bars chances for equilibrium. Instead, the individuated profits from disequilibrium in land use continue to attract the determiners of land use.(10)

The concept of equilibrium as a continuous space market dates back to the founder of location theory, Johann Heinrich von Thunen, who began his empiric studies on the subject in 1810. As Martin Beckman explains it,

> Long-run equilibrium requires that no activity could be profitably relocated; that no piece of land (or other immobile resource) could be more profitably used; that capital is earning the same rate of return everywhere; that no mobile resource (labor) could move to a location where extra benefits (wages and non-monetary income) exceed moving cost.(11)

This system casts centers of economic activity in terms of higher and lower orders. In a higher order center greater urban growth and energy demand prevail. Thus when the countryside becomes depopulated of its rural inhabitants by the encroachment of urban forms, the lower order centers must be eroded or even wiped out. The decline in the relative cost of transportation between the central city and the countryside and the expansion of growth in the high-order urban centers guaranteed this in the years between 1945 and 1980.(12)

The forces for disequilibrium are firmly built into any system that fragments the energy budget. Some people, for example, think that the public, through private choice, will cease using cars by either switching to mass transit or reducing their travel. They base this reasoning upon the congestion of auto traffic, with its delays and dangers, rather than upon the increasing rise in the price of fuel.

If this change should happen, it would greatly reduce the problems of traffic flow, the impaction of traffic from congestion, and the extension of urban sprawl. Unhappily, location economics has produced enough research to show the likelihood of automatic, self-regulatory mechanisms to be doubtful. Resistance to rising gasoline prices remains high and heavy reliance on the at-command convenience of the private car continues. The environmental and social problems raised by the private car loom small indeed in the eyes of their individual owners.

The addition of each new car further congests traffic unless a used car is simultaneously sent to the scrapheap. Still, the average delay that the driver of the new car will suffer is less than the additional delay that the new car will impose upon traffic. The consequence is that the social is greater than the private cost.

The driver of the additional car contributes to the loss of general amenities, or even necessities, within the urban environment. Air pollution and noise levels are increased, more space must be paved, and urban deterioration is intensified along the traffic arteries. But the car owner has gained the freedom and conveniences of impulsive portal-to-portal movement which far overshadow the imposition of high social costs. Indeed, car owners, will push for still greater support facilities. No society, of course, could ever provide enough resources in open space – or even in money – to fully provide all the demands of the private car owner and, at the same time, counteract the added social burdens.

Although larger social issues may concern the individual car-buyer, they are beyond personal control. The decision not to buy a car by itself is meaningless. Furthermore, the present condition of urban sprawl and the inadequacy – or unavailability – of urban mass transit make the choice not to acquire a car non-existent.(13)

The individual car owners are not persuaded that any connection exists among the loss of open space, the decline in the pleasantness in center city living, and their own private automobiling. Some location theorists argue ironically that, where physical movement and the economy are so dependent upon private automobiling, the best one could hope to accomplish might be a use of resources establishing the same level of congestion everywhere.(14)

The pity is that many location theorists have drifted away from von Thunen's early reliance on the almost physiocratic condition of the land. Location theory recognizes the importance of ecological fact in order to better attain equilibrium in land use. The theory need not operate only within limits set by fragmenting demands for high-energy cascades.

In land planning, for example, the soil scientist can serve as a resource person to identify the character of a given piece of land. Such information could save the subsequent embarrassment of saturating the soil with septic tanks, or lowering the water table by sinking many wells, or penetrating a high water table with basements.(15) Embarrassment is too mild a word to describe the social, personal and environmental costs such failures impose. But such consultation is the beginning of a total approach, merging economics and ecology, in a planning process that can resist grabbing isolated profit in disregard of the renewing environment.(16)

At the beginning of the nineteenth century, von Thunen understood that open space, sunlight, vista, air movements, and the historical ambience of a region are really common property. In a fragmented and segregating system, the premium goes to anyone who appropriates this common property for individual benefit. If nothing is done to plan for equilibrium in the relationship between the location of economic activity and the natural environment, then such activities can only harm all renewing systems and contribute to the grossest and most unstable kind of disequilibria.

This is not to make the sort of doomsday predictions, now so much derided, that prophesy all the structures built by urban sprawl will come tumbling down. It is simply to assert that urban sprawl, by ignoring these relationships, continues to exert a destabilizing effect upon the land environment.(17)

LEGAL ATTEMPTS TO CREATE LAND USE EQUILIBRIUM IN URBAN REGIONS

One often despairs of improvement when reading about the interrelated problems of protecting the renewing environment, conserving energy, and altering land use within urban sprawl. A belief that no institutional mechanisms exist to carry through basic shifts relative to energy usages, or ecologic systems, or land use seems justified. The impression is intensified that present legal structures cannot avert systemic disasters.

The impression, though, is a false one. Despair is not justified. Legal, economic, or political possibilities do exist for structuring changes from a situation of brittle deteriorations to one of flexible renewal. What is missing is the will of decision-makers to seek out these possibilities. Yet the possibilities of basic change are richly present for land use, as they are for environmental protection and energy conservation. And what helps or hurts one of these, helps or hurts the others.

One of these devices for change is the concept of land banking currently being put forward by The Trust for Public Land, based upon Stockholm's municipal practice since 1904. For the Swedes it has been a success, but one ought not forget that the Swedish society is homogeneous and, despite class differences, fairly well integrated. For this reason alone, land banking might not be so easily transported. But it is another of the possibilities leading to change which can work.

Under the concept of land banking, a municipal government buys up vacant, derelict, or open land, holds it out of use, and thereby slows decay, growth, or both. When the municipality determines that any part of its land is ready for use, this portion is leased to a private developer. Prior to any leasing of municipally owned land, a comprehensive land plan has to be developed, and all such leasing must comply with the plan. The turnover of land is maintained at a steady pace so that the rentals provide the necessary debt service to allow the acquisition of additional land.

These purchases do not occur under the municipality's power to exercise eminent domain and they are not forced sales. Instead, the municipality buys as the land comes on the market and competes with other, mostly private, buyers in its acquisition. The municipality thereby exercises two important functions as a regular institutional buyer of the land within the jurisdiction. By always being an available buyer, the municipality sets a floor on land prices. By always having land available for leasing, the municipality can act to dampen any threatened excess in land speculation.(18)

According to Professor Walter Lewis, this would enable the city to minimize pressure for zoning changes. By promptly taking open city land off the market as it is offered for sale through purchase, the municipal land bank could prevent urban sprawl from eating up increasingly scarce land.(19) Boulder, Colorado, by approving a tax increase in 1967, has already bought 4,500 acres to be kept permanently unused except as it serves as a kind of scenic "backdrop" for the city and by so doing confers an external value upon city real estate.

Interestingly, the Boulder puchases were outside the municipal limits. In order to be effective, municipalities clearly would have to be authorized to buy land outside their boundaries since this is where most open land lies. The problem is more one of legal power than political accountability. It was not hard for Boulder to display to every resident the importance of the scenic backdrop hanging over the city. Its existence justifies the expenditure of the taxpayers' money. But for many cities, it might be difficult to show the taxpayers the benefit of buying land lying outside city boundaries.

Of course, if the municipal boundaries are wide enough, the problem would be answered. Municipal government, however, is so fractured under conditions of urban sprawl that there is little likelihood of this possibility. A regional authority or state corporation, such as New York's lamented Urban Development Corporation, might be created or empowered to purchase open space. In this event, open space would be paid for by persons who, at least indirectly, would be within the normal zone of those benefited by tax expenditures.

Unfortunately for these alternatives, municipalities have been reluctant to let purchasing power pass to regional units. The depressing experience of the Urban Development Corporation in New York State has held back others from imitating it. What emerges from any cool scrutiny of land banking is that it, too, is dependent upon the basic social decision effecting the treatment of the urban environment. Barring a social decision for integrated behavior, land banks would be tools for social segregation and environmental fragmentation.   By itself, this is not sufficient reason to avoid such a legal and economic device as the land bank. But it is a reason to examine how the present fragmented situation could use the land bank as other institutions have been used, i.e., not for change but for more of the same conduct so harmful to the remaining environment, energy conservation, and open space.

The land bank, for instance, could become a means of unloading tax-delinquent property upon the city. Or the bank could be used as a device for a city to put unwanted activities, ranging from low-income housing to scavenger disposal areas, outside the municipal boundaries. When a society has social standards that seek higher consumption through fragmentation, it becomes hard to predict that the land bank would not be misused. A land bank could easily serve as a conduit for the exile of politically unwanted, but unavoidable or even essential, urban activities and functions. The land bank could be sunk, fiscally and every other way, by the weight of policies abusive of social and environmental purposes put forward by the high-minded promoters of the idea.

Certainly there are plenty of difficulties inhering in the way a land bank would have to operate under the demand conditions of urban-industrial growth. The initial outlay for the purchase of land could not be small and must compete with the already heavy municipal respon-sibilities for education, welfare, and health. The municipal tax rolls and debt burdens are currently high and this would make them higher.

Also, the municipality would have to be extraordinarily adept in setting prices, assessing, and taxing leased land. Otherwise the result of municipal acquisition over the decades would be a sharp rise in both the value of the land not yet bought by the city and the taxes paid by that land.(20) To prevent the latter, the city would be compelled to regulate the non-municipally owned land so that it would not become an Alsatia of activities not allowed on land leased from the municipality.

These, after all, are the same forces for fragmentation and segrega-tion which have kept zoning from more effectively slowing the rapidity of open space consumption. Barring basic changes in social attitude, they would work similarly in the case of the land bank. There really is no reason, under present circumstances, to believe that what has been true for municipal zoning could not also be true for the land bank. When proposed from 1910 to 1930, zoning offered much promise.(21) But the promise has been blighted by the events of urban sprawl. Even as the federal environmental protection legislation, most notably the Clean Air and Water Acts, have turned to zoning as a means of enforcement, zoning as an institutional device for saving land values is in poor repute.(22)

Consider what Gene Wunderlich has said about the relationship of scenic protection and zoning.

> The zoning game is a game of power, as are the games of right-of-way, mineral location, scenic protection, and tax deduction. Different players, different arenas, and different rules, but the prize is the same. Dominion over territory. . . (23)

With forces such as these continuing their dominant role, any land bank is far more likely to be used by growth promoters for their independent ends rather than managed in such a way as to exercise control over their activities.

Also other problems exist. They are not small ones and they too concern land banking, zoning, and local land use control. These problems relate directly to the fragmented character of municipal government, especially in the United States. Such governments lack expertise on land values as is perpetually revealed by an examination of property assessments. Still more important is the pervasive corruption existing in so many American cities in the handling of zoning, building permits, and land use. From the days when St. Tammany first made his deals with Aaron Burr's so-called water company, honesty has more often been a word cut into the outer walls of City Hall than a virtue practiced within them. The corrupt and fragmenting pressures on American local government make it unlikely that municipalities can operate a land bank as does Swedish local government. The market and social forces pushing toward urban sprawl offer little likelihood of success for the land bank as an isolated institutional device.

Implicit within the land bank concept, as compared to such a device as zoning, is the important idea that the whole title to land is vested in local government. Only the usufruct would become available to developers and could be managed similarly to the emphyteutic leases employed in some of the socialist countries of eastern Europe. This is a type of legal instrument dating back to the late Roman Empire. Today, as then, it seems to become popular when there are analogous relations concerning land and capital between government and the users of land.

Under such a lease, the government holds the title. A grant for a term is made for the land's use to a private person or to a group. The government may participate in providing some of the capital investment for development. In any event, the government shares in the proceeds, both as to current return and as the reversioner of the improvements.

Where government is strong vis-a-vis the private entrepreneur, it provides both an income outside of tax revenues and a corpus for taxation, insofar as the remaining income and assets of the lease are concerned. There also is the appreciation upon the improvements. Given the guiding role of government throughout, this increase need not be lost by the time the term expires.

As a land use system, the emphyteutic lease is an even greater determiner than the land bank operation. Government holds dramatically greater powers over land than those existing under an institution of private land ownership. But this lease is no autonomous solver of problems insofar as urban growth and the maintenance of the urban environment are concerned. Without the appropriate social decisions, the emphyteutic lease will not work any better than private land titles subject to public zoning and regulation.

There is no magic in any single process of land management. What government must contend with is pressure for land use. Government can control such pressure – if government wishes to do so – under systems of private land ownership, land banking, emphyteutic leases, or communalized title to land. But if government lacks the will, land use will be uncontrollable under any set of legal rules.

HIGH REGULATION OR GOVERNMENTAL OWNERSHIP: THE CHANCE FOR IMPROVED LAND USE

Nothing in the way land title is held predetermines how the land will be used. Even in a capitalist economic structure, government ownership of land can sometimes be cheaper than regulating private ownership. As a result of governmental efforts to respond to public dissatisfaction, private land ownership has been subjected to regulation, prohibition, and subsidy. All these legal approaches involve costs to the overall system. Should such costs continue increasing, the private ownership of land could be rendered economically inefficient.

Outright government ownership could greatly reduce these costs. Reflecting on this alternative might produce second thoughts in those profiting from the present high level of regulation of land held in private title. Government land ownership, on a scale approaching totality, is possible even in a social system dedicated to private capitalist economic forms and practices.(24)

The United States farm subsidy program is a prime example of the relation that costly programs bear to regulating a private title in agricultural land. From the inception of the federal soil improvement programs, the United States has relied on persuasion through the education of, and financial inducement to, the private farm owner. Americans have been assured repeatedly that this is far superior to a program of governmental ownership of the land in which farmers, as tenants, hold under leases whose terms had been set by government. Yet the Administrator of the Soil Conservation Service could say in 1972:

> Judged against current standards, 64 percent of the nation's cropland needs additional treatment. Some 67 percent of pasture and rangeland and 62 percent of forest land also has received inadequate treatment. . . .(25)

This is a terrible indictment of the effectiveness of the traditional American system in rural land management. Consider all of the federal money spent to maintain an "ever-normal" granary, and on soil banks, soil conservation districts, and other agricultural payment programs. What if that money, instead, had gone into buying on behalf of the United States government all rural land as it came on the market at full market price?

At that point, the government could have retired land unsuited for cultivation. No one would have been paid to make a selection of land to be retired. The prime choice would not be made by the one benefited.

The government could have reforested without having to fund pleading programs to encourage private forestry. Terms in the leases could determine how farming operations were conducted rather than the persuasion-through-education-cum-subsidy approach actually used.

There is no doubt of the inherent power for change in this alternative. Would the fiscal cost have been greater for the program of total federal governmental ownership and control? Possibly not. If such an alternative program had been pursued, would land conditions have reached the stage that they could not be honestly criticized today by someone insistent upon a comprehensive, integrated use of land?

Minimally, the answer is probably no. In the light of experience since the federal government began its subsidy programs, no program of federal land acquisition, ownership, and lease would have made the slightest difference to nature. The renewing environment would continue being broken up and processed into production and consumption units. Strong evidence exists that even federal land ownership itself has been managed to serve fragmented growth demands.(26) One-third of the land in the United States does belong to the United States.(27) Considering what has been done with so much of that governmental land, one cannot be sanguine as to how a federal program would have worked that gradually acquired all the farm land in America and then leased it back.

What has happened has been the imposition of a high burden on federally-owned lands, compelling the performance of economic functions valuable to private interests. The nation looks to the federal lands for its forest resources, recreation reserves, headland waters, and every other common value that private ownership of the remaining two-thirds of the land has no intention of supplying. But the pressure grows upon federally-owned land for more cutting of timber, more reservations of mineral lands, more acreage to be dedicated to the recreation industry, and for an ever-larger supply of water for mineral, industrial, and urban development.(28)

If the rural land acquisition program over the past forty years had doubled the amount of federally-owned land (so that the United States government owned two out of every three acres) would this pressure have been reduced? Or would the federal government have been under the same harsh pressure to use the natural powers of the land for maximum food and fiber production? It is very doubtful if such a program would have resulted in greater ground richness or greater preservation of open space.

Paradoxically, the bulk of the farmers would probably have prospered the most under such a program of total government ownership. They would have been relieved from the burden of their current huge capital investment in the land and the handicap of financing it out of annual yield. Under doubtlessly politically influenced lease payments, their economic position probably would have been quite good and would have benefited far larger numbers than are now productive farmers.

The mere ownership of land by government need not be a force for equilibrium in land use. The exploitation of soil, forests, and wildlife;

the depopulation of the rural areas; the growth of urban sprawl; and the deterioration of the urban environment could all have occurred under either programs of regional land banks or federal land acquisition. Indeed, the experience with lesser levels of formal governmental control indicate that they indubitably would have taken place.

The solution is not to throw in the towel. It is, for openers, incumbent on central planners to differentiate their responsibilities and to determine the key planning points for which urgent priorities must be established.(29) This is not to isolate these issues from the rest of the problems of the energy budget or from the living and renewing systems in nature. Too often concentrating upon key issues has been seen as just this sort of segregating activity. Difficulties have been treated as crash programs to be solved without regard for the larger whole.

Land is not a neat package, to be opened, sorted out, retied, and dropped comfortably in a nearby refuse bin. Open space is either everywhere or nowhere. Land is the fixed necessity that furnishes the locale for the activity of human culture. In the past, man assumed that nature, or tradition, or some process outside the scope of articulated human responsibility would take care of the provision of land and open space. It was inconceivable that land resources would not always be available for the taking, whatever the burden of the demand.

C. A. Doxiadis, who predicted that the future inevitably will produce the world-embracing city of ecumenopolis, insisted before his death that the land planning needed is for the universal garden. On a world-scale, he would classify land and water in interpenetrating categories, escalating from zones in which no human access would be allowed to those in which the densest, most demanding human activity would be concentrated. In this way land uses would be specified, differentiated public regulation or ownership would be possible, and a frame for negotiation on land use would have been established. Although no final solution, this institutional device opens the way to a stabilized land use.(30)

The present disequilibrium threatens the long-term availability of land. As future demands requiring land are formulated, the kind of low-quality consumption that a segregating urban sprawl now allows will prove a cost – and, for many demands, a barrier – to their accomplishment. The presently destabilizing operations going on in land use must ultimately be paid for; and the natural environment alone will not pay. The payment shall be extracted from the social and capital structures as well.

For these reasons, the time is now to create institutional devices in planning that will be capable of changing the present practices. And, most important of all, it is time to make the basic social decisions which can make worthwhile the creation of new institutional devices for environmental planners.

THE GROWING PERCEPTION OF THE IMPORTANCE
OF OPEN SPACE

Once land is perceived as a limited natural resource, its protection for the meeting of future human demand must rank high on the list of priorities. In this perspective, open space holds the key significance for both the maintenance of natural systems and the potentiality of their response to human demand. Under high-energy growth, open space tends to acquire an increasing general scarcity. This scarcity is intensified by urban sprawl. Open space, like any other function of land use, is limited, capable of extinction, and most valued when most limited.

In conditions of low-energy, little value is assigned to open space. Outside compressed settlements where a low rate of energy conversion exists, so much open space is present that it may even seem fearful in its brooding abundance. Low-energy usage makes such minimal demand upon open space for urban purposes that open space is hardly regarded as a natural resource.

With the arrival of a technology capable of high-energy potential, a transitional period occurs in which the old attitude continues to prevail. The first three quarters of the twentieth century was such a period. Urban sprawl was encouraged because open space was not highly valued in relation to other natural resources and to competing objects of capital investment.

As a result, urban growth has been permitted to spread in an undifferentiated way over the landscape. Vistas have been closed by high-rises and superhighways. Yet as all of this has occurred, the perception that open space should be cherished has been intensifying. As the existence of open space becomes most threatened, and it seems that the last vista for the urban eye will be closed, the great value of open space and the land environment at last come to the verge of acceptance by the urban-industrial demand structure.

In a growth situation, the price land can command in the market depends on attributes other than the natural stock. How land can produce cash output depends far more upon inputs of labor, capital, and human management. Under these conditions, an individual owner may very well see open land as a vacancy. Perhaps the land possesses a larger value because of this openness; but to the individual owner this is an externality conferring benefits upon other individuals, or to society at large. Except as they benefit as members of society, the individual owners of open land see their interests in conflict with all others.

The command price of open land is one sum to its owner. As land upon which urban forms have been imposed, it may command a far higher amount. It is scarcely surprising that the individual owner wants to receive the largest sum possible. Usually the private owner could care less about external diseconomies this imposes upon other individuals, society, or even upon the owner as a member of the general society. "Take the money and run" is a common epithet.

The general public is becoming more insistent upon controlling how land use is to be pursued in the future. Marion Clawson has given a straightforward explanation as to why this will be increasingly the case:

> . . .the number of persons who neither own nor use the land now, nor propose to do so in the future, but who nevertheless assert an interest in its use, is rising sharply. . .The rising demands for land use are encountering increasing resistance to change. . .with consequent turmoil.(31)

Nothing is inappropriate in non-land owners wanting to assert their interest, considering that much of the value in the land is the direct product of general social forces. What this public attitude will mean for the private landowner, Marion Clawson also pointedly summarizes:

> We can no longer let any producer produce what he chooses, in any way that he chooses. . .(W)e can no longer let every consumer consume anything and everything he may wish and can pay for.(32)

In short, the free days of undifferentiated urban sprawl over open space are coming to an end. Even under systems of private land ownership, a pressure is building for change. Increasingly, government is pushed into serving as a transfer agent. In this capacity, government shifts the use and control of land from its owners. The recipients of this shift are either persons who desire to own nothing more than an equity in land or persons who want to possess simultaneously far less and far more.

These beneficiaries of governmental intervention minimally want to assure that land be kept available to meet their demands into the indefinite future. Maximally, they want open space kept open and access, free of urban structure, guaranteed to the entire population. Unfortunately for this latter demand, the probability remains that urban form will continue to be imposed upon open space. Despite this, however, the implementation of these expectations would represent, at the least, a socialization of urban sprawl.

This is not to say the basic concept of private land ownership could not survive this shift. Those wanting their own equity in land would not oust entirely private interests in land. The issue of who holds title to land, and what title to land means, still keeps great operational resilience. For example, private ownership survived zoning. Private interests, as shown by the emphyteutic lease, have survived some countries' socialization of land. Even a communal land system may permit an assignment of personal plots or of apartments. It is perfectly possible for private ownership in land to survive the demands of the non-land owning public for open space, unconfinement, and low density.(33)

The preservation of open space and some degree of wildness in the natural landscape, however, should not be regarded as sufficiently served simply because urban access to them has been increased and made more generally available. Urban form is not confined to building structures.

The New England experience illustrates that prediction is perilous when made on the basis of how land was used in the past. At the opening of the nineteenth century, rural New England was an area of farms and a source of food for the growing industrial cities. Because of near proximity to urban centers, farmland appeared to have an assured future for appreciation in price. The opening of the Erie Canal in 1825 dashed those expectations; and the coming of the railroads sealed the doom of New England agriculture. The cheap, plentiful midwestern grain outcompeted the New England product in New England's very own cities, leaving those farmers little option except to abandon their now much depreciated (in price) farms.

By the mid-nineteenth century, New Hampshire had only twenty-five percent of its land still in forest. The local demand for timber made it seem likely the forest would diminish further. More importantly to the prophets of the early part of the nineteenth century, a need for increased tillage to feed the rising New England cities would certainly cut down the available timber. A reasonable expectation would have concluded that all the forests in the state would be gone long before the close of the nineteenth century.

Yet events external to New Hampshire changed all that. Western grain and beef made New England farming uneconomic in current market terms. The rising industries of the cities provided a place for the easy removal of the displaced farmers. Indeed, they could earn a higher cash income and enjoy greater amenities than when the farms were in their heyday. With the departure of the farmers, a demand for timber diminished until the much later arrival of the paper industry.

The canny Yankees left the land for sound reasons. Only city-earned income could maintain family farmsteads of substantial size, built from the fruits of the farm's own products. With the shrinking demand for agrarian land, the woods got their chance to come back, and old stone fences could again snake through the trees. By the early 1970s, New Hampshire was eighty-five percent wooded; and no prophet in the early-to-mid-nineteenth century could ever have predicted this.(34)

Forces external to the area completely altered the price of the land. Private ownership could not prevent the farmers from being swept away. It is equally doubtful if socialization of the title to the land, by itself, would have produced a different result.

No one is arguing, of course, that the present New England timber is virgin forest. Assuredly, it is second and third growth. But it is woodland, and woodland on a large scale. What is now threatening once again the trees and open space are economic forces as external as the one which made the return of the forests possible.

The national economy now sees this forested open space as appropriate sites to be cleared for summer and winter resorts, second homes, and for the ski industry. The ski slopes, lodges, and airports and highways to get the transient mass in, entertained, and out over weekends (or longer periods) are all making demands upon the resurgent woodlands. The rise in the price of energy once more makes the forest a source of fuel. While it is a highly replenishable source, replenishment may take more time than demand will easily grant to the supply. Traditionally, the preference has been to mine forests, not to farm them.

As there were shifts in energy nationally, so have there been shifts in the value of New England rural and exurban land. Energy shifts of this size are not uncommon with energy cascades. The pouring in of cheap and abundant energy in the form of food drove agriculture off the land. The pouring in of energy through the decentralization of electricity and automotive power has been a source of threat to the resurgent woodlands. Another externally caused change, the scarcity of petroleum, may reverse the situation again. The post-World War II exurban recreation industry may be damaged and a different sort of harm may come to the woodlands.

If all that is wanted is the simulation of a forest, then the environmental advantage gained by the first external energy surge in the nineteenth century may be offset by the twentieth century energy cascade. To recreate a concrete jungle in the new woodlands, duplicating in expanded form the suburbs of the Atlantic coast cities, would be an act of ultimate destruction. Just as destructive would be the denudation of the forests for fuel without adequate replanting. The continuing demand for cheap and abundant energy to support the impact of urban farms on rural northern New England would be the cause of the forest's loss.

In land use, the significant matters are whether a culture commands low or high levels of energy supplies, whether the energy budget is fragmented or unified, or whether urban form is indiscriminatingly imposed upon open land. These powerful forces set the limits within which decisions will be made for land use. Such social forces shape and move events far more than legal concepts and institutional devices, which are the means that the social forces employ to determine events.

Broad social interests are now working on behalf of open space and wildness in the land environment. Not all the economic forces are moving in the direction of continued consumption for urban-industrial growth. An interest is rising that turns away from patterns whose continued pursuit can destroy nature's resilience everywhere instead of in only a few areas. The value of open space is being gradually perceived even by the managers of urban-industrial growth.

THE UNIVERSAL INCREASE IN PUBLIC CONTROL
OF PRIVATE LAND USE

Changed attitudes are reflected in the way private land use is increasingly subjected to control not previously experienced. In the recent past, developers of housing or industrial tracts on open ground simply dedicated some of the blank space to the local unit of government. This was for the public support services. Thereafter, at the expense of the general fund or through assessments levied on the buyers, the local governmental unit was expected to fill the dedicated blank space with ditches, paving, lighting, or some other costly facility whose expense did not appear on the books of the developer. This no longer happens.

Today, in most instances, the developer is expected to provide these facilities for the project, although frequently the developer is permitted to do so in stages. Whereas the open space in the mid-1970s might have cost as little as $3,000 per acre in the United States, the costs for providing streets and utilities frequently ran over $15,000 per acre, with an initial commitment of one-third of that amount. Subsequent costs for both have increased substantially. The proportionate gap has remained however, between the price of raw land and the costs of municipal infrastructures.

As a result, the development period for new subdivisions is no longer brief, but often stretches over a period of fifteen years. Consequently, because time is money, the developer must have a long-term interest in the condition of the developed land and its environment.(35)

This relates to Lord Keynes' famous quip that compound interest was humanity's second greatest invention. As a corollary, one might argue that discounted cash flow for land development is practically in the same category of beneficent human inventions, even though it operates in a different way economically. Bernard Weissbourd has explained it graphically:

A dollar I am to receive 20 years from now is worth only six cents today if I can earn 15 percent on my money. . .(T)he question of future revenues from long-term transactions is crucial. . .(A) private developer, borrowing money at a rate of 8 to 10 percent, is not unrealistic in expecting a 15 percent return on his money. . .(D)uring this period of time, the difference between what a million dollars would earn at 6 percent and at 15 percent is in excess of $5.7 million.(36)

In a situation such as described, the "take the money and run" attitude acquires a much marked-down value. Planning becomes essential. The role of the government is determinative insofar as governmental actions affect the extension of cost of credit, taxes, deductions, subsidies, and requirements for expenditures.

Current support for the public interest is a need that surpasses in intensity anything experienced in the past. This is true in the United States, despite the popularity of initiatives for lowering real property taxes and cutting the rate of increase in public expenditures. A drive now exists to integrate land and development so that distant benefits can be discounted forward into an immediate advantage.

This sort of pressure is producing the drive for "open planning" of such a major land use as the location of electricity-generating stations. No longer are these to be concerns only of the electric utility, the vendor of the land, and some state regulatory agency. The time is passing for the "sweetheart negotiations" conducted in private and sprung on an unsuspecting public after the event without an opportunity for an opposing reaction. People who do not own land, but who are consumers of power and users of the land environment, are insisting that the planning process be opened from the beginning. If it is not, they are prepared to stop everything.

The open planning process adopted by the Northern States Power Company in Minnesota is exemplary of this changed attitude. As a logical first step, the company's planners catalogue all the factors contributing to an environmental impact. Not only do they catalogue the impacting developmental force, but they fully explore the situation this force impacts on. Only after this catalogue has been made can there be a meaningful investigation into alternative site locations for the proposed project.

The company is aware that this weighing of alternatives is destined to be rough at best. As they put it:

> . . .our complex and dynamic universe does not easily conform to an objective measure of interactions by a simple number.(37)

The resolution of conflicts can never be completely satisfactory. The weightings from one site to another cannot be varied, since this would make meaningless the values concerning the total impact. In addition, it is simpler to calculate the relative adverse environmental impact, including all positive benefits and social implications.

Yet opening up the planning process is worth doing, even though resolutions are hard to come by and even though they prove incapable of achieving universal acceptance. The Northern States Power Company's reasons for engaging in an open planning process are not altruistic. Rather they are self-serving and designed for a long-term operation. Their position is that:

> . . .a rational combination of the individual impacts with numbers representing radically different types of information (serves). . . : 1) to readjust for alterations arising from use of the maximum impact site concept, and 2) to answer more philo-sophical questions such as 'why is it we consider the HUMAN impacts to be twice as important as the NATURE impacts?'(38)

When a major electric utility planning the use of open space can ask such a question while pursuing self-interest, a change is occurring in the way human demands impact upon the natural environment.(39)

Of course not many industrial managers have understood this change. The mining industry, as one example, is having great difficulty in accepting public control for purposes of environmental protection. Their representatives are still talking about keeping mining "free" from "unnecessary restrictions" and making claims that "legislators must avoid the temptation to use land tenure laws to accomplish 'other' policy goals."(40)

Laments over a public presence in private land use decisions are, at best, only a delaying tactic. For environmentalists, these delays in fighting the public presence are a waste of time and money. It is a waste, even though in our presently fragmented system those delays doubtless profit some private individual interest. But the strengthening of public presence everywhere is precisely the direction social change is taking. To point to environmental requirements as threatening "the most basic requirement of mineral ownership," namely the "security of tenure," is to miss a very important fact: this is precisely what the mass of non-owners of the mineral interest are seeking. If there is no other leverage for an assertion of the public interest, then the public definitely will threaten the security of those now having tenure.

This is particularly true in the United States, where many mineral interests are exercised under claims entered on the public domain. The holders of those interests see a horrendous destructive process at work if anyone proposes to make their tenure on public lands subject to additional requirements. They do not want to be told that their holdings under the mining claims and mineral leasing laws should be conditioned upon compliance with environmental regulations. And assuredly they become highly agitated when it is suggested that their tenure on private land might be affected by environmental requirements.

The holders of mining interests view the value of the land exclusively in terms of mineral extraction. Any other values to the general public or the environment are regarded as arrant impositions of public requirements. Only an eventual economic threat to the well-being of the mineral extraction industry is regarded as significant.(41)

But the increasingly important social view is that the land has many significant values. Among these values is the ecologic. This is at least as important to large segments of the public as any economic demand for an exploitable resource. As Peter Flawn has observed, the public's future interest is likely to be in "the effects of environmental concerns – including legislative and public policy decisions – on the mineral industry."(42)

The reasons back of this claim by a prominent geologist lie in assertions of authority by those not directly owning land or the resources being taken from the land. These non-owners claim that value is conferred by the activities they pursue and that they are indirectly affected by what the owners do with the land. For both of these reasons, these social groups believe themselves fully justified in laying down the terms under which private land is to be used.

Any group which pressures the legislature to favor a single-use approach to land exploitation will find success costly in the long run. Soon the public will no longer tolerate a concentration upon single-use exploitation of the land resource, with its fragmenting and segregating effect on both the natural environment and social structure.(43) Given the accelerating energy supply pressures to use land for synthetic and biologic fuels, the drive in the direction of multiple uses of land will continue.

THE INCENTIVES FOR MULTIPLE SIMULTANEOUS USES
FOR THE LAND ENVIRONMENT

In bookkeeping, it is always easier to concentrate on the single use. Costs and benefits seem so much easier to calculate. It is not true, of course, because a single exploitation normally includes only the benefits to the exploiters and a mere handful of the costs involved in the operation.

Land use actions under conditions of high-energy growth require longer time frames for accomplishment. Consequently, more and more previously unincluded costs have to be internalized in the processes of human demand. The generators of economic activity are now starting to think in terms of internalizing these costs and of covering them by multiple, simultaneous uses of the land. When this is done, the single-activity exploitation will cease to appear the easiest or most effective method of bookkeeping.

The maintenance of the high-energy, urban-industrial demand structure itself has been taken for granted. This attitude must change under the impact of sharply rising energy costs, the presence of an increasingly fragile environment, and the effects of accelerating inflation accompanied by problems in the rate of production. These factors, which economic activity must accommodate, cannot tolerate an absorption of costs under conditions of underuse, misuse, or abuse of land, open space, and the dependent natural systems – as in the urban United States.(44)

It is tragic that the process of urban growth has been allowed to become urban sprawl and thereby to become an abuser and under-user of the land resource. All too frequently the open space has been lost in order to provide an ugly urban form unsuitable for long-term urban use.

> The tragedy. . .is that our cities are so unlivable, so unnatural, so unaesthetic. If we preserve the wildness of Vermont, that surely is no reason to destroy the humanity of our cities; both are essential parts of the balance.(45)

But balance is what the fragmented, segregating growth of urban sprawl cannot appreciate. The result has been an urban sprawl that represents a handicapped milieu for living.

Panayiotis Psomopoulos, a Greek city planner, has described the modern city dweller as one who:

> more readily 'fashions his environment to accommodate the limitations of a machine' than of a human being. 'Think of the car, which we can call a disabled machine because, although built for movement, it cannot go up and down stairs. . .However, the whole city is now conditioned by this disabled machine, as city streets are by definition nothing but ramps (almost exclusively meant to serve this disabled machine).'(46)

The social preference remains for making sacrifices to serve the demands of the automobile in city design. This is done rather than compelling such a force for energy transfer to accommodate urban growth comprehensively to the needs of nature as it responds to the extension of urban forms over open space.

Economic activity in urban-industrial society demands land in large quantities for many purposes. Many will continue to resist this demand. The individuated entity, seeking a profit from a particular land use, will rarely volunteer to internalize the costs for what it considers unwanted restoration. The mining industry has been traditionally an example of such an attitude. The greater return to nature and the general social structure from the land restoration seems of small importance to managers concentrating on the bottom line of the mining company's accounts on profit versus loss.

And yet, despite ardent resistence, a drive is mounting for multiple uses of land and toward both energy conservation and comprehensive environmental planning. The contrast is strong compared to the established way the resources of the land environment have been used in the past two centuries.

INTEGRATED LAND USE AS THE BASIS OF COMPREHENSIVE ENVIRONMENTAL PLANNING

The market, after all, knows the values of open space as evidenced by how it engrosses these values for individuated consumption units. The market has never treated the multiple values of light and air, vistas, and open space as anything other than values to be appropriated by individuals at no personal expense. The fact the market treated them as "free" goods supplied by nature does not mean that the market denied these environmental qualities market value. The market simply did not want to undertake any of the costs for their continued availability.

If government laid down the rules under which the engrossment of light, air, vistas and open space was to take place, and related these rules to the natural environment, such governmental action would occur at a crucial place in the market's operations. Far more than land would be affected. Unfortunately, government has not chosen to act to achieve a unified control of the land environment under the impact of growth demand. When government has seemed to act in that way, a close examination most often has shown it was for quite different purposes.

This is not to claim that every local decision against further urban growth constitutes an economic mask concealing unconfessible motives. Decisions against urban-industrial development have been too rare to write them off so cavalierly.(47) But decisions against urban growth, like the ones for it, ought to be taken as part of an interrelated use of the land environment. To do it on some ad hoc local basis may itself produce crisis.

Undifferentiated imposition of urban form upon open space has now reached the point where even the slow-down in the urban growth rate in the United States in the early 1970s could not stop land consumption in areas peripheral to metropoli or in regions remote from urban centers demanded by the recreation industry.(48) What is needed is large-scale, long-term, unified planning. The variety of functions possessed by land must be recognized.

Those who think selecting ultimate planning goals is an easy, uncontroversial task are confused. Either they do not think planning leads to action or they do not see how long-term goals have an immediate effect. Such past attitudes have put land use planning into ill-repute – an ill-repute in itself quite justified.

Staged land development is not a new idea. Phased development of new land projects has long existed. But now the employment of phasing action must be a vital part of every comprehensive environmental plan. The what and the how of the plan's processes must be spelled out. Otherwise planners are deceiving themselves, which is perhaps more significant than any lies told to the public. If no schedule is developed for change, then the plan itself is a synopsis of undifferentiated action. If the goals are so remote that action can be postponed on the beginning of their realization, then these are not planning goals at all. They are platitudes to soothe the agitated.(49)

Land use planning is basic to planning for energy, the total renewing environment, and the social crises of urban growth. Yet important as land use control is, it reflects only the basic social decisions as to how energy and the renewing environment are to be employed in a high-demand society. Truly, it was a social decision that concluded the problems of the city could be solved by simply "leaving" the city. As a social decision, it furthered the fragmentation of the energy budget and determined the creation of urban sprawl.

When the multiple uses of land and the value of open space are treated with contempt by suburban and exurban land developers, there can scarcely not be a crisis in energy, in the environment, and in the urban condition. Low density sprawl makes mass transit nearly an impossibility and wide-spread massive energy distribution a necessity. Given just these facts alone, neither energy nor environmental crises could have been avoided.(50)

In a fragmented growth-dominated demand structure, too much crisis-coping results in the institutionalization of every crisis, in lieu of solutions. Administrators too often have become personally committed to crisis preservation, but there is a limit in any system to the number of problems that can be institutionalized and turned into justifications for additional bureaucratic employment. The brittle quality of the conditions necessary for high-energy growth make such growth quite vulnerable to an accumulation of unresolved and institutionalized problems. Land use planning can be fruitful only when problems have not been permitted to accumulate to the point of systemic collapse. At that point, preserving anything is touch-and-go.

Urban forms are imposing on even the remotest regions in greater or lesser use levels. But the totality of the demand makes even the lesser uses too burdensome when taken in gross. The weight of these fragmented urban forms compels either the sacrifice to sprawl of the entire land environment, or else the decision to save the greater part through an acceptance of what such undifferentiated urban sprawl means. This game of blind-man's buff is dangerous nonsense.

8 Changing Environmental Views Under High Energy Growth

THE INTERSECTION OF ENERGY DEMAND AND THE RENEWING ENVIRONMENT

From the inception of high-energy conversion, the renewing environment has been seen either as a source for the supply of energy and materials or else as a sink for the wastes produced. The poet Goethe, at the very beginning of these massive demands on nature, was much troubled by the prospects. These actions represented to him an abandonment of nature as a series of visible phenomena. He could no longer find in humanity a concern for the relation between what these phenomena were inherently and what they humanly appeared to be.

Instead, the urban-industrial demand structure constituted an overflow of technical science that Goethe believed could only result in the destruction of nature. Human concern had been transferred exclusively to artificial effects quite alien to the operation of natural systems. For his pains, Goethe was simply regarded as pursuing old-fashioned, pre-Galileoan scientific concepts.

Yet as the twentieth century physicist Werner Heisenberg has said:

> In our time, when we know of the contamination of air and water, the poisoning of the soil by chemical fertilizers, and atomic weapons, we can understand Goethe's fear better than his contemporaries could. But Goethe's attempt did not really influence the course of science.(1)

Certainly the attitude of Goethe has had little influence. An economy increasingly dependent upon high-energy growth will respond to demand in disregard of nature's ability at handling wastes from burgeoning production and consumption. The atmosphere has been treated as a receptacle able to receive any quantity of aerial emissions. The deeps as well as the estuaries of the ocean have been treated in the same brutal and callous fashion.(2)

The centers of advanced urban-industrial growth produce conditions far worse than any figures based upon averages will indicate. The more investigators learn, the worse they discover the situation is. And when they look only at the centers of urban-industrial growth, the worse they perceive the situation is likely to become.(3)

Consequently, merely extrapolating a linear extension of averages into the future is misleading. However serious future conditions would appear, they still would be falsely optimistic. First of all, any prediction must include the consequence of each year's increase. Doing this shows that human demand upon a finite capacity grows faster than would a straightline projection.

But an action probably even more important needs to be pursued. The function of any predictor is best focused upon the centers that most perfectly reflect the present impact of events in the urban-industrial demand structure. In these centers those making predictions most likely will find the best evidence for what is both occurring and likely to occur. The risk exists, of course, if the concentration becomes tunnel-visioned. Important incidents for future predictions will be occurring elsewhere. But the centers for open-ended growth demands still deserve first attention in studies predictive of the future.(4)

A pleonectic demand has been imposed on nature to serve as a receiving body. Whether one is talking about water, air, soil, or the biomass, the by-product of waste under high-energy growth conditions demands the use of each as a sink. Against the finitude of nature only the growth in human demand remains the constant condition. On that subject, honest reportage must be grim. And to be honest, the reportage must center upon the points of urban-industrial growth rather than averages.

Air, soil, water, and the biomass are a single unity within a fairly tightly confined planet. Drawing its energy from the sun, this planet cannot be a closed system. Yet, insofar as the living environment is concerned, the interconnecting of relationships produces the effect of a closed system. In nature's dealing with humanly generated wastes, this result has been inevitable. Wherever one looks in this regard, the future for nature seems dolorous.(5)

The future cannot be different if profits continue to be segregated from costs and seemingly individuated to the profit takers. The costs under such a practice will then be shoved off on nature or the general fund. In the absence of an integrated approach to the burden of high-energy growth on natural systems, this will occur both routinely and in periods of crisis.(6) The focus upon energy throughout the 1970s resulted from problems of supply and price. Such attention treated energy as if it were unrelated to the renewing environment.

This was contrary to predictions of the United States Office of Coal Research in 1972. This prediction claimed that concern for the environment would be of the same kind that existed for energy.(7) When the two intersect, it asserted, the environment should receive for the first time a real chance of enough human attention to make an impact noticeable to nature. This sounds coolly rational. But one need not be a cynic to realize such an easy transfer of attention did not occur.

Throughout the 1970s, despite the repeated energy crises precip-itated by rising petroleum prices, little helpful attention to the intersection of energy conservation and environmental protection re-sulted. Nature continued to be used as a sink for waste from the transformation of energy. And in 1979, the United States government, responding to additional energy supply problems, permitted the burning of high sulfur coal and oil without uniformly requiring sulfur removal; the continual use of air-polluting additives in mobile fuel for better mileage; and other actions indifferent to the renewing environment. With permissions so highly responsive to continuing high-energy de-mands, where can a basis for optimism about the environment be found?(8)

PERSISTENT ENVIRONMENTAL ATTITUDES DESPITE HIGH ENERGY GROWTH

Understandably, when something is regarded as purely a burden upon the processes of production and consumption, the tendency is to continue the old habits. The recourse is rarely to look for possible opportunities in change if it is regarded as an unmitigated legal interference. Obdurate hostility to change is probably inevitable even though places exist where normal readings of soot, metal and carbon dust per cubic meter of air generally run three times the recommended level and where emergency readings, requiring the shutdown of indus-try, run more than fifteen times the recommended level.(9)

As long as there is venting of wastes and as long as loads go up the stacks without adequate control devices upon either the production or the smoke, then so long will there be a condition to which the law must respond with a treatment tuned to an emergency situation. Wiping out the legal and administrative regulations dealing with air pollution would merely shove the heads of the human ostriches back into the sand. What is needed is to bring such conditions to an end.

When nature is finite and the products of the human imagination that impinge upon nature are infinite, the course of history for natural systems can be sharply telescoped. In the event this telescoping proves still more urgent, then all other problems become bagatelles for the aesthete. But reform is made harder because no one can be certain what effect undifferentiated, open-ended human demand has upon the living environment as a waste sink.(10)

People fret about the costs of environmentally protective controls. But all the indications show that the present controls in the United States on sulfur oxides and particulate emissions have benefits ex-ceeding their costs. In benefit-cost consideration, a systematic ten-dency often overestimates the costs and underestimates the benefits. Perhaps in the last analysis, much of the purpose for enforcing stationary emission standards is to enhance the public health and postpone death.(11) Sadly there are not many ledgers where such social benefits appear compared to those account books in which the private outlays of the costs to procure the benefits bulk so large. Many prefer, therefore, to defer or resist action until some far future date.

So much talk has been concentrated upon the year 2000 that one would think it was a cutoff date. If one can reach 2000 reasonably intact, then one is safe: refuge has been reached. But 2000 is really a non-date. There is no evidence accumulating that conditions will suddenly be better then. Indeed, all evidence points to the opposite. Humanity will be well into the twenty-first century before many of the problems will be solved which the thoughtful today fear could be terminal of earth life systems. But at the very least, the current perception of nature has struck an alarm bell.

Some may challenge Jacques Cousteau's claim that the oceans face dire threat. Nevertheless, since 1950 somewhere between thirty and fifty percent of ocean life has been damaged by the activity of high-energy culture. If the rate established in that interval continues, Cousteau is convinced that the oceans shall cease to function as living organisms no later than 2025. Should Cousteau be even approximately right, such major reductions in living organisms occurring within the world's oceans would have consequences for the human economy alone that would be serious enough to warrant prompt preventive actions.(12)

People are continuously dividing up pollution-control as if polluting air, water, or soil were independent actions. Rarely is pollution of the biomass (apart from soil) mentioned, although it is at least equally important. But in any event, too much discussion treats the categories of air, water or soil as unrelated problems. But the planet is a single entity. Pollution of any kind is really of a oneness. The whole ecumene is being polluted by human activities and the demand structure of high-energy culture.

Presently, urban-industrial demand has reached such a point within only fourteen countries that they provide eighty-five percent of the world's pollution.(13) But the high-energy effect goes far beyond the boundaries of these fourteen countries. The rest of the nations of the globe are valiantly struggling to increase their own individual per-centages of this total; and in the gross amount of pollution impacting upon the systems of nature, they are succeeding.

For example, the Rhone and the Po rivers are known as the "lungs of the Mediterranean." These rivers, along with the undercurrents flowing through the Straits of Gibraltar, have been the main sources of regenerating oxygen for the whole sea. Today, the Rhone and the Po are sewers of debris and waste.

These two great rivers currently contain relatively little oxygen. The damage to the Mediterranean is intensified by the change in the discharge of the Nile produced by the enlarged Aswan Dam. The Rhone and Po, far from revitalizing a sea which takes eighty years to turn over its water content, now add to the ecological burden of the Mediterranean. Lord Ritchie-Calder has described that sea as in precarious ecological balance historically. Changes in the condition of the rivers debouching into this sea only imperil that balance.

The most polluted part is the Venice-Trieste area of the Adriatic. As Jose Stirn of the University of Zagreb has pointed out, this area cannot realistically be isolated. The whole Mediterranean basin is a single entity, even though more than fifteen nations share the shoreline. The ecological forces therein know nothing of national boundaries or of bays of the same water body which historical geography has mistakenly listed as separate seas.(14)

Similar facts apply to the Caribbean Ocean. Many tourists have viewed the West Indies as some halcyon refuge from urban-industrial demands. This is only because they have refused to see what was plainly all about them for seeing. If the West Indies had not been closely tied to high-energy conditions, these tourists would not have been there in such numbers. The inhabitants of those islands have had an experience of urban-industrial society that makes them want more of what they regard as its many benefits.

The West Indies have known only generations of comparative poverty in a relatively low-energy situation built upon the supply of raw materials to the world markets of high-energy growth. They now believe that transferring more of the production function directly to the islands will be to their financial gain. As a result, an American visitor can look at the Caribbean factories and exclaim, "My God, it looks just like Jersey."

But the natives think what they smell is the odor of affluence. Like other participants in urban-industrial economies, they want to use the atmosphere and the Caribbean as sinks for their industrial wastes and engross the profits and benefits to themselves alone. They associate a clean environment with the social "degradation" of tourism. The social characteristics of their decisions, therefore, become almost painfully clear.(15)

Few of those who have profited from using the environment as a waste-receiving body would voluntarily forego any part of those profits in order to internalize the costs of waste disposal within their operations. Regulation works best when prospects exist for an "internal subsidization," in which one part of the operation can be used to absorb the costs of another part.(16) But most often internalization occurs only if externally mandated. Merely because cost internalization is possible does not mean any production unit would voluntarily opt for it. As a Puerto Rican court ruled in 1972 in rejecting a conservationist lawsuit:

> There are materialistic considerations that upset the spirit, of course, but the right of fishermen must yield to the necessities of Puerto Rico's industrial development. The balance of convenience tilts in favor of the petro-chemicals.(17)

From the standpoint of most high-energy nations – or those aspiring to be – the statement of the Puerto Rican court is acceptable. From any "materialistic consideration" of the sort taken so seriously by the court, sacrificing the environment of the whole Caribbean island chain might well be justified. Of course, that type of justification leaves human populations and natural systems alike at the mercy of events. The islands and the sea in the Caribbean form a natural unity that will be broken only at great peril.

But such unity and such peril loom very small in the eyes of many local leaders. They persist in believing natural catastrophes cannot result. As they see it, "the balance of convenience tilts in favor of the petro-chemicals." One should not be surprised. It is the dominant attitude in far more heavily urbanized and industrialized high-energy situations than that prevailing as yet in the Caribbean.

Consistently, a refusal to perceive any inherent worth in nature has prevailed where cash flows and capital accumulations have been at stake. Any interrelatedness in nature tends to be denied at this point. If air, water, soil, or the biomass can be used as sinks for the waste of urban-industrial activity, they will be so used. Only when the crisis conditions reach such proportions that such isolation of benefit from cost becomes impossible will steps be taken to act in relation to those costs. Otherwise, obsolete environmental attitudes will persist. Even if the crisis stage is reached and decision-makers want to change course, neither sufficient time nor capital may be available to reorganize natural systems threatened with permanent interdiction.

HOW ENVIRONMENTAL ATTITUDES ARE INDIRECTLY CHANGED BY ACCUMULATING ENVIRONMENTAL KNOWLEDGE

Anyone concerned with the use of air, water, soil, the biomass, and natural ecosystems as waste sinks must focus on both monitoring and the accuracy of the monitors. The true state of affairs within nature's systems, rather than what human demand and aspiration would like it to be, must be the goal. The reaction of Jacques Cousteau to the constantly repeated assertions of some pundits that the ocean can provide reserves of food that are "unlimited, endless, of infinite fecundity" illustrates the need to insist upon environmental truth and nothing less, however tempting the preference for fantasy.

Evidence indicates that the ocean's potential productivity is based solely on a limited and fragile upper zone which is sensitive to alteration. Very slow changes might be accommodated, but rapid alteration seems beyond the capacity of what is, in comparison to the whole ocean, a small world. To be careless about harvesting in that fragile zone or about using it as a waste sink is among the worst human crimes.

The reason the ocean is saline is that it is the universal sink for nature as well as for humanity. But this means that all toxic wastes dumped inland ultimately must wend their way to the ocean. The exceptions are very small relative to the quantity that eventually reach the ocean. Primordially the ocean was a vast fresh-water body, which became salty through run-off from the land. This same run-off is now introducing all the wastes so generously produced by high-energy culture. Even what is dumped upon the ground within the continental interiors will in large measure eventually reach the ocean, including the chemicals that concentrate along the biological food chain.

Wastes must be stopped from entering the drainage process. Ultimately dumped waste has to concentrate within the ocean. The removal of toxic material at the source and its special disposal, preferably by as much recycling as would be physically possible, is needed.

Jacques Cousteau thinks this might account for as much as a five percent increase in the price of commodities in order to set up the means for excluding humanly originated toxicity from marine ecosystems. He claims:

> We must plant the seas and herd its animals. . . .That is what civilization is all about – banning hunting. Fishing as we do it is hunting and in the sea we act as barbarians.(18)

On a narrower scale, the same observations have been made about the major lakes and rivers. Wastes threaten these waters both as sources of food and as places where balanced native ecosystems can flourish. They too are sinks for wastes and are under stress.

The more severe the condition of a waterbody the less the market will do to salvage it. Degradation becomes acceptable. The research of Peter Davis on the Wisconsin River has shown, once pollution becomes severe enough, the chance of lawsuits over the pollution nearly disappears. Pollution becomes the "natural" condition of the river that all riparians expect eventually to exist. So many of the riverside landowners become emitters of pollution, or acquire close financial connections with emitters, that there is no incentive to shift the balance of equities from the polluters. The river is left to stabilize as best it can under the imposition of wastes, while the landowners see no reason to reduce voluntarily their discharge of effluents into the stream.(19)

Just to list environmental stresses summarizes the gross demands imposed by high-energy growth upon a receiving water body. These are:

> . . .the commercial fishery as a predatory process. . .; cultural eutrophication; the introduction of, or invasion of, nonindigenous aquatic species; tributary and shoreline restructuring. . .; turbidity and siltation caused by the continuing inflow of fine inert materials; the release of toxic materials from industrial sources, vessels, and vehicles; and the unintended introduction of biocides. No natural stress that has waxed and waned during the past 200 years has had a more profound, long-term, direct effect than any one of the above cultural stresses.(20)

This underscores the importance of accumulating knowledge in order to change attitudes concerning how the renewing environment has been impacted upon. Certainly the costs of fully monitoring conditions of severe pollution must be high. Techniques of improvement will have to be tailored to the natural systems peculiar to the receiving water, since no single method of improvement exists for all water bodies.

The economist Marc Roberts has concerned himself for many years with the techniques of accomplishing these ends and of paying for them. He eschews any ecologic standard of absolute restoration of previous conditions and aims at accomplishing a social value in the restored waterbody that would be equal to the costs of that restoration. This may be an overly modest goal, but it would be more of a start in the right direction than much of what is now being done. He explains the way change would operate in cleaning up receiving waterbodies:

> Theoretically it would be desirable to abate pollution to that point where the social value of additional cleanup is equal to the cost of that cleanup. However, it is difficult to anticipate either the costs of a given pollution program or society's desire for clean water. Since these factors are unknowns, the best solution to the question 'how much abatement?' can be reached by use of an iterative process. We do some cleanup, examine the costs and benefits, and decide whether we have done too much, not enough, the wrong kind, or whatever.(21)

To succeed, an iterative process needs a preceding decision defining the ultimate goal of the process. Otherwise the successive stages will simply be lost in just another open-ended series of incremental changes. Such unintegrated changes would only contribute to undifferentiated growth in an economy which thinks it battens on such a demand structure. The accumulation of knowledge is vital for changing such attitudes.

Both the accumulation of data and iterative action in relation thereto will require more than pious hope from the lawmakers. Exhortations have been issued for too long for all sorts of voluntary actions designed to improve matters. Voluntary actions have not occurred on a significant scale. Americans, particularly, have had a great deal of experience with the inefficiency of voluntary actions. Studies conducted on the history of voluntary compliance programs for improving water quality in the United States have shown, with practically no exception, that they accomplish no change whatsoever.(22)

The exact opposite proves to be the case when one turns away from voluntary compliance programs to mandated actions protecting the renewing environment. Studies show that a relatively high correlation exists between the severity of the legal system's demands for change and actual change in the quality of water. A willingness to mandate action and to put the pressure of money behind the enforcement techniques will statistically produce the greatest change for water quality in comparison with any other course of action.(23) In reviewing studies such as these, one can only conclude that Americans have been content in proving, over and over again, facts that ought to have been painfully obvious.

Increasingly, the condition of the world's waterbodies illuminates the inconsistency and the inappropriateness of the demands being put upon them, both as sources of extractive industries and as sinks for waste. Given the experience the urban-industrial world has had with its lakes, it should be a truism to say:

> Large amounts of toxic industrial wastes and plant nutrients from domestic sources cannot be accommodated in the future.(24)

At the present time, however, under the demand for high-energy growth throughout the world, nothing is trite about this statement. But the accumulating evidence of monitored conditions in the renewing environment is compelling a change in attitudes. Unfortunately, the change is slow compared to the swiftness of what is impacting upon the renewing environment.

OPHELIMITY AND THE WASTE LIMITS TO ENERGY DEMAND

It is true, of course, that there is "natural pollution."(25) Yet the better course is not to call this process pollution. It is better to focus upon the balance within ecosystems and the links in the life support chains than to talk about the "purity" of air and water. What some call "natural pollution" is of the same character as the imposition of urban-industrial wastes only when some catastrophic change has occurred to nature's systems and their existing balances.

Water and air are not the final sinks for waste. Rather, the biota of the planet, through whose functioning water and air are drawn, become the last sink. In consequence, they act as a means to concentrate the humanly generated wastes in the food chain, even in the eternal life-and-death recycling of living organisms.

This concentration threatens the life support upon which living organisms depend. In the final analysis, since humanity have made themselves the final stage in the food chain, they can expect to suffer more than any other cognizant organism. Humanity will be the final sinks for their own wastes. Renewing natural systems can no longer simultaneously cope with the waste burden and maintain a viable balance for themselves. Monitoring and data accumulation are needed to show the precise extent to which nature cannot accommodate these humanly imposed demands.

Very few would deny the value of measurement and the acquisition of comparative data; and those few are among the true pessimists. One of these, Roberto Vacca, asserts that it is already too late for the monitoring of natural events or the accumulation of data to be effectual. The struggle is already lost, and no chance remains to establish an equilibrating balance between the needs of natural systems and the demands of high-energy culture.(26)

If these pessimists are wrong, however, monitoring will have useful functions. The utility of monitors transcends providing an evidentiary back-up for prosecution. Uses of greater importance than courtroom service are the determination of background levels, the calculation of the impact upon natural systems of urban-industrial activity, and the establishment of the factual bases for the construction of models to serve as extrapolators in planning. At the same time, though, these efforts will help meet current needs for surveillance and enforcement and the assistance of law officers intent on making the present antipollution laws effective.(27)

Such extensions should enable officials, such as air pollution control officers, to provide useful services to a wide range of transportation, land-use, and general planning operations.(28) When monitoring can produce such fairly unanticipated results as showing that the total organic matter in storm water exceeded that in the same amount of raw sanitary sewage, one cannot dismiss the value of data accumulation.(29)

This does not deny the inevitability of multiple sources for error in monitoring and in model building based upon data accumulated. Calculating effective point source models includes uncertainties, and they can be gross enough to produce expectable errors in the model results of from twenty to one hundred percent. Before the potential for improvement is reached in the techniques of monitoring and model building, this wide a range of error should not be shocking. Many model calculations have had to rest on even larger margins for error.(30)

Formulating the background estimations in the cleaner air sheds generally must be done in a manner that allows great possibility for error two or more times the probability of correctness in the calculations. When working on so fluid a measure in a heavily populated air shed with a poor ambience, one simply has to accept as bearable the way such calculations work. Their potential inaccuracies must be borne in mind. Efforts must continue to remove those imperfections; but existing techniques must be used.

Error-less monitoring and model building will not evolve spontaneously. They must be attained by working through many stages which may encompass great, though unintentional, error. The slowness with which error can be eliminated is the direct result of the fragmentation and segregation of both energy and environmental usages.

Pending a different social decision, monitoring and model building are the only chances under the present system to do anything constructive about developing techniques capable of increasing the environment's ability to resist impositions of high-energy demands. A continuous accumulation of data occurs which otherwise would take too long to learn from the purely empiric experiences of urban experimentation. Even in the presence of gross error, this data justifies increasing reliance upon the techniques of monitoring and model building based upon the accumulations of the monitoring.

Although monitoring presently aids in keeping better records, it should do more. Those who program monitoring efforts must remember the destructive way urban-industrial society draws upon the quality of the air and water, and the ability of the land and sea to provide raw materials. Only the service of rising human expectations has been sought rather than any inquiry into how much nature can stand. Human expectations and satisfaction still press on with their accelerating, intensifying, open-ended burdens upon those renewing systems.

Given urban-industrial history, planners should not rely on a possible ophelimity limit, if they are concerned with either maintaining high levels of energy demand or establishing a balance with that demand able to support viable renewing natural systems. "Ophelimity limit" is the limit which humanity would reach when all their economic satis-factions had been met. Although psychologically and culturally relevant to any planner, ophelimity cannot provide the goal.

In its modern use, the etymology of ophelimity is ironic. It is related to the Sanskrit work, acharya, which means one who thoroughly knows the customary rules. One might well say that humanity, in their self-centered definition of ophelimity, have shown no mastery of any rules except some very narrow ones which have been egocentrically pre-determined to represent conditions of economic excellence. To any rules in nature, people have shown supreme indifference. Their own satisfactions and their own expectations have been permitted an absolute sway instead.

The irony in ophelimity is, therefore, a double irony. It stems from a word that describes human mastery over rules, even while human beings ignore how natural systems operate under the high-energy demands. The second irony has been perhaps even more profound: humanity seems never to reach a condition of ophelimity in the sense of fulfilling their economic satisfactions. Human imagination will always put expecta-tions beyond an ability to satisfy them. Goals keep fading in the distances of the human imagination.

Those interested in the survival of the urban-industrial demand structure, consequently, must forget ophelimity as a goal. High-energy demand itself – the transfer of energy from nature into human purpose and then back to nature – represents the culture's limitation. Oph-elimity is only a spurring force, and can be neither a goal nor a restraint.

Humanity has become a sort of extrabiosphere reservoir from which nutrients have been poured out for the stimulation of growth and the disequilibrium of nature.(31) Here human beings ought to learn how to become masters of the rules and find their ophelimity. The rules governing human relations to air, water, land and the living and renewing environment control the ties between life and energy.

Too often, instead, mechanistic terms have been relied upon that see energy as a mechanical model rather than a force sustaining the renewing and living structures within nature.(32) The thought that connects biology and energy is an alien one to too many who have great responsibility for the maintenance of high-energy culture. Their isola-tion from this thought is far more fateful than the division the novelist Lord Snow has decried between the literary and scientific cultures. The division Lord Snow has denounced, if it exists, is a cultural in-convenience. The division between those who see nature as a machine and those who see it as a living organism can be fatal for the future of both high-energy culture and nature.(33)

PRICE AS AN INSUFFICIENT REFLECTION OF ENVIRONMENTAL WORTH

Popular writers on economic subjects in high growth market conditions never tire of telling the world how price determines the way resources are shifted in the general market and how those shifts benefit every-one.(34) What they overlook in their zeal is that this price is only a thin reflection of the enormous worth of resources within the living and renewing environment. Indeed, one might better regard this worth in nature as being the object of the most concentrated attention. The whole grand superstructure of the growing high-energy cascades is based in nature.

Income taken directly from nature is relatively small compared to the totality of the gross product under high-energy conditions. The total value in the price system each year of agricultural commodities, forest products, and extracted minerals, has for long been added up to a figure that looked small beside the grand total of the gross product. Such disproportion cannot deny that natural products magnify enormously through the operation of the price system. The dramatic advance in the prices of oil and natural gas since the mid-1970s has illustrated the importance of these natural resources under high-energy demand. The value of these minerals has been magnified throughout the energy demand structure as a consequence of energy supply dominating energy price.(35)

The price structure, furthermore, may disguise the vital character of resources in nature. This occurs in many of the pricing mechanisms set for raw materials, or the valuelessness price assigns to so much of nature as a waste sink. A political cartel such as OPEC can assign prices in disregard of production costs or the impact of their action on either the world economy or the environment. Petroleum still remains substantially price resistant in a high demand energy situation and takes on a social appearance of an importance greater than the renewing environment.

In July 1979, an American governor reputedly said to the president of the United States that, in order to supply energy at acceptable prices, Americans have "the need to suffer 25 years of dirty air."(36) For people with this attitude, price and availability are paramount, while the renewing systems within nature can be ignored, temporarily or forever.

But this is human ignorance and not an operative fact inherent to nature. Unfortunately, the manner in which the pricing structure works upon raw materials taken directly from nature has a way of compounding the ignorance of people like the American governor. As an attitude, it relates to all raw materials extracted from nature. This activity provides such small figures in the total cash equivalent that urban-industrial society tends to forget the basic character of their sources in nature.

Someone concerned only with pricing might look at the gross national product of the United States in the 1970s and conclude that agricultural production was of no great significance. Throughout the 1970s the gross national product of the United States exceeded one trillion dollars by increasing amounts every year. Of that gross national product, the agricultural income shrank from a 7.5% share of national income in 1950 to a 3.6% share in 1975.(37) During this time, agricultural subsidies paid by the federal government provided a substantial, if minor, portion of this amount. How could any serious person, who looked only at how the price structure shifts resources through the market, consider the agricultural sector of the United States' economy as something of consequence?

In truth, such a market-oriented person would find that the economic condition of the agricultural sector is far weaker in comparison with other sectors of the urban-industrial economy of the United States than even the agricultural income figures would indicate. Of course, some agriculture economists rate the strength of American agriculture in terms of its having a capitalization of over $400 billion. For them, this means it is the largest industry within the country.(38) But this is a spurious comparative strength.

The agricultural economist Marshall Harris has observed that the United States' agricultural sector must live within an economy whose conditions are dictated by other sectors whose operating conditions are totally different. United States agriculture in the early 1970s, for an historic example, had yearly costs of about $2 billion or, in other terms, a $50 billion debt spread over twenty-five years. Again to the price-oriented, of course, this must seem small compared to national statistics on gross debt. But it is here that the vulnerability of those who draw directly from the living environment is exposed under conditions of high-energy demand.

The relationship between oil and agricultural produce makes the American farmer more sensitive to OPEC actions than most other American business interests. In 1970, the price of a bushel of American wheat at the Gulf of Mexico export docks was roughly comparable to the price of a barrel of Saudi Arabian crude oil. Because of this, American agriculture after World War II became heavily and increasingly dependent on investments of oil and natural gas. Petroleum makes biocides and diesel for farm machinery. Natural gas runs pumps, dries grain, and is converted to fertilizer. The successes of American agriculture, in large measure, have been the result of cheap and abundant energy supplies.

But OPEC's actions in the 1970s have placed American agriculture at peril. In that decade, the price of American wheat scarcely tripled. Even this rise was insecure since it could decline. But the price of oil in the decade – counting all price rises beginning in 1970 – had gone up ninefold, with little prospect of ever dropping again. It is no wonder that many rural Americans by 1979 were demanding the creation of a national grain trading board to command a barrel of oil for a bushel of wheat.(39) But even if this should happen, the rest of American agriculture would remain in danger from its dependence on a cartel-controlled price.

The American farmer, though, is not only part of a world economy and energy-pricing system that operates for the greater service of the urban-industrial demand structure. The farmer, even more importantly, is a part of nature. And nature affects the farmer more directly, more immediately and (at least initially) more significantly, than it does any other part of urban-industrial society.

Nature, in this instance, includes the fact that the farmer has only a mortal lifetime. The limitations of nature, as Marshall Harris has carefully shown, compel agriculture to amortize its debts in far shorter time-frames and under much more severe conditions than is true of the urban-industrial economy. The latter has far more flexible ways of amortizing debt since it creates its own crises.

Crises in the agricultural sector are often produced by nature as well as OPEC oil ministers or the world economy. In the United States, as a result, well over twenty-five percent of agricultural sales were supplied by scarcely more than one percent of the farms; over half of the total number of farms, on the other hand, were too small to be self-sustaining under the demands for credit in an economy organized to meet the terms of "normal" urban-industrial conditions.(40)

All of this has still greater applicability in other living resource sectors under high-energy conditions. The price system reduces the production of the forests and the fisheries to seeming insignificance in the total economic system. The so-called "free goods" of air and water have a similar slight fiscal recognition. It seems as if anyone who expressed a concern for the renewing environment was stooping to pick up pins in terms of the gross national product.

The way value is assigned relative to gross national product produces an indifference to the manner in which nature is used as a universal sink. Many of those who have helped to prepare the apparently interminable United Nations Law of the Sea Conference have concluded that there is a world wide "brick wall of indifference" to everything concerning the oceans except the wealth people hoped to extract from the waters or the bed of the ocean. The indifference of the nation states to the ecological problems of the ocean could scarcely be more profound.(41)

In terms of price structures, the vastness of the ocean makes a very small impact on the world's gross product. Knowing the urban-industrial experience with agriculture and forestry under this condition of low appearance in the price structure, there is no room for optimism about the ocean. The roles of price and gross product will always play down the sectors of activity that do not look large for these roles, especially when such activities can be shoved over into what the pricing system wants to consider a "free good."(42)

In the case of the world's ocean, the international law specialist Brian Johnson said,

It is as though ecology and Stockholm had never happened. It looks like business as usual, pending annihilation.(43)

Government and industry alike are intent on extracting oil, gas, and minerals. At the same time, they see no reason why they cannot increase the amount of marine life taken by the world's fisheries. Nor do they see why they cannot increase the amount of waste coming into the ocean as a universal sink. Similarly overlooked is what all this will mean to the ocean as a supplier of oxygen, or as a place for any sort of marine life, or even as to how baseline data will ever be established against which to measure effects once all these demands start to skyrocket.

Right now, the ocean simply fails to constitute a sufficient fiscal size to seem of much economic significance. The economic comparisons of urban-industrial growth dwarf it. The same is true of the products of agriculture and the forests, of water and the atmosphere.

The United States, however, is beginning to focus on the fiscal worth of renewable resources such as weather, water, soil, and forests.(44) The products of field and forest are experiencing a magnifying effect.   Agricultural and forest products serve increasingly as the concentrated sources for the foreign income that partially counterbalance an otherwise disastrous balance of trade from the magnified effect of higher energy prices. The market system suddenly has catapulted the monetary value of these living resources to the forefront.

Aside from this, however, the mechanistic view remains far more common today, equating the values of fiscal sums, as determined by the market's pricing system, with worth in nature. This technique cannot sufficiently take into account the measurement of the full risks involved in handling the renewing environment. The boundless demands for high-energy growth are guaranteeing this appearance in the price system of the comparative low value of any part of the renewing environment.(45)

The continuation of "business as usual" can only make the present situation far worse than it is. Pricing techniques work very well upon certain assumptions. These assumptions include such beliefs as thinking that nature can be treated as a "free good", that nature has an infinite capacity to serve as a waste sink for urban-industrial by-products, that human activity assigns a value to anything in nature, that everything in nature exists essentially as a resource awaiting human use, that fragmenting and processing the unities in nature can be done with impunity, and that nature can easily carry the burden of the human imagination.(46) The existing techniques would work very well if these assumptions were right.

The source of the present crisis, or series of interlocked crises, is that these assumptions are wrong. Nature is finite both as a source of supply for resources and as a receptacle of urban-industrial waste. Nature has an inherent worth independent of any humanly-assigned value. Systems in nature are not simply waiting to become human resources. Nature cannot be fragmented and processed with impunity, and nothing comes from nature "free."

Under the present conditions of high growth demand, environmental protection is not an amenity. Protecting the environment is essential for the survival of the whole energy-demanding, growth-focused system of modern urban-industrial society. Everything else ought to be a secondary consideration.(47)

It is much the way Willard Hurst expressed the situation for the late twentieth century in a letter to Wythe Holt, another legal historian:

> (C)urrents of policy moving in our time are not just "humanitarian,". . .they are, rather, demands for a more rational economic calculus, and reflect distrust of the legitimacy of the corporation as not truly fulfilling even its utility role, because it doesn't properly calculate its costs compared with its gains. . . .In any given span of living, men's available stock of energy, perception, and intelligence, and courage to strive against chaos, are so limited compared with the total pressure of experience that directed effort must be expected to be of marginal effect, and. . .most directed effort must be expected to generate unforeseen costs and fresh problems which will in considerable measure subtract from such gains as may be made.(48)

The old techniques are failing because their assumptions have proven false. Immediate change may only be marginal at first, but radically different assumptions and techniques for effectuating them are now necessities. To quote Willard Hurst once again:

> . . .those effects are humanly important and. . .in any case, our human dignity requires that we make the effort.(49)

NATURE AND DEMAND: WHICH IS WHOSE ENEMY?

A common, traditional view of nature that remains important in determining the human use of nature, was expressed at a convention of the American Meteorological Society. Succinctly defining this position, the speaker said:

> The enemy is the innate intransigence and inscrutability of nature.(50)

Historically, it has been a common way to view nature whether the talk was of the climate, the ambience of air and water, or some other part of the dynamic renewing environment.

When one says that the human "enemy" is hail, blizzards, floods, droughts, or hurricanes because these operate according to terms outside of either human understanding or control, we throw nature into mortal danger. The way people have treated their "enemies" in nature illustrates a kind of combat that has been abusive, degrading, and most often fatal to the natural systems on the receiving end of the assaults. When nature is not a series of interlocked systems to be worked with but, instead, comprises seried opposition, human enterprise will impose demands of the harshest sort upon those "inimical" structures.

The law, which is a part of any culture, can react to nature only as determined for its internal processes by basic cultural attitudes. Given the fragmented view of nature held under conditions of high growth demand, and associating with that the view of the concomitant regard of nature as the human enemy, the result must be a set of laws that would see nature as simply a source for free exploitation. The legal system cannot be attuned to seeing nature in a different light, except as contrary views have been thrust upon law and administration by constituencies who insist that a different attitude must be adopted if high-energy culture and humanity are to survive within viable natural systems.(51)

The practices of high-energy demand upon nature still too often treat nature as a "free" good. Considering the demands for energy within the rest of the century, combined with the probable need to reduce the previously established pace for increases in growth of energy transfers, one can see that the intensity of the demand on the renewing environment can only increase.(52) Competition for capital, the uncertain supply of energy, and the shakiness of natural systems are all factors that ought to be causing a reassessment of the economy's "needs."

At a time when institutions are still taking a frugal view of how much is to be invested in environmental protection, compared with what these same institutions would put into environmental exploitation, it is hard to be optimistic that nature will receive the necessary attention. When the president of the United States in 1979 proposed to freeze American reliance on imported oil as of 1977 by simultaneously investing in the development during the 1980s of both solar energy and synthetic fuels, optimism for the environment fades in light of the capital costs involved. As a concurrent Rand Corporation study showed, there were "awesome economic complications" that could only prompt opposition from environmental groups.(53)

The wise and, in the long term, realistic lawmaker ought to perceive under present conditions the interrelationship of demand and its impact. To continue accepting projections that are described as "needs", believing that thenceforward every action must be accommodated to meeting those "needs", is no longer acceptable public conduct. In the remainder of the twentieth century, sufficient capital, energy, time, or response within natural systems will each prove insufficient.

Legal and administrative processes have meaning to nature only insofar as they impact upon the way the demand structure imposes upon nature. Intent is without significance, however graciously phrased the statutory intent may have been. Distinctions may matter very much to the legally trained; but nature perceives only urban-industrial demands.

How demands are justified culturally, or what may be the human definitions of legality or illegality, are of little consequence if not enough is done to positively protect renewing natural systems. The practice is too strong that sees only the evidence that seems to show ecosystems are not suffering. An insistence remains dominant that either all is well or else all is in the process of becoming well again. Neither is true.

To recognize that present urban-industrial accomplishments have resulted from the interaction of the demand structure and the environment would represent a step forward. If the legal system supplied a structure within which there could be thorough understanding of the consequences of managerial decision, a better technique would have been initiated. The legal and administrative processes, after all, must deal comprehensively and integratedly with the rise in human expectations, the increase in the demand for energy and materials, and the ability of natural systems to accommodate to the burden of the human imagination.

This means that an effort must be made to pace the rate of growth in high-energy conditions, since there is no indication that the trend will end. At the same time, the renewing resources must be managed so that they can viably sustain the pace of this growth. They are two halves of the same responsibility. The one cannot be discharged without the other.

THE NECESSITY OF ENVIRONMENTAL PLANNING
AROUND A UNIVERSAL GARDEN

An acute crisis exists between demands for high levels of energy use and the renewing environment. The leaders of urban-industrial society must realize that there is unity between what they expect and demand on the one hand and the limitations of nature, with which they must deal, on the other. Planning and doing cannot be carried on by asserting the existence of separate institutional cures for these asserted problems.

When a planner says, "long-range plans must not only anticipate. . .changes in water use patterns, but must actually induce transfers to higher value uses," the planner must be thinking about air and land as well as water or the planner is not thinking at all.(54) If planning fails to remember these relationships, it merely engages in the old common practice of institutionalizing problems in separate, problem-vested bureaucracies. The oneness in the renewing processes of nature must be recognized.

Planning that perpetuates a violation of the unity among natural systems, and between human demand and nature, cannot have a positive component for environmental protection. However attractive a planner's standards of aesthetic vision purport to be, such planning is no different than some of the uglier ways for exploiting and destroying ecosystems for the narrowest of human advantages. Planning can be oriented to maintaining high-energy growth and to extending urban-industrial growth. But planning cannot be turned in those directions without simultaneously taking into account the relationship they have, and will continue to have, with natural systems.

There was no planner more city-oriented than the late C. A. Doxiadis, the founder of the form of planning known as ekistics. He has been criticized for seeing the modern individual as best served by planning for a future of city living. He accepted the value of high-energy usages and appreciated the benefits of the urban-industrial demand structure. He did not idealize traditional rural life.

But these attitudes do not indicate any indifference on the part of Doxiadis to nature. He is without the beliefs that people can live only in the city, or always expand energy expectations, or endlessly increase material demands upon nature, or disregard nature's own needs and limitations as these are brought under the impact of the human imagination. He believed, rather, that high levels of energy usage and urban-industrial demand must accept the unity of natural systems and the relationship between human demand and nature.   High-energy culture is in the process of establishing a single ecumene for the planet, drawing all of nature's ecosystems within it. But for Doxiadis, this process greatly increased human responsibility and in no way diminished it.

He boldly recommended dividing the world into three parts. The preserve for nature would cover half the earth's surface and would be for the maintenance of forests, deserts, mountains and wetlands. The agricultural area would be forty-five percent of the earth's surface, excluding those ocean areas not used for marine farming. While the natural moiety would have very little human population, about two billion people would reside in the agricultural zone. It would be no haven for traditional mores, but would be tightly organized as an industry. And finally, only five percent of the earth's surface would be reserved for the universal city.(55)

For this reason Doxiadis could legitimately claim that he was calling for the universal garden rather than the universal city. He predicted that there ultimately would be a continuously built up city along the ocean coasts and the major water bodies of the continental interiors. But the worldwide city will not exist without a universal garden to sustain it. Nature, according to Doxiadis, must be viewed as a living organism, and the imagery should not be that of mechanics but of biology.

Whether he was correct concerning the ultimate future of the growth of urban zones, Doxiadis was likely right in his views concerning energy. The continuance of high-energy usage, much less its greater increase, is as dependent upon the ability of nature to cope with its demands as such usage is dependent upon the human imagination to shape its form and direction. Under the intensifying unity of the globe, as more and more of the ecosystems are drawn into a single ecumene with a burgeoning human population, there has to be a concern with nature's viability transcending any previously known human interest in how nature functions.

Today the general rule is still to ignore the essential relatedness of the renewable resources, even the hydrologic cycle itself. The behavior of those doing the ignoring has been so outrageous that their actions illustrate what it means to ignore the unity in nature. Such ignorance violates the foundations of the universal garden and threatens to lay the garden waste. But if there is no universal garden, there will be no viable urban-industrial society, either. Building and maintaining the universal garden is the prerequisite for any worldwide city that is a product of high-energy demand.

THE RENEWING ENVIRONMENT AS THE WEALTH BASE FOR HIGH-ENERGY DEMAND

As long as the unity of nature is resolutely ignored or denied, tragic events must repetitively occur to the renewing environment and human beings must suffer economic loss. The urban-industrial demand structure must incur otherwise unnecessary expenditures to counteract natural events that, with foresight, could have been taken into account and avoided. Unity in nature is ignored at human peril and at great human cost.

Strangely, the quicker natural systems lash back, the less damage they are likely to suffer. But when the reaction in natural systems is delayed or concealed, the most massive harm accumulates. Building in a flood plain or constructing into a water table are actions that produce their own consequences in quick succession. Other denials, however, of the unity of nature and the interrelatedness of human demand and nature's responses may not produce such swift reactions. When their reactions come, doing much about them can be an impossibility.

Humanity makes a serious error in believing that so much wealth has been accumulated by urban-industrial society that it will be sufficient for every future action that may be required for environmental protection and maintaining energy supplies. Even now, too little worrying is going on under conditions of high-energy growth that takes into account either the adequacy of the renewing environment or of sufficiently relating energy demand to energy supply. Too many continue to believe that the economic and ecologic strengths are present for more of the same under only a slightly altered guise.

The emphasis remains upon sustaining more of the same energy demands and at rates not so much greater than those of the past. In all the talk in the United States about the federal government developing alternative mobile fuel sources to gasoline, too few point out that these fuels likely will cost more than any price OPEC might set below $40 per barrel in 1979 dollars. The capital may be present to pursue these alternative fuel courses, but the likelihood is not as great as the leaders of urban-industrial society want it to be. No politician wants to tackle the problems created by America's dependence on gasoline and diesel engines. Instead, it seems safer to seek ways to support that dependence. As one Dallas County official said of the 1979 proposals for an American synthetic fuel program, "We may have to run over a few ecologists to do it." The tradition of treating the renewing environment as a cheap, even "free," resource for urban-industrial demands is well entrenched.

High-energy demand in the United States and other advanced urban-industrial economies operates on the premise that the renewing environment has its value determined by what it can command in the market – and in a politically controlled market, at that. It is a social decision that simply cannot see the inherent worth of natural systems. Each natural element is treated as if it came from nowhere, went nowhere, and had no value except what human demand should assign it. Gross disparity exists between the value assigned to such elements in terms of cash and the worth that they have to their natural ecosystems.

As early as the 1852 Report of the United States Land Patent Office, the deteriorating condition of soil in the country as a result of the demands made upon it had been noted:

Of the land cultivated in this country, one hundred million acres are damaged to the extent of three dollars per acre per annum; or, in other words, a complete restitution of the elements of crops removed each year cannot be made short of an expense of $300,000,000.(56)

This situation has not been reversed. The restitution has not been made. Much of what was then agricultural land has been driven from later markets by its inability to compete with lands subsequently brought into cultivation; and perhaps this has been of help to renewing systems.

Only very recently does the government seem to be aware of the impact of demand upon natural systems. What may be emerging could be the beginnings of a realization of the unity in nature. However, even the laws to protect the environment, with their individual attention to air, water, and solid waste, maintain a fragmented view. Each law often works at cross-purposes to another as the administrators apply these different statutes to uses affecting air, or soil, or water quality. Administrators of the laws for environmental protection cannot themselves claim immunity from nature's unity.

The techniques are very modest leading in the direction of unified action by urban-industrial institutions. They are techniques that still represent the exception to the way high-energy demand and urban-industrial growth are encouraged to carry on. But the connection of resources, economic activity, and human satisfaction is more clearly seen and acted upon than has previously been the case.(57)

The movement is still almost glacial, being far too slow and slight in relation to what needs to be accomplished. But something is happening in urban-industrial institutions. Even a little is more than what nature has experienced previously from those institutions in the way of recognizing the unity of natural systems. One ought not, therefore, despise the changed techniques until any ultimate inadequacies should emerge.

9 The Inseparability of Energy and Environmental Decisions

THE BOUNDS OF LAND RESOURCES UNDER HIGH
ENERGY DEMAND

If a different relationship is to be established between the human demand structure and nature, then the prejudice that sees nature as boundlessly able to meet high-energy demands must be abandoned. This prejudice lies at the root of modern economic thought and represents a rejection of the views of the eighteenth century physiocrats and the disciples of Quesnay. These economists of the Englightenment romanticized the place of land in the economy, although whether or not they overrated the land's importance in the natural scheme of systemic processes is increasingly questionable.(1) In any event, their views were in ill-repute by the early nineteenth century, and David Ricardo laid these ideas to an apparent rest with a definition of land that for a long time was regarded as ample in scope.(2)

The increasing pressures of the interface between high-energy demands and the renewing environment revealed the insufficiencies of the Ricardian definition of land. Henry Carey, an American economist with primary concern for the role of energy in the economy, was dissatisfied by the middle of the nineteenth century with the adequacy of Ricardian land for descriptive purposes. Carey's views, however, did not prevail. Nevertheless, the inadequacies of the range of the Ricardian land definition have become clearer as the pressure of demand upon the renewing environment has accelerated and grown more intense.

One must understand that "land" to Ricardo included air and water as well as the resources which could be extracted from the ground. Yet despite all the elements Ricardo included in the term, he saw their only unity in the economic connections through which they met human demand. Ricardo was convinced that "land" had a boundless capacity to satisfy present and future demands.

Ricardo's view of a boundlessness in nature that would be at every entrepreneur's disposal dominated the views of economists throughout the nineteenth century. As he expressed it:

The brewer, the distiller, the dyer make incessant use of the air and water for the production of their commodities; but as the supply is boundless, they have no price. . .No charge is made for the use of these natural aids, because they are inexhaustible, and at every man's disposal.(3)

In the Ricardian view, "land" was immune to qualitative change. It was merely empty space waiting to be filled by economic activity. Consequently, economic models based on the Ricardian definition of land lack a variable that can substitute for the perennial contribution of nature. Since nature in his definition is composed of "free" goods that make up the content of "land" prior to the imposition of human activity, Ricardian land can only be an emptiness waiting to be filled by human activity.

From Ricardo's colorless view of nature's value to economic systems, Karl Marx borrowed his "dogma that everything nature offers us is gratis."(4) When so radical and probing a philosopher as Marx could be captured by the Ricardian definition of land, one can begin to realize the power Ricardo's idea exercised over economic thought for nearly two centuries.

Not everyone, however, accepted this narrow definition of land. Henry Carey, as already noted, found Ricardian "land" unable to take account of the role of energy in the exploitation of resources or of Carey's own view that resources ultimately are only energy. John Stuart Mill, with his view of the stationary state, assigned a far greater function to the renewing role of nature than was to be typical for urban-industrial society in the exploitation of the resources its demands identified in nature. Friedrich Engels, in his Dialectic on Nature, produced a work rich in appreciation of nature's inherent worth as well as to the human economy.

But the fate of Engels' work illustrates the minor character of such views. While Carey and Mill suffered a public rejection, Engels was sufficiently subdued to leave his manuscript incomplete and for posthumous publication. Although groping and mechanistic in its imagery, the book should not be denounced as "vulgar," as Octavio Paz says some have described it.(5) For those who operate within the confines of Ricardian land, an emphasis upon nature will always be denounced as sentimental and vulgar. But the bitterness with which a position is held does not vouch for its truth.

The demand structure for energy growth has seen the renewing environment as a factory provided free for expropriation. Every element has been taken as something freely granted without limitation as to what may be demanded. But the renewing resource which has been paradigmatic for all natural resources is water. Its importance to high energy growth has been set forth by the French political theorist Bertrand de Jouvenal:

It is an important feature of today and factor of tomorrow that the Western learning which is now being diffused throughout the world, which is sought everywhere, irrespective of political and social regimes, as characteristic of industrial society and as key to prosperity, is a learning formed in countries where water was not a cause for worry, was a quite unsignificant theme.(6)

High-energy demand developed in water-abundant regions, treating it in the Ricardian manner as a boundlessly free good. This demand has now gone out to the rest of the world, where water is not in such ample supply. And the attitude classifying water as a free good has accompanied it.

High-energy demand sees everything in nature as a flowing stream incapable of intermission. Even so insightful a man as the Utopian socialist Robert Owen could see only the image of the factory in nature – "devote equal attention to our vital machine, the circuits of nature, which are so much more wonderfully constructed." His metaphor shows the ethos for high-energy growth was established early and firmly.(7) Since nature, unlike the factory, has the power of continual renewal, the accuracy of the metaphor is fatally undermined.

No valid comparison can be made between nature and the humanly made machines that are so pitifully incapable of self-renewal – or even able, despite repairs, to survive in the long-run. The image of nature as a machine can only maintain the momentum of human abuse of the environment. This poverty of imagery conceals the social decision to fragment and process nature the way machines macerate and blend what is fed into them. Ricardo notwithstanding, there is no boundlessness in the land for feeding open-ended demands.

THE INTERRELATION OF HIGH-ENERGY DEMAND
AND THE RENEWING ENVIRONMENT

Views of the interrelatedness between high-energy growth and the renewing environment have long existed. Even during the heyday of David Ricardo's definition of land, these views existed. One description of this interrelatedness has been preserved for us by Henry Carey.

Another 19th century economist, E. Peshine Smith, a friend of Carey's, insisted on showing the close interconnection of increasing energy conversion, demand growth in urban-industrial activity, the renewing environment, and the institutional administration of all of these as interconnected forces. Considering the commonality of views then and now, his views are as well worth quoting today as they were in the 1870s. Peshine Smith stated his concerns about the shift from low to high-energy usages comprehensively:

From the indestructibility of matter, as the physical premise, it obviously follows that what we term production and consumption are mere transformations of substance. Whether fossil coal is converted into heat, smoke, and ashes, corn into hogs' flesh, turnips into mutton; corn, pork, turnips, and mutton into human muscle and brain; the uniform phenomenon is alteration of matter in its quality merely, without increase or diminution of its quantity.

In every transition of matter from one condition to another, force is employed, or, as we say, consumed, and force is also evolved or produced. When we regard any commodity as an object, the forces necessary for its production are summed up and measured by value. When we regard it as an instrument, the forces capable of being generated – set free would be the more accurate expression – by its consumption are summed and measured by utility. . . .The consumption of a product is nothing else than its passage from a state of inertness to one of activity,. . . .It is only through this transition, and at the moment of its occurrence, that a commodity becomes the pabulum to production, and that its utility, which was before latent and potential only, becomes manifest and efficient. . .

Between the production of any commodity whatsoever, and its consumption, the interval, long or short, is one of inertness. It stands the monument of human power and natural forces which, having expended themselves in bringing it into shape, slumber in suspended animation, communicating no impulse to the incessant activity which. . .is the essential characteristic of vitality, but is itself a clog and obstruction, involving a draft upon the vital force to put it in motion. . .The growth of wealth, therefore, depends upon the rapidity of circulation; not the rapidity with which products are transported in space, nor the frequency of mere changes of ownership, but the continuity of transformations through the immediate succession of actual consumption to production.(8)

This outlook brims with energy, and is at least as suitable for the future of high-energy growth in the twenty-first century as it was when it was written in the Age of Steam. Although based on the premise that matter is indestructible, this proposition differs greatly from Ricardo's boundlessness in nature. Matter might be indestructible in the mass, but in individual manifestations Peshine Smith found it very vulnerable to transformations that could utterly wipe out certain forms without much benefit to the whole.

Consumption to Peshine Smith was a matter of energy. Production was also a matter of energy, as was waste. Energy was his measure of value and utility. Not accidentally, his term for the stuff upon which industrial activity operates is "pabulum," the instrument of nourishment in its literal derivation. Smith believed that nature is drawn into the growth of high-energy demand and purposefully homogenized.

Time was the element of inertness in this energy-based view. The real source of wealth was the rapidity with which transformations could occur through the force of energy upon the functions of production and consumption. Peshine Smith, in brief, summarized the conditions for high-energy growth and how those conditions inevitably impacted upon nature, social structure, and the individual human being.

Still, dependent as his explanation is upon turning nature and human effort alike into the "pabulum" of production and consumption, Smith perceived that all of it depends upon nature and draws its content from nature. Nor is nature seen as being "free" in the provision of this service. As Henry Carey observed, the enjoyment of wealth by humanity is in direct proportion to the extent they have energy at their command in order to draw upon the richest resources of nature. When the energy is not available, then humanity has been, and will be, driven back upon the poorer resources.(9)

For those who see energy, demand, and nature inextricably intermixed, no long-run belief in the boundlessness of nature is possible. The potential burden of the human imagination imposes an eventual responsibility to keep the flow of interchange between human demand, energy transfer, and the responses of natural systems in motion. Once these interrelatednesses are found to exist, it is only a question of time before the determination of goals becomes of primary importance in the operation of the relations subsisting between humanity and nature.(10)

PLANNING FOR THE INTERRELATEDNESS OF HIGH-ENERGY DEMAND AND THE RENEWING ENVIRONMENT

Once an interacting-reacting kind of relationship has gotten underway between the high-energy demand structure and natural systems, decisions could be made upon a far broader scale than has existed for even the most rational decisions in the past. The result would revise the actions that have imperilled the continuance of the cycles affecting various ecosystems. As the United Nations Food and Agriculture Organization has said:

Although in any broad attempt to bring together economic and social development needs (and) various environmental requirements...there are a vast number of difficult conflicts to resolve, there would seem to be no reason why scientific insight, technological capability, and the relevant institutional mechanics cannot accomplish this within a reasonable time span.(11)

One cannot disagree with so bland a statement that recognizes the unity between humanity and nature. Yet, if it is all so "reasonable," why the indifference and the delay? If so easily achievable, why does not such unified planning exist in the world? The reason is that the recognition has been of an abstract kind, with little existence at an operational level. When only bureaucratic announcements are made, nothing is really done to tie together humanity and nature. What seems to have been so widely recognized, in practice has not been recognized at all.

There is a perception of the consequences of high-energy demand that is given lip-service by public announcements. After all, it was not young radicals but two elderly, conservative senators, Herman Talmadge and George Aiken, who made the following comment in the early 1970s on urban-industrial society as it has operated in the United States:

> . . .our nation has compressed its people – without any planning at all – into a bone-hard catacomb of steel and asphalt. . .It is an amazing commentary on the content of this modern civilization that the trip to work for American commuters each morning is more perilous and tension filled than it was for the pioneers to troop out from St. Louis to settle the West.(12)

The kind of planning these conservative senators were calling for is of a unified, environmentally related sort – a planning approach that has been conspicuously absent. They may not fully have realized the kind of planning their stated goals required. But whatever their perceptions, more and more people are perceiving the problems incident to fragmented action and are asking for unified planning.

The need for unified planning is gaining recognition among those who see planning as something more than a chronic reaction series to seemingly unrelated, successive problems. The belief is growing that much can still be done to protect the environment from extravagant human demand. What has not manifested itself has been the social decision to undertake the needed changes. The decision continues to be delayed because the newer perceptions have not prevailed. The grip of the past remains too strong.

The land definitions of David Ricardo still carry a profound influence. Within Ricardo's definition of land is embraced what he called the "original and indestructible power of nature." This includes not only the ground, other than the exhaustible minerals and aggregates, but also the crop seed and the source of germination of plant life.(13)

The world treatment of the forest resource illustrates how this mistaken principle has been fully acted upon. What has been ignored has been the life-support aspect of land as a maker of soil, a retainer of water, and a producer of forest and the ecosystems living within the forest. Even when high economic productivity is occurring permanent ecologic destruction is possible and is even likely when one is dealing with living nature.

True, the location of the germinal parental stock of a forest, at which point the trees find their powers of regrowth intermitted, can be hard to determine. But it seems plain from experience that a point does exist at which the forest resource cannot be swept into the "indestructible" attribute of Ricardian land. If nothing else has been learned from experience, it is that forests, plant life, seed stock, and all elements pertaining to the working of ecosystems are highly destructible.

For Ricardo, the original natural power in land might be indestructible in terms of the whole economy. But any brief account of human experience has to show that particular destruction is not merely possible but rather common. Ecologic history offers a contradiction to the Ricardian statements about the boundlessness and indestructibility of nature. The world's histories as to how humanity has dealt with ground cover and water offer numerous examples of a refusal to engage in integrated environmental planning under conditions of either low or high-energy demand.(14)

One source of this dismay would be a study of the Iberian forests. There are few more desiccated lands in near humid conditions, which historically were forest covered, than are those of the Iberian peninsula. The accumulated effects of deforestation in erosion, stream sedimentation, and the desiccation from rapid run-off penetrated to even the royal court. Yet the perception meant little for the peninsula's renewing environment.

One can only note with regret that the Spanish experience is claimed to be environmentally universal. Paul Chabrol, an ecologic historian, asserts that Spain's experience with her living environment is merely exemplary. Indeed, he draws together a comparison of air, land, and water. Like Plato's description of the Attic deforestation, Chabrol's is an excellent critique of Ricardo's claim for an inherent indestructibility in land value. Drawing on a Spanish Moslem source on conditions in the eleventh century under the Omayyads, Chabrol makes some striking comparisons between Moslem Spain and the remainder of the Islamic world. Spain is then said to be:

> . . .as Syria in the agreeability of its climate and the purity of its air, as the Yemen for her equable and agreeable climate, as the Indies for their penetrating scents, as Persia for the importance of fiscal revenues, as Aden for the production of its coast-line.(15)

Much remains of interest for a twentieth century observer of these eleventh century comparisons. Of interest a thousand years later – always excluding the Persian oil royalties – is that the same countries might reasonably be compared with Spain on these same points. There would, however, be striking differences.

The experiences when placed side by side would reveal comparable poverty in natural resources and the lack, rather than the plenty, of what had been recited in the eleventh century. In every country – Syria, Yemen, Persia, and Aden – the ultimate desiccatory ruin of the land has resulted, as it has in Spain, from economic practices that seem to reflect in their consequences a hostility to nature. Reaping isolated benefits from the water, soils, and forests of the Mediterranean has imposed the costs of arid, barren lands on succeeding generations. Not all the profits from the oil of western Asia can restore the ancient lushness of the Fertile Crescent and its Mediterranean littoral.

Further examples of this sort could be legion. An example of high-energy demand, destructive of the renewing environment, can be drawn from socialist Russian experience under a legislative system that claims to protect woodlands and forest ecosystems. According to the newspaper Sovietskaya Rossiya, one of Russia's major woodlands, the Zhiguli, has been reduced in half a century from four hundred thousand acres to fifty thousand. This has been done by one special exception after another allowing encroachment upon the forest lands by a nearby expanding industrial city. The fact that the forest contained over seven hundred species of plants and had the richest variety of wildlife and flora in central Russia was not allowed to be controlling over the social decision for urban-industrial growth.

Forest ponds in the Zhiguli were eliminated, because the nearby growing urban industrial zone needed water. The Volga was cut off from the forest animals by a barrier of industrial plants, dachas, and other urban structures. Species such as the brown bear and the wild boar have become extinct. The consequent shortage of water, since neither the ponds nor the river are available to support wildlife or the forest itself, brings the chance for survival of what remains close to nil. It happened not because the environmental laws are not phrased in tough language but, in the words of the Russian newspaper, because "enforcement often yields, as in the case of Zhiguli, before the march of industrial progress."(16)

With evidence accumulating that urban-industrial demand interdicts natural systems, the need grows for energy and environmental planning that takes a unified view of the interleaved actions and reactions of both high-energy demand and the renewing environment's ability to cope with the burden.(17) What complicates the prospects of success for even this kind of planning, however, is that the boundless and indestructible Ricardian land has proved to have far fewer renewable powers than previously attributed to it. Little by little, nature's seemingly massive reserves have been consumed, even as the leaders of urban-industrial society neglect to initiate integrated energy and environmental action.

Plant life is only one example that the renewing environment offers of a worth far beyond the price any crop can command. Plants are smog-eaters, sinks for urban-industrial wastes. Their suffering to the acid rain now coming down upon them may indicate plants have reached their limits as sinks. But sinks for the wastes of high-energy growth, plants have been and will be. Both for the environment and human health and amenity, it is difficult to overestimate the value of just the forested land. Russell Seibert of the American Horticultural Society implored Americans in 1970 to:

> . . .plant plants at every opportunity. They are smog eaters and the more plants we plant, the better our chances of breathing fresh air. . .(P)lant at every opportunity those plants that not only enhance the setting but also tolerate the most adverse metropolitan conditions.(18)

This recommendation encompasses the role of plant life for the whole world. Perhaps it reads like a tacit acceptance of the present high-energy demand structure. Since matters are not going to improve in the future, it seems to imply, the wise horticulturalist will plant to provide both a green counteraction and a selection of plants capable of resisting inescapably adverse air pollution.

Yet to justify even such minimal expenditures, one must part company forever with David Ricardo's views of boundlessness. No boundlessness is present in the renewing environment nor any element of indestructibility inherent in air, water, or the biomass. Matter is indestructible in terms of energy transfers — at least until one reaches the moment known poetically as the "energy death." But that indestructibility has little to do with maintaining life support systems and the flow of the hydrologic cycles, the jet stream, or climatic gradients.

Thornton Wilder has expressed the great slowness with which nature works in a poetic passage in his novel, The Eighth Day.

> What stretches of time are required to complete the procession of a marsh to a forest. The professors have drawn up the time plan: so much for the grasses to furnish humus for the bushes; so much for the bushes to accommodate the trees; so much for the young of the oak family to take root under the grateful shade of the wild cherry and the maple, and to supplant them; so much for the white oak to replace the red; so much for the majestic entrance of the beech family, which has been waiting for its propitious hour — the war of the saplings, so to speak.(19)

And how long does it take high-energy demands to undo all of that? Only a comparative handful of years.

When in 1979 the United States proposed to launch an energy program substantially freeing the country of dependence on foreign oil in 1990, the emphasis was all on the maintenance of the energy supplies for mobile power uses, the generation of electricity, and space heating. They were decisions consistent with a war for energy. But they were decisions only accidentally providing any degree of protection to renewing environmental systems.

Whatever urgency is imposed by energy supply problems, energy and environmental planning must be recognized as comprising the same interrelated actions. Nothing can be planned for the one that will not affect the other. Demands that indicate the environment is subordinated to energy supply, as in suspending the Clean Air Act to permit conversion to high sulfur coal by industry and electric utilities, must be altered.(20)

Such a change will not happen soon. Perhaps, as the economist Paul Craig believes, the United States "could lower our consumption (of oil) by ten to fifteen percent without chaos in our social fabric."(21) But the leaders of urban-industrial society remember that their society was built on the promise of plentiful energy, and they do not wish to risk social chaos. Perhaps they privately identify more with the American manufacturer of recreational vehicles, who remained optimistic in 1979 on the future supplies for mobile energy on the basis that, "You aren't going to be able to take away sex, booze, or weekends from the American people."(22) Under pressures existing and impending, however, fragmented decision making will fail on a scale even greater than it has traditionally, whatever social chaos ensues.

HIGH-ENERGY DEMAND AND THE MAINTENANCE OF A LIFE-SUPPORT ENVIRONMENT

Behind life stand the life-support systems of the renewing environment: air, water, and the constituents of soil. Non-life they may not all be, but neither are they all living entities. Some life, of course, is anaerobic and needs an atmosphere lethal to other life forms.

But the worth of the renewing environment for life support can find no other adequate description than essential and basic. Consequently, the changes which the waste and supply demands of urban-industrial society impose upon the renewing environment require constant attention.

Life cannot sustain itself on its own wastes. The environment has self-cleaning properties which permit the dilution, reconstitution, and reuse by other natural processes of waste. These self-operative properties produce the flow of dynamic change that renews what is renewable within nature. But the forces for renewal are not infinite. Nevertheless, humanity has found the means to disrupt the renewing forces in part and, unless steps are promptly taken to counteract the present trends, high-energy demand will inadvertently and indifferently risk its total disruption.

In this light, the Air Conservation Commission of the American Association for the Advancement of Science in 1965 made a then dramatic announcement about what they considered a necessary limitation upon human conduct.

Any environment must be self-cleaning in order to sustain life. Unless the environment can dispose of life's by-products, life will cease.(23)

What prompted this proposition and turned a truism into a melodrama was the condition of the metropolitan atmosphere impacted by four major sources of pollution in high-energy culture: motor vehicles, thermo-electric power generating stations, industry, and households, because of their space heating and trash incineration. The atmosphere had been turned into a sink and conditions, previously known only indoors, had been made a commonality in the open air supply for urban regions.

Much of this air contamination had been due to the efforts of urban-industrial society to introduce amenities within the home and factory by displacing objectionable substances into the outside air. At first the effect on the outside air, similar to a small amount of pollution discharged into a flowing stream, was not noticed. But as industrial development and urban concentrations progressed, the outdoor conditions acquired noticeably deteriorated characteristics that had once been known only in tightly confined spaces. It was understood even as early as the 1950s that such amenities as indoor comfort and the luxury of private motor cars had been purchased at the price of polluting the formerly clean, common air supply.(24)

Throughout most human biological history, the human environment was "characterized by the virtually unlimited availability of what we now refer to as 'pure air'."(25) Only after humanity learned how to release the energy stored in plants and fossil fuel was this sort of environment modified by emitted waste. However, for thousands of years this energy conversion took place under conditions of low control of energy applications. Not until the advent of high demand for applied energy usages did the products of combustion, along with other by-products of human activity, form the massive pool of substances in the atmosphere to which humanity must now genetically adapt themselves. The significance of this is as yet unknown.

The time to accumulate a perhaps fatal experience has been insufficient. Furthermore, the atmosphere still possesses a truly formidable capacity to dilute, disperse, and destroy an enormous list of substances urban-industrial society indifferently discharges into it. The renewing environment's powers of indulgence are drawing rapidly to a close, if they have not done so already.

Yet it is no wonder that emitters cling to a treatment of renewing natural systems as a free good. The pressure on profits grows greater in urban-industrial society. Inflation and the related rise in energy costs impel some to try to shuffle these costs, too, onto the environment. "Why now?" "Why me?" are the common queries of people who cannot understand nature's inability to accept the result of grandfather clauses, exempt categories, variances, and special exceptions. If synthetic fuels in the 1980s should cost the $40 per barrel some consumer advocates say they shall,(26) who will happily pay a higher premium per barrel to protect the environment from the making and the use of those fuels? Will it not seem easier to do what previous energy decisions so often did and let the environment renew itself as best it can?

Probably, under the burden of higher energy costs, decision makers in urban-industrial society will seek to give the environment short shrift. If so, the mistake will be tragic and, in some instances for individuals as well as for the environment, irreversible. After all, in 1965 the AALS Air Conservation Commission certainly did not take a position favoring environmental purity. Far from advocating atmospheric purity, they defined pollution as the condition that

. . .Occurs when these processes cannot keep up with the rate of discharge, and when. . .(there) is. . .a susceptible receptor, such as man.(27)

Short shrift was extended to other life organisms. Air was viewed by this commission of scientists in terms of its physical properties. These had importance, it seems, only insofar as they affected human well-being. Pollution was not something emitted into the atmosphere. Pollution was the result of the aerial processes being unable to keep up with the pace of the emission. Nature rather had the value, it seems, of a caged canary in a mephitic mine.

This attitude concerning atmospheric emissions under conditions of high-energy growth was underscored in the commission's six-point air pollution control and air conservation program. Even these would be regarded as too extreme, of course, by those zealous advocates of all the "benefits" and "amenities" of high-energy culture who delight in denouncing all critics of those individuated pleasures as "eco-freaks" or "doom-sayers."(28)

The commission's proposals were very minimal. Subsequent legislation has gone further, though how much more it has accomplished is being questioned. The proposals were meant to:

> . . .take into account (i) the volume and mobility of the air mass overlying the area where emissions occur; (ii) the interaction of pollutants and the self-cleansing attributes of the atmosphere; (iii) the topography of the region and any effects it may have on dispersing pollutants; (iv) the variables of meteorology; (v) the existing pattern of industrial practices, transportation, use of land, production of energy, and all matters that pertain to their further development; and (vi) the range of sensitivity of human beings, plants, and animals in the region.(29)

The political process cannot fail to be an intimate part of what even scientists will recommend in relation to the environment, nor should it be. Little is perceivable in the form of public events except as they are looked at through political lenses. Until the basic social decision to adopt a different attitude toward growth is taken, the attitude will remain dominant that everything in nature must be accommodated to urban-industrial demand. No reexamination of the scope of that demand will otherwise be called for. Under such conditions, it has proven most difficult to push effectively beyond the 1965 proposal of this private commission of scientists.

Collective benefits, such as clean air and water, have a far lower value in the political arena than individuated ones. Where all benefits are counted – and discounted – as specific benefits in the form of public contracts or new industry, politicians can be expected to be cool toward collective benefits which they cannot accrue to their personal advancement. There is no way to direct the distribution of clean air and water among the inhabitants of a region as contrasted to specific benefits such as jobs. Pinpointing the source of a collective benefit is difficult since normally it is impossible to identify the origin of a collective harm.

For this reason, what Jeremy Bentham called "contrabandists" – persons who commit offenses against a hard-to-define general good – are rarely subject to the same degree of public ignominy as those who perpetrate crimes against specific persons.(30) They may commit a social harm far greater than the sum total of Jack the Ripper's career, but they will not be labeled wrongdoers in the public eye because they will have escaped identification.

Just as collective doers of wrong escape identification, so do the conferrers of collective benefits. And political brokers, naturally, have little desire to become committed to self-effacedly providing collective goods or eliminating collective harms. In these areas, they are often content to pay lip service to collective social goals.

In outlining the American air pollution situation as long ago as 1971, Mathew Crenson concluded that people who control political influence will not usually make trades in behalf of collective benefits.(31) Those who do show this willingness promptly run into the difficulty of trading collective benefits. This difficulty results from the fact that collective benefits cannot easily be fit within the existing homogenization process.

This failure to fit is an inescapable result of the essentially fragmentary situation under present conditions of high-energy growth. Under such fragmented conditions, where everyone seeks to individuate profits and to shove the costs off onto others, it is most profitable of all to be a freeloader and to care nothing for collective benefits – at least in the short and highly personal run.

Under these conditions, the emphasis falls upon the specific benefits rather than on the collective ones. Anything that can be made to flow in the form of easily identifiable personal profits will prompt immediate responses of gratitude and/or obligation. Out of these responses come the yield for an ongoing political brokerage. This brokerage indirectly provides a few collective benefits which more direct efforts might never accomplish. It is, nevertheless, primarily a brokerage that rests upon the provision of specific benefits.

Monitoring services and enforcement of the laws for environmental protection and energy conservation are themselves benefits. They are also costly, both to the general economy and to persons in their private activities. Nevertheless, they confer a collective benefit, however hard it is for any individual to ever see that benefit personalized.

The greater the specific benefits conferred by urban-industrial growth, the harder it must be to obtain support for the collective benefits of clean air and water. The presence of specific benefits submerges the potential collective good to be obtained from improving the response of the renewing environment. Mathew Crenson from his research could only conclude that the "dirty air issue" was a hard one to focus support around when industrial influence was strong.

Indeed, the more open the political processes to the influence of various constituencies involved in the operations of high-energy culture, the more veto power each of these units likely would exert to block collective good and to assure for its own small bloc whatever specific benefits could be commandeered from political brokerage. So pessimistic is Crenson on this issue that he has come to see political pluralism and citizen preference for specific benefits over collective goods as imposing:

> . . .an important limitation upon the alleged openness of pluralistic political systems, tending to obstruct the expression of collective interests and the political progress of collective issues.(32)

Under high-energy demand, it seems as if political histories were accumulated for the purpose of showing how correct an analysis this is. Pleased as one can be about the strength of the insistence on environmental protection in the presence of the demand levels for high-energy growth, the old attitudes exert a pervasive influence.

BROKERING DECISIONS FOR ASSURING ENVIRONMENTAL RENEWABILITY UNDER HIGH-ENERGY DEMAND

Political operations make it impossible to create a constituency for nature. Nature is a collectivity peculiarly subject to what Theodore Lowi describes as "disaggregability." The human concept of nature is a phenomenon of human artifice. The "disaggregability" of natural systems is the result of an inability of human institutions.

Human institutions, whether urban-industrial or some other societal form, cannot compel a wider decision until there has been an accumulation of enough specific benefits. The consequence is an episodic and disordered character to decision making that acts upon natural systems as a disaggregating and, hence, destructive force. But it is the human institutions, not the natural systems, which are essentially disaggregated.

Government finds it extremely difficult to focus on issues of collective good. The aggregating of enough specific benefits is a time consuming and costly process. The mobilization of masses of specifics is required in order to produce motion in the direction of preserving the otherwise ignored collective good. The stress for mobilizing as much specific support as possible acts to shove the decision making function into the larger, central units of government.(33)

Sometimes in this way, persons may find a fulcrum upon which to rest the levers of their pressure for protecting some aspect of nature as a collective good. A means is provided for forcing decisions and conferring on the political brokers counters for negotiation. What had been non-decisions are exchanged for decisions redistributing responsibilities and penetrating the previously unbreakable opposition of divided interests indifferent to the collective good.(34)

The larger, central governmental units are, by this much, better able to aggregate enough specific benefits to more effectively intervene in production and consumption processes. Alternatively, govern-

ment can set constraints that comprise limitations upon those processes. At the larger, central levels, however, the constituencies that have
to be aggregated are more complex. What is aggregated has to be
conjoined to form the levers political brokers can use. They must be
pressed against whatever fulcrum can be found in order to attain the
collective action needed. At these larger spheres, locally tiny numbers
aggregate into significant forces. When such aggregations reach a
sufficient point, they can assist unifying decision making to a degree
far larger than their absolute numbers would indicate. Those concerned
with environmental protection find their political effectiveness in this
last aggregated group. Indeed, it is at this level of aggregation that the
motive force can most frequently set in action the political brokerage
able to bring together both contending and complementary forces.

This aggregated interest is important because the "experts" within
the governmental institutions usually fail in a unifying function because
of the fragmentary character of their expertise. As individuals, these
experts may well perceive the need for unifying decisions. Yet, the
whole fragmentary character of the present urban-industrial situation
denies them either training or legitimacy as the brokers for unifying
social decisions.

Traditional political brokers do not look with favor upon the
bureaucratic experts as their competitors in this role. In fact, experts
can very well find their security attacked not only by the political
brokers but by fellow experts in the bureaucracy. Both groups will base
their attack on the charge that to go outside a narrow area of technical
knowledge is to act inexpertly and to sacrifice the authority of the
expert.

As J. R. Mahoney has observed, the training of experts commands
both an individual and a corporate responsibility. The individual makes
the choice of expertise out of all the disciplines which might be chosen.
Only later will the individual decide whether to extend the core of
asserted competency over a wider or narrower range of the technical
areas which constitute the claimed expertise.

But of far greater importance is the corporate or social responsibility that determines what constitutes a specialty of study. Here the
decision is made as to what can be expertise, how broad the training
must be, and what sort of investment is to be made to permit
individuals to effectively elect an area as a subject for expertise. For
these reasons, the bureaucratic expert can rarely play much of a part in
the brokering of decisions capable of piecing existing fragments together into a unifying decision for the collective good.(35)

Perhaps too much has been said about the necessity of aggregating
specific benefits in order to accomplish the collective good. This is not
the only way. Negative costs can also be aggregated to the degree that
they force upon specific interests the knowledge that the collective
good must be served if their specific benefits are to be sustained or
restored.

High-energy demand routinely imposes and aggregates these negative costs. Even though the potential beneficiaries of environmental

protection are widely dispersed portions of the population, there are still those who can be specifically identified as bearing many of the costs of environmental exploitation. As such, they suffer a diminution in their own specific benefits.(36)

The very collectiveness of the good served by protecting the environment not only prevents nature from forming a politically effective constituency, but also acts as a baffle for bureaucratic interest. All institutions want to simplify their work. This means that they tend to exclude from their considerations all effects external to their jurisdictional limits.

Bureaucratic institutions, whether those in public administration or private corporations, commonly plead lack of time, limiting statutory directives, or a sharp border round their expertise. They resist in the name of simplicity all orders to encompass in their planning their general relationship to nature on the one side and the production and consumption functions on the other.(37) This resistance, however advocated in the name of simplicity, expertise, or some other abstract virtue, must be met by counter-pressure.

There has to be an insistence that it is precisely this broad inclusion of data and experience which "experts" must take into account. A narrow "simplicity" feeds the flourishing fragmentary forces pushing for high-energy growth. Like so much else in the structures of urban-industrial society, the confining of the interests of the environmental bureaucracy to narrow jurisdictional areas of alleged technical expertise will be in the not very long run diseconomic and malecologic for the collective good of both urban-industrial society and the renewing environment. It is absolutely essential to broker the human capacity to span future time,

> to exercise foresight and hindsight, to imagine future accomplishment and to review past errors. . .(to learn from experience that) the bigger the job, the bigger the problem of investment and risk, since a longer series of decisions must be negotiated over a longer period of time.(38)

THE TOTAL ENERGY AND ENVIRONMENTAL PLANNING REQUIRED

Nature demands a total approach. Steadily, the reaction of natural systems imposes this requirement upon the humanly constructed demand structure of high-energy growth. Humanity cannot continue to make no provision for a constituency representative of nature. Urban-industrial society can only for a time continue to refuse the investment in brokering the demands of high-energy growth against the systemic demands of nature.

The fragmentary, processing approach may still seem for many to be cheaper and every other variety of action far too costly. But increasingly the meaning of what is cheap and what is costly in nature's terms is being brought into prominence. The renewing environment may or may not have a constituency in urban-industrial politics. Still, changes in the patterns of high-energy growth are going to occur in the pricing of energy, the allocation of resources, the generation of goods and services, and the impact of the costs, including inflation, on consumption.

An interesting foreshadowing of changes leading in the direction of unified environmental management was a method put forward in the 1960s for calculating the self-purification capacity of a stream. The proposal of the bio-engineer, A. Syniolis, although not yet practicable, marked the beginning of a shift in attitude. Syniolis insisted on basing his parameters of calculation upon real values that consist of:

> 1) the coefficients of the actual reductions. . .of BOD. . .of the river, which does not take into account the effect of dilution; 2) the conversion power of the river. . .on the stretch investigated, given in kilograms of BOD reduced per unit time. . .in the 1-hourly volume of flow through a given cross-section; 3) the degree of self-purification. . .along the stretch of water, providing for the dilution effect as well. . . .(Part of the equation employed) characterizes the intensity of the self-purification processes taking place in the stretch of water investigated under the influence of all the natural factors.

All this would seem to be quite enough. Most technologists would feel replete to have been so supplied by the bureaucratic institutions in charge of data collection. For Syniolis it was only a start.

In addition, he demanded statistics on:

> 1) the abundancy and activity of the biological factors, primarily bacteria; 2) the nature and degree of dispersion of the organic compounds present in the wastes; 3) degree of contact of water with the bottom and banks as well as with the biological films covering these surfaces and the vegetation of the higher order. . . .(Thereby) the total oxygen uptake and the amount of oxygen consumed by a given stretch of water are obtained. The amount of oxygen acquired comprises the oxygen in the upstream water, re-aeration, oxygen from photo-synthesis and that present in water entering the stream from the drainage area. The oxygen consumed comprises that consumed by BOD, that used for COD (chemical oxygen demand), change of water saturation, for aeration of inflows low in oxygen and for respiration of the fauna and flora.(39)

Contemporary expert opinion is content to be far more modest than to insist on real values in the equation. Financial resources are modest and enforce modesty. Far from hoping to have total knowledge, the emphasis is upon designing short-cuts in order to calculate the costs of protecting the environment through such schemes as process changes, emission cleaning equipment, or a change in fuels. What these short-cuts seek is the chance to expand the impact of scarce allocations of money so that relatively significant benefits can be obtained for the environment at low investment rates.(40)

One cannot be surprised, therefore, when the experts, who know nature is without a constituency powerful enough to push budget allocations through the governmental system, limit their attentions. Perhaps modestly thinking of efforts such as the decentralization of treatment facilities is better than contemplating a total kind of energy and environmental planning. This, of course, is much less than what a Syniolis might want.

But, most experts still see the perfect world of total energy and environmental planning as being remote from any near employment.(41) Given the modesty of resources, the problem of an environmental expert operating in an institutional setting is not how to enlarge the bases for computation but, rather, how to reduce larger difficulties to subproblems for computation within operational and institutional limits.(42)

The present social decision still increases the scope and intensity of the pressures energy growth imposes on the environment.(43) The hope remains among many decision-makers of cutting to the marrow of the bone any funding that would deal with resulting difficulties.   The expert, thereby, is driven to the expedients of smaller plant, smaller model, smaller subproblem in order to be allowed any contribution to environmental protection. Experts can only hope that their small, individuated efforts will aggregate into a merged effect of major proportions. But this is hope only and not an assurance.

One cannot harshly criticize the institutional expert who tries to do much with the small fiscal resources allocated for such work. Proceeding on an informed hunch is better than waiting for perfect knowledge. Working with little has been a necessity, but it cannot substitute for a program that would include all the appropriate data sources touching upon the demand structure's impact. The experts may have to work without the information denied them, but the usefulness of their work has been, and will be, reduced by such denial.(44)

A broad spectrum is needed for viewing the impact of human demand and the burden of the human imagination upon natural systems. Technically ingenious short-cuts, compelled by the smallness of the funds allocated for environmental protection, cannot substitute for a social decision to move from a fragmented to a unified treatment of the renewing environment under conditions of open-ended growth. Today, experts think more in terms of waste treatment than in process change, much less in terms of demand reduction. More than that, experts have been pushed into protecting their own institutions, so that individuals only occasionally realize the overall obligation of the environmental expert. This obligation must be the protection of natural systems from the impact of human demand rather than the institutional protection of the expert's own institutional position.

Regretfully, appreciation is lacking that sees environmentally beneficial land use, protective resource exploitation, and more efficient
energy usage as helping humanity even more than they help renewing
natural systems.

The more massive the demand upon nature, the larger the scale of
the effect of the demand. An increased likelihood results of a break up
in the parts of natural systems upon which heavy resource reliance has
been placed by urban-industrial demands and the insistence for a high-
energy supply.

The effects of growth in the 20th century can be seen by the
observant in the water and the atmosphere, soil and soil cover, wildlife,
and the whole of renewing systems in nature. Yet in much of that
period, the environmental burdens of maintaining high-energy usage
have been small compared with what they now are or soon will be.
Anyone who thinks ahead must wonder at the intensity of the future
impact upon nature if the choice is made to make every sacrifice to
substantially maintain the high-energy demand curves that have been
pounding steadily upward. The lack of past universal breaks can be no
assurance that breaks will not occur universally. And nothing can assure
that universal breaks may not be universally fatal.

THE AUTONOMY OF BOTH ENERGY AND THE RENEWING
ENVIRONMENT FROM URBAN-INDUSTRIAL GROWTH DEMAND

Nature has an irreducible autonomy. Outside everything urban-
industrial society proposes, under a system that willfully ignores the
unity in nature, lies nature's absolute veto. Nature exercises that veto
when a breaking point has been reached in a biological system or in the
means for physically renewing a flowing process.

The word "human" expresses an inherent limitation. Translated, the
word means, "a being pertaining to the earth," and is of the same root
as the Latin word for soil. This perception is similar to the directive
under which the economist H. H. Liebhafsky says humanity must
operate:

> We are all tenants for life of the environment and our possession
> is rightful. The environment is an essential part of the inher-
> itance, and uncontrolled pollution constitutes a destruction or
> improper deterioration of that inheritance. Those who may from
> time to time be in a position to make use of governmental power
> to preserve the inheritance stand as trustees.(45)

For a species whose name in one major language means belonging to
earth, it makes an excellent directive.

On a modest scale in the past, humanity experienced the unity that
nature imposes through scarcity. The experience was modest because it
involved low applications of controlled energy conversion. But the
desiccation and deforestation of land illustrates the sort of dependency

that arises when a resource humanity has depended upon becomes scarce. This previous experience may prove exemplary of the future should high growth in the energy curves continue its course without regard for the limits of renewability.

Where resources do not appear scarce, not only is there no incentive to save, there is an incentive to extravagantly utilize. This is the primary way in which the human economy confers value upon elements in nature, destructive as it must be to the worth these elements have in existing natural systems. Once the element becomes scarce, those whose very lives are dependent upon it find ways of careful measurement and of operating social institutions so as to best use the scarce resource. At that point, there is no room for the kind of one hundred percent error that a more plentiful nature might not only permit but treat as imposing no immediate consequence. Everything, then, must be done in terms of the inherent worth in natural systems, with little margin for error being tolerable in relation to what is, or has become, the survival of the culture.(46)

Only where a resource is both scarce and vital to a culture will an effort be made to deal with it conservingly. Otherwise, its abundance may be even frightening. This has occurred to one forest ecosystem after another that has been brought under human control. Humanity first moved into the uninhabited forest and their reaction was one of fear, of being excluded, of being in a place sacred to gods.

When the American settlers crossed the Ohio in the 1780s, they felt overwhelmed by the awesomeness of the deciduous forest awaiting them. How does Conrad Richter, in the first volume of The Awakening Land, his great trilogy on the settling of the Old Northwest Territory, describe their reaction? By comparing the forest to a sea and the settlers to people who follow the sea:

> For the moment Sayward reckoned that her father had fetched them unbeknownst to the Western ocean and what lay beneath was the late sun glittering on green-black water. Then she saw that what they looked down on was a dark, illimitable expanse of wilderness. It was a sea of solid treetops broken only by some gash where deep beneath the foliage an unknown stream made its way. As far as the eye could reach, this lonely forest sea rolled on and on till its faint blue billows broke against an incredibly distant horizon. . .(47)

America moved in quick succession from the initial fear of the wild forest, to extravagant cutting purely for the purpose of clearing, to the market glut of timber, to concern for conservation of deforested areas. All this occurred within the span of two centuries. This includes three dates significant for conservation: 1863 when Yosemite Park was created; 1872 when Yellowstone Park was founded; and 1890, when President Harrison set aside the first federal forest preserve. In a brief span high-energy demand turned the American forest problem from one of "settlement and subjugation" to one of conservation.(48)

As the forests approach exhaustion, the attitude shifts. From being awesome, they become pitiful. From being something to be wantonly destroyed, they become something to plant. From being a commodity for export, they are aided by efforts to move the burden off native forests and to import the cuttings of others.

The human tendency is to save what is left and to stop the kind of activities that created the condition of scarcity. Some call this a natural saving. But this "natural" saving occurs only where conditions impose a unity of dependence and where the scarcity is such that the demand structure cannot act to conceal scarcity.(49)

Forests and wildlife mostly differ on this latter point from such portions of the renewing environment as water and air. Important as the green cover of the earth and the ecosystems of animal life are to life maintenance on this planet, they do not have the immediacy of an air or water shortage. The result is that cultures can conceal some resource scarcity in their demand structures either by going to imports, moving to domesticated species, or changing the economic dependence upon them. This shuffling action is not available when water and air supplies are imperilled.

What is in nature has been seen by urban-industrial society as a source of supply or as a sink for waste. If one is a critic of such behavior, renewing systems are simply the victims of such decision-makers. A far rarer perception sees that energy itself may be subject to an analogous exhaustion.

This is not a matter of sufficiency of fuel supply. Rather, it is a question of the energy flow itself. As the ecologist Paul Colinvaux has observed about the energy in biological systems,

> . . . .energy cascades through our system from trophic level to trophic level, and must lose something of its ability to do work at each bounce in that vital cascade, just as the second law of thermodynamics tells us it does. As the energy flow proceeds, so the flow gets less.(50)

Risk can arise in this lessening. The process of energy degradation that occurs is crudely analogous to the entropy law. This is especially evident when one considers that wastage or conservation of ergodic powers may not have determined the evolutionary success of individual species.

And yet, increasingly, some are beginning to wonder if nature will assert its irreducible autonomy in relation to energy as well as in connection with the renewing environment. More will matter than what high-energy growth imposes upon environmental systems. Indeed, urban-industrial society's own high-energy growth demands may control the ultimate limits. Most solutions for curing the harm of high-energy demands to nature involve the continued availability of energy cascades. But what if the possibility of the energy cascades' very existence were threatened?

For this reason, the work of Ramon Margalef has been viewed with hope by the speculatively minded. He has attempted to identify the relationship between ecosystems and how an identity between information and negative entropy results. In this way the structure would be maintained for the most efficient use of energy and the reduction of entropy, according to his theory.

It is with reluctance that many view this theory with dubiety. Aside from the occurrence of evolution in species rather than ecosystems, the theory's major flaw is allegedly the assumption of a closed information system capable of reducing energy degradation. This purportedly ignores what happens to present production whose consumption is foregone as the result of information received into ecosystems intent on maximal benefit from energy. As Paul Colinvaux describes the fate of that excess production:

> Some goes to decomposers; some is used to enable large plants to hold space; some accumulates as litter.(51)

In short, the criticism is that energy must be lost in the energy transfer process. Can information be properly identified with the forces that counteract the loss of energy? Ecosystems seek maximal benefit from energy. Hence, they can neither be a closed system that reduces energy degradation nor accumulators of information that constitutes a negative entropy. Yet it is in negentropy that the optimistic, far-seeking mind of Buckminster Fuller finds great hope.(52)

But as an ecologist, Paul Colinvaux calls "litter" what others might describe as information, negentropy, or any sort of energy conservation. Unlike the optimism inherent in the theory of Margalef, Colinvaux seems compelled to conclude that this "litter" is another part of the energy-degradation process of life, converting free to bound energy. At best, the life systems are low entropy demandants, but they do not produce negentropy. Perhaps, as argued by Buckminster Fuller, the human mind is a source of this negentropy; but natural ecosystems, as said by many, do not serve the hopeful purpose put forward by Margalef.

Philosophically, there is nothing particularly new in any of this. Since the middle of the nineteenth century it has been assumed that a force exists in the life principles for bringing on energy, death and chaos, a termination through an irrevocable procedure. The basis of the pessimism of the brothers Brooks and Henry Adams, and of their circle in Boston, was predicated on this. It was no accident that the dynamo plays such a malevolent role in Henry Adams' writing about the Virgin and the Dynamo.

The attitude, however, was considered extravagant as a basis for any routine worry since energy had been degrading for a long time. The time until chaos and the energy death seemed to contemporaries of the Adams brothers in Boston in the Gay Nineties to be very far away, indeed. In any event, there was no reason to spoil dinner by a contemplation of how much energy the cook-stove had irrevocably degraded from the earth's total store.(53)

The knowledge of ecologists concerning the irrevocable degradation of energy lacks dominating current importance. Rather, how high-energy demand impacts upon, and may speed up, natural processes bids fair to be more significant. If the high-energy demand structure is speeding up the degradation of energy, this may pose the severest natural limitation of all.

The imagery may yet seem extreme, but, still, the accelerations make one unsure. The argument is made that economics should abandon its imagery borrowed from classical mechanics, and shift to an imagery of energy degradation or entropy. In this way, the governing of the economy by biophysical processes would be given adequate reflection in economic thinking. The agreeable merit of this would be to bring into full recognition the irreversibility of certain actions relative to life and energy. The emphasis upon the reversible character of actions in mechanics would be muted.

Qualitative change in the universe takes order continuously and irrevocably toward disorder. This may have special importance for a high-energy demand structure based on an open-ended expectation of increasing energy cascades. The working out of this natural degradation process is slow, but it is ceaseless and cumulative.(54)

In the terms of energy degradation, waste is the product of human economic processes and must increase in greater proportion than the increase in economic activity. Nature cannot be a sink, therefore, in which these "spillovers" can ever be "lost." The limitation on a high-energy demand structure is the stock of low entropy on the planet, which turns all renewable flow resources eventually into the non-renewable stock resources. Persons holding this view would use up the stock of low entropy at a minimum rate of depletion. However, the pattern of human behavior, under the conditions of high-energy growth, has been that of a "fantastic spendthrift" who has carelessly satisfied non-vital demands at the expense of a fuller life in the future.(55)

Maybe Buckminster Fuller, optimistically harking back to the transcendental view of his great-aunt, the philosopher Margaret Fuller (Marchesa Ossoli), is right when he insists that information can counteract the loss of energy. But maybe he is wrong.

The possibility, even if centuries removed, of the unavailability of energy for a human culture, by then totally dependent on pulsating energy cascades, ought to cause a certain pause for reflection. If the possibility exists, then the truly ultimate sink for the waste products of the present high energy demand structure is not really the renewing environment at all. It will be the irreversible procedure called so poetically, "the energy death." This would be the ultimate material boundary for human imagination. One can only hope that those are wrong who believe the expanding levels of demand for energy can appreciably hasten that day.

10 Integrating Future Energy and Environmental Actions

BOUNDLESS DEMAND AND THE LIMITING ENVIRONMENTAL RESPONSE

Urban-industrial society, having segregated the costs imposed upon nature from the accumulated profits, insists that high-energy growth has successfully mastered nature. To make such a success positive, a belief in an infinitude of potential resources is required. Then it would follow that the sort of high-energy growth the long established urban-industrial economies have pursued in northwestern Europe, North America, and Japan will be possible on a global scale.(1)

The demands for high-energy growth have so far doomed efforts to stabilize growth and preserve environmental interrelationships. Resistance by nature has not been permitted by urban-industrial society, if resistance could be overcome. As it has long existed, the dependency of the demand structure for high-energy growth has rested upon open-ended and undifferentiated expansion.(2)

For urban-industrial society under the conditions of high-energy growth, technology has become a social magic. Technology has supposedly mastered nature, with technology having tighter feedback requirements for evaluation than even magic. Through technology, urban-industrial society purports to have compelled the adaptation of the renewing environment to the demands made upon it.(3)

The French economist Jean Fourastie, even as he conceded that technical innovation alone is not sufficient to sustain life-support systems, claims that technology exclusively can move the mass of the world's population from misery to affluence. Technology is the talisman of the future. The American economist Sidney Pollard invests technology with a magic property: people must believe this is the way to a technically brightened future, or they will despair totally.(4) Substantial silence remains, however, on what all this means for the sustainability of the renewing environment.

The scheme presently renders any cost-benefit ratio analysis nearly impossible. In most talk about "weighing gains and losses," or arguing that "more means better," urban-industrial society has chosen to glide over the degree to which the present discounts the future. All views alleging technology as the solution of every future problem make optimistic assumptions about both energy and the renewing environment.(5)

People who hold this sort of faith in technology think energy will be abundant. They believe – or at least hope – that technological costs can be cheap relative to the costs of capital and labor. They are convinced that technology will cause no entropy problem in the conversion of sources into energy cascades. And they act as if natural systems will have an unlimited capacity to serve as sinks and traps for the various kinds of off-fall. When technology is magic, rigorous qualitative comparisons become part of a magic-lantern slide show.

It is simple to serve the future by projecting old trends or narrowing the terms upon which predictions are to be made.(6) But determining what values are being freighted in the extrapolated figures is much harder. Because values are concealed therein, the prediction works as if a demon had gotten into the calculator. As the historian Warren Wager describes this demon, it represents a flaw

> . . .of unintended and unforeseeable growth, too rapid and too complex to be assimilated by mortal man in the time allowed. . .(E)verything has happened and everything has been demanded and everything has been unveiled and unleashed all at once, (so that) knowledge, power, commodities, people, desires, and wastes (have exploded). . . .We are simultaneously at the zenith of history and on the brink of total and irreparable catastrophe.(7)

Suddenly some of humanity have realized that the demand for open-ended energy growth has processed the renewing environment without assisting the natural restorative strengths inherent in nature. Urban-industrial society has waxed on its demands without foreseeing apparent growth limits. Natural systems are now showing severe and perhaps irreversible disturbances.

The demands for high-energy growth have put the seal of urban-industrial society upon the renewing environment. In so doing, the vulnerability of the latter has been revealed, along with the steady increase in the vulnerability of the high-energy demand structure itself. Humanity, in setting a seal upon nature, has once more underscored its own dependence upon renewing natural systems. The human appetite for energy and goods has been shown to be infinite. The finitude of the renewing environment under the burden of that appetite has been increasingly revealed.(8)

The North American Review stated in the early 1970s, "Perhaps it is time to convene an environmental Nuremburg to establish that ecocide is morally and legally as culpable as genocide."(9) But why an accused whose actions had involved personal survival in the acts inciting the charge of ecocide?

Technological and institutional innovation offers humanity hope as well as grounds for despair in this situation. How else can one talk about human responsibility if one does not believe in the importance of the products of human ingenuity? Perhaps it is an egoistic position, but it is a defensible egoism.

The responsibility of urban-industrial society for the renewing environment is not a total responsibility. Since humanity did not invent an organism called "Nature," they are not liable for all nature's actions. But urban-industrial society, like all living things, is part of an interactive-reactive systemic operation in nature. Hence, there is far more responsibility in the high-energy demand structure than many want to be the case.

Nor will the size of the responsibility diminish. Once this is socially perceived and acted upon, a movement toward urban-industrial survival will develop. The endless discount operation, trading the renewing environment for ephemeral current profits, will then cease.

THE RELATION OF TECHNOLOGICAL INNOVATION TO THE RENEWING ENVIRONMENT

Conditions of high-energy demand have made much of the world's population dependent upon brittle relationships with the renewing environment. Many see the problem only as a creature of the OPEC oil cartel's arbitrary power to fix supply and price. But artificial energy problems, such as a cartel can impose, are not the grave crisis urban-industrial energy usages have created relative to nature and the society's own survival.

In some ways, humanity's natural milieu has been turned into something as alien and artificial as a spaceship. Many in urban-industrial society have become passive recipients of the benefits of high-energy growth.   Anything that interrupts the energy cascades could represent a fatal result. Fatality could occur directly by stopping energy supplies in the midst of winter. It could also occur indirectly by affecting the quantity or price of food as a result of the diminution in energy for farm operations.

The essential purpose of urban-industrial society has been to impose a seeming order upon natural systems. The wild order and variant richness in nature have not been appealing to those for whom organization means the reduction of complex problems to simple decisions. As H. van der Haas has said in describing urban-industrial society, such organizers believe that they base their decisions upon facts and only facts.(10)

Consequently, decision-makers in urban-industrial society dissect their values by analyzing them in terms of facts which they have concluded exist. The facts are then made part of a pattern for preferred simplicity, never more simply than when the decision-makers insist their values have been determined by those alleged facts. The process totally ignores how matters have been viewed so as to define them as facts, and denies that the alleged facts are pregnant with values.

A rhetorical question, posed by the National Coal Association in the United States, exemplifies how this process relates to energy:

Can a nation stand further marginal improvements in the quality of its natural environment at the expense of draining its energy strength and stalling its economic development?(11)

What is at issue, however, is neither a "marginal improvement" of the environment nor a "draining of energy strength." The issue is the ability of the environment to sustain its powers of renewal and the steady delivery of energy. If these fail, there will be considerably more happening than a "stall" in economic "development." Urban-industrial society itself would be at issue.

The importance of energy, and of the demand that nature both supply energy and absorb the wastes of the conversion process, has not occurred culturally in any jammed up time-frame. As William McNeil, a historian of western civilization, informs us, the history of that civilization has been a "series of breakthroughs toward the realization of greater and greater power." For that reason, the power that can protect both the source of energy supplies and the ability of the renewing environment to deal with the rise in energy cascades must be enlarged and exercised. The constant and intensifying self-transformation of society under conditions of high-energy growth must mean an

. . .institutionalization of deliberate innovation in the form of industrial research laboratories, universities, military general staffs, and planning commissions of every sort, an accelerating pace of technical and social change.(12)

Under conditions of high-energy growth, William McNeil has said a dominant "radical rationality" prevails. Under such conditions, the entire population, the rich and the powerful as well as the poor and weak, are completely uncertain as to their chances for individual survival should the high-energy demand structure collapse. In order to protect themselves from such a "radical rationality," a demand has developed for

. . .a heavy weight of bureaucratic routine. . .to set powerful brakes upon the dizzy pace of change which gives men vertigo today. . .(13)

At a time when technology is coming up with continual changes, the market is concerned only with marginal utility, financial institutions care only for a maximum return on investments, and the renewing environment shows clear signs of stress, people have been turning to the state to provide all the certainty, predictability, and ultimate security that is elsewhere so singularly lacking.(14) Yet what the state can provide under continuing demands for open-ended growth is extremely precarious.

The institutions that exist under conditions of high-energy growth represent, after all, a bias that is more developmentally oriented than environmentally protective. For decades, many of these government institutions have pursued policies of market saturation and unconfined growth. Recently concerns have been expressed for energy efficiency, even more recently than the interest in environmental protection. But the institutions have scarcely begun to adequately respond to these changes, assuming such changes in attitude have indeed occurred.

Institutions in the past have found it sufficient to merely invoke such terms as "security" and "affluence" in order to justify their growth-intended actions.(15) A task force of the Rockefeller Brothers Fund described such conduct:

> . . .historically, public opinion has favored development almost irrespective of the cost to the environment. Our laws and institutions. . .reflect a pro-development bias. . . . Processes that allow for sensitive accommodations and balances. . .are not yet in effect in most areas.(16)

The pollution of the renewing environment has not been a minor externality aberrantly imposed. Instead, the consequence of concentrating only on servicing the demand for growth in energy conversion and materials' exploitation has been accompanied by an indifference to the ability of natural systems to handle conversion and exploitation at such rising levels. If this had been the result of some easily adjustable economic disequilibrium, then one could only insist that the minor adjustments be made.

This is precisely the insistence of Herman Kahn, because he does see these as "unresolved problems" that will be adjusted with fair simplicity in a manner not disruptive to current urban population concentrations, the demands of existing lifestyles, or the types of public investments being made. These "unresolved problems" include such subjects as a growing likelihood of world famine, the pollution and subsequent shortage of air and water, and the destruction of the bio-equilibrium.

But in the Kahn lexicon, technological innovations will also treat the polluted air and water, desalinate the ocean, provide chemical agriculture, and make urban life better.(17) Presumably, no shortage of energy for accomplishing these salvaging actions would occur, nor would the renewing environment find it difficult to deal with the side-effects of so much energy application. In its result, this view matches popular attitudes that focus only on the allegedly temporary character of shortages in the energy supply and their consequent economic dislocations. The popular mind, too, focuses on quick technological fixes for alternative energy supplies and anticipates that any larger problems will be resolved so as to comfortably maintain the present system.

One might not be a blind, bigoted pessimist to think these "unresolved problems" mentioned by Herman Kahn could prove resistant to bland solutions. Simply increasing applications of technology, even if one believed technology could ultimately rescue both a high-energy society and the renewing environment, will not likely prove an adequate solution. However, if one is to be critical of such optimism, one cannot base reservations simply on the optimists' cheerful extension of today's apparent amenities as the wave of the future. The basis for a view less than cheerful lies in the scant evidence from past human behavior that urban-industrial society will prudently undertake even the minimal actions which Herman Kahn proposes to solve his "unresolved problems."

Technical innovation, on the basis of past experience, is therefore far more likely to further upset any existing equilibrium than to establish stability. A belief that successful technical innovations in the future will not be accompanied by unforeseen and unwanted costs is unjustified. The fanfare cannot be only for the intended benefits. Buckminster Fuller in 1979 might lament the public reaction to the unpredictable drop of Sky Lab: "They think scientists are a part of the problem, not the solution."(18) But when Sky Lab roared across the night skies of southwestern Australia, like a vast heavenly freight train on fire, one might have excused the local population for holding that attitude as they headed for whatever shelter each could personally find.

Indeed, if the economist E. J. Mishan is right when he claims, "the villain. . .is technology itself irrespective of the economic system," then hope that technology will salvage the high-energy demand structure and the renewing environment is destroyed. Mishan even proposes that it will not matter at all whether the world should be capitalist or socialist in its economic organization. Technology impinges on either system's ability to come to grips with the relationship between high-energy growth and natural systems impacted by that growth.(19)

Some would charge that such a position is merely the revival in the late twentieth century of Ludditism. Perhaps it is, but another critic of prevailing fashions, F. R. Leavis, refuses to be daunted by the charge:

> To point out these things is not to be a Luddite, it is to insist on the truth that, in an age of revolutionary and constantly advancing technology, the sustained collaborative devotion of directed energy and directing intelligence that is science needs to be accompanied by. . .the livingness of the deepest vital instinct;. . .(20)

In short, if this be Ludditism, then make the most of it, because the charge of lapsing into intellectual Ludditism will always be laid at the door of anyone skeptical of technical salvation along the lines of Herman Kahn's extrapolating tables.

One need not be a Luddite to take a unified view of the impact of the high-energy demand structure on natural systems. Under this structure, people are influenced by their experience to consider only the restricted choices of existing growth-oriented institutions. Any critic of this structure can expect to be denounced under one pejorative rubric or another.(21)

As the scientific historian Giorgio de Santillana has said:

> . . .(W)hen we are willing to suppose anything that will "work" when nothing is too far-fetched to try, we have surrendered choice of thought and entered a phase that has some of the aspects of intellectual nihilism.(22)

Science and technology under such a prevailing attitude could scarcely have been used except to process natural systems into units of production and consumption for stepping up the tempo of growth. Indifference to the effect upon the systemic relationships being processed made any critic of this process a non-person.

Santillana insists that the essence of the history in high-energy growth over the past two centuries has been one of change, uninterrupted and profound, with a steadily accentuating rhythm, a continuing turbulence that has deprived natural systems in the renewing environment of any chance at equilibrium. Using the alleged tranquility of the eighteenth century as his take-off base for the present, he asserts:

> . . .if one takes the happy eighteenth century. . .as a median point of equilibrium, and if one seeks to make this the focal point round which move the next two centuries, one has told a story of a headstand, in which all words lose their meanings. It has been the force of the Industrial Revolution which has created this headstand: certainly from 1760 to 1960, it has done so to the very utmost, notwithstanding the commonality and continuity of culture, notwithstanding all that still lives in us so fully of Diderot, Goethe, and Stendhal. And today when there is a necessity to have in some degree an understanding of the whole matter, it is appropriate that the organs of comprehension have come to be wanting.(23)

Urban-industrial society, consequently, has been moved into a world in which few simple variables exist. All the variables have become interrelated, and the systems linking the natural and social phenomena have great complexity. This complexity is so convoluted that many avoid the task of accurately and comprehensively describing the web connecting both ecologic and economic activities – much less doing anything to respond to that connection. But the pressure of that connection is denying the present the opportunity to defray factual investigations to the future. The decision-maker, despite the vaunted claims of science and technology, is being thrust back upon the ancient human resources of intuition and good judgment.(24)

Humanity has been moved by a society built on high-energy usages and unlimited growth into a complex series of variable relationships. But no guide has been provided to those relationships, nor a warning posted of the risks involved. Although information concerning those relationships and risks is being developed, the gathering comes at too slow a rate to wait until the entire mosaic has been laid.

What makes lack of knowledge so severe a problem is that the whole demand structure is constructed to block the acquisition of the very kind of knowledge most needed to facilitate the necessary unifying functions. The high-energy demand structure creates masses of new knowledge, even to the point where invention has become a routine. And yet this new knowledge remains serial, discrete, fragmenting, and itself an imposition of further open-ended demand for growth.

The least such processes of automatic invention have called for are profound changes in institutions. It is insufficient to join in the chant, "Men have become Gods."(25) Such a chant is merely hubris.

Technology has been the means to subject nature to the rational control of the human scientific mind. Most of the conflict and turmoil, ensuing from that endeavor, have come from a too narrow base of knowledge about nature. The narrowness of this base makes the exercise of the human will irrational, even as the self-confident assertion of rationality is made.(26) This narrowness for rational action limits technology as well as intensifies the limitations inherent in the operation of the renewing environment.

Technological innovation can take an important part in establishing a viable relationship between high-energy demand structure and the renewing environment. Certainly it cannot be dispensed with, whatever the risks involved. But there must be modesty in technology's use and not mythic nonsense about acting divinely. With this more humble perspective, technological innovation may save both the high-energy demand structure, of which it is a necessary part, and the renewing environment upon which all aspects of human life depend.

ARTIFICIAL REGIMES AND THE RENEWING ENVIRONMENT

As early as 1877, Ernst Kopp observed that human culture seeks to turn all of nature into an artificial environment. Based upon what he saw happening in the age of steam, Kopp argued that humanity wanted to draw both its own ideas and nature into an urban-industrial society, thereby making humanity the unique artificer of nature. Everywhere in nature, urban-industrial society had put the concrete print of its demands as a memorial. And Kopp saw this as the beginning of a shift from a natural to an artificial environment.(27)

Philip Wagner, in pointing up this historical insight of Kopp's, noted a generation ago that the human relationship to nature is mediated by artificial agencies. Humanity's traditional security and independence have been correlated with the amount of artificial control the individual could exert over natural forces. Humanity and nature have long established a general symbiosis as the result of the increasing artificial control human demand structures have asserted over the whole of the environment.

Society puts artificial structures of its own making between itself and nature in order to mediate human contact with natural systems. The result is a symbiosis, a state of mutual dependence between human demand and natural systems. But above all, it is a symbiotic state that is primarily of human manufacture.

With the rise of the energy cascades, artificial environments have spread over the entire globe. The urban-industrial social form has been carried to the most remote places. Its specializations, its widening generalization of consumption patterns, its material affluence that is privatized from the total costs of its processes, and its accompanying vulnerability to renewing environmental limitations, have become a global set of phenomena. The rigorous, broad, and accelerating assertion of humanity's influence over nature guarantees an environmental artificiality. Technical means are part of an artifice designed to raise the productivity of labor, the unit output of the industrial plant, the rate of mineral extraction, the yields of land, the production of energy, and the intensity of investment to previously unparalleled degrees. As Philip Wagner summarized, the resulting

> . . .artificial environment. . .is the new harvesting ground of consumers, who stalk. . .as the nomad Semang prowl the forest in quest of natural products.(28)

The consequence for the renewing environment could only be one of accelerating pressure to sustain these rising levels through the institution of urban sprawl, the supply of the networks to sustain it, and the maintenance of the flow in the energy cascades. Under these conditions, government has generally been only the means of financing the facilities for holding together this sprawling, disconnected, intensely consuming demand structure.(29)

The result has been the imposition of heavy costs upon the renewing environment which the demand structure has refused to internalize in its processes. The limitations operating within renewing systems ultimately will require a redistribution of the relationships which have so carelessly passed on these costs and refused to recognize them. Because of the open-ended, undifferentiated character of the present demand for growth, the public authority will have to concentrate the force necessary to carry through this redistribution of relationships. To do differently jeopardizes the balance needed to sustain the renewing environment and the energy supply upon which the urban-industrial demand structure directly depends. Since humanity has insisted on going at cross-purposes to natural systems, the burden of the costs previously put upon nature will have to be deflected directly onto the machinery of law and government.

Government will respond traditionally by creating artificial regimes to minimize the social change needed under conditions of high-energy demand. These regimes will seek to increase the ability to accommodate this demand. The effort to guarantee energy supplies, and the reception of wastes in natural systems, jeopardizes the viability between urban-industrial society and the renewing environment. Government will go in this direction, even if resented; and these artificial regimes cannot be entirely benign, however valuable they prove themselves. In the foreboding words of Philip Wagner:

> . . .authentic redistributive agencies often invoke as much violence. . .and show as little respect for individual "rights" and interests, as do criminal and predatory raiders.(30)

Such words make grim predictions. But they do not seem inapposite when taken in relation to the burden of urban sprawl, the dispersant and demanding networks holding together the functions transpiring in the disconnected urban space, and the environmental pressures that will likely compel a redistribution of priorities under conditions of high-energy dependence. An already substantially artificial environment has been created, thanks to human ingenuity. Where artifice ends and nature begins can scarcely any longer be determined. This is a highly vulnerable condition, since the artifice up to this point has taken so little of nature into account.

The need for further human intervention, along the lines of consciously created artificial regimes interleaved with natural systems, is becoming more and more apparent. Operationally, the historian William Irwin Thompson assures us that the so-called radical suggestions of the Club of Rome for limitations on growth are in this category. The Club proposes, he says, nothing more than an artificial regime for all of nature. This solution would be technical, require management and bureaucracy on an international level, and merely exchange the goal of an expansionist economy for a stationary one.

Simply put, Thompson sees critics like the Club of Rome as only interested in a little change to save high-energy demand. He sees artificial regimes as adjustments to what has existed for over two centuries in urban-industrial society. It is just a shift in the direction of public finance, meant to do nothing more than save the large investment in what presently exists.(31)

Obviously, people such as Thompson believe something far more profound than any of the proposals of the Club of Rome is needed. They resent the dominance of the guardian-scientists, implicit in the artificial regimes of the Club's proposals:

> ...who can promise to keep the life-support systems of Space Ship Earth working — at the price of absolute scientific control over environments and populations.(32)

But Thompson believes that people, though they have not reached the limits of the human imagination, have come to some boundaries in nature's present systems, including the supply of energy for a high-energy demandant society. Thompson, far from turning to artificial regimes sustained by technological innovation, has lost hope in technology's ability to solve problems.

If nothing is done to alter the present course, then breaks will occur eventually in both the flow of the energy cascades and the operations of natural systems. If changes are made, there may still be irrational interim responses that would produce similar kinds of breaks, though the hope is that these would be transient. Certainly unified planning, connecting the demand for greater energy with the capabilities for renewal in the environment, has not previously been pursued by urban-industrial society. The energy and environmental problems of the late twentieth century have resulted from this lack of unified planning. Their manifestations have become clearly visible, even though the growth biases of urban-industrial society have obscured their causes.

The belief is growing, however, that either a change in urban-industrial demand patterns will occur or else artificial regimes will require massive investments accommodating natural systems to those patterns.   Perhaps the future will represent a pastiche of both. The future may see an incremental adaptation as foreseen by Warren Johnson, in which urban-industrial society will adapt to an age of scarcity, as that society similarly adapted to an age of affluence.(33) Or Barry Commoner may have been right when he said that, by 1990 the United States could supply all its mobile fuel users with plant-derived alcohol.(34) Or Armand Hammer, of Occidental Petroleum, may have been correct when he said these same mobile fuel users would receive a substantial portion of their supplies after 1986 from domestic shale oil.(35)

One might hope for such changes. A permanent break in either the energy supply or renewing environmental systems must be avoided. Bringing viability to the relationship of the high-energy demand structure and nature is an accomplishment that may have one, or more, of the solutions some optimistically offered in the 1970s.

But however optimistic one tries to be, one can be sure of none of these possibilities. The construction of artificial regimes for saving both the renewing environment and the demand system impacting upon it may be truly essential. Yet, despite this potential significance, little is being done to build such regimes. Technology still offers slight evidence of a capability of sustaining the renewing life-support systems on the same scale with which technology supports the growth in open-ended, undifferentiated demand.(36)

At one time, a cultural historian such as Arnold Toynbee could confidently write that humanity had "command over non-human nature."   He could belittle such a question as being "a side issue," denominated by him as "the obviousness of the fact that man is relatively good at dealing with non-human nature." For Toynbee in those years, "Man has been a dazzling success. . . ."(37)

But scarcely twenty years later, Toynbee's views on this subject had altered dramatically. By concentrating upon human self-centeredness in relation to nature, he argued, that urban-industrial society had sought to make the human species secure. But humanity had not thereby been made secure. Conditions of high-energy conversion had imposed enor-mous costs upon nature, showing the human inability to positively manage non-human nature. In pursuing human security through open-ended, undifferentiated growth, urban-industrial society had created a far greater vulnerability than previously feared. And Toynbee no longer believed that humanity had dealt at all well with non-human nature.(38)

Such human artifacts as radioactivity, industrial wastes, and the weight of demand for material resources have created the sort of burden that has endangered the survival of life forms on the planet.(39) As urban-industrial society had sought mastery over energy and the environment, the inadequacies of its technological artifice were exposed. Urban-industrial technology is an artifice, ranging from such process systems as pricing to megalopolitan sprawl, that seemed to eclipse nature.(40) But nature's reaction now offers the promise of undermining the magnitude of much of what this high-energy demandant social structure has accomplished.(41)

The humanly constructed environment of artificial regimes is bearing down upon the present generations in the world at gathering speed. This need not result in what Toynbee has called "the reckless game of overwhelming and obliterating Nature by the imposition on her of an artificial environment created by technology."(42) It can instead result in an alteration of the way high-energy demand impacts upon nature, and can produce the kind of innovation that would reinforce the renewable characteristics in the environment.

Perhaps artificial regimes would be only a negotiated incremental change. They may not be the means to the basic reordering of activity that many believe necessary. Still the changes these artificial regimes would introduce ought not to be despised. Even if in themselves inadequate to redress the situation, these regimes might construct the avenues upon which later, needed, basic changes could take place.

Of course, perhaps not even artificial regimes are perceived as necessary by some. For them, nature continues to have her plentiful aspect, careless of any human ophelimity and able to support any pleonectic demand. The economist Wilfred Beckerman has spoken at length on behalf of this view:

> (T)he whole of the "finite resources" argument against continued economic growth is based on a series of logical muddles, dubious moral judgments, a scant respect for the historical facts, and a complete ignorance of the way that economies adjust to changes in demand and supply. . . . (T)he "ecodoomster" case (may) go by default because, in the end, the public is exasperated by its basic exaggerations, moral confusions, and pseudo-scientific methods.(43)

Anyone concerned with the ability of the renewing environment to respond to the challenges of high-energy society can only conclude that a good many "experts" are walled off from the ideas challenging their expertise. As a result, their judgments tend to operate in a pre-selected manner making them acceptable to the growth-oriented system that granted them the status of "expert."

While in the late twentieth century one can talk of collective knowledge, one cannot talk of unified knowledge. Indeed, there is even a hostility to the "experts" becoming collectively aware of the extent to which corporate actions threaten either nature or the high-energy growth conditions. If knowledge were unified, then the mediatory power of artifice would be increased through the application of knowledge possessed in urban-industrial society.(44) At least, this would permit focusing upon the problems in the renewing environment as well as upon what might be done through economic investment and technological innovation to solve them.(45)

If urban-industrial society now fears the products of its artifice, then society can only be cavilling at a condition created by its own demands. In a great reversal of responsibilities, society must become liable for the maintenance of nature's renewing system, even as the demand structure remains far from exhausting its ability to generate more demands.

And as for nature, as Rene Dubos has said, "resources don't exist until we invent them."(46) Urban-industrial society has found its material wealth in the "invention" of these "resources." Yet at the moment, even all this accumulated wealth may not be sufficient to sustain the natural systems under the impact of high-energy demands. There is, still, a limit to what artificial regimes can do.

These artificial regimes will not make Gods of men. Science and technology, the institutions of law and government, the mechanisms of politics and the market under planned artificial regimes will, at best, assist in a shift in the way contemporary society views nature relative to demands made upon renewing systems. So long as the renewing environment is viewed basically as a universal sink for waste and an endless source for energy and materials, artificial regimes can only incrementally palliate the more severe conditions. If urban-industrial society could view nature as a partner with limited capacities, then artificial regimes could play more than a marginally mediatory role.(47)

Many of the energy and environmental problems now being experienced are the direct consequence of social constraints or economic practices, rather than biophysical limitations. These can be alleviated by changes in the operation of the market or by amendments to the legal system that would clear the way for different action.(48) But not all energy and environmental problems fall into this category; and these problems will prove the most nearly intractable.

Wastes introduced into the biomass, working their way up the food chain and using humanity as the final waste sink, are among these tougher problems.(49) Also in this group are such reactions as changes in the atmospheric ozone layer or the ability of the oceanic plankton to sustain themselves when systemically insulted by steady accretions in pollutants. These threats to environmental renewability call most strongly for reaction in the growth demandant urban-industrial society.

The institution of artificial regimes for dealing with energy and environmental dangers will not be sufficient. Basic changes in the operation of the demand structure are ultimately needed. But in the interval, artificial regimes that can assist the functioning of naturally renewing systems must be constructed. At the very least, artificial regimes will help to temporarily preserve human options.

THE ENERGY AND ENVIRONMENTAL COMPULSIONS FOR NORMATIVE PLANNING

Little has been done through law to create bargaining arenas within which proposed technological innovations could be prospectively evaluated.   If such arenas could be provided, decision-making could be negotiated concerning change before society became attuned to both individuated benefits or distressed by the shunted-off costs. But the dominant practice has been the steady, routinized stream of technical activities, that shut out the opportunity for a negotiated, consciously willed, particularized decision.(50)

Rather than trying to negotiate alleged differences to a comprehensive conclusion, the over-arching tendency has been for decisions to come smoothly from pre-established routines designed to serve fairly narrow missions. This has given technology the appearance of a momentum of its own. It is as if social institutions had appointed technology as their surrogate for making hard decisions concerning values, goals, and justifications. Deferring to automatic systems has become the easy preference.(51)

Some accountants have argued, in lieu of such deference, that the managers of production units ought themselves to undertake the assessment of what their work does to the environment. They believe that it is a mistake to leave this accounting to government alone.   Superficially, this resembles the environmental impact statement; but it is quite different.

First of all, this form of social cost accounting would not be limited to statutory purposes. And, perhaps still more important, the task would be an internally imposed one, not an effort undertaken solely to satisfy an external bureaucracy. Although their concern for the renewing environment may be slight relative to other interests, the accountants who propose this form of accounting would urge production units to consider the impact of technological innovation capable of harming the operations of these units.(52)

Because it seems folly to wait for self-generated internalized comprehensive business analyses, the pressure has grown for some kind of governmentally mandated, prospective assessment system.   The United States Congress has created an Office of Technology Assessment to guide it. Others have proposed a Science Court. Given the fact that the enlargement of scientific knowledge has become a synonym for the enlargement of humanity's coercive power over nature, the protection of nature requires that regular assessment mechanisms be created to examine the prospects when innovation is first proposed.

The action forcing procedures of environmental impact statements (EIS) required under the National Environmental Protection Act have been used for this purpose. Although they have produced far more juridical activity than was first anticipated, the EIS has encouraged self-analysis to some extent. Certainly, if no effort is made for either internally generated or externally mandated, prospective judgments, there can only be a continuous chronic recurrence of crises initiated by automatic, unforeseen, and consequentially indifferent technological change.(53)

It has become increasingly apparent that further change affecting the flow of energy and the renewing environment must not be considered as only the intentional product. Also to be considered is the potentiality of costs and burdens, never intended by those proposing changes, which foresight can reasonably predict. Refusing to do so threatens not only renewing environmental systems, but human life – assuming human life has a significance independent of its life-support systems.(54)

A basic social decision is required; and if not made, Hasan Ozbekhan, the information specialist, assures us that humanity will be replaced in decision making by their own technology. In this epigrammatic way, he summarizes the risk humanity will run if human purpose is no more than perpetually innovating new technologies. To maintain the present modes of conduct in this manner, and to project them into the future without any effort to alter unreasonable burdens on energy and environmental systems, is to subordinate the human imagination to the operations of technical artifices.

Much of the present situation has arisen, claims Ozbekhan, because humanity has been led to believe that all fundamental constraints relative to the renewing environment have been overcome:

> . . .by multiplying our means, by discovering ways of using them efficiently, that is economically, by getting to understand the nature of maximizing processes, by expanding through cumulation and substitution the ensemble of our techniques.(55)

Compellingly, this expert on computers says planning should not see its future limited by information already known, focusing concern only upon present operational dimensions. What Ozbekhan demands is normative planning, a decision to act upon determined values.

Planning that merely extrapolates present experience will likely result only in a self-regeneration of the current situation. An insistence on measuring everything by present rules unexposed to criticism will determine future modalities by the application of unexamined rules. Simple extrapolation represents, in short, a fundamental unwillingness to consciously shape any aspect of the future and surrenders this generation's decision making to an automatic incorporation of the fragmented decisions of an earlier period of high-energy growth.(56)

Humanity must not believe that they can delegate the responsibility for decision making to technology. Values are external to technological actions. If no unifying knowledge is present when technology is applied, then decisions will go by default to the most discrete, isolated, and individuating units in society.(57)

To cut off dialogue, to leave matters of decision with technological routine, and to refuse to make conscious, normative decisions will expose urban-industrial society to the dark risk predicted by Giorgio de Santillana:

> (I)nevitably, if science were to insist on presenting itself as an assemblage of devices for pragmatic power and economy of thought. . .(just) the researcher's business simply to go ahead. . .(wherein) the scientist has ceased taking part in the great dialogue as a cultural being. . .(then) the little gusts of revolt blowing through society are the kind that the statesmen might find worthy of attention. . .(W)hat is left of tradition has a way of turning against those who disregard it.(58)

In the case of normative planning, should there be a shift to it, a distinction must be made between the basic purposes of planning and regulation. Simply put, planning should operate in an anticipating mode, with consideration for a long perspective. It should include within its functioning a determination of values to be served. Regulation, on the other hand, proceeds incrementally in response to directly presented problems.

Values are the heart of normative planning. In a dynamic high-energy system, any tendency to simplify the inherently complex problems has to be dangerous activity. Many people attracted by systems analysis are drawn to the seeming simplicity in its programming. But they risk omitting the multi-value choices truly present in such hard-to-summarize items as aesthetic, ecological, and non-economic cultural values. Yet this multi-value choice analysis is what is most needed in planning.(59)

The normative planner wishes to draw the future into the present, at least to the extent of a simulation. In order to do that, this planner must seek a time-invariant data base against which the plan, at some presently remote time, can be tested. Otherwise, the plan will react spastically to future shock.

During a period of value-dissonance, such as has characterized the twentieth century, the problem of selecting the values upon which a normative plan can be based is particularly difficult. This is most true when the value-dissonance is synchronous with the technological innovation of an open-ended, high-energy system. But values do exist and their selection is not a matter of de gustibus.

Value dissonance is the greatest threat to normative planning. This inability to agree on values as they concern the course of future energy demands and the ability of the renewing environment to respond to those demands could abort normative planning at its inception. The field of planning could thereby be left to the automatic routines of technology and the high-energy demand structure. Certainly there exists no current social agreement on the need for, the worth of, or the chance at fully articulated, previously agreed upon social values of even the most immediately pragmatic sort.(60)

Normative planning, however, believes in ways to attain a consciousness of the possible. The possible limitations in the resources
drawn from the environment are its concern, as well as alternative,
practicable solutions to problems that define the possible consequences
of future actions. The normative plan is not just an extension of
production figures, although normative planning requires specific
knowledge. Under such a plan, urban-industrial society would engage in
comprehensive actions, requiring value choices.

For example, in 1979, the Battelle Memorial Institute had worked
out plans to assist local communities to react to constrictions in energy
supplies. Actions like this community energy management plan are
value-based planning. It requires the initial governmental decision
against continued urban sprawl. Spreading suburbs can be stopped and
the percentage of gasoline used in private cars lowered. Such plans
mean developing "islands of density," either in the central city or in the
suburbs, that take advantage of the "village concept" in concentrating
retail stores and services institutions. Concentrations of this kind make
public transit, car pools, and bicycling feasible alternatives to the
private car with its one user at the wheel. The city, under such
normative planning, ceases to be so much the victim of growth and
becomes more of a beneficiary.(61)

At the moment, predicting the future consists of predicting the
future of technology. Certainly the future of technology cannot be
omitted from normative planning. But technology's future need not
exhaust all the possibilities for the future of the world, as something
like the community energy management plan illustrates.

Even so, the current trends in the present high-energy, growth
demandant system seem well established. They still lead in the direction of subordinating the energy supply and the environment's renewability to the surge for further rises in the energy cascades and the
exploitation of resources. Under these conditions of furious growth,
everything must remain at a level of extreme adaptability.(62)

As Hasan Ozbekhan insists: "The future should be viewed as a
solution to the present, not as our extension of it."(63) This is, of
course, a goal and not an accomplished kind of normative planning. In
the 1960s many planners claimed that as early as the 1970s there would
be fuller and fuller integration of forecasting and planning, to the point
that the technological forecasting function would be "dissolved" in the
planning function.(64) But systemic long-term planning of world scope
remains only a dream. Aurelio Peccei, a founder of the Club of Rome,
describes what does not exist when he insists planners must:

. . .promote the development of the capacity of synthesis, a
capacity that has been neglected so far. . .(I)n the present,
pluralistic, and hectic world, the desideration is the capacity to
incorporate the essence of disparate elements in a synoptic
view. . .combining and reconciling disharmonious elements, situations, problems and phenomena of a technological, social,
economic, psychological character, which originate and develop

independently of one another, possess disparate natures, resilience, dimensions, speeds and trends, but collide and interact to
form the integrated, complex, and changing contemporary
world.(65)

To call this task "difficult," as well as "serious" and "urgent" the
way Peccei does, can only bring a sardonic smile to the lips of anyone
who has tried the most modest variety of planning for the future. After
all, planning for the future is already an integral part of urban-
industrial society under all forms of capital organization. But most of
this planning is intended to produce more of the same, and does not
select values around which, in the words of the physicist Denis Gabor,
humanity can "invent the future."(66)

Any future balance between demands for high growth in energy and
materials' exploitation, on the one hand, and the renewability of nature,
on the other, will not automatically emerge as the work of an invisible
hand. Syncretistic, normative planning is needed because of the complex behavior occurring in the energy demand structure and the
renewing environment. Planning such as this is awesome in its scope,
both absolutely and in relation to the quantity and quality of the
planning actually going on at present. But it will be required, unless a
condition of great pain and distress is preferred.

THE COSTS OF OPEN-ENDED GROWTH IN
THE ENVIRONMENT

To an Aristotelian, and perhaps also to a Marxist, a point exists beyond
which human demand will peak. Thereafter, matters would be fairly
simple for the normative planner of the future, since the demand
structure would operate under stable production and consumption
conditions. All "necessities" having been provided, people would turn to
leisure time recreation for themselves. With need and scarcity overcome, human beings would realize their full potential for thought and
fantasy.

Unfortunately for these prospects, experience under conditions of
high-energy growth indicate that material aspirations can be stimulated
up to a state of pleonexy. The steady acceleration of demand has
effectively denied the possibility of a natural terminus for human desire
at some future time. Indeed, when a society recognizes no limits to
growth, as is the case with the urban-industrial demand structure, any
cessation in growth is a cause of profound fear. Talking about satisfying
"needs" in a structure that simply wants more growth and more
affluence is a pointless exercise.

World conditions, however, are indicating the limitations within the
environment of an unstated policy of open-ended growth. So complex is
growth, and so demanding is it of capital for its accommodation, that
the famous 1950 dicta of the French economist Jean Fourastie seems to
be coming to pass. He predicted that:

. . .technological progress tends wherever it operates, i.e., mainly in the primary and secondary sections, to elimination of
absolute rent (i.e., profits).(67)

The cost of complexity is increased by the need to react to the
research-oriented, routinely inventive urban-industrial system which
works most efficiently in situations described by the sociologist Robert
Merton as "multidimensional interaction." A Soviet-Polish symposium in
1966 at Lvov claimed that the increased cost of infrastructure support
for this system of complex technological self-invention under conditions
of high-energy growth must "lead to a drop in effectiveness directly
proportional to the number of staff raised to the fourth power."(68)

This may, indeed, mean that Fourastie is right. The increasing costs
of absorbing technological innovation in a high-energy demand structure
required to account for its impact upon the renewing environment
might impose costs considered impossible except by those who think in
terms of survival. Profit could become the victim. Anyone favorably
impressed by the capital cost figures of Amory Lovins for providing
varying energy sources must be dismayed at the potential capital risk
that the 1979 proposed United States energy program would incur by
simultaneously developing so many kinds of fuel supplies.(69) This
proposal is like a declaration of war, not on energy but on capital.

Those who are indifferent to such costs, therefore, will still be
compelled to watch them spiraling upward in the effort to maintain the
present urban-industrial system. In order to sustain the automatically
induced traditional growth patterns, there will have to be increased
inflation. The inflation will occur in the numbers engaged in such
support activities as administration, regulation, research, and maintenance of both the demand structure and the renewing environment.
Even when urban-industrial society creates artificial regimes for the
renewing environment, they too will often demand more in the way of
support than they shall return as assistance.

Some insist that this sort of expanding growth, which has been
associated with the rising energy cascades, is necessary for a free,
open, pluralistic society. For them, a stationary state can produce only
an authoritarian governmental structure. Any attempt to prospectively
assess technology would simply substitute bureaucratic committee
intrigue. And what then?

(T)he unknown is the unknown and does not become known
through the vote of a committee – least of all a committee
which. . .would be composed of agents of political power.(70)

Humanity can scarcely call for only "good" inventions and claim that
they can deny licensure to inventions with "bad" future consequences.
As long as there is demand for a geometric progression in the growth
curve of energy cascades and affluence, the accompanying difficulties
cannot be avoided by simply setting up bureaucratic review committees.(71) The unknown may be the unknown; but there is nothing

unforeseeable about the incompatibility of aspirations that want only the "good" from innovations and none, please, of the "bad."

The fact remains, whatever the dangers of trying to cope, that open-ended growth has imposed massive costs upon both the demand structure and the renewing environment. Even those who have enjoyed the bounty realize actions must be taken to deal with the unaccounted costs.(72) As a result, the most individually affluent have been the ones calling for conservation, zero growth, the stationary state, equity rather than growth, and a constitutional right to the quality of life.

Of course the affluent in urban-industrial society continue making heavy demands for growth. But their personal demands are largely either in the tertiary economic stage for services or in the quarternary stage for leisure expenditures. And these latter demands require urban-industrial society to provide what Gerald Piel has called "the common of the wilderness and of the urban ambience."(73)

Conditions have brought these affluent people up against what Lord Keynes described as the "paradox of the aggregate." What are individually desirable – for example, a fast car, a detached suburban villa, a vacation home – have turned out to be frustrations, once they were widely attained. The only ways to maximally enjoy such attainments are either to cut down on the numbers of persons who can find access to them (which threatens the support mechanisms of those already possessing these amenities), or to demand that the government "do something" to insure that there will be a "common of wilderness and urban ambience."

This causes the currently affluent to review once more the proposal of John Stuart Mill for a steady or stationary state. For them it would not mean an end to the cessation of technical innovation, so long associated with the concepts of improvement. The gross national product could keep growing, in the sense of nonmaterial service inputs. The fears of authoritarianism are allayed by the belief that politically the interests of all persons would be made effective through automatically operating processes. The only limitations would be relative to the growth in population, energy conversion, and the consumption of natural resources.(74)

Under the commitment of promises such as this, who would not opt for the steady state instanter? If they believed in its possibility, of course, they would. But somehow one doubts that such a choice really exists. Is it possible for the affluent to have a steady state along with ski lodges in the wilds and scuba vacations in the West Indian reefs? Can the gross national product (GNP) increase from nonmaterial service inputs without requiring a great increase in energy transfers and a greater demand on the renewing environment? One certainly can doubt it. When individuals steadily increase what they regard as resource "needs," they will demand satisfactions so complex that satisfying these new "basic demands" would undercut the chance for a "steady" state.(75)

The current common demand, of course, is _not_ for a steady state. The motif for growth remains as strong as we move toward the end of the twentieth century as when the century opened. Particularly, growth in energy transfers is the expectancy of the future. Growth in the twentieth century has become a social demand and individual desires simply intensify that demand.(76)

Urban-industrial society offers little evidence of a willingness to mute voluntarily its demands upon the renewing environment. The society's decision-makers are not yet in any position to replace "the quantitative framework of exchanges, interactions, and organizations" which are a necessity in the operation – and, hence, the preservation – of the ecosystem. A study group at the University of Wisconsin well described the present situation:

> It is a gigantic one-way flow of elements, essential to life, from the earth into the air and the sea.(77)

Unfortunately, human accounting systems demand simplicity. Yet the test of an ecosystem's health – or its chance at survival under stress – lie in the system's complexity. The stability of any ecosystem is degraded when compelled to serve singly as a source of supply or as a sink for waste. The complexity of urban-industrial society's own demands, instead, have forced simplification upon natural ecosystems, thereby destroying any approximation of ecologic stability. No chance exists, under these conditions, for a natural re-establishment of systemic equilibrium based upon self-regulating mechanisms operating at steady rates and keeping energy in a cycled balance.(78)

Clearly, even should the demand structure do nothing about normative planning for different future behavior, the costs imposed by that demand would continue accumulating. These costs would rise both within the economy and in the operationally renewing systems in the environment. Some individuals, such as Barry Commoner, believe these costs could prove sufficient to overwhelm the economic basis of the current demand structure.(79)

Assuredly, if normative planning dealing directly with these costs is consciously adopted, it would heavily impact upon the urban-industrial demand structure. What previously had been shunted off onto the renewing environment would then be reabsorbed by the system generating the impacting demand. The reverse effect might be as great or greater to the demand structure as the once shunted costs had previously proven to nature. But at least society has the opportunity for conscious choice.

Perhaps the present demand structure wants only a short discount time for itself and the planetary life-support systems. Wilfred Beckerman has only contempt for those who think the earth's resources finite in relation to the potential of high energy demand upon them. But he is prepared to admit he might be wrong and that there could be fatal limits. He is not impressed:

> Furthermore, suppose, that as a result of using up all the world's resources, human life did come to an end. So what? What is so

> desirable about an indefinite continuation of the human spe-
> cies. . .? It may well be that. . .everybody has an instinctive fear
> of death. But one must not confuse this with the notion that in
> any meaningful sense, generations who are not yet born can be
> said to be better off if they are born than if they are
> not. . . .(T)o ensure that successive generations of people must
> be brought into this world is not so obviously a big deal for
> anybody.(80)

No other answers are acceptable to the person taking this view.
Perhaps there is even stoic nobility in thinking in this stark way.
Assuredly such an economic attitude deals comprehensively with the
problems of cost. No need would be present, under these discounting
functions, to spend a cent on extending the energy supply, protecting
the renewing environment, or doing any other sustaining action beyond
a preselected cut-off date for planetary life.

The mass of humanity may be ready to make this trade. If they are
not, then they must begin to consider the costs of change. This will
require choosing values, setting priorities, undergoing expenses – all in
the hope of having a future of greater length than one shortly
discounted.

Perhaps as a prestigious business review said in 1975, "the social
audit is near death."(81) If so, action had better be under way to
resuscitate it. The time is running out in which the urban-industrial
demand structure can provide for the costs that must be incurred to
salvage many of the renewing systems within the environment.

THE IMPORTANCE OF TECHNOLOGY FOR NORMATIVE
ENERGY AND ENVIRONMENTAL PLANNING

It is both artificial and unwise to separate an organism from its
supporting environment. Society under the conditions of high-energy
supply has separated itself cognitively from the renewing environment.
Those within urban-industrial society, who have individually profited
from this separation resist any effort at terminating this separateness.
As Gregory Bateson has said in discussing whether a human being or a
computer "thinks":

> What "thinks" and engages in "trial and error" is the man plus the
> computer plus the environment. And the lines between man,
> computer, and environment are purely artificial, fictitious
> lines. . . .The unit of survival is organism plus environment. We
> are learning by bitter experience that the organism which
> destroys its environment destroys itself.(82)

The failure to take advantage of the potentiality for change has
been most evidently a part of the urban-industrial demand structure.
The result has been a freezing of variables routinely automated to

strengthen the rise of open-ended growth in the use of energy and materials. A refusal to attempt other variables which would lend support to the renewing systems in nature has resulted.(83)

A technology has been created that serves as a mechanism of necessity, with normative planning being denied a significant role once technological innovations had begun. An operation was set in motion at the beginning of the rise of the energy cascades two centuries ago, and it has not been altered since that time.(84)

Ironically, one of the people most insistent on getting in control of this process is the advocate of technological innovation, Buckminster Fuller. He insists on creating artificial regimes that would reform the biophysical environment of urban-industrial society, rather than trying to impose and enforce codes of negative penalties meant to limit the thrust of high-energy demand. For him, the major recourse now available would be to bring:

> . . .to full success the social-support function of world industrial-ization, which consists of all the externalized metabolically regenerating organics of man. . . .(It) must be undertaken with the intent of permitting man's innate faculties and facilities to be realized with subconscious coordination of his organic pro-cess. Reform of the environment's purpose is to defrustrate man's innate capabilities, whether the frustration be by physical environment or by the coordinated reflexes of other humans induced in those humans by the inadequacies of the environ-mental advantages.(85)

In essence, Buckminster Fuller insists upon the externalization of functions originally integral to human beings. He means to integrate the whole of the biophysical environment, all of human knowledge and experience, and the totality of humanity in a conscious, global, decision making process. This decision making would account for what the presently accelerating demands are doing to the stressed environment.

The conscious action Fuller calls for would, as a beginning, increase in high-energy societies the efficiencies of energy transfers which he believes are at present "appallingly low."(86) But most importantly from the point of view of those who indict technology as the jailer of human choice, Fuller insists that, humanistically, the high-energy rise has failed to develop a situation negating the entropy that these tech-nologic innovations have steadily increased.(87)

The technologic imagination has raised the demands for energy transfers which, in turn, has increased entropy and the randomness of events. The reluctance of a demand structure, which derives its profits from such conditions, to adopt a program of either sufficient energy conservation or accountability for renewing environmental systems, has created the severity of the present situation. Technologists such as Fuller insist that actions can be taken to reduce the randomness of events and the consequent entropy.

A great risk is involved, of course, in normative planning as well as in continuing to submit to routinized drift. With all the technology now available — and which will be even more available in the future — the opportunity exists not only to make wise, preserving decisions but also to make hugely destructive ones. A normatively willed future could be as bad or worse than anything a self-generating demand structure might spin out of its own internal routines. Much is imminent in the future, and it could be ecocide as well as irenic models of perpetual bliss.(88)

But if humanity is to accomplish anything positive at all, there must exist a belief that "social institutions and human aspirations can conspire to solve the most daunting problems."(89) Only those who think humanity is predetermined to salvation or extinction could think otherwise. Yet the problems will prove daunting if action adequate to maintaining environmental renewability should continue to be postponed or avoided.

Ecosystems, once exhausted, rarely can be revived by either applications of capital or technology. Until now, the demands for high energy cascades and the exploitation of the environment have produced their worst effects on isolated areas. The inhabitants of exhausted places have been able to emigrate elsewhere or to seek support as dependents from the centers of affluence concentrated by urban-industrial demand. But if exhaustion of the renewable elements within the environment ever became a worldwide phenomenon, then there would be no escape for anyone, however ruthless they might be.

Despite recurring energy supply problems in the 1970s, many continued to insist that humanity are on the verge of universally easing into leisure and affluence through new energy transfers. Growth in human demand and expectation will be paced, according to these clear-eyed visionaries, by concurrently available energy transfers. If they are right, then all will be well. If they are wrong, this is like playing Going to Jerusalem without any chairs at all in the game. When music stops, nobody gets a safe seat. There will be none to take and everyone will go sprawling.(90)

As Lord Keynes has said:

The social object of skilled investment should be to defeat the dark forces of time and ignorance which envelop our future.(91)

Since "investment" in this context must include planning, or forecasting, or inventing the future, one suspects that this would be at least one of the purposes for skill at investment. For this reason, this quotation should be the cause of considerable reflection and supplementation.(92) Anyone who has known great responsibility has known also the fear that events may overwhelm that responsibility. Every effort to penetrate the future with predictions or to control the direction of events — which often constitute the same purpose — has to be taken with the consciousness that failure may always be at hand.(93)

The observation of Lord Keynes clarifies the perilous position of those easily assured by the claim that the future will be more of the same, and that more of the same will be just what a happy future would need. In Keynes' sense, they are thereby part of the "dark forces" who veil the future and who refuse to account for it in their actions. Too often their only response to those expressing doubt about the future's automatically provided joy is one of petulant anger in lieu of their normal indifference to self-query. The suggestion of normative planning for the future bounces off them like hail off concrete.

Options are being shortened. Entropy, despite informational negentropy, proceeds. Energy demands show no limit in the prospect of their growth. The side effects in the dispersal of the effects of energy transfers become more apparent. Although irreversible disaster may not be an immediate possibility, there are upper limits in all natural systems beyond which human demand can only break them. Compared with such breaks, any talk about the ability of nature to "satisfy" the demands of high-energy growth becomes empty wind.

THE VALUE OF DOOMSDAY FOR ENERGY AND THE ENVIRONMENT

During the decade of the 1960s, the urban-industrial demand structure discovered the renewing environment.(94) During the decade of the 1970s, that same demand structure has had to realize the ultimate importance of energy. In both instances, there has been reaction by government at every level throughout most of the world. Perhaps even a beginning has been made in dealing with the energy and environmental problems that currently exist. They are problems that threaten to become far more excruciating over the next generation than has been the case until now.

Initiatives have been undertaken in urban-industrial countries since 1973 to conserve the employment of energy, at least pending the obtaining of larger sources of reliable supply for future increases in energy usage.(95) These efforts need to be profoundly expanded, if a sufficient response is to be made as well to the continuing environmental need.(96) The pollution of the atmosphere, the water, and the ecosystems of the ocean, as well as the potential capital and energy costs of rectifying or preventing such damage, had become a concern by the 1970s.(97) Plainly, the rest of the twentieth century will be involved in dealing with the interrelatedness of the urban-industrial demand structure, the rising energy cascades, the constraints of the renewing environment or the expansion of those constraints through the imposition of artificial regimes, and the impact of both inflation and a capital crunch.

Getting from the late twentieth century to any subsequent one still remains a problem for humanity. In the centuries yet to come, there should be all the paraphernalia of a high-energy culture capable of providing a range of options for humanity far greater than any available for even the most privileged sections of the human race today. It is important that this generation carry through on the interstitial development of that high-energy promise.

But it is far more important for future generations that the present generation carry through the tasks sufficient unto the present day. And those tasks include nothing less than the preservation of both the conditions for urban-industrial society and the renewing environment needed to sustain life.

An additional burden of foreboding must be borne by urban-industrial society, including a sense of individual danger for those within that society. No guarantee was ever given to this society that it need never consider a tragic sense to life. This burden cannot be laid down. The potential joy in human life cannot be realized until actions have been taken to reverse the established impact high-energy demands have been making directly upon the renewing environment and reflexively upon human existence.(98)

The imagination of decision-makers in urban-industrial society has been concerned with increasing the levels of demand, most of all in the usages for energy and in functions for the renewing environment. The result has been an implicit acceptance of a compulsion to continuously seek freedom from any confines nature might impose upon growth in production, in the consumption of that production, and in energy transfers. Ultimately, it has been a view of freedom limiting to the scope of the human imagination. Conventional wisdom in the late 1970s still viewed the protection of the renewing environment as a "non-productive" cost.(99)

In such deliberately narrowed terms, "non-productive" might be adequate for defining the word "costs." But no quantitative product of the imagination can free either individuals or societies from the biophysical systems that compose nature. The very imbalance between humanity and nature assures this. So long as human beings breathe, so long as they need water and nutrition, so long as they cannot command either the supply of the energy cascades or the capacity of the environment's systems to handle the consequences of those energy transfers, then for so long will humanity not be free of nature. And from that vantage point, these costs are highly "productive."

Humanity must decide if they want a future. If they do not, then they should determine the termination date and discount in relation to it. One seriously questions how much pleasure would be enjoyed by those who would apoplectically crowd into their private lives all the enjoyments planetary life might ever have shared. Certainly the deathbeds of those making Beckerman's choice might offer some impressive scenes, if any but God were present to be impressed. But such a conscious, willed selfishness is not a likely preference for most of humanity, however much they might unself-consciously slip in that direction through inertia.

If the decision is to seek survival, humanity must decide to do at least some planning in relationship to values. Norms cannot be dispensed with in planning. Perhaps the indispensability of normative planning is most present in technological action. Technology requires a purpose, if no other reason than to assist in committing the capital for its realization; and behind purpose lurks value.

A society dependent upon high-energy flows, upon growth, and upon the stimulation of demand must accept the fact that it neither produces nor consumes. Society is only part of a perpetual transfer process. Already urban-industrial society has imposed artificial regimes upon the renewing environment. Once the full consequence of production and consumption as a perpetual transfer process is accepted, then the institution of artificial regimes will expand. Within that expansion, there will be the consequences in action of previously determined values.

Urban-industrial society must accept that its impact upon the renewing environment has gone past the possibility of ignoring it, just as society's dependency upon energy requires matching energy supply with demand. There still exists the possibility of a viable relationship between the continuing demands for energy and the limitations within the renewing environment. But the chance is slipping away.

Doomsaying? Yes, in several senses of the word "doom." For some, it means death, as used in "ecocide." For others, it means a prophesy of the future. But originally this word signified nothing more than a complete description of the present. Urban-industrial society right now needs its own "Doomsday Book," at least as much as William the Conqueror needed his in the eleventh century following the Norman Conquest.

Unfortunately, given what is now known of the present situation, "doom" has more pejorative meanings. As such, there is immanent within it a prediction of the future, a prophesy of possible death, and a judgment on the society that has allowed itself to come to such a pass. Out of the present conditions of high-energy demand could come great promise – or the extinction of the planet's life-support systems. One sort of "doom" could spell the end of the living portions of nature upon this planet. Another "doom" could, conversely, mean ushering in the only Golden Age humanity will likely ever know.

This is extravagant language, but it is not without truth. The human imagination has the capacity to make a conscious choice between such "dooms." Slowly, grudgingly, it seems to be swinging in the direction of the second meaning. To turn back now from the responsibility for the conditions high-energy demand imposes upon the renewing environment would be a fatal mistake. Serendipity will provide no rescue. Only value-laden, future-oriented, self-monitoring, judgmental decisions will serve. Whether or not such decisions get made over the rest of the twentieth century will determine the "doom" of humanity.

Notes

CHAPTER 1

(1) On the allegations of capital shortfall, see James J. Needham, "No More Exchange – So What?", Wall Street Journal, November 27, 1974, and Growth and the Environment, Selection of Materials for the United States House of Representatives Merchant Marine and Fisheries Committee (Washington, D.C.: Government Printing Office, 1974), pp. 75-85.

(2) Charles T. Unseld, "Social Impact Assessment of Energy Policy: Behavior, Life Style, Values and Priorities" in Energy Policy in the United States: Social and Behavioral Dimensions, ed. Seymour Warkov (New York: Praeger, 1978), pp. 220-33.

(3) Barry Commoner has written extensively – and, for many, persuasively – on the unavoidance of such costs, The Poverty of Power (New York: Knopf, 1976), and The Politics of Energy (New York: Knopf, 1979).

(4) For the happy view, see Herman Kahn, William Brown, Leon Martel with the Hudson Institute, The Next 200 Years: A Scenario for America and the World (New York: William Morrow, 1976). These views have been updated with an increase in pessimism for the 1980s, in Herman Kahn and the Hudson Institute, World Economic Development: 1979 and Beyond (Boulder: Westview Press, 1979).

(5) Choix des Rapports, Opinions, et Decisions, vol. I (Paris: A. Eynery, 1818), pp. 351, 357.

(6) Jean Jaures, Histoire Socialiste de la Revolution Francaise, vol. II, ed. A. Mathiez (Paris: Ed. de la Libraire de L'Humanite, 1922), p. 9.

(7) In the contemporaneously published version of this speech by the Abbe Sieyes in Le Moniteur Universel, these ideas were excised. As the later editor of this first publication said, it "did not put forward equally the opinions of orators. . . ." (Reimpression de L'ancien Moniteur, vol. I ed. Leonard Gallois (Paris: au Bureau Central, 1860), p. 411, note.)

(8) As one of many examples, see statements reported from the Fourth International World Wildlife Fund Conference, Gladwin Hill, "Waste of Resources Called Peril to Man," New York Times, December 1, 1976, p. A18. Valuable work on how society determines levels of energy usage has been done by Linda Mulligan, see especially her "The Social Definition of Energy: Resources and their Institutionalization", a paper for the 72nd Annual Meeting of the American Sociological Assoc., September 7, 1977. See also the interview with Hazel Henderson in Calypso Log, vol. 6, no. 2 (June 1979), 14-16, 21: "The whole problem is that there are still an enormous number of very educated people in all countries – people who have Ph.D.'s in physics and engineering and all kinds of things – who still think that the oceans are for human use and convenience. . . .This is not only ignorant and greedy, but it's going to be disastrous."

(9) George Simmel as quoted in Ward E. Y. Elliott, The Rise of Guardian Democracy (Cambridge, Mass.: Harvard University Press, 1974), p. 257.

(10) This view has been especially associated with the efforts of Jacques Cousteau and the work of his Cousteau Society. But it is not unique to him; see Howard T. Odum, Environment, Power and Society (New York: Wiley-Interscience, 1971).

(11) Dennis L. Meadows, Alternatives to Growth – I: A Search for Sustainable Futures (Cambridge, Mass.: Ballinger, 1977). Some would say the shrinkage will come and the quality of life will change drastically, William Ophuls, Ecology and the Politics of Scarcity: Prologue to a Political Theory of the Steady State (San Francisco: W. H. Freeman, 1977). See also Charles F. Park, Jr., with Margaret C. Freeman, Earthbound: Minerals, Energy and Man's Future (San Francisco: Freeman, Cooper, 1975).

(12) Ian Burton, Robert W. Kates, and Gilbert F. White, The Environment as Hazard (New York: Oxford University Press, 1978). The close relationship between impact on the renewing environment and the demand for increased energy was most clearly revealed by the character of the deterioration of air quality in the United States between 1952 and 1977, Associated Press, Columbus Dispatch, June 10, 1972, quoting Thomas G. Ellestad of the United States Environmental Protection Agency.

(13) Noel Mostert, Supership (New York: Knopf, 1974); R. Richard M'Gonigle and Mark W. Zacher, Pollution, Politics, and International

Law: Tankers at Sea (Berkeley: University of California Press, 1979); and D. W. Abecassis, Oil Pollution From Ships (London: Butterworth, 1978. The Law of the Sea Conference has not been successful, Margaret L. Dickey, "Should the Law of the Sea Conference Be Saved?" 12 The International Lawyer, 1978, pp. 1-19. She believes whatever success the conference has enjoyed "have proceeded successfully by sidestepping the fundamental choices," p. 19.

(14) John Herman Randall, A World Community (New York: Frederick A. Stokes, 1930), pp. 3-5; Odum, Environment, Power and Society, Chapter 1.

(15) Joseph A. Schumpeter, History of Economic Analysis, ed. Elizabeth Boody Schumpeter (New York: Oxford University Press, 1954):

> For it is quite true that our common impression to the effect that general undervaluation of the future does exist in modern society may be in part a simple consequence of the existence of interest and that, hence, the task of establishing that there is also independent undervaluation, capable of "causing" interest, is not so easy, especially since apparently contradictory evidence is not lacking. Such a discussion would also have to take issue with the many objections that have been raised. A particularly interesting one must, however, be mentioned. Some writers seem to believe that, if there existed systematic undervaluation of the future, society would have to plan for economic doom or general liquidation. But this is precisely what society actually does, and it is one of the most profound problems of economic analysis to show why capital equipment nevertheless expands instead of dwindling. This problem is obscured by the practice of postu-lating that the economic engine is being maintained, or is maintaining itself, as a matter of course. (Ibid., p. 929, note his emphasis)

(16) This has produced a situation in which the world economy, on the bases of energy use, supply, and demand for growth in both, can be divided into a few regional superpowers, Douglas Evans, The Politics of Energy (Toronto: Macmillan of Canada, 1976). The United States economy between 1860 and 1960 changed fuel bases three times, each time taking a 40-year transition period to do so. It may be on the verge of a fourth shift in fuel base to nuclear, solar, or some other energy source. A 40-year transition time may not be available.   Howard Bucknell III, "Energy and National Security: A Midwestern Perspective," Occasional Paper, April 27, 1979, Energy and National Security Project, The Ohio State University's PEREPS, Mershon Center and Battelle Endowment, pp. 10-13.

(17) Urban-industrial demand, however modest its managers may view it in terms of its potential growth, has long since profoundly altered

nature, Loren Eiseley, The Invisible Pyramid: A Naturalist Analyzes the Rocket Century (New York: Scribner's, 1970), pp. 14015, 20-21; Catherine Roberts, The Scientific Conscience: Reflections on the Modern Biologist and Humanism (New York: George Braziller), 1967.

(18) The physical problems alone make a total energy budget seem an impossible goal, American Physical Society, "Efficient Use of Energy: A Physics Perspective" (1975) in Energy and Natural Resources Law, ed. William H. Rodgers (St. Paul: West, 1979), pp. 370-1.

(19) Serious efforts are being made in the planning of future buildings and settlements to avoid treating heat as a waste product, see Part III, "Shelter and Movement", in Strategies for Human Settlements: Habitat and Environment, ed. Gwen Bell, (Honolulu: The University Press of Hawaii, 1976), and Human Settlements and Energy: A Seminar of the United Nations Economic Commission for Europe. ed. C. I. Jackson (Oxford: Pergamon Press, 1978).

(20) Chemical and Engineering News, November 18, 1974, p. 48, reporting on the Rand Corporation's energy situation study for the National Academy of Sciences. There is, indeed, no agreement on what is "used" and what is "lost" energy. R. B. Kidman, R. J. Barrett, and D. R. Koenig, Energy Flow Patterns for 1975 (Los Alamos, N.M.: Los Alamos Scientific Laboratory, June 1977), p. 8.

(21) Robert Stobaugh and Daniel Yergin, eds., Energy Future, The Report of the Harvard Business School Energy Project (New York: Random House, 1979). It argues primary reliance should be placed upon energy conservation and solar power. The Administration of President Carter believes that if by the year 2000 a doubling of the price of oil in real terms after 1978 had produced a 25% drop in consumption, then solar power could provide 20% of the United State's energy needs, Steven Rattner, "President Setting Solar Power Goal", New York Times, June 19, 1979, p. D-13.

(22) An exhaustive survey on the character of urban growth and suggestions for controlling it is the 3-volume study, Randall W. Scott, Management and Control of Growth, David J. Brower and Dallas D. Miner, eds. (Washington: The Urban Land Institute, 1975). "Growth management" has become very important, see Chapter 7 in Planning and Control of Land Development, Daniel R. Mandelker and Roger A. Cunningham, eds. (Indianapolis: Bobbs-Merrill, 1979): "Probably no innovation in planning and land use control strategies has caught the public imagination more than the growth management, or growth control, movement. . . ." (P. 987). See also Lawrence Burrows, Growth Management (New Brunswick: Rutgers University Center for Urban Policy Research, 1978).

(23) "First, there was the mistaken notion that energy was a kind of master force in determining where people live, how they live, and what they think. Indeed, as history shows, the use of various energy forms and technologies is a cultural choice. Energy, then, follows culture as much as if not more than culture follows energy. . . ." (James O'Toole and the University of Southern California Center for Future Research, Energy and Social Change (Cambridge, Mass.: The MIT Press paperback "addition", 1978), p. 70.) We shall see.

(24) "Confusion and disorder on land can be seen by flying over it and even in some places by driving through it. It is also evident in the oceans and the atmosphere. . . ." (C. A. Doxiadis, Ecology and Ekistics, ed. Gerald Dix (Boulder, Colo.: Westview Press, 1977), p. 15.) See also Richard F. Babcock, Billboards, Glass Houses, and the Law – and other Land Use Fables (Colorado Springs: Shepard's Inc., 1977), for a zoning lawyer's acerbic view of sprawl.

(25) Lewis Mumford, The Pentagon of Power (New York: Harcourt, Brace Jovanovich, 1970), p. 191. For a later statement of some of these views, see Lewis Mumford, My Works and Days: A Personal Chronicle (New York: Harcourt, Brace, Jovanovich, 1979).

(26) It is a phenomenon scarcely peculiar to urban-industrial society with a high energy demand. Compare J. Donald Hughes, Ecology in Ancient Civilizations (Albuquerque: University of New Mexico Press, 1975), for the environmental effects, with the impact in high energy culture of abrupt lowering of energy supply, Kenneth E. Boulding, "The Social System and the Energy Crisis", Science, vol. 184, April 19, 1974, pp. 255-7. See also, Mulford Q. Sibley, Nature and Civilization: Some Implications for Politics, The Loyola University Series in Political Analysis (Itasca, Ill.: F. E. Peacock, 1977).

(27) A philosopher's exploration of the gulf between nature and the artificial reasoning concerning it is Max Oelschlaeger, The Environmental Imperative: A Socio-Economic Perspective (Washington: University Press of America, 1977).

(28) The energy product under such conditions is not cheap at all on a more comprehensive analysis. Amory B. Lovins, "Cost-Risk-Benefit Assessments in Energy Policy," 45 George Washington Law Review August 1977, 911-43. See also his later, "Soft Energy Technologies," 3 Annual Review of Energy 477, 1978.

(29) The continued importance in environmental matters of municipal government remains, however, Manual of the Council of Europe (London: Stevens & Son, 1970), pp. 295-98; Francoise Carton de Wiart, Inventaire . . . en Matiere d'environemente (Brussels: Interenvironnement, 1973).

(30) Traditionally any interest in the renewing environment having the characteristic in economics of non-specificity and in loss of a common title has suffered the abuse of over-use and/or indifference, see Managing the Commons, ed. Garrett Hardin and John Baden (San Francisco: W. H. Freemen, 1977).

(31) Environmental Effects of Complex River Development: International Experience, ed. Gilbert White (Boulder: Westview Press, 1977). This is the product of a July 1976 symposium held from Rostov to Kazan, in itself a learning experience.

(32) The opportunities are vast. For one example, see Stephen J. Fitzsimmons, Lorrie T. Stuart, and Peter C. Wolff, Social Assessment Manual: A Guide to the Preparation of the Social Well-Being Account for Planning Water Resources Projects (Boulder: Westview Press, 1977). Inevitably, these are land use projects as well.

(33) ". . . even after filtration, the drinking water of certain New Orleans residents that originates in the Mississippi river and the drinking water of certain Cincinnati residents that originate in the Ohio river have been linked to several types of cancer." (Paul R. Portney, "Toxic Substances Control", Resources, No. 59, April-July 1978, pp. 5-6, reprinted from Current Issues in U.S. Environmental Policy (Baltimore: Johns Hopkins University Press for Resources for the Future, 1978).) See also R. H. Harris, T. Page, and N. A. Reiches, Carcinogenic Hazards of Organic Chemicals in Drinking Water (Washington: RFF Reprint Series, 1977). It is a world-wide problem. "Anticipating the Effects from Chemicals in the Environment", Environment Directorate, Organization for Economic Cooperation and Development, Paris, 1977.

(34) For a critique, see Ivan Illich, Energy and Equity (New York: Harper & Row, 1974); Allan Schnaiberg, "Obstacles to Environmental Research by Scientists and Technologists: A Social Structural Analysis," Social Problems, vol. 24, no. 5, June, 1977, pp. 500-52.

(35) Jacob H. Beuscher, "An Ideal Natural Resources Law Future," in Fran Thomas, Law in Action: The Work of Professor Jacob H. Beuscher (Madison: Land Economics Monograph No. 4, 1972), pp. 80-84; Marvin E. Olsen, "Conserving Energy by Changing Societal Goals," Illinois Teacher, September/October, 1976, pp. 19-24.

(36) Under the present divided system, though, they are very heavy, Hugo Osvald, The Earth Can Feed Us, introduction by Lord Boyd-Orr, B. Nesfield-Cookston, trans. (South Brunswick, N.J.: A.S. Barnes, 1966). In 1978, for example, the United States Soil Conservation Service estimated the cost at $35 billion 1978-2018, compared to $15 billion spent 1937-1977, Don Kendall, "Slow Soil Erosion," Columbus Dispatch, 5 February 1978, an AP dispatch. See also the excellent article, William Tucker, "The Next American Dust Bowl — and how to avoid it," Atlantic Monthly, vol. 244, no. 1, July 1979, pp. 38-49.

(37) Already it is being alleged by many economists that these costs on behalf of environmental protection are major contributors to current inflation. About the best they can say is, "The costs imposed by governmental regulation. . .when Congress responded to demands for cleaner air and water. . .'tended to come on the books at exactly the wrong time' – amid the inflationary shocks of 1973-74. . . .(Richard J. Levine, "Price of Progress?", Wall Street Journal, June 19, 1979, quoting the Harvard University political economist Richard Zeck-hauser.)

(38) On the effect of human activity upon the hydrologic cycle, K. Acuthan, "Man on the Hydrologic Cycle," Water Resources Bulletin, vol. 10, no. 4, pp. 756-8, August 1974; on natural balances, see Andre Missenard, In Search of Man, Laurence G. Blockman, trans. pp. 168-73. See also Chapter 18, "Conflicting Demands For Allocation of Water," in Water Needs for the Future, Ved P. Nanta, ed. (Boulder: Westview Press, 1977) and Ven Te Chow, "Water as a World Resource," 4 Water International, 1979, pp. 4-8, 24, especially his remarks about future modification in the hydrologic cycle.

(39) See how this is explored in This Little Planet, Canon Michael Hamilton, ed. (New York: Scribner's, 1970).

(40) See the chapter, "The Need to Establish Priorities," in It's Not Too Late, ed. Fred Carvell and Max Tadlock (Beverly Hills: Glencoe Press, 1971), pp. 127. The establishing of energy priorities is an emphasis of Lee Schipper, see Lee Schipper and Allan J. Lichtenberg, "Efficient Energy Use and Well-Being: The Swedish Example," Science, vol. 194, no. 4269, December 3, 1976, pp. 1001-13. An interesting book tying energy and environment together by way of the entropic theories of Nicholas Georgescu-Roegen – and arguing for a re-ordering of priorities in urban-industrial society – is Norman Metzger, Energy: The Continuing Crisis (New York: T. Y. Crowell, 1977).

(41) The impact of the public perception of how a change in the value of energy affects community action is described in Energy and the Community, ed. Raymond J. Burby III and A. Fleming Bell (Cambridge, Mass.: Ballinger, 1978).

(42) The description of an annual electrical energy-growth rate of ten percent as a "need" has already been denounced as a "dogmatic projection, in the total absence of any rational examination. . . ." (John W. Goffman and Arthur R. Tamplin, Poisoned Power (Emmaus, Pa.: Rodale Press, 1971), p. 1972.) On the role of advertising in energy consumption, Wilson Clark with David Howell Energy for Survival: The Alternative to Extinction (New York: Garden City: Anchor Books, 1975), pp. 128-32. An excellent book on cost projections, conceived from a different view from either of the above, is Russell G. Thompson, James A. Calloway, and Lilian A. Nowalanic, The Cost of Energy and a Clean Environment (Houston: Gulf, 1978).

(43) One of the most stimulating and insistent exponents of this viewpoint is Rene Dubos. Among his many works, there is his book with Barbara Ward, Only One Earth: The Care and Maintenance of a Small Planet (New York: Norton, 1972), and his book Of Human Diversity (Barre, Mass.: Clark University Press, 1974). It is not a view that has earned universal acceptance, see the acerbic essay "Ecological Panic," in Paul Johnson, Enemies of Society (New York: Atheneum, 1977), pp. 85-101.

CHAPTER 2

(1) John McHale, The Ecological Context (New York: George Braziller, 1970), p. 115. On the growth rates from 1950 to 1972, and how one can predict future energy growth, Energy: Global Prospects, 1985-2000, Report of the Workshop on Alternative Energy Strategies, Carroll L. Wilson, director (New York: McGraw-Hill, 1977), pp. 83-84.

(2) Harold J. Barnett, Energy Uses and Supplies, United States Bureau of Mines Information Circular 7852, October 1950.

(3) Environmental Reporter, vol. III, no. 15, August 11, 1972, p. 444, quoting a report of the United States Senate Commerce Committee. By 2000 it was predicted that the total energy use in the United States would go from 73.1 quadrillion BTUs in 1974 to 163.4 quadrillion BTUs, "Electricity: Pricing a Critical Resource in an Energy-Short Environment," At Issue, ser. 3, October 1976, p. 14. All similar scenarios depend upon the future price, efficient engineering and social use, technical innovation and physical and political availability of sources for energy conversion. Energy: Use Conservation and Supply, ed. Philip H. Abelson (Washington, D.C.: American Association for the Advancement of Science, 1974). See also Philip Abelson, Energy for Tomorrow (Seattle: University of Washington Press, 1975). John McHale, The Future of the Future (New York: George Braziller, 1969), p. 210, indicates the American experience was paralleled in Great Britain. In 1911, a British family of five had twenty energy units at their disposal. By 1963 it was 405.

(4) Joel Darmstadter, Joy Dunkerly, and Jack Alterman, How Industrial Societies Use Energy: A Comparative Analysis (Baltimore: Johns Hopkins University Press for Resources for the Future, 1977), shows how to make comparisons internationally.

(5) Sam H. Schurr and Bruce C. Netschert, with Vera T. Eliasberg, Joseph Lerner and Hans H. Lundsberg, Energy in the American Economy, 1850-1975: An Economic Study of Its History and Prospects (Baltimore: The Johns Hopkins Press for Resources for the Future, 1960), p. 16. The decade 1910-20 was a transitional period.

(6) Vaclav Smil, China's Energy: Achievements, Problems, Prospects (New York: Praeger, 1976), p. 136. See fig, 6.1, p. 142. It seems 1.83 kilograms of coal equivalent have been required in this twenty-five-year period to generate each additional United States (1973) dollar equivalent in the GNP.

(7) Environmentalists believe that "we need not fear dire economic consequences from cuts in energy usage," Conservation Foundation Letter, March 1978. "A continuation of the trend toward a 'post-industrial economy' should lead to a further gradual reduction in the energy-GNP ratio. . . ." (Ibid., p. 7.) The disaggregated character of energy, however has meant that in the United States between 1940 and 1970, "for the matured end uses, such as electrical drives, the rate of growth of electricity consumption matches closely that of Gross National Product," Thomas H. Lee, "The Case for Evolutionary Optimization," in Future Strategies for Energy Development: A Question of Goals (Oak Ridge: Oak Ridge Associates Universities, 1977), pp. 229, 233. One ought not confuse, either, energy relative to each unit of GNP and per capita energy use. In the United States, the latter rose from a per capita energy consumption of .05 percent per year from 1870 to 1940 to 2.7 percent per year from 1960 to 1970. Ibid., p. 232.

(8) McHale, Context, p. 118, 9. But see Darmstadter et. al., Industrial Societies, pp. 8-9.

(9) Lester Brown, "Rich Countries and Poor in A Finite, Interdependent World," The No-Growth Society, ed. Mancur Olson and Hans H. Lundsberg (New York: Norton, 1973), pp. 153-64. The World Bank believes that developing nations – excluding those in OPEC – will experience a 6.2 percent annual increase in energy demand until oil consumption reaches 17.75 million barrels a day in 1985 as opposed to 9.69 million barrels per day in 1975. Because sixty of these countries have little capital to invest in oil and natural gas, the Bank will provide loans and technical assistance. Atlas/World Press Review, vol. 26, no. 7, (July 1979), p. 56.

(10) National Commission on Materials Policy, Final Report (1973), Washington, 1973, Fig. 2.2.

(11) Amory B. Lovins, Soft Energy Paths: Toward a Durable Peace (Cambridge, Mass.: Ballinger, with Friends of the Earth International 1977), p. 66. See also The Energy Controversy: Soft Path Questions and Answers, ed. Hugh Nash (San Francisco: Friends of the Earth, 1978).

(12) Statement of Congressman James F. Howard (D., N.J.), Chairman, United States House of Representatives Public Works Sub-committee, at hearings conducted August 3-9, Environmental Reporter, vol. III, (1972), p. 433. In the United States the winters of 1977 and 1978, with their shortages of natural gas, coal, and electricity, underscored this

while the reaction of the truckers in 1979 to the rise in the price of diesel fuel reinforced it.

(13) Harper Leech, The Paradox of Plenty (New York: Whittlesey House, 1932), is especially dramatic in recounting this situation and its resolution.

(14) Ibid., p. 197.

(15) Paul H. Earl and Steven G. Phillips, "Alternative Energy Policies' Impact on Industry Price Behavior," Econometric Dimensions of Energy Demand, A. Bradley Askin and John Kraft, eds., (Lexington, Mass: Lexington Books, 1976), pp. 111, 122. A publication of the American Society for International Law was sanguine that the long-run exhaustion of the earth's finite resources should not be a major concern since fossil fuels and nuclear power would be sufficient until at least 2025 by which time price pressure will have brought on line new energy supply technologies. Mason Willrich and others, Energy and World Politics (New York: The Free Press, 1975), pp. 59-60. See also Providing for Energy, A report of the Twentieth Century Fund Task Force on United States Energy Policy (New York: McGraw-Hill, 1977).

(16) Henry Carey, The Unity of Law (Philadelphia: Baird, 1872), p. 116; Carey, "Wealth: Of What Does It Consist?" in II Misc. Writings (1870); Frederick Soddy, Wealth, Virtual Wealth and Debt (New York: E. P. Dutton, 1926), Chapter 3; Soddy, The Role of Money (New York: Harcourt, Brace, 1935) on "ercosophy," p. IV.

(17) What Henry Carey did not foresee was the division of the world into countries with an energy demand far exceeding domestic supply and other countries with a surplus of energy supplies. The latter have a very different attitude than the former as to how to reconcile this division. I Energy Policies of the World, ed. Gerald J. Mangone (New York: Elsevier, 1976). This volume concerns itself with the purposes of countries that have surplus supplies for energy conversion.

(18) The consequences of a world divided between energy users and energy suppliers, between countries with long-established high energy usages and those whose expectations for energy are still in early stages of acceleration, are explored by some of the most thoughtful writers on energy policy in The Energy Question: An International Failure of Policy, ed. Edward W. Erickson and Leonard Waverman (Toronto: University of Toronto Press, 1974), 2 vols.

(19) There are modern, serious energy policy writers who might agree, Sidney Sonenblum, The Energy Connections: Between Energy and the Economy (Cambridge, Mass: Ballinger, 1978).

(20) If the dispersed energy of the sun, tides, wind, ocean thermal decline, and biomass (assuming the last four are not part of solar energy) could be increasingly harnessed, the crisis in energy supply might be resolved at least for a time, Denis Hayes, Rays of Hope: The Transition to a Post-Petroleum World (New York: Norton, 1977).

(21) Ester Boserup, The Conditions of Agricultural Growth. Introduction by Nicholas Kaldor (Chicago: Aldine, 1965), p. 73.

(22) Isaac Asimov, "Prospects for the Year 2000," Columbus Dispatch, January 6, 1975.

(23) The Energy Crisis and the Environment: An International Perspective, ed. Donald R. Kelley (New York: Praeger, 1977).

(24) A return to a primarily renewable energy source is discussed in Perspectives on the National Energy Plan: A Mid-Course Appraisal (Washington, D.C.: International Economic Policy Association, September 1977), pp. 22-23 and is the subject matter, in great part, of Lovins, Soft Energy Paths; Hayes, Rays of Hope, and many exponents of alternative energy sources.

(25) Leech, Paradox of Plenty, pp. 27, 40-41.

(26) Peter D. Junger, "Book Review," 22 Case Western Reserve Law Review, 1971, 598, p. 603.

(27) Russell G. Thompson, James A. Calloway, and Lilian A. Nawalanic, The Cost of Energy and a Clean Environment (Houston: Gulf, 1978), p. 25.

(28) Carol Ann Lease, "Industry Should Burn Wood, Not Coal," Columbus Dispatch, March 2, 1979, describing a Battelle Memorial Institute Study for the Industrial Environmental Research Laboratory of the USEPA, which did allege the output of sulfur dioxide would be lowered; "Gasohol 'Crop' May Benefit Local Farmers," Indiana Rural News, June 1979, p. 23; Warren Hoge, "Brazil Is High on Alcohol Fuel," New York Times, June 14, 1979, which does call alcohol "a clean-burning fuel" compared to gasoline. But the emphasis is upon an abundant energy source.

(29) Mulford Q. Sibley, "The Relevance of Classical Political Theory for Economy, Technology, and Ecology," 2 Alternatives: Perspectives for Society and the Environment, no. 2 (1973), p. 14.

(30) H. C. Pereira, Land Use and Water Resources (New York: Cambridge University Press, 1973), p. 26. The source cited from Plato is now regarded as a product of the Academy, though not too long after Plato's death.

(31) Howard T. Odum, Environment, Power and Society (New York: Wiley-Interscience, 1971), p. 214.

(32) Ibid., pp. 216-17, 218.

(33) Ibid., pp. 274, 213. Just to list the current policy objectives of the United States is to reveal the governmental reflection of this mandate. Robert B. Krueger, The United States and International Oil (New York: Praeger, 1975), p. 10. See also Krueger, "The Future Availability of Oil," Second Annual Conference on Financing World Energy Requirements, Honolulu, Hawaii, December 1, 1977.

(34) The convergence of crises relative to energy and the environment make it urgent that these problems be simultaneously addressed, George L. Tuve, Energy, Environment, Population, and Food: Our Four Interdependent Crises (New York: Wiley-Interscience, 1976).

(35) Kenneth J. Arrow, "The Rate of Discount for Long-Term Investment," Energy and the Environment: A Risk-Benefit Approach (New York: Pergamon Press, 1976), pp. 113, 129.

(36) It is not a flow with an easily predictable rate.

We can intuit that the functions provided by energy...are closely variable with economic activity. Since the energy required to provide these functions is determined by equipment and system efficiencies and since we know from practical experience that these efficiencies can be improved, the relationship of energy use and economic activity is nonlinear and may be discontinuous. . . .

(Roger W. Sant "Adjusting Capital Stock to Higher Energy-Using Efficiencies," in Energy Conservation and Economic Growth, ed. Charles J. Hitch (Boulder: Westview Press for AAAS Selected Symposium, 1978), no. 22, p. 153.)

(37) Fred Cottrell, Energy and Society: The Relation Between Energy, Social Change, and Economic Development (New York: McGraw-Hill, 1955), pp. 54-56.

(38) Fred Hirsch, Social Limits to Growth (Cambridge: Harvard University Press/Twentieth Century Fund, 1976), pp. 84-85.

(39) Wilson Clark, "U.S. Agriculture," Smithsonian, January 1975, vol. 5, no. 10, pp. 59-64.

(40) Cottrell, Energy and Society, pp. 12-13.

(41) Ibid., pp. 113-14. See also p. 96 and pp. 108-09.

(42) Linda W. Mulligan, "Energy Regionalism in the United States: The Decline of the National Energy Commons," Energy Policy in the United States, ed. Seymour Warkov, (New York: Praeger, 1978). pp. 1-10.

(43) Steven Rattner, "Environmental Agency Softens Rules in Bid to be More Moderate and Efficient," New York Times, January 19, 1979, indicates "softening" and "moderating" go in one direction.

(44) Although energy relative to Gross National Product has declined since 1920, high energy-intensive services could reverse this. As yet one cannot be certain. Sam H. Schurr and Joel Darmstadter, "The Energy Connection, RFF Resources, no. 53, Fall 1976, p. 2, Table, and p. 6. Darmstadter does not believe there must be such an increase, see his "Lessons of History and Other Countries," in Hitch, Energy Conservation, pp. 113, 115, though he criticizes people who do believe an increase in energy is always needed to support an increase in GNP. See John G. Winger and Carolyn A. Nielsen, "Energy, the Economy, and Jobs," Energy Report From Chase (Chase Manhattan Bank, September 1976), p. 2.

(45) Herman Kahn believes the shift to services will lower the use of energy. Herman Kahn, William Brown, Leon Martell with the Hudson Institute, The Next 200 Years (New York: William Morrow, 1976), p. 62. See also Martin Mayor. Today and Tomorrow in America, (New York: Harper & Row, 1976), pp. 79-86.

(46) "Energy is perceived as a public good." (Bucknell, Energy and National Security p. 15.) It could scarcely be otherwise in the United States with its increasing per capita use of energy in the 1970s, despite the energy alarms.

(47) Cottrell, Energy and Society, p. 2.

(48) Leech, Paradox of Plenty, p. 2. One need not mention the anguish such a view brings to the Historic Preservationists of much later decades.

(49) Ibid., pp. XV-XVI. Barry Commoner, of course, has argued against the substitution of synthetic for natural goods because so many synthetics are made from petro-chemicals and the transformation so often requires massive amounts of energy.

(50) Ibid., p. 107.

(51) C. C. Furnas, The Storehouse of Civilization (New York: Bureau of Publications, Teachers College, Columbia University, 1939), pp. 292-3.

(52) John Chamberlain, "Philosophies Clash on Energy Actions," Columbus Dispatch, January 10, 1975. See also William F. Baxter, People or

Penguins: The Case For Optimal Pollution (New York: Columbia University Press, 1974), and its review by Peter D. Junger, 37 Ohio State Law Journal, 1976, pp. 965-85.

(53) This, at least, seemed a common view among those attending the Fifth Economic Summit's Conference in Tokyo in 1979. Richard J. Levine, Philip Revzin, Mike Tharp, and John Urquhart, "Test at the Top," Wall Street Journal, June 25, 1979.

CHAPTER 3

(1) Lawrence Friedman, A History of American Law (New York: Simon & Schuster, 1973), p. 583; Richard Cloward and Frances Fox Piven, The Politics of Turmoil (New York: Pantheon Books, 1974), pp. 33-34. See also Michael E. Tiger with Madeleine R. Levy, Law and the Rise of Capitalism (New York: Monthly Review Press, 1977), Chapter 22.

(2) The argument is also made that government should go beyond regulation and itself be the sole producer and transmitter of energy so as to control both demand and supply. Michael Tanzer, The Energy Crisis: World Struggle for Power and Wealth (New York: Monthly Review Press, 1974).

(3) Fred Cottrell, Energy and Society (New York: McGraw-Hill, 1955), pp. 265-7, 211-12.

(4) The sharpening of this conflict is one of the reasons for the United States to move to greater energy conservation and greater utilization of current energy sources, Energy Future, The Report of the Harvard Business School Energy Project, Robert Stobaugh and Daniel Yorgin, eds. (New York: Random House, 1979).

(5) Jules Loh, "Lamm Is A Lion," Columbus Dispatch, January 12, 1975.

(6) Interestingly enough, however, neither the Steering Committee of the National Urban Coalition nor its National Priorities Project Staff for an important effort to set priorities for the United States in the 1970s even mentioned energy as among national problems to be dealt with. Counter-budget: A Blueprint for Changing National Priorities, 1971-1976, Robert S. Benson and Harold Wolman, eds. (New York: Praeger, 1971).

(7) M. Ray Thomasson, "Energy Supply and Demand Challenges and Some Possible Solutions," in Energy Delta, Supply vs. Demand, ed. George W. Morganthaler and Aaron R. Silver (Tarzana, Calif.: American Astronautical Society Publications Office, 1975), pp. 1-30, although much else in this excellent volume is pertinent to this point.

(8) Wall Street Journal, August 22, 1972. This led to a boom in the refining oil industry. Wall Street Journal, March 11, 1976. See also
Douglas Martin. "Hostile Reception," Wall Street Journal, June 27,
1979, for the long-term persistence of the situation. Still every source
in both industry and government expressed surprise at shortfalls in 1979
in the domestic American refining of gasoline, diesel oil, and home
heating oil, Associated Press survey, Columbus Dispatch, June 24, 1979,
and a far scantier version in the New York Times, June 25, 1979. Some
blamed low refinery utilization levels. Washington Post, June 22, 1979,
interview with James R. Schlesinger, Secretary of Energy.

(9) Of course, this had not prevented Congress from "attempting to
enact a synthetic fuels bill for years," nor from trying to authorize two
billion dollars for such a program, described as "the tip of the iceberg"
since such a program would minimally cost well above twelve billion
dollars. Dissent of congressman Ron Paul, Report no. 96-165, United
States House of Representatives Committee on Banking, Finance, and
Urban Affairs, (May 15, 1979), pp. 44-50. In July 1979, although a price
tag of $88 billion had been placed on President Carter's proposed
synthetic fuels program, the United States House of Representatives
Education and Labor Committee wanted a $200 billion "synfuels"
program, CCH Energy Management, no. 332, July 24, 1979, p. 2.

(10) This delay is disputed by such a persuasive work as Medard Gobel,
Energy, Earth and Everyone: A Global Strategy For Space Ship Earth
(San Francisco: Straight Arrow Books, 1975). See also R. Buckminster
Fuller, "Preparing for a Small Town World," Strategies for Human
Settlements: Habitat and Environment, ed. Gwen Bell (Honolulu: The
University Press of Hawaii, 1976), pp. 5-14.

(11) Growth in United States energy consumption through at least the
early 1980s has been regarded as unavoidable by most observers,
however costly the environmental and other impacts. Richard B.
Mancke, Squeaking By: United States Energy Policy Since the Embargo
(New York: Columbia University Press, 1976), p. 80. See also p. 154.
There are important exceptions such as Amory Lovins and William
Ophuls.

(12) Cottrell, Energy and Society, p. 2. This results in an energy subsidy
for urban-industrial development, Paul Ehrlich and Dennis C. Pirages,
Ark II: Social Response To Environmental Imperatives (New York:
Viking Press, 1974), p. 8.

(13) Wall Street Journal, January 6, 1975, p. 17.

(14) One wonders when the issue of natural gas sufficiency and price
will be resolved. The Economic Regulatory Administration of the
United States Department of Energy pushed hard for industry to switch
from oil to natural gas, even in preference to other fuels, CCH Energy

Management, April 10, 1979. p. 3, at the very time that the Energy Information Administration in the same Department predicted that in the years 1979-90: (1) energy prices would rise faster than the general rate of inflation and (2) the price of natural gas would rise the highest of any energy source, Ibid., May 23, 1979, p. 7.

(15) Carey, "Wealth," Miscellaneous Writings, vol. II, in which the pamphlet of 1870 is bound, separately paginated, as reprinted from the Penn Monthly Magazine, October 1870.

(16) See Don E. Kash and others, Our Energy Future: The Role of Research, Development, and Demonstration in Reaching a Consensus on National Energy Supply (Norman: University of Oklahoma Press, 1976).

(17) "The Potential for Energy Conservation," United States Office of Emergency Planning, 1972. The Federal Energy Administration targeted ten industries for energy efficiency improvement, 41 Federal Register 48169-71, November 2, 1976. See also Oscar L. Dunn, "Energy Conservation – Top Priority," NAM Reports, vol. 21, no. 17 (November 1976), p. 11. It would be impossible to list the sources stressing the importance of energy conservation.

(18) R. Buckminster Fuller, "Energy Economics," Ekistics, vol. 45, no. 269, May 1978, pp. 164-71.

(19) John McHale, The Future of the Future (New York: George Braziller, 1969), pp. 215, 219, fig. 69. An interesting book on how present technology could conserve energy is Joel Darmstadter, Conserving Energy: Prospects and Opportunities in the New York Region (Baltimore: Resources for the Future by Johns Hopkins University Press, 1975).

(20) Thus, electricity, though not a thermally efficient energy form, may greatly multiply the efficiency with which capital and labor are used and be justified accordingly. Sam H. Schurr and Joel Darmstadter "The Energy Connection," RFF Resources, no. 53, Fall 1976, pp. 1, p. 2. An extraordinarily useful work on how energy is used is Joel Darmstadter, Joy Dunkerly and Jack Alterman, How Industrial Societies Use Energy: A Comparative Analysis, (Baltimore: Johns Hopkins University Press for Resources for the Future, 1977). On the burden of the gasoline-powered car, see Emma Rothschild, Paradise Lost: The Decline of the Auto-Industrial Age (New York: Random House, 1973).

(21) ". . .the frustration over lack of progress and consensus in energy policy arises from . . . interrelated concerns about, or conflicts with, economic growth, social equity, foreign policy, technology, and environmental impacts. . . ." (Charles J. Hitch, "Foreward," to Sam H. Schurr, Joel Darmstadter, Harry Perry, William Ramsey and Milton Russell, An Overview and Interpretation of Energy in America's Future (Washington: Resources for the Future, 1979).)

(22) See National Commission on Materials Policy, Final Report, (Washington, D.C.: Government Printing Office, June 1973, p. 4D-6: This report was criticized by J. Stansbury and E. Flattaw, Cleveland Plain Dealer, September 4, 1973. See Charles F. Park, Jr., Earthbound (San Francisco: Freeman, Cooper, 1975), pp. 43-46. The material recycling of renewable resources presents severe problems, Commission on Natural Resources, National Research Council, Renewable Resources for Industrial Materials, A Report of the Committee on Renewable Resources for Industrial Materials, Board of Agriculture and Renewable Resources, (Washington, D.C.: National Academy of Sciences, 1976), pp. 59-60.

(23) An interesting book illustrating this is Corbin Crews Harwood, Using Land to Save Energy (Cambridge: Ballinger, 1977). See also P. Psomopoulos, "The Natural and Man-Made Physical Environment of Tomorrow," The Child in the World of Tomorrow: A Window into the Future, ed. Spyros Doxiadis, Jaqueline Tyrwhitt, and Sheena Nakou (Oxford: Pergamon Press, 1979), pp. 19-26.

(24)In looking at energy conservation possibilities. . .not only are there many ways to "save" or "conserve" energy (a fact that becomes obvious from the most cursory analysis of energy use), but. . .there are also many ways for conserving energy that pay for themselves in money terms. These savings have remained unrealized through consumer ignorance or institutional inertia.

(Bruce C. Netschert, "A Parallel – Energy and Minerals," National Materials Policy, Proceedings of a Joint Meeting of the National Academy of Sciences-National Academy of Engineering, October 25-26, 1973, (Washington, D.C.: National Academy of Sciences, 1975), p. 35.)

(25) Henry Carey, The Harmony of Interests (1868), pp. 13-14 in Miscellaneous Works, vol. I.

(26) Ibid., p. 4.

(27) Allen V. Kneese, "Energy Conservation Policies," 18 Natural Resources J. (1978), pp. 815-23. See also Talbot Page, Conservation and Economic Efficiency: An Approach to Materials' Policy (Baltimore: The Johns Hopkins University Press for Resources for the Future, 1977); and Hendrik Houthakker and Michael Kennedy, "Demand for Energy as A Function of Price," Energy Delta, pp. 529-54.

(28) Some of the reasons can be found in the impact upon the United States' economy by the higher energy prices of the 1970s, not even considering the impact of 1979 price rises in oil. "This impact is not limited to a reduction in the growth of energy consumption, but it has also resulted in a slowdown in economic growth, a weak recovery in capital spending, a substantial increase in employment, and a decline in

the growth of productivity. . . ." (Edward A. Hudson and Dale W. Jorgenson, "Energy Prices and the U.S. Economy," 18 Natural Resources Journal, 1978, pp. 877-97.)

(29) A very informative study was done for the Federal Energy Administration, R. Lind and R. Nathans, The Benefit-Cost Methodology for Evaluating Energy Conservation Programs, (Science Applications, Inc., 1975) reprinted in part in Energy and Natural Resources Law, ed. William H. Rodgers, Jr. (St. Paul: West, 1979), pp. 366-8. Petroleum products in the United States were price controlled after August 15, 1971. Robert T. Deacon, "An Economic Analysis of Gasoline Price Controls," 18 Natural Resources Journal, 1978, pp. 801-14, does not believe the controls constrained the price of gasoline in comparison with the market's influence. But then the market was constrained generally by governmental control and activity.

(30) Walter J. Mead, "Political Economic Problems of Energy – A Synthesis," 18 Natural Resources Journal, 1978, pp. 703-23.

(31) Energy conservation programs currently try to counter this; see Charles A. Berg, "Energy Conservation through Effective Utilization," Science July 13, 1973, vol. 181, no. 4095, pp. 129-30. See HUD Minimum Property Standards, vol. I, July 1974, pp. 6-7-3 to 6-7-7, vol. II, January 1975, pp. 6-7-4 to 6-7-8; vol. III, April 1977, pp. 6-7-4 to 6-7-8; 24 CFR (1978) sec. 200.925-933 and Appendix, July 17, 1974. A Time to Choose, America's Energy Future (Cambridge: Ballinger, 1974), dissent of William Tavouleas. pp. 402-3, points out the trouble in changing construction practices for any purpose. The Federal Energy Administration, through varying trade associations, pushed for substantial improvements in energy efficiency, 41 Federal Register pp. 51866-69, November 24, 1976. Both the Energy Policy and Conservation Act (P.L. 94-163, December 22, 1975) and the FEA Authorization Act (P.L. 94-385, August 14, 1976) were steps in the right direction. See also, Papers for a Seminar on the Impact of Energy on Considerations of the Planning and Development of Human Settlements, Economic Commission for Europe, Committee on Housing, Building, and Planning, Ottawa, Canada 3-14 October 1977; and see the debate on energy policy, National Academy of Public Administration Foundation, June 22-23, 1976, excerpted in Federal Energy Organization, September 1976, pp. 117-31, A Report prepared for Senator Percy for the Senate Committee on Government Operations, 94 Congress, Second Session, by the Congressional Research Service.

(32) William J. Weaver, President, Ohio Energy Systems, Inc., address to the American Gas Association, Columbus Dispatch, May 11, 1971, p. 13A. See E. McBean, D. Haycock, and J. Gorrie, "What Price Reject Heat?" 15 Water Resources Bulletin, 1979, pp. 684-91.

(33) A Time to Choose, dissenting opinion, p. 410.

(34) Berg. "Energy Conservation," p. 134. See A Time to Choose, dissenting opinion of Dean Abrahamson, pp. 355-7. There is a very useful nine-country analysis of transformation losses in Darmstadter et al., Industrial Societies, pp. 136-40.

(35) An idea of the energy "cost" can be found in R. B. Kidman, R. J. Barrett, and D. R. Koenig, Energy Flow Patterns for 1975 (Los Alamos, N. M.: Los Alamos Scientific Laboratory of the University of California, June 1977).

(36) Oil in the United States has received the greatest share of governmental incentive funds, coal the least, with natural gas, nuclear energy, and hydropower receiving intermediate amounts of funding. Between 1918 and 1978 the federal government provided somewhere between $123.6 and $133.7 billion in incentive funds. Of these, 42% "could be categorized as the action of levying a tax on the elimination, exemption or reduction of an existing one"; 26% "was in the form of disbursements for which the Federal government received no direct or indirect good or services in return"; 12% was "money expended to create incentives. . .through nontraditional services such as exploration, research, development, and demonstration"; 12% "involved government market activities such as TVA"; and the rest was described, in Bruce W. Cone and Roger H. Bezdek, "Incentives Report Overview," in Proceedings, First Seattle Workshop on Incentives Used to Stimulate Energy Production, ed.   Bruce H. Cone with the Battelle Incentive Team, (Richland, Wash.:   Pacific Northwest Laboratory-Battelle Memorial Institute, February 1979), pp. 1-1-1-7. This has been called a "first-rate data collection effort," "the first time a consistently calculated dollar estimate of the various incentives used in the past to stimulate all forms of energy production" had been put together, Thomas Sparrow, "The Policy Issues of Equity and Efficiency," Ibid., p. 2-1, his emphasis, in B. W.   Cone and others, An Analysis of Federal Incentives Used to Stimulate Energy Products (Richland, Wash.: Pacific Northwest Laboratory-Battelle Memorial Institute, March, 1978).

(37) Joseph H. Wherry, Automobiles of the World (Philadelphia: Chilton, 1968), p. 21. Siegfried Marcus was tutor to the Crown Prince. In 1864 the police had forbidden his car the use of the streets, Ibid., p. 17.

(38) Ibid., pp. 87, 106; see also Lord Montague of Beaulieu, Lost Causes of Motoring (New York: A. S. Barnes, 1971), vol. II, pp. 55-6. In terms of the ideal of speed, the best the steam car could do by 1930 was 15 seconds to start and the electric car had a top speed of about 60 miles per hour – which might seem fair by the late 1970s when the speed limit had been set at 55 miles per hour.

(39) American Petroleum Institute, Petroleum Facts and Figures, Washington, D.C.; 1971, p. 203. The relatively greater importance of gasoline in the United States energy situation is evidenced in Darmstadter et al., Industrial Societies, pp. 168-69.

(40) The article by Edward A. Hudson and Dale W. Jorgenson indicates clearly what they called the "dramatic impact" of higher oil prices on the United States economy, 18 Natural Resources Journal, 1978, p. 877, see note 28 supra. The same, or even more severe, impact is perceived in other urban-industrial societies.

(41) Bureau of the Census, Statistical Abstract of the United States for 1976, 97th ed., Washington, D.C., 1976, Table 912; Wall Street Journal, January 16, 1975, pp. 1, 4, stated one-third of the oil went to gasoline for private cars.

(42) Time, January 20, 1975, pp. 69-70. See also Wilson Clark with David Howell, Energy for Survival: The Alternative to Extinction (Garden City: Anchor Books, 1975), Chapter 3; World Energy Outlook (Paris: OECD, 1977); and Vincent E. McKelvey, "World Energy – The Resource Picture," 10 Case Western Reserve Journal of International Law (1978) pp. 597-612. The OECD has pursued a consistent view, Flora Levin, "European Harmony on Oil," New York Times, June 23, 1979.

(43) Congress has several times mandated improved fuel economy for the 1980s as well as for studies to improve energy efficiency. See for example P.L. 93-319, June 24, 1974; P.L. 94-163, December 22, 1975; P.L. 95, August 7, 1974; Clean Air Act, as amended to June 1, 1978, 42 U.S.C., section 4701.

(44) Time, January 20, 1975. Nearly five years later, however, the same magazine could report: "It has become a commonplace that America has scarcely begun to conserve", Marshall Loeb, "How To Counter OPEC", Time, July 9, 1979, p. 23.

(45) And even Norway's hopes have had to be reduced, Bjartmar Gjerde, Norwegian Minister of Oil and Energy, in Organization of Arab Petroleum Exporting Countries News Bulletin, April 1978, p. 33.

(46) Earl Finbar Murphy, "The Future of the Law for Energy and the Environment," 39 Ohio State Law Journal, 1978, 750, pp. 771-2. An excellent brief survey of the pros and cons of gasoline rationing is in the Conservation Foundation Letter, June 1979.

(47) Karen Elliott, "5-Year Delay," Wall Street Journal, January 16, 1975, p. 4. Subsequent events have shown that mileage can be improved by American car manufacturers, just as it has been elsewhere in the world.

(48) Barry Commoner, The Closing Circle (New York: Knopf, 1971), Chapter 12.

(49) The picture, in terms of national gaps, has been said to worsen as one moves further past 1980, Wilson et al., Energy: Global Prospects,

1985-2000, WAES Report (New York: McGraw-Hill, 1977), and United States Central Intelligence Agency, The International Energy Situation: Outlook to 1985, E. R. 77-10240U, April 1977.

(50) A Time to Choose, p. 399. Profesor Sax is not committed to the view that the federal property clause represents unrestrained power.

(51) Final Environmental Statement for Prototype Oil-Shale Leasing Program, vol. 5 (Washington, D.C.: Government Printing Office, 1973. Even a good strip mine reclamation program can be effectively dismantled, Marc K. Landy, "What Price Strip Mining?", RFF Resources, no. 53, Fall 1976, pp. 3-5. See the further work, Argonne National Laboratory for the United States Department of Energy, National Coal Utilization Assessment: An Integrated Assessment of Increased Coal Use in the Midwest, October 1977.

(52) A book surveying the technical means and problems of energy conversion from various sources is Jesse S. Doolittle, Energy: A Crisis – A Dilemma – Or Just Another Problem? (Champagne, Ill.: Matrix Publishers, 1977).

(53) A book exploring some aspects of a selection of these problems is Energy and Environment: Cost-Benefit Analysis, R. A. Karam and Karl Z. Morgan, eds. (Oxford: Pergamon Press, 1976). See also, R.   C. Seamons, Jr., J. L. Liverman, and F. D. Ordway, "National Energy Planning and Environmental Responsibility," 6 Environmental Affairs, 1978, pp. 283-300.

(54) A review of the problems of extracting coal, including the demand for water and land reclamation as well as other matters, is John P. Holdren, "Coal in Context": Its Role in the National Energy Picture," 15 Houston Law Review 1978, pp. 1089-1109.

(55) A survey of what the six Rocky Mountain states are trying to do to accommodate strip-mining while protecting the environment is Robert E. Peck, "Surface Coal Mining in the Western United States: How Does It Provide for Wildlife?," 54 North Dakota Law Review, 1978, pp. 337-64.

(56) For the efforts of the Federal government in the United States, D. Michael Harvey, "Paradise Regained? Surface Mining Control and Reclamation Act of 1977," 15 Houston Law Review, 1978, pp. 1147-74. Paradise seems very distant in this article.

(57) An article dealing with these and other issues in the context of one energy-obtaining technology, R. K. Olson, "Coal Liquefaction: Issues Presented by a Developing Technology," 12 Tulsa Law Journal, 1977, pp. 657-81.

(58) See dissent of D. C. Burnham, A Time to Choose, pp. 262-371. A description of the breeder reaction energy system and President Carter's decision to abandon plutonium as a fuel source is in John F. Shea III, "New Nuclear Policy and the National Energy Plan," 29 Baylor Law Review, 1977, pp. 689-738. See Victor Futter, "The Case for Multinational Reprocessing Centers – Now," 16 Columbia Journal of Transnational Law, 1977, pp. 430-50.

(59) William D. McCann, "Northern Ohio Becoming Nuclear Power Hotbed," Cleveland Plain Dealer, September 4, 1973. The expectancies of the size of nuclear power generation has since been revised downward, see notes 6-8 in Amory Lovins, "Invited Testimony" before Environment, Energy and Natural Resources Subcommittee of the Committee on Government Operations, U.S. House of Representatives, September 21, 1977. One also must take into account the far greater costs for atomic-fission power than those anticipated which may make them a risky investment for utilities, Robert Gillette "Nuclear Energy Cost Cause for Concern," Indianapolis Star July 25, 1976, quoting an MIT Center for Policy Alternatives study. Frank G. Dawson, Nuclear Power: Development and Management of a Technology (Seattle: University of Washington Press, 1976), argued "reactors with large power ratings are required in order to compete economically with fossil-fuel plants," p. 271. Amory Lovins, Soft Energy Paths (Cambridge, Mass.: Ballinger, 1977) generally attacked centrally-generated electricity, p. 87.

(60) Carolyn Brancato, "New Approaches to Current Problems in Electric Utility Rate Design," 2 Columbia Journal of Environmental Law, 1975, pp. 40-100, 54-55.

(61) On these costs, J. Michael McGary III and Troy B. Conner, Jr., "Nuclear Alternative: An Analysis of Paralysis," 28 Hastings Law Review, 1977, pp. 1209-43.

(62) Many world powers certainly have decided to proceed with nuclear power whatever costs or risks have been brought to their attention.

(63) Lovins, Soft Energy Paths, Part III, and Lovins, "Energy Strategy: The Road Not Taken," Not Man Apart, vol. 6, no. 20, November 1977.

(64) Allen Kneese, R. U. Ayres, and R. D'Arge, "Economics and the Environment," Environmental Law and Policy, Eva Hanks, A. Dan Tarlock and John Hanks, eds. (St. Paul: West, 1974), pp. 715-21. Lovins agrees with this, Not Man Apart, p. 7. See also William J. Lanouette, "Energy Report," National Journal October 1, 1977, pp. 1532-34.

(65) In 1972, it ranged from 150-350 acres for oil-fueled to 100-200 for gas-fired; to 200-400 for nuclear, to 900-1200 acres for coal-fired energy plants, Environmental Reporter, vol. III, p. 444. Water demands

even for power from sources alternative to fossil-fuels can be large. M. M. Eisenstadt, "Water Problems of Solar Hydrogen Production," 18 Natural Resources Journal, 1978, pp. 521-44, and Kenneth O. Kauffman, "A New Challenge for Western Water Supplies," 15 Water Resources Bulletin 1979, pp. 387-95.

(66) "Acid rain," as one example, is so serious that the First International Symposium on Acid Precipitation and the Forest System was convened in May 1975 at Ohio State University; and the New York State Assembly Standing Committee on Environmental Conservation and the Adirondack Park Agency jointly conducted a public meeting on the Acid Precipitation Problem at Lake Placid, New York, May 4-5, 1978.

(67) Ralph Borsodi, "A Plan for Rural Life," Agriculture in Modern Life, Baker Brownell, ed. (New York: Harper & Brothers, 1939) pp. 187-211.

(68) C. A. Doxiadis and John G. Papaioannou, Ecumenopolis: The Inevitable City of the Future (New York: Norton, 1976).

(69) On energy issues, this was not in doubt, Steven Terry, "Energy Needs of the Poor: A Saga of Ongoing Legislative Neglect and Local Abuse," 11 Clearinghouse Review, 1977, pp. 331-42.

(70) Sierra Club's 1972 Power Policy Conference (San Francisco: Sierra Club Special Publications, 1973). Amory Lovins believes this accomplishable without a necessary accompanying change in lifestyle, Soft-Energy Paths, Chapter 2. William Ophuls, Ecology and the Politics of Scarcity (San Francisco: W. H. Freeman, 1977) does not.

(71) Peter J. Wyllie, quoted in Environment Midwest, January 1975, p. 11, was an exception.

(72) "Energy and the Environment," Environmental Facts, July 1973, United States EPA. Also on energy conservation, see the report of the Environmental Quality Laboratory of Cal Tech which claimed the United States could get a 15-year "breathing space" on the energy crisis if it slowed the annual energy growth from 4.2% to 2.8% and by 1995 saved seven billion gallons of oil yearly through lighter-weight cars and improved heating and cooling in buildings, Columbus Dispatch, September 17, 1973, p. 8B. For these and similar reasons, many have urged a national energy policy on the United States, Robert B. Krueger, The United States and International Oil (New York: Praeger, 1975), pp. 83-108.

(73) Amory Lovins, Soft-Energy Paths, and Barry Commoner, The Politics of Energy, most notably.

CHAPTER 4

(1) Quoted in Atlas World Press Review, vol. 22, no. 7, January 1975, p. 8.

(2) Ivan Illich, "The High Life on Low Energy: II," New York Times, September 18, 1973.

(3) H. G. Wells, Anticipations (New York: Harper & Brothers, 1902). These articles first appeared in the Fortnightly Review, vols. 69-70 (N.S.), 75-76 (O.S.), April-December 1901, and in the North American Review, vols. 172-173, June-November 1901. At any rate, it is how the inhabitants of these houses are described when seen at their best by Mr. Wells.

(4) On how in the United States after 1933 these opportunities for suburban living were made available to an enlarged middle class through alterations in the credit system, as well as other institutional reforms, see E. Carter Macfarland, Federal Government and Urban Problems HUD: Successes, Failures, and the Fate of Our Cities, Boulder: Westview Press, 1978.

(5) The pioneer work on the impact of inflation on Europe after 1500 is Earl J. Hamilton American Treasure and the Price Revolution in Spain, 1501-1650 (New York: Octagon Books, 1970).

(6) Henry Homes, Lord Kames, Sketches of the History of Man, vol. III, (Hildesheim: Georg Olds, 1968), pp. 116-17. This decree was reaffirmed as late as 1672 by Louis XIV, indicating royal power even then did not perceive changed circumstances.

(7) Ibid., vol. III, pp. 118-19.

(8) Ibid., vol. III, pp. 117-21.

(9) The Spanish Crown in the Indies, which exercised a power far greater than any effective control over their capitals by the French or the far looser English authority, had pursued similar policies meant to delineate the edges of towns from the country around them. The move from country to town was to be clearly ascertainable for towns set up and maintained according to this plan, although the use of urban space in the New World was more generous in comparison with the traditional cities in Europe. See, "Royal Ordinance for the laying out of new cities, towns or villages," July 3, 1573, Article 129, in Zelia Nuttal, "Royal Ordinances Concerning the Laying Out of Towns," 5 Hispanic American Historical Review, 1922, 249. When Latin American cities began to participate in high energy culture, they then grew, sprawling into the countryside without regard to ancient plans meant to demarcate city from countryside.

(10) Homes, History of Man, vol. III, p. 131.

(11) George L. Hersey, Alfonso II and the Artistic Renewal of Naples, 1485-1495 (New Haven: Yale University Press, 1969).

(12) Homes, History of Man, vol. III, p. 125. Lord Kames, ironically, was not the last futurist to find a problem insoluble that later changes he did not foresee would totally alter.

(13) Daniel J. Boorstin, The Americans: The Democratic Experience (New York: Random House, 1973), p. 105. See also, Sam B. Warner, Jr., Streetcar Suburbs: The Process of Growth in Boston, 1870-1900 (New York: Atheneum, 1969).

(14) Address to the Southhampton (New York) Garden Club, quoted in Elizabeth Barlow, "The Battle for Southhampton," New York Magazine, September 24, 1973, p. 10. On the impact of the career of Robert Moses, see Robert A. Caro, The Power Broker: Robert Moses and the Fall of New York (New York: Vintage Books, 1975).

(15) Theodore H. von Laue, The Global City: Freedom, Power, and Necessity in the Age of World Revolutions (Philadelphia: J. B. Lippincott, 1969), p. 130.

(16) Ibid., pp. 127, 132, 137, 139.

(17) William F. Hueg, Jr., "Food for All," The Torch, vol. XLVII, no. 4, October 1974, pp. 18-22.

(18) Ibid. Lester Brown believed anyway in 1979 that the world was reaching the limit in biological erosion of forests, grasslands, and croplands. Resource Trends and Population Policies: A Time for Reassessment (Washington: Worldwatch Institute, 1979). Jan Schneider believes international procedures, though needing improvement, have prevented a worse situation, World Public Order: Towards an International Ecological Law and Organization (Toronto: University of Toronto Press, 1979), p. 107.

(19) Hueg, "The Torch" p. 19. A valuable critical article is Pierre Crosson, "Demands for Food and Fiber: Implications for Land Use in the United States," Land Use: Tough Choices in Today's World (Ankeny, Ia.: Soil Conservation Society of America, 1977), pp. 49-61.

(20) Fred Cottrell, Energy and Society (New York: McGraw-Hill, 1955), noted this disparity a generation ago.

(21) Barry Commoner, The Poverty of Power (New York: Knopf, 1976).

(22) Kenneth Boulding has emphasized the disaggregated character of energy at the same time that he has recognized the utility of the more modestly purposed integrated energy systems. Kenneth E. Boulding, "Determinants of Energy Strategies," Future Strategies for Energy Development (Oak Ridge, Tenn.: Oak Ridge Associated Universities, 1977), pp. 16-33.

(23) Edward Higbee, Farms and Farmers in an Urban Age (New York: Twentieth Century Fund, 1963), and especially United States Department of Agriculture, Contours of Change: The Yearbook of Agriculture, 1970, Washington, D.C.

(24) Roger Revelle, "Pollution and Cities," The Metropolitan Enigma, ed. James Q. Wilson, (Washington, D.C.: United States Chamber of Commerce, 1967), p. 88 for the stack pumps; p. 101 for the combined sewers.

(25) Some are turning away from this, however, see Harwood, Using Land to Save Energy, and Gary O. Robinette, Landscape Planning for Energy Conservation, A Study for the American Society of Architects Foundation (Reston, Va.: Environmental Design Press, 1977).

(26) Dick Netzger, "Financing Urban Government," Wilson, ed., The Metropolitan Enigma, p. 61.

(27) Quoted in New York Times, September 26, 1973, p. 17, and by Earl Finbar Murphy, "The Child and Changing Human Settlements," The Child in the World of Tomorrow, Spyros Doxiadis, Jaqueline Tyrwhitt, and Sheena Nakou, eds. (Oxford: Pergamon Press, 1979), pp. 421-2.

(28) Serious proposals have been put forward to avoid dire environmental consequences, Frederick R. Anderson, Allen V. Kneese, Phillip D. Reed, Russell B. Stevenson, and George Taylor, Environmental Improvement Through Economic Incentives (Baltimore: The Johns Hopkins Press for Resources for the Future, 1977); but the follow-up to such proposals could leave one a pessimist. See also Sydney Howe, Environment and Equity: A Survey of Metropolitan Issues (Washington, D.C.: Potomac Institute, 1977).

(29) The substantial rise in energy costs in the 1970s has forced an increase in integration of energy usages, Scott Fenn, Energy Conservation by Industry (Washington: Investor Responsibility Research Center, January 1979). It is, at best, a beginning.

(30) For example, see John Tarrant, "The End of the Exurban Dream," New York, December 13, 1976, p. 51. Richard Babcock is a vigorous opponent of fragmented urban land management, "Regulating Land Development: Some Thoughts on the Role of Government," Tough Choices, pp. 34-36. For a mixed report on gentrification, see Fergus Bordewick, "Future City", New York, July 23, 1979, pp. 32-40.

(31) Netzger, "Financing Urban Government" Wilson, ed., Metropolitan Enigma, p. 61.

(32) Scott Buchanan, Embers of the World: Conversations with Scott Buchanan, Harris Wollford, Jr., ed. (Santa Barbara: Center for the Study of Democratic Institutions), Center Occasional Paper, vol. III, no. 2, February 1970, p. 100.

(33) C. Northcote Parkinson, "How to Plan a City with Human Affection," The Knickerbocker News Union-Star September 18, 1971.

(34) James T. Maher, The Twilight of Splendor (Boston: Little, Brown, 1975), p. 25 for the references to Greber's work, and p. 73 for the quotation.

(35) See David R. Godschalk, "State Growth Management: A Carrying Capacity Policy" in Randall W. Scott with David J. Brower and Dallas D. Minor, eds., Management and Control of Growth, Washington, D.C.: Urban Land Institute, 1975, vol. III, pp. 328-339.

(36) Alexander B. Leman, "Neighborhood in Megalopolis," CBC-Radio Canada Interview, December 18, 1974. Planners in this situation talk about separating population into "communities" organized according to whether the persons within them are single, married couples without children, couples with children under age eight, or the aged. To use the word "community" for these social bits and pieces is to bankrupt the language. Vance Packard, A Nation of Strangers (New York: David McKay, 1972), p. 305. For an historic American view to the same effect, Daniel Boorstin, The Americans: The Democratic Experience (New York: Random House, 1973), pp. 130-36, 281. A more radical critique is in Hugh Stretton, Urban Planning in Rich and Poor Countries (Oxford: Oxford University Press, An OPUS Book, 1978), pp. 147-56.

(37) H. Wentworth Eldredge, ed., Taming Megalopolis, vol. I (New York: Anchor Books, 1967), p. 3.

(38) C. A. Doxiadis, Building Entopia (New York: Norton, 1976).

(39) Christopher Tunnard, "America's Super Cities," Eldredge, Taming Megalopolis, p. 17.

(40) An excellent book on one nation's efforts is Daniel R. Mandelker, Green Belts and Urban Growth: English Town and Country Planning in Action (Madison: University of Wisconsin Press, 1962). See also the pioneer American study by Charles Haar, Land Planning Law in a Free Society: A Study of the British Town and Country Planning Act (Cambridge: Harvard University Press, 1951).

(41) Mitchell Gordon, Sick Cities: Psychology and Pathology of American Urban Life (Baltimore: Penguin, 1965). The preface is dated June 1962. On the underpricing of public services demanded by the automobile, see Joe W. Russell, Jr., Economic Disincentives for Energy Conservation (Cambridge: Ballinger, 1979), pp. 82-85.

(42) See Melvin and Carolyn Webber, "Culture, Territoriality, and the Elastic Mile" in Eldredge, Taming Megalopolis, p. 40, p. 45. For related experiences in a socialist economy, see Jiri Musil, "Sociology of Urban Redevelopment Areas," in Human Identity in the Urban Environment, Gwen Bell and Jacqueline Tyrwhitt, eds., Baltimore: Penguin, 1972, pp. 298-299. Webber, loc. cit., p. 53, says "at the same time that social organization of cosmopolitan groups is being largely freed from the restraints of territorial place, the 'urban villagers' live out their lives in territorially bounded and territorially perceived structures."

(43) For example, consider the impact of high-energy mobility on popular recreation, A Program for Outdoor Recreation Research, Washington, D.C.: National Academy of Sciences, 1969; and Robert W. Douglass, Forest Recreation, New York: Pergamon Press, 2nd ed., 1975, as to motorcycles, p. 26; snowmobiles, 189-192; motor cars, 171 and elsewhere.

CHAPTER 5

(1) Gideon Sjoberg, "Cities in Developing and Industrial Societies," H. Wentworth Eldredge, ed., Taming Megalopolis, vol. I (New York: Anchor Books, 1967), pp. 142-43.

(2) Wilbur R. Thompson, "Urban Economics," Ibid., pp. 157-58.

(3) During the period of some of the most land-consuming suburban development in the United States in the 1950s private rates of interest for the building of single family residences ran at rates around 3-4% per year on fixed rate mortgages. By the end of the 1970s, such mortgages were running over 11% on variable rate mortgages permitting a maximum allowable increase of 2.5% over the life of the mortgage, with the expectation that by the early 1980s the base rate on such VRM residential mortgages would be 14%. Margaret Josten, "Variable Rate Mortgages: Betting On the Future," Cincinnati Enquirer, July 1, 1979, p. D-1.

(4) Gwen Bell and Jacqueline Tyrwhitt, eds., Human Identity in the Urban Environment (Baltimore: Penguin, 1972), p. 30.

(5) Mitchell Gordon, Sick Cities: Psychology and Pathology of American Urban Life (Baltimore: Penguin, 1965), p. 13.

(6) A. K. Campbell and Seymour Sacks, "Administering the Spread City" Eldredge, Taming Megalopolis, p. 299. A superb book sets forth a seemingly justifiable base for optimism in refocusing the American city in a more concentrated manner during the remainder of the twentieth century, Wolf von Eckardt, Back to the Drawing Board: Planning Livable Cities (Washington: New Republic Books, 1978).

(7) For the impact of past practices, Richard F. Babcock and Fred Bosselman. "Land Use Controls: History and Legal Status" Management and Control of Growth vol. I, 1975, pp. 196-210.

(8) J. M. Richards, "Lessons from the Japanese Jungle," Bell and Tyrwhitt, eds., Human Identity, p. 591.

(9) Ibid., p. 594.

(10) An excellent, comprehensive overview of how government does, and could, act on land use decision is Daniel R. Mandelker, Environmental and Land Controls Legislation (Charlottesville, Va.: Bobbs-Merrill, 1976).

(11) C. H. Waddington, "Biology and the Human Environment," Bell and Tyrwhitt, eds., Human Identity, p. 59. See also C. H. Waddington, The Ethical Animal, Chicago Phoenix Science Series, 1967.

(12) Paul Shepard, Man in the Landscape: A Historic View of the Esthetics of Nature (New York: Knopf, 1967), and J. Donald Hughes, Ecology in Ancient Civilizations (Albuquerque: University of New Mexico Press, 1975).

(13) Campbell and Sacks, "Spread City," note 6, supra.

(14) An excellent work on how to conserve energy even under such conditions of urban sprawl is Joel Darmstadter, Conserving Energy: Prospects and Opportunities in the New York Region (Baltimore: The Johns Hopkins University Press for Resources for the Future, 1975).

(15) S. Giedion, "Man in Equipoise," Bell and Tyrwhitt, eds., Human Identity, p. 225. See also Siegfried Giedion, Space, Time, and Architecture: The Growth of a New Tradition, 3rd edition (Cambridge, Mass.: Harvard University Press, 1954), part 4.

(16) This idea is explored by Kenneth E. F. Watt, Institute of Ecology, University of California, Davis, in a draft of a project dated January 5, 1975. It is also basic to the idea of Amory B. Lovins, Soft Energy Paths, especially on competitive capital requirements. See also K. E. F. Watt, The Titanic Effect: Planning for the Unthinkable (Stamford, Conn.: Sinauer Associates, 1974).

(17) New York Times, September 24, 1973, p. 17.

(18) This sense of malaise may account for the 1976 living preferences of Americans: 13% preferred a large city, 29% a small city, 21% a town or village, 37% rural life, see Jane O'Reilly, "Where Would You Live If You Could Live Anywhere?", New York, December 13, 1976, p. 144. For the first time in United States' history (except briefly in the 1930s), population movement in the late 1970s was away from metropolitan to rural areas. The momentum could slacken because populations in these "nonmetro" areas is almost totally dependent on the internal combustion engine. But other factors work strongly in favor of strengthening this trend, Glenn V. Fuguitt, Paul R. Voss, and Joseph C. Doherty, Growth and Change in Rural America (Washington: Urban Land Institute, 1979).

(19) Theodore von Laue, The Global City (Philadelphia: J. B. Lippincott, 1969), p. x. See also ibid., pp. 6-7. See also The State of the Cities: Report of the Commission on the Cities in the '70's (New York: Praeger with the National Urban Coalition, 1972).

(20) J. P. Thijsse, "Conurbation Holland," Eldredge, ed. Taming Megalopolis, p. 339.

(21) Boris Pushkarev and Christopher Tunnard, Man-Made America: Chaos and Control (New Haven: Yale University Press, 1963).

(22) S. B. Zisman, "Open Spaces in Urban Growth," Eldredge, ed., Taming Megalopolis, p. 294.

(23) Jane Jacobs may be right when she says that a park is where the citizen goes to get mugged. But even if she is right, so that they become areas into which only the caretakers can venture while armed, their other ecologic and economic work would still be performed. Jane Jacobs, The Death and Life of Great American Cities (New York: Vintage Books, 1963). Chapter 5, "The Uses of Neighborhood Parks," is not really that negative. See the update on her views in, Roberta Brandes Gratz, "An Interview of Jane Jacobs", New York February 6, 1978, pp. 30-34.

(24) Colin Buchanan, "The Outlook for Traffic in Towns," Eldredge, Taming Megalopolis, p. 374.

(25) It is not necessary to place economic usages in an adversarial relationship with the renewing environment, of course – only very common in the demand structure of open-ended, undifferentiated, and supposedly isolable patterns of growth. An example of how natural systems can be enhanced by industrial activity is Ave Buchwald, "Waste Heat Utilization from Thermal Power Plants in New York State," 1 Sea Grant Law Journal, 1976, pp. 211-54. See also Taylor A. Pryor,

"Growing Seafood on Shore," Bell, ed., Strategies, pp. 67-78. These offer rich possibilities.

(26) This is dealt with in Earl Finbar Murphy, Nature, Bureaucracy, and the Rules of Property: Regulating the Renewing Environment (Amsterdam: North Holland Publishing Company, 1977).

(27) Edwin T. Haefele and Allen V. Kneese, "Residuals Management and Metropolitan Governance," in Metropolitanization and Public Services, Lowden Wingo, ed. (Baltimore: Johns Hopkins Press for RFF, 1972), p. 59.

(28) For a harsh criticism based on somewhat different grounds, Murray L. Weidenbaum, Reno Harnish with James McGowan, Government Credit Subsidies for Energy Development (Washington, D.C.: American Enterprise Institute, 1976).

(29) For a view that sees state and national planning being able to take different courses, see Helmut J. Frank, "Arizona's Energy Economy," Arizona Energy: A Framework for Decision (Phoenix: Arizona Academy, April 1976), pp. 14-18.

(30) There are excellent insights in Carl E. Bagge, "Coal and the Nation's Energy Future," 15 Houston Law Review, 1978, pp. 1081-1088, p. 1086. He apparently would strengthen the staff of the Office of Management and Budget, as well as the Office of the President, for strong central coordination of Federal energy and environmental programs. This has little to do with the practical problems of counsel advising corporations as to the panorama of law involved in environmental law enforcement in the United States, see "Air and Water Act Enforcement Problems – A Case Study," 34 The Business Lawyer, 1979, pp. 665-723.

(31) For a brief statement of Jacques Cousteau's views, Calypso Log, vol. 4, no. 4 supplement, July/August 1977, p. 4.

(32) Barry Newman, "The Sea," Wall Street Journal, October 2, 1973, p. 1.

(33) E. J. Mishan on the "Panglossian effect" in his "Ills, Bads, and Disamenities: The Wages of Growth," The No-Growth Society, Mancur Olson and Hans Landsberg, eds. (New York: Norton 1973), p. 83.

(34) The limitations of energy supply and requirements for environmental protection were being reflected in the 1970s in regulations that were regarded as difficulties imposed externally on energy users, Government Institutes, Energy Users and Government Regulations, Linda E. Buck, ed., Proceedings of the Third Annual Energy Users Law Seminar, Washington: January 26-27, 1978.

(35) As an example of what government does for water as a resource for economic utilization, see Luis V. Cunha et al., Management and Law for Water Resources (Fort Collins, Colo.: Water Resources Publications, 1977).

(36) An interesting work on the breadth of science relative to governmental decision making is Mary E. Ames, Outcome Uncertain: Science and the Political Process (Washington: Communications Press, 1978).

(37) Haefele and Kneese, "Residuals Management," pp. 66-67. For the economic importance of keeping resource bases intact see the summary of his work by Talbot Page, "Sharing Resources with the Future." Resources, no. 56, September-December 1977.

(38) Sjoberg, "Cities," p. 122.

(39) C. A. Doxiadis, "Anthropocosmos," Bell and Tyrwhitt, eds. Human Identity, pp. 158-59.

(40) von Laue, Global City, p. 19.

(41) See Chadwick F. Alger, "The Impact of Cities on International Systems," Ekistics, vol. 44, no. 264, November 1977, pp. 243-53. See also Chadwick F. Alger and David G. Hoovler, "You and Your Community in the World", Learning Package Series no. 23, (Columbus, Ohio: Consortium for International Studies Education, International Studies Association, 1978).

(42) Campbell and Sacks, "Spread City," pp. 317, 319.

(43) The best argument for the incremental approach to urban problems was made by President Lyndon Johnson's last Secretary of Housing and Urban Development, see Robert C. Wood, "The Contributions of Political Science to the Study of Urbanism," Eldredge, Taming Megalopolis, p. 199.

(44) "Uniform effluent standards expand the demand for scarce clean petroleum fuels, in the face of rising costs, to inflate greatly the fuel cost component of production costs. Much of this inflation can be moderated by prohibiting the use of natural gas and oil products in new electric power plants. However, this prohibition increases considerably the capital requirements of the electric power industry to build new coal-fired operating plants." Russell G. Thompson, James A. Calloway, and Lilian A. Nowalanic, The Cost of Energy and A Clean Environment (Houston: Gulf, 1978), pp. 25-26.

(45) Barry Commoner, The Closing Circle (New York: Knopf, 1971). There are those, of course, who remain unpersuaded, Samuel McCracken, "Solar Energy: A False Hope," Commentary November 1979, pp. 61-67, which ranges critically over Commoner's work.

(46) Roger Revelle, "Pollution and Cities," The Metropolitan Enigma, James Q. Wilson, ed. (Washington, D.C.: United States Chamber of Commerce, 1967), p. 87.

(47) A governmental attempt to protect a scarce series of integrated resources is described in Protecting the Golden Shore: Lessons from the California Coastal Commission, Robert G. Healey, ed. (Washington: The Conservation Foundation, 1978).

(48) The historic origins of this human contradiction are philosophically discussed by Mulford Q. Sibley, Nature and Civilization: Some Implications for Politics, Loyola University Series in Political Analysis (Itasca, Ill.: F. E. Peacock, 1977).

(49) Gordon, Sick Cities, p. 407.

(50) An exploration of some of the regulations government has been impelled to in the United States as a result of the rise in the cost and the uncertainty in the supply of energy is in John A. Carver, Jr., "Governmental and Regulatory Aspects of the Energy Crisis," 20 Institute on Mineral Law, 1978, pp. 105-121.

(51) Dale Rogers Marshall, "Metropolitan Government: Views of Minorities," Minority Perspectives, Lowden Wingo, ed. (Baltimore: Johns Hopkins Press for RFF, 1972), p. 24, where it is not expected before the mid-1980s.

(52) C. A. Doxiadis, "Anthropocosmos," Bell and Tyrwhitt, eds., Human Identity, p. 161. See also, C. A. Doxiadis, Action for Human Settlements (New York: Norton, 1977).

(53) Richard Babcock would treat urban land as a public utility, Tough Choices, pp. 37-38. Others stress the value of its private ownership, Brian Robson, "Property Ownership," Habitat, vol. 1, no. 4, July 1976, pp. 36-39. Others, of course, would socialize it.

(54) Eleanore Clark, "Return to Rome," New York Review of Books, December 12, 1974, pp. 48-50.

(55) The difficulty of such adjustment appears most clearly in such a work as R. K. Jain, L. V. Urban and G. S. Stacey, Environmental Impact Analysis: A New Dimension in Decision Making (New York: Van Nostrand Reinhold, 1977).

CHAPTER 6

(1) W. Edward Wood, "'Last Chance' for Block I.?", Providence Journal, November 17, 1973, p. 1.

(2) "The Demands for Land: A Panel Discussion," Tough Choices, pp. 94-101.

(3) Wall Street Journal, February 10, 1975, which was up only from 33% in 1960. Viscount Etienne Davignon, chairman, International Atomic Agency, has said, ". . .the average American now uses twice as much energy as the average European, but at half the cost." Robert Keatlye, "Europe Doesn't Want a Grand Design." Ibid., January 4, 1977. Much more sophisticated comparisons appear in the tables in Darmstadter et al., Industrial Societies, though much of the data still is drawn from the early 1970s.

(4) Land Use Digest, vol. 11, no. 1, January 1978, p. 3. See also United States Department of Housing and Urban Development, Final Report of the Task Force on Housing Costs, Washington, 1978. This report is discussed by Wilson J. White, "What Price Shelter?", Urban Land, vol. 37, no. 7, July-August 1978, pp. 9-13. For a forecast of some of these costs through 1980, see Richard Ellison, "Another Perspective on Growth Management," Urban Land, vol. 38, no. 1, January 1979, pp. 3-8. This relationship of land cost to sale price is predicated, of course, on a continuation of the type of residential housing offered from 1945 to 1980. This is unlikely. Among other changes predicted for residential houses sold in the United States in the 1980s will be: (1) smaller in total square footage with smaller rooms; (2) more energy efficient; (3) closer to major employment centers; (4) built at much higher densities so that more dwelling units are on a parcel of land; (5) replacing private attached garages with communal parking structures or some other means to diminish the cost and prominence of the private parking structure; and (6) possessing "mega" rooms, combining several functions in one, remarks of Sanford R. Goodkin to the 21st Pacific Coast Builders' Association, in James L. Adams "Not 'Easy New World', Needn't Be 'Desolate'", Indianapolis Star, July 8, 1979.

(5) The role of the federal government in traditional land use decisions is covered in Part IV of Tough Choices.

(6) American economic history is replete with evidence of the dominance of this attitude in the popular mind, and in the minds of economic and political decision-makers, Joseph M. Petulla, American Environmental History (San Francisco: Boyd and Fraser, 1977).

(7) Nicholas Georgescu-Roegen, Energy and Economic Myths (Oxford: Pergamon Press, 1977), brilliantly reveals the costs others have not seen.

(8) John T. McIntyre, Steps Going Down (New York: Farrar and Rinehart, 1936), p. 27. The events occur in 1933 in the novel.

(9) John Keats, The Crack in the Picture Window (Boston: Houghton, Mifflin, 1957).

(10) Leif Bruneau, "Change in legislation and the procedures for granting concession to industry," Swedish Water and Air Pollution Research Laboratory, (undated). See also Environmental Policy in Sweden (Paris: Organization for Economic and Community Development, 1977).

(11) David J. Brower and James H. Pannabecker, "Growth Management Update: An Assessment and Status Report," 19 Natural Resources Journal, 1979, pp. 161-81.

(12) Emrys Jones, Towns and Cities (New York: Oxford University Press, 1966), p. 64.

(13) William Gillespie, consultant to the Scottish Development Board, speaking to the British Road Federation – British Tourist Authority Conference on Roads and Leisure, London Times, July 16, 1970.

(14) Usually though the relative scales were small by modern comparison, Arnold Toynbee, An Ekistical Study of the Hellenic City-State (Athens: Athens Technological Organization – Athens Center of Ekistics, 1971), pp. 24-26.

(15) Jones, Towns and Cities, pp. 95-96.

(16) The control of air pollution from mobile sources in such places as California is extraordinarily difficult when these land use conditions prevail, James R. Krier and Edward Ursin, Pollution and Policy (Berkeley: University of California Press, 1977), for the California experience, 1940-1975, on controlling auto exhaust emissions.

(17) Jones, Towns and Cities, pp. 62-63. For what this means for the high-energy city, see Corbin Crews Harwood, "The Role of Land Use in Energy Conservation," in Energy Conservation and the Law, Proceedings of the Annual ABA Standing Committee on Environmental Law, April 30-May 1, 1976, pp. 59-63.

(18) See Walter J. Mead, "Political-Economic Problems of Energy – A Synthesis," 18 Natural Resources Journal, 1978, pp. 703-23, which describes the energy crises of the 1970s as the product of the political economy.

(19) P. Auberson, "Urban and Regional Planning in the Western Greek World in Archaic Times," Ekistics, vol. 35, no. 206, January 1973, p. 43.

(20) C. A. Doxiadis, "Closing Remarks," Ibid., p. 51.

(21) Marion Clawson, "A Look to the Past and a Look to the Future," National Land Use Policy, Proceedings of a conference sponsored by the Soil Conservation Society of America, November 27-29, 1972 (Ankeny, Ia.: Soil Conservation Society of America, 1973).

(22) See Percival Goodman, The Double E (New York: Anchor Books, 1977).

(23) Lewis Mumford, The City in History: Its Origins, Its Transformation, and Its Prospects (New York: Harcourt, Brace, 1961), pp. 505-11.   See also Lewis Mumford, My Works and Days: A Personal Chronicle (New York: Harcourt, Brace, Jovanovich, 1979).

(24) Peter House, The Urban Environmental System (Beverly Hills: Sage, 1973), p. 65.

(25) H. G. Wells, Anticipations (New York: Harper & Brothers, 1902), pp. 50-54. The writing was done in 1900. I have previously noted that this book had already appeared in 1901 in the Fortnightly Review and the North American Review.

(26) Ibid.

(27) Ibid., p. 67.

(28) Ibid., pp. 112, 235-36, 282 respectively.

(29) See House, Urban Environmental System, pp. 245-49, on the varieties of urban migration.

(30) Richard D. Lamm and Steven A. G. Davison, "The Legal Control of Population Growth and Distribution in a Quality Environment: The Land Use Alternative," 49 Denver Law Journal 1972, pp. 4-6.

(31) People who do this are what Wendell Berry calls "nature consumers," Wendell Berry, The Long-Legged House (New York: Audubon/Ballantine, 1971), pp. 30-43.

(32) See C. A. Doxiadis, The Great Urban Crimes We Permit By Law (Athens: Athens Technological Organization, 1973).

(33) E. E. M., Book Review, Urban Land, vol. 31, no. 4, April 1972, p. 22.

(34) In June 1979 in the United States, at a time when sales of large and intermediate cars had dropped by an average of 20%, sales of the Rolls-Royce held up or increased. A Rolls dealer in Philadelphia, when asked how this was possible for a car getting only ten miles to a gallon of gas, reportedly replied, "The man who buys a Rolls has the tank filled at the pumps of some factory he owns." Radio News Report, June 30, 1979, WOSU-AM.

(35) Columbus Dispatch, January 24, 1971.

(36) ". . .the sheer quantities of land involved are the multiplying effects of changing land use patterns from energy activities," The Ford Foundation, Exploring Energy Choices, A Preliminary Report of the Ford Foundation's Energy Policy Project, Washington, D.C., 1974, p. 23.

(37) Kenneth E. F. Watt et. al., Land Use, Energy Flow, and Decision Making in Human Society (Davis: University of California Interdisciplinary Systems Group, 1974), p. 50.

(38) Ibid., p. 40.

(39) Ibid., p. 3. Ideas similar to this are greatly developed in Kenneth E. F. Watt, L. F. Molloy, C. K. Varshney, Dudley Weeks, and Soetjipto Wirosardjana, The Unsteady State: Environmental Problems, Growth, and Culture (Honolulu: University Press of Hawaii, 1977).

(40) Land Use Digest, vol. 5, no. 8, August 21, 1972, p. 3.

(41) Mihajlo Mesarovic and Eduard Pestel, Mankind at the Turning Point (New York: E. F. Dutton, 1974), p. 180. This is the second report of the Club of Rome. For the post-1973 impact through 1976 of energy prices, see Edward A. Hudson and Dale W. Jorgenson, "Energy Prices and the U.S. Economy," 18 Natural Resources Journal, 1978, pp. 877-97.

(42) Brian J. L. Berry, Megalopolitan Confluence Zones, ACE Publications, series report no. 10 (Athens: Athens Center of Ekistics, 1971), p. 2. The mixed character of suburban population and land use is explored in H. James Brown and Neal A. Roberts, Land Owners at the Urban Fringe (Cambridge: CRP Publications, Department of City and Regional Planning, Harvard University, 1978).

(43) This is why sharply rising energy prices discriminate so harshly against some segments of the poorest population in the United States in comparison with both other poor people and still more prosperous levels of society, Steven Ferry, "Energy Needs of the Poor: A Saga of Ongoing Legislative Neglect and Local Abuse," 11 Clearinghouse Review, 1977, pp. 331-42. On this topic, a book of considerable value is Energy and Equity: Some Social Concerns, Ellis Cose, ed. (Washington: Joint Center for Political Studies, 1979).

(44) Berry, Megalopolitan Confluence Zones, pp. 1-2, 4-5.

(45) Ibid., p. 6.

(46) It has been suggested that in the United States "changes in urban structure and settlement patterns" may be needed because of "the interactive nature of energy supply, delivery, and utilization with virtually all aspects of society and economy," Interim Report of the Committee on Nuclear and Alternative Energy Strategies, Assembly of

Engineering, National Research Council (Washington, D.C.: National Academy of Sciences, January 1977), compare p. 13 with p. 2.

(47) Mesarovic and Pestel, Turning Point, p. 146, distinguishing "organic" growth.

(48) Jean Barraud, "Faudra-t-il nationaliser l'espaceloisirs?", Le Figaro, July 17, 1970.

(49) Andre Fontaine, Book Review, Le Monde, August 1, 1970, p. 13. With post-1979 petroleum prices and Italy's need for foreign exchange to import petroleum (combined with the high cost of Italian goods in the world markets), one wonders if such auto traffic, on third thought, would remain so appealing.

(50) Barraud, "Faudra-t-il nationaliser," quoting.

(51) World Conference of Mayors, Milan, Italy, April 15-17, 1976, in Ekistics, vol. 42, no. 252, November 1976, p. 288.

(52) Dernieres Nouvelles D'Alsace, June 27, 1972, p. 42, recounting the abortive efforts of the Association for the Protection of Nature to save the Parc Baumann.

(53) See "Squeeze on Earthly Space," in Robert Rienow with Leona Train Rienow, Man Against His Environment (New York: Sierra Club/Ballantine, 1970), pp. 47-55. See also Lester Brown, Resource Trends and Population Policy: A Time for Reassessment (Washington: Worldwatch Institute, 1979).

(54) In land use, this attitude, and the efforts to avoid acquiring it, has an impact for beyond the problem of urban sprawl; and for parts of the world, the consequences pose more immediate disasters, Social and Technological Management in Dry Lands: Past and Present, Indigenous and Imposed, Nancy L. Gonzalez, ed., AAAS Selected Symposia Series No. 10 (Boulder: Westview Press, 1978).

(55) Guy Mountford, "How Tourists Menace Tourism," Atlas World Press Review, vol. 22, no. 2, February 1975, p. 62, discussing ideas of the World Wildlife Fund and the International Union for the Conservation of Nature and Natural Resources. See also Fred P. Bosselman, In the Wake of the Tourist: Managing Special Places in Eight Countries (Washington: Conservation Foundation, 1978).

(56) Whenever government acts to constrain the market or to shift established social values, it can expect resistance and reluctance to change. These problems, and how regulation seeks to cope with them, are explored in Robert A. Kagan, Regulatory Justice: Implementing a Wage-Price Freeze (New York: Russell Sage Foundation, 1978).

CHAPTER 7

(1) Richard Lamm and S. C. G. Davison, "Legal Control" 49 Denver Law Journal, 1972, 1, p. 37, quoting.

(2) Ibid., p. 51.

(3) E. Carter McFarland, Federal Government and Urban Problems, HUD: Successes, Failures and the Fate of Our Cities (Boulder: Westview Press, 1978).

(4) See Charles Haar, ed. Land-Use Planning 3rd edition (Boston: Little, Brown, 1977), pp. 519-21.

(5) Christopher Tunnard and Boris Pushkarev with Geoffrey Baker, Dorothy Lefferts Moore, Ann Satterthwaite, and Ralph Warburton, Man-Made America: Chaos or Control? (New Haven: Yale University Press, 1963), p. 23, quoting the English Architectural Review in the early 1950s.

(6) Ibid., p. 386.

(7) Guy Mountford, "How Tourists Menace Tourism," Atlas World Press Review, vol. 22, no. 2, February 1975, p. 62.

(8) See "Appalachia: Again the Forgotten Land" in Peter Schrag, Out of Place in America: Essays for the End of an Age (New York: Random House, 1970), pp. 125-40 and Albert J. Fritsch, The Contrasumers: A Citizen's Guide to Resource Conservation (New York: Praeger, 1974), Chapter 3.

(9) The population pressure upon the large urban regions induced some federal planners to seek to relieve that pressure by redirecting settlement to areas of current low population. This was most openly expressed in the work between 1970 and 1974 of the Commission on Population Growth and the American Future. An essential element in their work was to head off further emigration from other areas to what they defined as big cities, that is, urban regions with populations in excess of 400,000 persons. The commission believed that small towns in America, when they were not being swallowed in the waves of urban sprawl, were shrinking steadily in population and social significance. As a result, the Commission wanted to encourage a pattern establishing so-called medium-sized growth centers. They would not be Brian Berry's "spontaneous" nucleic centers in the zones of confluence forming in the expansion of metropoli which generate urban sprawl. They would be, instead, an effort by the Federal government to found centers of economic attraction away from existing magnets of urban-industrial growth. To be recommended a site had to be more than 75 miles from a metropolitan area of two million or more people. It had to have had a

combined population in the site's county of less than 350,000 people in the 1970 census and population growth average greater than the 1972 national growth average of 13.5 percent. And the site had to have geographic and resource potential to absorb a "massive dose of federal assistance to foster growth." The Commission issued seven volumes of research reports and statements of hearings. They are dated 1972, though some volumes were not issued by the Government Printing Office until 1973 and 1974. A report, subject to later change, was issued in 1972, Population and the American Future, The Report of The Commission on Population Growth and the American Future (New York: New American Library, 1972). The plans for growth centers in depressed rural areas are set forth at pp. 221-24. This Commission and its staff built on work done by the National Commission on Urban Problems whose report is Building the American City, 91st Congress, Second Session, House Document, no. 91-34 (1969). But the problem in locating land use and rechanneling population shifts through the establishment of other growth centers, as the Commission recommended, is that it is still a fragmentary and isolated approach. It is in no way comprehensive. As one of the Commission's critics, Niles Hansen, said about the possible success of the proposed growth centers, ". . .with it (success) there'll come all the problems of traffic congestion, inadequate recreational facilities, instant slums, pollution, ecology disruption, and so on," quoted in Franklynn Peterson, "Goodbye Guysville, Hello Growth Center," Columbus Dispatch Magazine, February 25, 1973, p. 11.

(10) See Erica Mann, "Habitat Postmortem," Build, vol. 1, no. 5, August 1976, pp. 7-8.

(11) Martin Beckman, Location Theory (New York: Random House, 1968), p. 105, and see also p. 110.

(12) Ibid., p. 120. It is predicted that in the 1980s rising costs will exert pressure to reduce travel by automobile, both to conserve gasoline and to protect air quality, and push in favor of redevelopment of downtown urban cores, Sanford R. Goodkin, remarks to the 21st Pacific Coast Builders Conference, Indianapolis Star July 8, 1979.

(13) Some very pertinent observations on these attitudes appear in James O'Toole and the University of Southern California Center for Future Research, Energy and Social Change (Cambridge, Mass.; The MIT Press, 1978).

(14) Beckman, Location Theory, pp. 97-98.

(15) Tunnard and Pushkarev, Man-Made America, p. 386.

(16) Walter Isard and others, Ecologic-Economic Analysis for Regional Development (New York: Free Press, 1972).

(17) The point is well made in C. A. Doxiadis, Ecology and Ekistics, Gerald Dix, ed. (London: Elek Books Ltd., 1977).

(18) Urban Growth and Land Development: The Land Conservation Process, Land Use Subcommittee, Advisory Committee to the United States Department of Housing and Urban Development, National Academy of Science and National Academy of Engineering (1972) in Donald G. Hagman, ed., Public Planning and Control of Urban and Land Development (St. Paul: West, 1973), especially pp. 111-14.

(19) Gary Washburn, Knight News Wire, Houston Post, October 14, 1973, quoting Professor Lewis and Huey Johnson, President, The Trust for Public Land.

(20) Ibid., quoting Robert K. Widdicombe, Jr., Executive Vice-President, Home Builders Association of Chicago.

(21) The history of this promise is set out in Land Use and Controls, 3rd rev. ed., Charles Haar, ed. (Boston: Little, Brown, 1977), pp. 185-87.

(22) Regulation and zoning have been the commonest approaches taken to land use control in the United States. They have been so unsuccessful that many doubt the ability of either the local units of government or of the states to ever perform successfully the administrative and political burdens of land use control. See, Fred P. Bosselman, "Elements of State Planning," National Land Use Policy, Soil Conservation Society (1972), p. 184. See Leonard U. Wilson, "Coping with Intergovernmental Confusion," Tough Choices, pp. 412-18.

(23) Norman Wengert, "Legal Aspects of Land Use Policies," quoted in National Land Use Policy, p. 159. In her address to the American Society of Planning Officials, Ann Louise Strong would avoid the "game" by regulating land, air, and water as public trusts and nationalizing development rights on the basis that spillover effects of land use decisions require such public changes. Land Use Digest, vol. 10, no. 7, July 1977, p. 2.

(24) Earl Finbar Murphy, "Private Rights versus Public Welfare," Land Use Course for Local Government Officials, April 26 and 27, 1979, sponsored by the Ohio Department of Natural Resources, The School of Natural Resources of The Ohio State University, and the Cooperative Extension Service of The Ohio State University.

(25) Kenneth E. Grant, "Land Use – Past and Present," National Land Use Policy, p. 18-19. Since then nothing has changed for the better according to a study on farm practices prepared by the United States Department of Agriculture, Don Kendall, "$35 Billion Effort May Slow Soil Erosion, Experts Believe," Columbus Dispatch, February 5, 1978.

(26) The Federal thrust for a continued fragmented treatment is recounted, in part, in J. McNamara "Integrating Energy Development and Land Management Goals in the National Forests, Or How Geothermal Resources Got Lost in the Woods", 11 Natural Resources Lawyer, 1978, pp. 325-41, producing an unintended but de facto moratorium, Ibid., p. 336. For a recent general treatment of problems in the United States concerning geothermal power, Owen Olpin and A. Dan Tarlock, "Water That Is Not Water," 13 Land and Water Law Review, 1978, pp. 391-440.

(27) Clawson, National Land Use Policy, p. 26.

(28) The pressure affects many kinds of resources in which there is a Federal ownership or sovereign superior presence, see as recent examples drawn from a huge potential of examples, Robert E. Peck, "Surface Coal Mining in the Western United States: How Does It Provide for Wildlife?", 54 North Dakota Law Review, 1978, pp. 337-64; R. K. Olson, "Coal Liquefaction: Issues Presented by a Developing Technology," 12 Tulsa Law Journal, 1977, pp. 657-68; Dale D. Goble, "Increasing the Use of the Sun: A Potential Role for Energy Utilities," 14 Ibid., 1978, pp. 63-108; and Selected Works in Water Resources, Asit K. Biswas, ed. (Champagne Ill.: International Water Resources Association, 1975).

(29) Doxiadis, Ecology and Ekistics, Chapter 3.

(30) C. A. Doxiadis and J. G. Papaioannou, Ecumenopolis: The Inevitable City of the Future (New York: Norton 1976).

(31) Clawson, National Land Use Policy, pp. 31-32. As Richard Babcock says, ". . .I am suspicious of proposed solutions that reject the necessity of occasional showdowns. Nowhere is this more evident than in land policy." Richard F. Babcock, Billboards, Glass Houses and the Law (Colorado Springs: Sheppard's, 1977), pp. 165-66.

(32) Clawson, National Land Use Policy, p. 36. See also Housing for all Under Law: New Directions in Housing; Land Use and Planning Law, Report of the American Bar Association Advisory Commission on Housing and Urban Growth, Richard P. Fishman, ed. (Cambridge, Mass.: Ballinger, 1978), pp. 9-11.

(33) These ideas are discussed extensively in Earl Finbar Murphy, Nature, Bureaucracy, and the Rules of Property: Regulating the Renewing Environment (Amsterdam: North Holland Publishing Co., 1977).

(34) Grant, National Land Use Policy, pp. 21-22, for the New Hampshire forest figures. As of 1978, it is calculated the national forests in the United States are worth $42 billion. Marion Clawson, "What's Ahead for the Forest Service?" American Forests, vol. 84, no. 1, January 1978, pp. 16, 50, even though private forests are predicted to have a greater

relative future value, William E. Towell, "Making the Best of It." Ibid., pp. 19, 56.

(35) Bernard Weissboard, "Satellite Communities," Urban Land, vol. 31, no. 9, October 1972, pp. 3, 9-10. For later concern with cost problems by major private, academic and governmental institutions, Land Use Digest, vol. 9, no. 9, September 1976, p. 2.

(36) Weissboard, "Satellite Communities", British new towns in the past were a "success" if their return on profit was 9 percent. In the United States, because of development demanding "properties with all problems solved," land by 1977-78 had reached record prices, Land Use Digest, vol. 10, no. 12, December 1977, p. 2. In 1979, the price of land was still rising, see Don Priest and Allan Borut, "HUD National Conference on Housing Costs," 38 Urban Land, no. 6, June 1979, pp. 5-11.

(37) "Environmental Analysis System," prepared for the Northern States Power Company by Commonwealth Associates, Inc., September 1972, p. 3.

(38) Ibid., pp. 7-9

(39) This is not to claim that the process now works in an atmosphere of unusual agreement, as is exemplified by recent Minnesota litigation, see PEER v. Minnesota Environmental Quality Council (Minn., 1978), 266 N.W. 2d 858. Subsequently, another public interest group, ECCO, sought to intervene on the remand to the Council and on appeal to the district court was summarily dismissed. Private communication to the author, May 21, 1979.

(40) Stanley Dempsey, "Land Management and Mining Law," in The Mineral Position of the United States, 1975-2000, E. N. Cameron, ed. (Madison: University of Wisconsin Press, 1973), pp. 109, 122. Mr. Dempsey was an attorney for Climax Molybdenum Company.

(41) The call in August 1979 by the Executive Council, AFL-CIO, for nationalization of such energy sources as oil and natural gas is the ultimate claim of a public interest which private mineral interests must always treat with seriousness.

(42) Peter T. Flawn, "Impact of Environmental Concerns on the Mineral Industry," Cameron, ed., Mineral Position, 95. This volume is a symposium of the Society of Economic Geologists.

(43) The author believes much of this is borne out in the United States by the Federal Land Policy and Management Act of 1976, PL 94-579, October 21, 1976, 90 Stat. 2793; the National Forest Management Act of 1976, PL 94-588, October 22, 1976, 90 Stat. 2958; the Clean Air Act

of 1977, P.L. 95-95, August 7, 1977 and 95-190, November 16, 1977; and the Surface Mining Control and Reclamation Act of 1977, P.L. 95-87, August 3, 1977. See the exhaustive Legislative History of the Federal Land Policy and Management Act of 1976, Committee on Energy and Natural Resources, United States Senate, Publication No. 95-99, April 1978, as an example of the effort needed for such legislation.

(44) For what the abandonment of central parts of American cities has done – and what its cause may be – see Robert W. Lake and Thomas E. Fitzgerald, Jr., Real Estate Tax Delinquency in the Central City: Private Disinvestment and Public Response (New Brunswick: Rutgers Center for Urban Policy Research, 1977).

(45) M. R. Durchslag and P. D. Junger, "HUD and the Human Environment," 58 Iowa Law Review, 1973, 805, p. 808, note.

(46) Address to an international conference on multihandicapped adults sponsored by the International Cerebral Palsy Society, quoted in the New York Times, October 14, 1973. Indeed, fragmenting demand does even worse things to nature. The multiple-terrain vehicle makes all the outdoors a playground of sacrifice. This new toy with its limited practical use is without the handicap of the auto, with its need for a pavement. It is the machine without the sort of handicap pointed out by Psomopoulos; and because it lacks such a limitation, nature, open space, and the entire land resource is allowed to be compelled to accommodate to its demand. Only a society that gave no regard to the entirety of the consequences imposed upon the environment by a particular human demand could be so casual about the land resource exposed to such an energy demanding vehicle. David Sheridan, Off-road Vehicles on Public Land (Washington: Council on Environmental Quality, 1979), exhaustively recites pros and cons, but his final conclusion is negative to the off-road vehicle for almost all natural surfaces.

(47) Goldner v. Planning Board of Ramapo, 30 N.Y. 2d 359, 284 N.E. 2d 291 (1972); Construction Industry Association v. City of Petaluma (Ninth Circuit, 1975) 522 F.2d 897: Metropolitan Housing Development Corporation v. Village of Arlington Heights, 429 U.S. 252 (1977), remanded, 598 F.2d 1283 (Seventh Circuit 1977), cert den., 434 U.S. 1025 (1978), consent decree of April 2, 1979, 312D. 245. On the judicial role in the United States in land use, see Richard Babcock, Billboards, pp.   49-64. For courts nonparticipation elsewhere, see Daniel R. Mandelker "Putting Together the Policy and Legal Decisions" Tough Choices, p.   421. See David J. Brower and James H. Pannabecker, "Growth Management Update: An Assessment and Status Report", 19 Natural Resources Journal, 1979, pp. 161-81.

(48) The Census Bureau reported in 1973 that "urban" growth had slowed since 1970. The growth rate for all metropolitan areas in 1971-73 was 2.2% and, if continued at that pace for the 1970s, growth in the "large

urban centers would be only about 11% compared with the 16.6% growth rate they had in the 1960s." One expert said this was due to job opportunities in (1) "the peripheral areas around big cities" and (2) "in remote rural areas where resort and recreationally oriented development projects are drawing year-round residents," Land Use Digest, vol. 6, no. 10 October 22, 1973, p. 1. On the other hand, metropolitan areas continued to gain population, while non-metropolitan areas continued losing, Table no. 14, p. 15, in Statistical Abstract of the United States (1976). The high cost of gasoline will not likely cause a change in this pattern.

(49) In today's current availability of the litigation process to challenge governmental action, this becomes particularly inappropriate, see Bert De Leeuw, "Energy and the Poor: The Role of Legal Services," 12 Clearinghouse Review, 1978, pp. 28-33.

(50) In testimony before the House Banking Subcommittee on the City, Frank H. Spink, Jr., of the Urban Land Institute said, ". . .very low densities and a pattern of 'urban sprawl' is (sic) probably energy inefficient. . .(E)nergy conservation should be made an integral part of all federally supported planning programs. . . ." However, as pointed out by Robert A. Burley of the American Institute of Architects, ". . .effective mechanisms for coordinating urban development with energy plans do not exist. . .", Land Use Digest, vol. 10, no. 11, November 1977, p. 3. This remains a basically accurate appraisal. In 1979, for example, the United States Council on Environmental Quality believed that the long-term easing of both energy and environmental problems lay in more efficient fuel productivity, Council on Environmental Quality, The Good News About Energy (Washington, D.C.: Government Printing Office, 1979).

CHAPTER 8

(1) Werner Heisenberg, "The Great Tradition," Encounter, vol. XLIV, no. 3, March 1975, pp. 52, 56. The change in the attitude of science is made very clear in Hans Reichenbach, The Rise of Scientific Philosophy (Berkeley: University of California Press, 1951), Chapter 7.

(2) An interesting series of papers on technology's impact on the oceans is in Technology Assessment and the Oceans, Proceedings of the International Conference on Technology Assessment, Monaco, October 26-30, 1975, Philip D. Wilmot and Aart Slingerland, eds., London and Boulder: FPC Science and Technology Press/Westview Press, 1977. See also Peter Nachant Swan, Ocean Oil and Gas Drilling and the Law (New York: Oceana, 1979).

(3) A controversial study by the Southern Indiana Health Systems Agency, which examined vital statistics for 1971-1975 in eighteen

southern Indiana counties (there are 92 counties in the state) showed the Ohio River counties, including the one for the city of Evansville, exceeded the state average for air-pollution rated deaths by at least 30 percent in three of six categories. Vanderburgh County (Evansville) was 60-200 percent above the state average in deaths caused by emphysema and 50-100 percent above the average in arterial deaths, while this county was in the top ten percent of counties in the United States for incidents of larynx cancer. The Indiana State Board of Health insisted "air pollution in the area is not that bad." Indianapolis News, July 7, 1979. But the Ohio River valley is a corridor in much of its length for air movement and so pollutants may well move through from elsewhere.

(4) This way to prediction relates to what Fred Hirsch has called "defensive goods" and a "qualitative hierarchy of output." Hirsch, Social Limits to Growth, a Twentieth Century Fund Study (Cambridge, Mass: Harvard University Press, 1976), pp. 57-8.

(5) See the grim predictions in Kenneth E. F. Watt, The Titanic Effect: Planning for the Unthinkable (Stamford, Conn: Sinauer Associates, 1974), pp. 157-58.

(6) A study of the disposal of trash in the United States showed long-standing strong evidence of this, see Katie Kelly, Garbage: The History and Future of Garbage in America (New York: Saturday Review Press, 1973). In a high energy situation, such as exists in the United States, about half the trash is paper products, since almost half of the paper produced in the United States goes into packaging. Because of this substantial quantity of paper in the trash under high energy growth, the quantity of solid waste is fairly price conscious to any fall in the general circulation of goods within the economy. When this happens, the amount of solid waste accordingly can be expected to go down. On the other hand, this affects the price of paper which, in turn, rebounds upon the efforts of government to recycle paper picked up by their municipal scavenging services. This means that overstrained municipal budgets have to find the money each year to dispose of what have become unwanted by-products. As a result, some in 1979 were considering burning the trash to generate electricity.

(7) BNA Environmental Report, vol. 3, no. 12, p. 343, July 21, 1972. This is reiterated in A Preliminary Assessment of the Health and Environmental Effects of Coal Utilization in the Midwest, Argonne National Laboratory for the United States Department of Energy, January 1977.

(8) The claim is made that the United States could maintain its present life style even though using forty percent less energy and more solar power, so that greater conservation in usage rather than greater production of energy supplies is seen as the answer. Energy Future, the Report of the Harvard Business School Energy Project, Robert Stobaugh and Daniel Yergin, eds. (New York: Random House, 1979).

(9) Cleveland Plain Dealer, July 24, 1972, took these statistics from Steubenville, Ohio. It is only one of many possible examples though recent evidence may have appeared of generally improved air conditions. See 8th Annual Report U.S. Council on Environmental Quality (1978). Others deny it, NRDC Newsletter, Vol. 6, nos. 2-3, March/April/May, 1977. Reports in 1979 indicate the United States had made little improvement in atmospheric conditions from air pollution, see interview with Dr. Thomas G. Ellestad of the United States Environmental Protection Administration, "Visibility Declines As U.S. Air Quality Worsens," Columbus Dispatch, June 10, 1979. As to how the "soup" is measured, see Frank Corrado, "Midwest 'in the soup': Hazy Blobs Abound," Environment Midwest, July 1979, pp. 12-16.

(10) Paul Colinvaux, "An Ecologist's View of History," Yale Review, spring, 1975, vol. LXIV, pp. 357, 365, is not impressed with threats. He says,

> Catastrophe is supposed to come from interfering with the air or with swamps or with the oceans, or else mass starvation is said to be imminent. All these predictions can be disposed of by logic or measurement or both. . . .Realistic models show that doubling the carbon dioxide content of the air as we are doing is unlikely to heat the earth enough to melt the Antarctic ice cap. I find this sad, for what exhilarating times we could have with the sea coming in, Miami Beach flooded, the continents changing shape and many cities to be planned anew.

(11) See Lester B. Lave and Eugene P. Seskin, with Michael J. Chappie, Air Pollution and Human Health (Baltimore: The Johns Hopkins University Press for Resources for the Future, 1978).

(12) Parker Bauer, "Outdoor Report," Columbus Dispatch, November 3, 1971, p. 54A, quoting Jacques-Yves Cousteau, address to the International Conference on Ocean Pollution. Captain Cousteau has not lessened his pessimism since this address. His comment on the efforts of the United States Government in 1979 to help the American fishing industry in order to triple current fish harvests: "It will work for a few years and then accelerate the depletion of natural stocks. The fishing problem is a question of imaginative, long-term planning for good, global management of the living resources of the ocean. No country has yet started to implement such a policy." Calypso Log, vol. 1, no. 5, July 1979, p. 2.

(13) Bauer, "Outdoor Report," Columbus Dispatch. See also the speech by the late Phillipe Cousteau to National NAACP Convention, June 30, 1977, Calypso Log, vol. 4, no. 5, supplement, September/October 1977.

(14) New York Times, October 23, 1971, p. C9. The 80-year turnover figure is from Arthur R. Miller of Woods Hole Oceanographic Institute.

The material from Jose Stirn is from the same article. In the succeeding years the conditions have not improved and many were wondering at the end of the 1970s if there was a basis for the hope that anything protective of the oceans ever would emerge. Margaret L. Dickey, "Should the Law of the Sea Conference Be Saved?," 12 International Lawyer, 1978, pp. 1-19.

(15) Puerto Rico, with its Operation Bootstrap, has been an outstanding example. An environmental group in that commonwealth, the Guaypao Conservation Association, reported in the early 1970s that the southeast coast of the island around Tallaboa Bay had "excessively high and unhealthy levels of various air pollutants." They reported that the water pollution levels there were also very high. Of course, as Alister Hughes of the Caribbean Conservation Association has said,

> . . .if industrialists would drop their active hostility and join the fight to save the environment, it would be a wise investment in their own futures.

Yet where in the development of the urban-industrial demand structure has this wisdom ever existed on any significant scale? See Ben Funk, "Industries Pollute Caribbean Shores," Columbus Dispatch, October 22, 1972, p. 16A.

(16) W. S. Comanor and B. M. Mitchell, "The Costs of Planning," 15 Journal of Law and Economics, 1972, 177, p. 185. Carl J. Dahlman, "The Problem of Externality," 22 Ibid., 1979, pp. 141-62, deals with the important role of transaction costs generally and in the need for endogenous institutional change in order to lower them.

(17) Funk, "Industries," Columbus Dispatch, The Puerto Rican case involved a suit of 125 fishermen against CORCO-Union Carbide. This was apparently a part of the trial judge's opinion. Apart from the newspaper account, I have not seen another report.

(18) Jacques-Yves Cousteau, Columbus Dispatch, August 4, 1971, p. 3B. See also his "The Causes for Concern," Mainliner, vol. 21, no. 1, January 1977, pp. 40-41.

(19) Peter N. Davis, "Theories of Water Pollution Litigation," Wisconsin Law Review, 1971, 731, pp. 777-79. See pp. 810-16 for riparian ownership.

(20) H. A. Regier and W. L. Hartman, "Lake Erie's Fish Community: 150 Years of Cultural Stresses," Science, vol. 180, June 22, 1973, pp. 1248-49.

(21) Marc J. Roberts, "River Basin Authorities," 83 Harvard Law Review, 1970, 527, p. 1555. On monetary costs, p. 1551 note. For more

recent work by this economist on what helps to determine public interest costs, see Marc J. Roberts and Ted Bogue, "The American Health Care Systems: Where Have All the Dollars Gone?" 13 Harvard Journal of Legislation, 1976, pp. 635-86.

(22) L. L. Roos and Noralou Roos, "Pollution, Regulation, and Evaluation," 6 Law and Society, 1972, pp. 509, 513.

(23) Lettie M. Wenner, "Enforcement of Water Pollution Control Law," Ibid., pp. 481, 495, though the facts are very complex. See also Lettie McSpadden Wenner, One Environment Under Law: A Public Policy Dilemma (Pacific Palisades, Calif.: Goodyear, 1976).

(24) Regier and Hartman, "Lake Erie's Fish Communities," Science, p. 1255. On the "good and bad news" on water pollution in the United States late in the 1970s, see Gladwin Hill, "The Water Pollution Fight," New York Times, December 24, 1978.

(25) On the "aqueous solution" that permits an "integrated system of biologic metabolic reactions" within it, see Patrick R. Dugan, Biochemical Ecology of Water Pollution 2nd ed., (New York: Plenum Press, 1975).

(26) Roberto Vacca, The Coming Dark Ages, J. S. Whale, trans. (New York: Doubleday, 1973), pp. 194-5.

(27) Some technologies, such as nuclear power, are believed by their critics to be too dangerous for monitoring but, instead, require abolition. Robert Jungk argues that only a regimented society could mobilize the resources adequately to control the risks of nuclear energy, see Robert Jungk, The New Tyranny: How Nuclear Power Enslaves Us (New York: Fred Jordan/Grosset & Dunlap, 1979).

(28) J. R. Mahoney, "A Regional Air Quality Monitoring System for New England," New England Consortium on Environmental Protection (NECEP), June 23, 1972, p. 2.

(29) Edward H. Bryan, "Quality of Storm Water Drainage from Urban Land," 8 Water Resources Bulletin (1972), pp. 578, 583. See also Isaac Yomtovian, "Optimum Alternatives for Controlling Combined Sewage Outflows – A Case Study," 15 Water Resources Bulletin, 1979, pp. 628-43.

(30) J. R. Mahoney, "Models for the Prediction of Air Pollution," Study Group on Models for the Prediction of Air Pollution, Organization for Economic Cooperation and Development (OECD), DAS/CSI/A.70.86, Paris, October 20, 1970, pp. 47-59. This was an early paper pointing out limitations and yet arguing the value of going ahead despite such a lack. Since then, improvements in environmental monitoring have been of

major consequence, but perfection remains, in many cases, both distant and elusive.

(31) Dugan, Biochemical Ecology of Water, p. 37.

(32) Nicholas Georgescu – Roegen, Energy and Economic Myths: Institutional and Analytical Essays (Oxford: Pergamon Press, 1977), pp. 237-42.

(33) "The combined effects of industrialization, population growth, and urbanization achieved. . .particularly since the end of the Second World War. . .brought us nearer to the brink of irreversible ecologic disasters and the depletion of some essential resources." Ignacy Sachs, "Human Environment," Jan Tinberger, RIO: Reshaping the International Order, A Report to the Club of Rome (New York: E. P. Dutton, 1976), Annex, p. 286. Lord Snow's observations are in, The Two Cultures, And a Second Look (New York: Cambridge University Press, 1969).

(34) For example, Harry Brown, You Can Profit From a Monetary Crisis (New York: MacMillan, 1974), pp. 23-24. The "bibliography," pp. 373-87, and Chapter 33, "Where To Go For Help," may be the most interesting parts of this book.

(35) The world price of petroleum quadrupled in 1973-1974. This enlarged price rose over seventy percent in 1979. The price of natural gas also rose, dramatically so in terms of percentages because of Federal price regulation of interstate transmission prior to November 1978, Natural Gas Policy Act of 1978, P. L. 95-621 November 9, 1978. In the mid-1970s the price of coal also rose sharply, but by mid-1979 the coal industry in the United States had fallen into a depressed condition which caused that industry to look forward to a Federal coal liquefaction and gasification program in the 1980s.

(36) Reported in Rowland Evans and Robert Novak column, Field Newspapers Syndicate, in the Indianapolis News, July 13, 1979.

(37) Bureau of the Census, Statistical Abstract of the United States (1976), 97th edition, Table 640, p. 399. It is difficult to find agreement among sources on agricultural income or very recent ones. It is only about 3% of the gross national income in the United States and is probably still shrinking in relative size, see Bureau of the Census, Statistical Abstract of the United States (1978), 99th edition, Table 715, p. 443, and Table 1191, p. 698.

(38) W. F. Hueg, Jr., "Food for All," The Torch, October 1974, p. 19.

(39) Dan Morgan, "U.S. Should Consider Food Cartel Against OPEC," Washington Post News Service, in the Indianapolis Star, July 15, 1979.

(40) This information, as well as references to his ideas, are taken from a speech of Marshall Harris at a seminar held in September 1970 at Indianapolis Law School. See his, "The Institutional Face of the Environmental Coin," 54 Nebraska Law Review, 1975, pp. 299-314.

(41) The meetings of the International Whaling Commission in July 1979 voted for a world wide moratorium on whaling by factory ships, "the boldest conservationist measure in any of its 31 annual meetings." But all the great whales except the sperm (blue, fin, humpback, and gray) have been depleted nearly to extinction; and the sperm has only a chance at survival. The minke whale, a small species, was exempted from the ban. New York Times, July 15, 1979

(42) See the materials gathered in Managing the Commons, Garrett Hardin and John Baden, eds. (San Francisco: W. H. Freeman, 1977).

(43) Barry Newman, "The Sea," Wall Street Journal, October 2, 1973, p. 1. The "brick-wall" reference is also from here. See also Oscar Schachter, Sharing the World's Resources (New York: Columbia University Press, 1977), pp. 37-51.

(44) Weather modification, partially because of the greater importance of agricultural and forest products to the general American economy, has received increased attention in the United States, see Weather Modification: Technology and Law, Ray Jay Davis and Lewis O. Grant, eds., AAAS Selected Symposia Series No. 20 (Boulder: Westview Press, 1978).

(45) The economist Nicholas Georgescu   Roegen is one who has consistently argued differently, see his highly original The Entropy Law and the Economic Process (Cambridge: Harvard University Press, 1971).

(46) A beautiful, impressionistic series of essays of what this means to wilderness and scenic America was written in the 1960s by Berton Roueche, What's Left: Reports on a Diminishing America (New York: Berkeley Medallion Books, 1970).

(47) This is the basic idea that I have been re-iterating since my book Governing Nature (Chicago: Quadrangle Books, 1967). Subsequent events have reinforced my conviction of the fundamental character of this view.

(48) Letter of February 22, 1971 in Wythe W. Holt, Jr., Book Review, 1971 Wisconsin Law Review, pp. 982, 988, 993.

(49) Ibid., p. 989.

(50) Walter Orr Roberts, president, University Corporation for Atmospheric Research, Boulder, Colo., to the 1965 convention, American

254   ENERGY AND ENVIRONMENTAL BALANCE

Meteorological Society, quoted in CF (Conservation Foundation) News-letter, January 1973, p. 5.

(51) An excellent book relating to how the law, public administration, and private management do relate to renewable natural resources, as well as some material on how they can, is Allen-Randolph Brewer-Carias, Derecho y Administracion de las Aquas y otros Recursos Naturales Renovables (Caracas: Coleccion Derecho y Desarollo, 1976). The author has produced a valuable amalgam of North and Latin American ideas on the subject.

(52) Mike McCormack, Schmitt Lecture, Notre Dame University, April 14, 1975, in Congressional Record, vol. 121, no. 59.

(53) The Rand Corporation study on synthetic fuels immediately preceded President Carter's proposals, Edward Merrow, Stephen Chapel, and Christopher Worthing, A Review of Cost Estimation in New Technologies: Implications for Energy Process Plants, Rand Corporation, July 1979. The study thought such a program could cost as much as $400 billion. This compares with the fact that the entire United States economy raised in 1978 less than $400 billion in capital. On the other hand, some thought an adequate program, though apparently not the sort of "all-out" program President Carter later called for, might cost as little as $40 billion. Even this "low" figure exceeds by several factors what Congress was thinking about for this program as late as May 1979. The Rand Corporation study was discussed, and these figures drawn out of it, in an editorial in the Wall Street Journal, July 13, 1979. President Carter's energy proposals in this regard were first set out in his Address to the American People of July 15, 1979, see 15 Presidential Documents, 1979, pp. 1235-41, as well as his two additional addresses on this subject on July 16, 1979, Ibid., pp. 1241-58.

(54) Frank Maloney, Richard C. Ausness, and J. Scott Morris with Frank D. Schwenke, A Model Water Code (Gainesville: University of Florida Press, 1972), pp. 74-75 for the quotation and the water illustrations.

(55) For an early expression of these ideas, see International Conference on Water for Peace, vol. 1, May 23-31, 1967 (Washington, D.C.: Governmental Printing Office, 1968) pp. 42-43, C. A. Doxiadis, "Water and Environment." See his map for both ecumenopolis and the universal garden in Ekistics, vol. 41, no. 247, June 1976, p. 335. See also C. A. Doxiadis and John G. Papaioannou, Ecumenopolis (New York: Norton, 1976), and C. A. Doxiadis, Ecology and Ekistics, Gerald Dix, ed. (London: Elek Books, Ltd., 1977).

(56) Dr. Daniel Lee, "Report on Agriculture," quoted in Henry Carey, The Unity of Law (Philadelphia: H. C. Baird, 1872), pp. 209-10, note.

(57) An important example is Decision Making in the Environmental Protection Agency, Committee on Environmental Decision Making, Commission on Natural Resources, National Research Council, Washington, D.C., National Academy of Science, 1977. The American Bar Association Special Committee on Energy Law has undertaken a study for the United States Department of Energy on how the American states make governmental decisions on short and long-term electric power demands, "Preliminary on the National Energy Project," August 1979.

CHAPTER 9

(1) On the "resurgence of romanticism" in analyzing land value, see Robert Dorfman, "An Afterward," When Values Conflict: Essays on Environmental Analysis, Discourse and Decision, Laurence H. Tribe, Corinne Schelling and John Voss, eds. (Cambridge, Massachusetts: Ballinger for the American Academy of Arts and Sciences, 1976), pp. 160-61. For the romantic impact on technology and nature, see Jan Huizinga, In the Shadow of Tomorrow, J. H. Huizinga, trans. (New York: Norton, 1936). This is "not suggesting some wishy-washy, romantic attitude toward land", Carl H. Reidel, "The Unfulfilled Agenda: Land-Use Planning," American Forests, vol. 85, no. 8, August 1979, p. 6, reprinted from G. Tyler Miller, Jr., Living in the Environment, 2nd ed. (Belmont, Calif.: Wadsworth, 1979).

(2) The development of the analytic views of these and other economists in their historic contexts is recounted in Joseph A. Schumpeter, History of Economic Analysis, ed., Elizabeth Boody Schumpeter, (New York: Oxford University Press, 1954).

(3) Bertrand de Jouvenel, "Water and the Future of Man," International Conference on Water for Peace, Washington, D.C.: Government Printing Office, 1968, vol. I. See also Bertrand de Jouvenal, Human Futures, (Atlantic Highlands N.J.: Humanities Press, 1974).

(4) Nicholas Georgescu-Roegen, The Entropy Law and the Economic Process (Cambridge: Harvard University Press, 1971), p. 2.

(5) Octavio Paz, Alternating Currents, Helen R. Lane, trans. (New York: Viking, 1973), p. 183. Nadezhda Mandelstam, however, disbelieves anyone could be genuinely enthusiastic about Engels' Dialectic of Nature, see her Hope Abandoned, Max Hayward, trans., (New York: Atheneum, 1974), p. 4. Paul Johnson in his Enemies of Society (New York: Atheneum, 1977), calls it "a characteristic specimen of pseudo-science," p. 152.

(6) Bertrand de Jouvenel, "Future of Man", vol. I, p. 71. He was a founder in Paris in the 1960s of Les Futuribles, a group organized for studying the development of the future.

(7) Ibid., vol. I.

(8) Quoted in Henry Carey, The Unity of Law (Philadelphia: H.C. Baird, 1872), pp. 127-29. Carey, whose business was publishing, printed his own work in versions filled with interesting material that an editor would have struck as extraneous or redundant to his main argument. But this little essay written by his friend Peshine Smith, adviser to the Japanese government after 1868 and later president of the University of Rochester, would otherwise have been lost.

(9) Ibid., pp. 391-92.

(10) Howard T. Odum, Environment, Power and Society, Table 8-1, p. 244, "Ten Commandments of the Energy Ethic For Survival of Man in Nature." See also George L. Tuve, Energy, Environment, Population and Food: Our Four Interdependent Crises (New York: Wiley-Interscience, 1976).

(11) Pollution: An International Problem for Fisheries, Rome: FAO 1971, p. 82. This is reprinted from FAO's annual report, The State of Food and Agriculture, and cites heavily from papers given at the FAO Technical Conference on Marine Pollution and its Effects on Living Resources and Fishery, Rome, Italy, December 9-18, 1970. The very datedness of the event, combined with the experience of what has happened since then, reinforces one's pessimism about the ease of effective action for environmental protection.

(12) Herman E. Talmadge and George D. Aiken, "On Regaining Paradise," American Forests, vol. 78, no. 9, September 1972, p. 8.

(13) Georgescu-Roegen, The Entropy Law, p. 216.

(14) Such works include Paul Bigelow Sears, Deserts on the March (Norman, Okla.: University of Oklahoma Press, 1935); Walter Clay Lowdermilk, The Conquest of the Land Through 7000 Years, 3rd ed. (Washington: United States Soil Conservation Service, 1953); and Edward Hyams, Soil and Civilization, The Past in The Present Series, ed. Jacquetta Hawkes (London: Thames and Hudson, 1952). And in the years since these books have appeared, the situation has not improved. As just one dreary example pulled from what could be many, the condition of the public rangelands in the United States at the end of the 1970s was called "deplorable." In the United States, not the Sahel, 83% of rangelands managed by the Bureau of Land Management of the United States Department of the Interior were in "unsatisfactory" condition, while over thirty percent of the range managed by the National Forest system produced at less than forty percent of capacity. Range management in the United States by its Federal government was described in 1979 as having been in a state of "paralysis" for the previous thirty years. See Maitland Sharpe, "An Appetite for Destruction," Outdoor America, vol. 44, no. 4, July/August 1979, pp. 6-9.

(15) Paul Chabrol, "La Desertification de L'Espagne: Est-elle Historique ou Climatique?", Memoires, Academie des sciences, inscriptions, belles-lettres de Toulouse, vol. 131, series 14, tome X, 1969, pp. 77, 79.

(16) Ray Moseley, "Soviet Woodland is Disappearing," a United Press International dispatch quoting heavily from Sovietskaya Rossiya, in the Columbus Dispatch, July 22, 1973, p. 64A.

(17) A conference, such as "Beyond Pollution Control," offered some hope. Sponsored by the United States EPA and the Department of Commerce, it was designed to indicate the aspects of environmental protection directly beneficial to industry, Gladwin Hill, "Some Factories Gain by Abating Pollution," New York Times, January 20, 1977. The same may be said for the ideas of Milton Wessel as applied in Tom Alexander, "A Promising Try at Environmental Detente for Coal," Fortune, February 13, 1978, pp. 94-102. See Milton R. Wessel, The Rule of Reason: A New Approach to Corporate Litigation (Reading, Mass.: Addison-Wesley, 1976). See also David O'Connor, "Environmental Mediation: The State of the Art," 2 EJA Review, 1978, pp. 9-17. But too little has come from any of this.

(18) Russell J. Seibert, chairman, environmental committee, American Horticultural Society, in Philadelphia Inquirer, September 16, 1970, p. 42.

(19) Thornton Wilder, The Eighth Day (New York: Harper & Row, 1967), p. 12.

(20) Interview with Senator Henry Jackson, Chairman of the United States Senate Energy and Natural Resources Committee, July 16, 1979, National Public Radio, WFIU-FM. Senator Jackson had earlier introduced legislation that proved predictive of President Carter's July 15, 1979 energy proposals, except for the Energy Security Corporation, Warren Weaver, Jr., "Revisions Appear Likely," New York Times, July 17, 1979, pp. 1, 13.

(21) Interview with Paul G. Craig, professor of economics and public administration, The Ohio State University, The Ohio State Lantern, July 6, 1979.

(22) Interview with John Hanson, founder, Winnebago Industries, quoted in the Indianapolis News, July 7, 1979.

(23) Air Conservation, Report of the Air Conservation Commission of the American Association for the Advancement of Science, publication no. 80, AALS (Washington, D.C.: AALS, 1965), p. 3.

(24) Ibid., p. 24.

(25) Ibid.

(26) Interview on National Public Radio, July 17, 1979, WFIU-FM, with a representative from Energy Action, a consumer advocacy group in the field of energy.

(27) Air Conservation, p. 36.

(28) Such a critic has been John Crosby, The Observer, September 13, 1970, quoted in Roberto Vacca, The Coming Dark Ages, J. S. Whale, trans. (New York: Doubleday, 1973), pp. 2-3. See also Eugene Bardach, "Save Energy, Save a Soul," Commentary, vol. 61, May 1976, p. 54 and his follow-up letter, Ibid., vol. 63, January 1977, pp. 23-25. There are others too numerous to list who hold these views.

(29) Air Conservation, pp. 9-10. The United States EPA proposed "selling the right to pollute to the highest bidder. . .to let the market-place determine which uses of a particular pollutant should continue." Wall Street Journal, December 30, 1977. The agency has followed through with its "bubble concept," which would allow facilities to meet air quality goals by increasing the level of control for emission sources having low marginal control costs while decreasing the level of control for sources with higher marginal control costs. CCH Pollution Control Guide, no. 283, April 2, 1979, p. 146.

(30) For a fuller discussion, Earl Finbar Murphy, Water Purity: A Study in Legal Control of Natural Resources (Madison: University of Wisconsin Press, 1961), p. 64.

(31) Mathew A. Crenson, The Un-Politics of Air Pollution: A Study of Non-Decisionmaking in the Cities (Baltimore: The Johns Hopkins Press, 1971).

(32) Ibid., pp. 137-40, citing Edward Banfield.

(33) In energy situations, all this is further complicated by the disaggregated character of energy supply and the consequent problem of trying to assemble even an approximate total energy budget. This seems evident in A National Plan for Energy Research, Development and Demonstration: Creating Energy Choices for the Future, United States, ERDA, 2 vols. 1977.

(34) Crenson, Un-Politics of Air Pollution, pp. 157, 178, 183-4.

(35) James R. Mahoney, "Multi-Disciplinary Training of Air Pollution Meteorologists," paper presented to the April 1971 joint meeting of the American Meteorological Society and the Air Pollution Control Association, p. 114.

(36) Norbert Dee, Gary Stacey, John Bowman, Syed Qasein, "Financing Abatement of Mine Drainage Pollution," Water Resources Bulletin, vol. 8, no. 3, June 1972, pp. 473, 474. For a study of how mineral exploitation taxes have operated and whether they have diverted the burden, see O. William Asplund, Severance Tax and Impact Trust Funds (Salt Lake: Utah Office of Legislative Research, 1976).

(37) These are the distortions in urban-rural interactions that have been common. Michael J. Webber, Impact of Uncertainty on Location (Cambridge, Mass.: M.I.T. Press, 1972), pp. 56-57.

(38) Stephen Rosen, "The Future of Hindsight and Foresight," Wall Street Journal, February 10, 1972. The "support. . .by social values of the nation" is essential in any analysis, Executive Summary, "An Analysis of Federal Incentives Used to Stimulate Energy Production" (Richland, Wash.: Battelle Pacific Northwest Laboratories, March 1978), p. 8.

(39) B. Koziorowski and J. Kucharski, Industrial Waste Disposal, trans. J. Bandrowski, ed. G. R. Nellist (New York: Pergamon Press, 1972), pp. 6-8. No one who has read regularly in the Water Resources Bulletin could underestimate the importance of work done in research in water quality and in practical applications of that research. At the same time, it seems to this author to fall short of the perfect conditions for counseling in management for which the scheme of A. Symolis calls.

(40) Mahoney, Models, p. 3. The data required for a model is described at pp. 60-67.

(41) But there are researchers working steadily in this direction of greater knowledge in the management of water quality, for example, see Stephen J. Fitzsimmons, Louie I. Stuart, and Peter C. Wolff of Abt Associates, Social Assessment Manual: A Guide to the Preparation of the Social Well-Being Account for Planning Water Resources Projects (Boulder: Westview Press, 1977).

(42) Paul E. Pugner and Trevor C. Hughes, "Regional Water Supply Planning by Interactive Systems Analysis," 14 Water Resources Bulletin, February 1978, abstract, p. 157.

(43) This sort of pressure is at least partially revealed in Econometric Dimensions of Energy Demand, A. Bradley Askin and John Kraft, eds. (Lexington, Mass.: Lexington Books, 1976).

(44) Mahoney, Models, pp. 71, 68, respectively.

(45) H. H. Liebhafsky, "'The Problem of Social Cost' in an Alternative Approach," 13 Natural Resources Journal, 1973, pp. 615, 676.

(46) This issue of inherent worth in nature as not necessarily being adequately reflected in the market, at least soon enough to protect both renewing systems and the economy dependent on them, is more fully discussed in Earl Finbar Murphy, "The Future of the Law for Energy and the Environment," 39 Ohio State Law Journal, 1978, pp. 750-87, 753-55, and in his Nature, Bureaucracy, and the Renewing Environment: Regulating the Renewing Environment (Amsterdam: North Holland Publishing Company, 1977).

√ (47) Conrad Richter, The Awakening Land, vol. I., The Trees New York: Knopf, 1940, pp. 8-9.

(48) Luther H. Gulick, American Forest Policy (New York: Duell, Sloan & Pearce, 1951), p. 19. For a brief, but informative, article on American forest resources, see Dorothy Behlen, "Are We Running Out of Forests?", American Forests, vol. 85, no. 7, July 1979, pp. 12-15.

(49) A comprehensive work that deals in historic context with the development of attitudes and shifting policies toward exploitation and conservation in the United States is James M. Petulla, American Environmental History (San Francisco: Boyd and Fraser, 1977). It does not reflect an easy optimism about what has happened.

(50) Paul Colinvaux, Introduction to Ecology (New York: Wiley, 1973), p. 230.

(51) Ibid., p. 568. His discussion of Margalef is at pp. 564-69. For a statement of Margalef's views, see Ramon Margalef, Perspectives in Ecological Theory (Chicago: Phoenix, 1975); and also the earlier book, Le Teoria de la informacion en ecologia, memoria lefda por Ramon Margalef y Discurso de contestacion by Francisco Garcia del Cid Arias, Mem. de la Real Academia de Ciencias y Artes de Barcelona, ter. epoca, vol. 32, no. 13, 1957.

(52) R. Buckminster Fuller with E. J. Applewhite; Synergetics: Explorations in the Geometry of Thinking (New York: MacMillan, 1975), pp. 86-89, for his use of entropy. He has stated a predictive quality in this and in other related regards appears in the work of his great-aunt, Margaret Fuller, the Marchesa Ossoli.

(53) See the amused account in Ellery Sedgwick, The Happiest Profession (Boston: Little, Brown, 1946).

(54) These ideas are restated from Nicholas Georgescu-Roegen, The Entropy Law and the Economic Process (Cambridge; Harvard University Press, 1971), p. xii, pp. 3-17. See also his Analytical Economics: Issues and Problems (Cambridge: Harvard University Press, 1966).

(55) Georgescu-Roegen, Entropy Law, pp. 19-21. See also Chapter VI, "Entropy, Order, and Probability," p. 141 ff. His ideas are explored in Scarcity and Growth Reconsidered, V. Kirby Smith, ed., (Baltimore: Johns Hopkins University Press for Resources for the Future, 1979), Part I.

CHAPTER 10

(1) The basis for such confidence was summarized by Rene Albrecht Carrie, The Meaning of the First World War (Englewood Cliffs, N.J.: Prentice Hall, 1965), pp. vi-vii. "The old view that the totality of resources was limited and constant had long ago been destroyed by the incontrovertible fact that industry is a creator of wealth," Ibid., pp. 3-4. As Leslie Paul wrote during World War II about modern man: "He wills the conformation of his nature to the ends he has come to regard as good, he seeks to compel as much of the non-personal world as he can master to the service of those ends." Leslie Paul, The Annihilation of Man: A Study of the Crisis of the West (New York: Harcourt, Brace 1945), p. 205.

(2) Francis A. Schaeffer, Pollution and the Death of Man, The Christian View of Ecology (Wheaton, Ill.: Tyndale House, 1972), pp. 83-4. The philosopher Iredell Jenkins has argued that all nature is interpreted for humanity by means of paradigms so that the data of occurrences within the human consciousness has motivational force for humanity rather than nature's direct impact. Nature appears to humanity, therefore, as a series of discrete resources to be exploited. Nature has no reality to people except as they generalize their experiences with nature, systematize those generalizations, turn this knowledge into a teaching tool, and then internalize the knowledge as a rule of conduct. Humanity in the formation of its moral universe has not yet accepted all the implications of high energy demand in a restricted system of environmental renewability. For some of these ideas, see Iredell Jenkins, Book Review, 16 American Journal of Jurisprudence (1971) 302, p. 317; Iredell Jenkins, "Nature's Rights and Man's Duties," Law and the Ecological Challenge, ed. Eugene E. Dais, (Buffalo: William S. Hein, 1978), pp. 87-92.

(3) Samuel Z. Klausner, On Man in His Environment (San Francisco: Jossey-Bass, 1971), p. 66. For some of his more recent views, see his "Household Organization and the Use of Electricity," in Energy Policy in the United States: Social and Behavioral Dimensions, ed. Seymour Warkov, (New York: Praeger, 1978), pp. 45-59.

(4) W. Warren Wager, Good Tidings: The Belief in Progress from Darwin to Marcuse (Bloomington: Indiana University Press, 1972), p. 317, quoting Jean Fourastie; p. 318, note, quoting Sidney Pollard. See also P. B. and J. S. Medawar, "Revising the Facts of Life," Harper's, February 1977, vol. 254, no. 1521, pp. 47-60.

(5) See the article by Peter D. Junger, "A Recipe for Bad Water: Welfare Economics and Nuisance Law Mixed Well," 27 Case Western Reserve Law Review, 1976, pp. 1-335.

(6) There is a refusal to do this in Ervin Laszlo, Goals for Mankind: New Horizons of Global Community, fourth report to the Club of Rome (New York: E.F. Dutton, 1977).

(7) Wager, Good Tidings, pp. 355-6.

(8) The complexities of this potential conflict are explored in C. S. Hollings, "Myths of Ecology and Energy," Future Strategies for Energy Development: A Question of Scale, ed. Irene Kiefer (Oak Ridge, Tenn.: Oak Ridge Associated Universities, 1977), pp. 35-48.

(9) Joseph W. Meeker, "Nature's Constitutional Rights," North American Review, new series, Spring 1973, vol. 258, No. 1, p. 11.

(10) Andre Teissier du Cros, L'Innovation pour une morale du Changement (Paris: Robert Laffont, 1971), p. 11.

(11) The quotation is from a study prepared by the accounting firm of Coopers and Lybrand for the National Coal Association and appears in a statement of the Ohio Valley Coal Operators Association in Ed Heinke, "Worry Pervades Coal Mining Country," Columbus Citizen-Journal, February 27, 1974, p. 15.

(12) William H. McNeil, The Rise of the West (Chicago: University of Chicago Press, 1963), p. 567; on power, p. 804. The establishment of this pace in European history goes back at least to the fifteenth century. Lynn White, Medieval Technology and Social Change (New York: Oxford University Press, 1962), p. 79, is replete with examples of what led to the industrial and energy revolution in the eighteenth century.

(13) McNeil, Rise of the West, pp. 803-4. One doubts if any events since 1963 would cause Professor McNeil to alter these words.

(14) Teissier du Cros, L'innovation, pp. 158, 237.

(15) Kenneth E. F. Watt, The Titanic Effect: Planning for the Unthinkable (Stamford, Conn.: Sinauer Associates, 1974), pp. 219-20.

(16) The Use of Land: A Citizens' Policy Guide to Urban Growth, A Task Force Report Sponsored by the Rockefeller Brothers Fund, ed., William K. Reilly (New York: Crowell, 1973), p. 14. On the social attitudes favoring uncontrolled use of land for urban sprawl, see Peter O. Muller, "Suburban Takes Over," Temple University Alumni Review vol. 27, no. 2, 1976, pp. 22-26.

(17) Teissier du Cros, L'innovation, p. 22, citing Herman Kahn. For a further Kahn view, see Herman Kahn, William Brown, Leon Martel and the Hudson Institute, The Next Two Hundred Years: A Scenario for America and the World (New York: Morrow, 1976).

(18) Interview on National Public Radio, June 30, 1979.

(19) E. J. Mishan, Making the World Safe for Pornography and Other Intellectual Fashions (LaSalle, Ill.: Library Press, 1973), p. 225. His ideas are technically presented in his Cost-Benefit Analysis (New York: Praeger, 1976).

(20) F. R. and Q. D. Leavis, Lectures in America (New York: Pantheon, 1967), pp. 21-22.

(21) Mishan, Making the World Safe, pp. 231, 262. The "Buddhist economics" of the late E. F. Schumacher, with their "production of local resources for local needs," is a response, Small Is Beautiful: A Study of Economics as If People Mattered (New York: Harper & Row, 1973). See also E. F. Schumacher and P. N. Gillingham, Good Work (New York: Harper & Row, 1978).

(22) Giorgio de Santillana, Reflections on Man and Ideas (Cambridge, Mass.: MIT Press, 1968), pp. 67-68.

(23) Ibid., p. 315, my translation.

(24) Walter Izard and others, Ecologic-Economic Analysis for Regional Development (New York: Free Press, 1972), p. 233.

(25) W. S. Robertson, The Future of Man in a Technological World (Edinburgh: St. Andrews Press, 1968), pp. 9-11, quoting Dr. Leach, Provost, King's College, Cambridge University.

(26) Frank H. George, Science and the Crisis in Society (London: Wiley-Interscience, 1970), p. 166.

(27) Philip Wagner, The Human Use of the Earth (New York: The Free Press, 1960), pp. 9, 241, note.

(28) Ibid., p. 226.

(29) Ibid., pp. 241-2, citing the 1901 views of Edmond Desmoulins. Public administration has worked more to intensify and accelerate the fragmentation of the renewing environment than to protect systemic operations, see Lajos Szamel, Legal Problems of Socialist Public Administration Management (Budapest: Akademia Kiado, 1973), p. 80, pp. 145-6.

(30) Wagner, Human Use of the Earth, p. 69. A similar foreboding prediction may be found in Frances M. Lappe and Joseph Collins, Food First: Beyond the Myth of Scarcity (Boston: Houghton, Mifflin, 1977).

(31) Interview with William Irwin Thompson, Time, August 21, 1972, vol. 100, no. 8, pp. 50-52.

(32) William Irwin Thompson, At the Edge of History (New York: Harper & Row, 1971), pp. 99-101. See also Ted Morgan, "Looking for Epoch B," The New York Times Magazine, February 28, 1979, pp. 32-33, 65-66.

(33) Warren Johnson, Muddling Toward Frugality (San Francisco: Sierra Club Books, 1978).

(34) United Press International dispatch, July 25, 1979, reporting on his Congressional testimony.

(35) New York Times, July 24, 1979.

(36) Resources Defense, A Report from the National Wildlife Federation, Washington, 1979.

(37) Arnold J. Toynbee, Civilization on Trial (New York: Oxford University Press, 1948), pp. 261-62.

(38) Arnold J. Toynbee, Experience (New York: Oxford University Press, 1969), p. 285.

(39) As long ago as 1936 C. C. Furnas warned that the long "life" of radioactive wastes would be a major problem for nuclear energy, The Next Hundred Years: The Unfinished Business of Science (Baltimore: Williams & Wilkins, 1936), p. 189.

(40) An exploration of many of the legal, tax, and economic aspects of this technology was undertaken by the Committee on Energy and Natural Resources, Section on Business Law, International Bar Association, part of which appeared in a special issue, International Business Lawyer, March 1979.

(41) Arnold J. Toynbee, Science in Human Affairs: An Historian's View (New York: Institute for the Study of Science in Human Affairs, 1968), pp. 13-14. See also Ibid., pp. 6, 8, 10, and 12.

(42) Toynbee, Experience, p. 294, note.

(43) Wilfred Beckerman, "The Myth of 'Finite' Resources," Business and Society Review, no. 12, Winter 1974-75, 21, p. 25.

(44) In the United States, some see environmental impact statements as partially serving this unifying purpose. Others are dubious. "Defining 'better decisions' under NEPA (National Environmental Policy Act) is difficult because there is no convincing argument that environmental concerns should in fact have ascendancy over other pressing national concerns. This precludes any approach other than requiring decision-makers to systematically weigh the priorities, costs, and benefits of their action." Melanie Fisher, "The CEQ Regulations: New Stage in the Evolution of NEPA," 3 Harvard Environmental Law Review, 1979, pp. 347-48, 380.

(45) Arnold J. Toynbee, Surviving the Future (London: Oxford University Press, 1971), pp. 29-30.

(46) Paul London, "Rene Dubos, The Eternal Optimist," Business and Society Review, no. 12, Winter 1974-75, 4, p. 9. See also Rene Dubos, A God Within (New York: Scribner's 1972), p. 224.

(47) For example, it has been suggested that water parliaments be internationally created to operate hydrologic regimes, see Ralph W. Johnson and Gardner M. Brown, Jr., Cleaning Up Europe's Waters: Economies, Management and Policies (New York: Praeger, 1976), p. 295.

(48) Wilfred Beckerman, Two Cheers for the Affluent Society (New York: St. Martin's Press, 1976). Views similar to his – such as those of Colin Clark, Herman Kahn, and Anthony Wiener – are vigorously attacked in Rene Dumont, Utopia or Else, Vivienne Menkes, trans. (London: Andre Deutsch, 1974).

(49) This was long ago noted by Jorgen Birkeland. "Primitive man removed himself from the neighborhood of his wastes: modern man removes his wastes from the neighborhood of himself." Microbiology and Man (Baltimore: Williams and Wilkins, 1942), p. 224.

(50) Roy Burke III, James P. Heaney, and Edwin E. Pyatt, "Water Resources and Social Choices," Water Resources Bulletin, vol. 9, no. 3, June 1973, pp. 433, 438-9, 441-2, and 444; Leon S. Mickler, "The Abyss," American Forests, vol. 84, no. 3, March 1978, pp. 13, 38, and 40.

(51) Fred L. Polak, Prognostics (New York: Elsevier, 1971), p. 199.

(52) Frederick Giggey of Peat, Marwick, Mitchell & Co., head of their project for the National Science Foundation, quoted in Arlen J. Large, "Learning to Discipline Technology," Wall Street Journal, May 2, 1972. See also Douglas M. Branson, "Progress in the Art of Social Accounting and Other Arguments for Disclosure on Corporate Social Responsibility," 29 Vanderbilt Law Review, 1976, pp. 539-683.

(53) On technology assessment, Technology Assessment Act of 1972, P.L. 92-484, October 13, 1972, 86 Stat. 797, 2 USCA sec. 471: on the prevention in advance of adverse environmental effects of technological innovation, Exec. Order No. 11472, May 29, 1969, 34 Fed. Reg. 8693, as amended; on the Science Court, see P. M. Boffey, "Experiment Planned to Test Feasibility of Science Court," Science, vol. 193, p. 129, July 9, 1976 and E. Callen, "A Reply," Ibid., p. 950, September 6, 1976; and on the environmental impact statement requirement, the National Environmental Protection Act of 1969, P.L. 91-190, January 1, 1970, 83 Stat. 852, 42 USCA sec. 4321: Fisher, loc. cit., note 44 supra.

(54) The Brazilian educator Darcy Ribeiro insists there is a ". . .necessity for a rationalization of social life, for an intentional construction of culture, and for intervention into the world of values that motivate behavior," since there are limits to both human endurance and natural systems, The Civilizational Process (Washington, D.C.: Smithsonian Institute Press, 1968), pp. 149-51.

(55) Hasan Ozbekhan, Technology and Man's Future, Rand Corporation, 1966, pp. 5-6.

(56) Ibid., pp. 9, 11-14.

(57) Doxiadis, Ecology and Ekistics, ed. Gerald Dix, (1977), Chapter 6.

(58) Santillana, Reflections on Man, p. 69.

(59) Alexander N. Christakis, "The Limits of Systems Analysis in Economic and Social Development Planning," Ekistics, no. 200, July 1972, 37, pp. 38-39.

(60) See Alfred Willener, The Action-Image of Society: On Politicization, A. M. Sheridan-Smith, trans., (London: Tavistock Publications, 1970), pp. 293-4. He sees normative planners as technicians who base their solution ". . .on a consciousness of the possible. . .defining the ends. . .according to the resources available. . .as defined in statistics. . . .(They are compelled to) offer practicable solutions. . .In their concern to take into account the resources, and possibly the social aspirations, within the system, they define, in fact,. . .their own image of the future society."

(61) Interview with John R. Hagely, energy planner, Battelle Memorial Institute, Columbus Dispatch, July 22, 1979. The Institute had worked on energy management plans similar to that described here for seventeen cities in the United States by mid-1979.

(62) Robert Waelder, Progress and Revolution: A Study of the Issues of Our Age (New York: International Universities Press, 1967), p. 290.

(63) Aurelio Peccei, The Chasm Ahead (New York: MacMillan, 1969), p. 229, quoting Ozbekhan.

(64) Ibid., quoting Eric Jantsch, p. 225. The prediction was even more premature in 1945 of Gaston Berger that it was "essential" for planning to be general, social and humanistic, Ibid., p. 228.

(65) Ibid., pp. 257-58.

(66) Dennis Gabor, Inventing the Future (New York: Knopf, 1964). See also his The Mature Society (New York: Praeger, 1972).

(67) Jean Fourastie, Le Grand Espoir du xxc Siecle (1950) quoted in Radovan Richta and a Research Team, Civilization at the Crossroads: Social and Human Implications of the Scientific and Technological Revolution, 3rd ed., Marian Slingova, trans. (Prague: Svoboda, 1969, p. 72, note.

(68) Richta, Civilization at the Crossroads, pp. 228-29. The conference at Lvov was concerned on how this would affect costs in hierarchical industrial administrative structures. The ideas of Lev Kritsman, set out in 1918, are stimulating, Ibid., p. 255, note. For some important insights, see Robert K. Merton, "Social Knowledge and Public Policy: Sociological Perspectives on Four Presidential Commissions," in Sociology and Public Policy: The Case of Presidential Commissions, ed. Mirra Komarovsky (New York: Elsevier Scientific Publishing Company, 1975), pp. 153-77.

(69) Amory B. Lovins, Soft Energy Paths: Toward A Durable Peace (San Francisco: Friends of the Earth International, 1977). See also Sam H. Schurr et al., An Overview and Interpretation of Energy in America's Future: The Choices Before Us (Washington: Resources for the Future, 1979), pp. 28-34.

(70) Waelder, Progress and Revolution, p. 94. He sharply distinguishes on this basis between "pluralist" and "regimented" societies.

(71) "Additional information may not by itself. . .lead to an acceptable overall energy policy. It may fail. . .because divisions exist over goals and values, and present institutions enable protagonists to prevent adoption of programs they oppose even if they cannot implement those they seek. . . .(D)isruptive change. . .may be on the horizon. . .," Milton Russell, "Energy: Policy Statement in an Eventful Year," Resources, no. 57, January/March 1978, pp. 3, 5. The successive trade-offs by the United States government in the spring of 1979 of diesel-fuel between farmers and truckers illustrated both bureaucracy as a cause of disruption and how expensive disruption can be, CCH Energy Management, no. 327, June 26, 1979, pp. 1-2.

(72) Gerard Piel, The Acceleration of History (New York: Knopf, 1972), p. 17.

(73) Ibid., p. 358.

(74) Ibid., pp. 368-69. The second home is made a particular case in point by Fred Hirsch, Social Limits to Growth, pp. 32-36.

(75) Energy use could drop, even as economic growth increases. This is, indeed, the likely scenario for the future. This would not exemplify the steady state. In fact, a controversial study has found, "Increase in energy prices increase the demand for labor relative to the demand for capital, thus increasing the return to labor relative to the return to capital," David J. Behling, "U.S. Energy Consumption and Economic Growth," in Energy and Equity: Some Social Concerns, ed., Ellis Cose, Washington: Joint Center for Political Studies, 1979, pp. 15-23. Considering what this would mean for productivity rates and inflation, it would usher in, at any rate, a very different sort of steady state than anyone in the early 1970s might have anticipated.

(76) Richta, Civilization at the Crossroads, p. 75, note: ". . .impulses to actions do not appear as definitive wants connected with man's personal self-assertion, but as abstract economic interests, external stimuli, mediating a variable context."

(77) Institute of Ecology, Man in the Living Environment, A Report of the Workshop on Global Ecological Problems (Madison: University of Wisconsin Press, 1972), p. 20. See also Ibid., p. 95.

(78) Ibid., pp. 271, 117, 169, 207. The rapidity of technological innovations has required a stretching of the powers of human adaptibility for which tradition offers few guides. See Loren C. Eisely, in Man and the Future, ed. James C. Gunn (Laurence, Kans.: University Press of Kansas, 1968), pp. 41-2. An interesting report on medieval man's fears in an unexpectedly similar regard is Peter Brimblecombe, "Attitudes and Responses Towards Air Pollution in Medieval England," Journal of the Air Pollution Control Association, vol. 26, no. 10, October 1976, pp. 941-45.

(79) Barry Commoner, The Poverty of Power (New York: Knopf, 1976). He is, perhaps, more optimistic in The Politics of Power (New York: Knopf, 1979).

(80) Beckerman, "The Myth of 'Finite' Resources," Business and Society Review, 1974-75, pp. 21, 22.

(81) John Paluszek, "The Top Ten Corporate Responsibility Happenings of 1974," Ibid., p. 27. The announcement was premature, considering what an advisory committee on increased coal production and use was

later required to consider, 43 Federal Regulations January 16, 1978, pp. 2229-40.

(82) Gregory Bateson, Steps to an Ecology of Mind (New York: Chandler, 1972), p. 483.

(83) Ibid., p. 503.

(84) Jacques Ellul, A Critique of the New Commonplaces, Helen Weaver, trans. (New York: Knopf, 1968), pp. 174-75.

(85) Buckminster Fuller in Gunn, ed., Man and the Future, p. 129.

(86) Ibid., p. 140. See also Amory B. Lovins, "Scale, Centralization and Electrification in Energy Systems" in Future Strategies, pp. 88, 127. The Environmental Defense Fund has claimed increased end-use efficiency, more efficient conversion processes, and such alternative energy sources as co-generation of electricity from various wastes would eliminate the need of most proposals for coal and nuclear power expansion, see David N. Carvalho, "Energy Conservation Through the State Public Utility Commissions," 3 Harvard Environmental Law Review, 1979, pp. 160-86, p. 182. See also Randall J. Fenerstein, "Utility Rates and Solar Commercialization," 1 Solar Law Reporter, 1979, pp. 305-68, and Robert W. Gilman and Richard E. Meunier, "Electric Utilities and Solar Energy: The Service Contract in a New Social Context." 30 Mercer Law Review, 1979, pp. 377-94.

(87) Fuller, Man and the Future, pp. 268-73.

(88) Bateson, Ecology of Man, p. 485.

(89) John Maddox, The Doomsday Syndrome (New York: McGraw-Hill, 1973), p.v. Danilo Dolci, The Man Who Plays Alone, Antonia Cowan, trans. (New York: Pantheon, 1969), explores what can happen if society loses faith in this attitude that Maddox so confidently treats as universal.

(90) On future energy supplies for the rest of the twentieth century and the possibility that higher prices could provide a supply through lowering demand, though the risks are substantial, see Schurr, Energy in America's Future, pp. 4-9, 15-19, 20-23, 52-4.

(91) Quoted in "Adam Smith," Supermoney (New York: Random House, 1972), pp. 76-77. The same quotation appears more fully in "Adam Smith," The Money Game (New York: Random House, 1968), pp. 219-20.

(92) Tim Congdon, "Are We Really All Keynesians Now?", Encounter, Vol XLIV, no. 4, April 1975, p. 23, on the contrary claims, "A quote from Keynes, no matter how slight and trivial, appears to silence

opposition. . .It can. . .sometimes serve as a substitute for thought." That is not my purpose here.

(93) Paul Colinvaux, Introduction to Ecology (New York: John Wiley, 1973), p. 580, says it is not sudden disaster which must be feared, ". . .but a steady and perhaps irreparable loss of our chances for a satisfying life."

(94) Although as a Japanese legal specialist insists is still the case in environmental exploitation, "It is the actual differences in. . .technology or economic power. . .and not any legal institutions which dictate the (results). . . .(T)he underlying rationale of free competition has been one of the basic values endorsed by modern history"; Shigeru Oda, I The Law of the Sea in Our Time (Leyden: Sijthoff, 1977), p. 194.

(95) Allan A. Hodges, "Do We Have the Energy to Conserve?" Urban Land, vol. 36, no. 2, February 1977, p. 10, reprinted from Mortgage Banker, February 1977. See Proceedings, Conference on Financing World Energy Requirements, Honolulu, November 30-December 2, 1977. The examples after 1978, especially, could be legion.

(96) See Strategies for Human Settlements: Habitat and Environment, ed. Gwen Bell, (Honolulu: The University Press of Hawaii for the East-West Technology and Development Institute, 1976), Part I. Item F for the VII Conference of Mayor's of the World's Great Cities, Turin and Milan, April 14-19, 1978, included "single cities. . .and ecological disasters."

(97) See the excerpts in La Presse, Brian and Jacqueline Morton, eds., (Lexington, Mass.: D.C. Health, 1972), part IV; and, one among many examples, Stockholm International Peace Research Institute, "The Dioxin Curse", Atlas World Press Review, vol. 24, no. 11, November 1977, pp. 13-15. A careful study of the environmental and public health problem is David A. Doniger, The Law and Policy of Toxic Substances Control: A Case Study of Vinyl Chloride (Baltimore: The Johns Hopkins University Press, 1978).

(98) Mireille Delmos-Marty, "Droit Penal et Protection de l'Environnment," Environmental Policy and Law, vol. 2, no. 4, December 1976, pp. 161-7. See also the Conservation Foundation Letter, January 1978, "A Growing Worry: The Consequences of Development."

(99) The United States Conference Board said, "If cleaner air and safer work-places were given explicit values and counted in output, productivity behavior would look better," John Cunniffe, Associated Press Business Analyst, "Improved Industrial Environment is Being Purchased at High Price," Columbus Dispatch, February 14, 1978. With the use of wood for fuel in the United States having expanded since 1973 at the rate of 15 percent per year, until in 1979 the United States Department

of Energy reported wood supplied Americans with half as much energy
as did nuclear power, American environmentalists might well be concerned over the maintenance of the renewable environment related to
wood as a resource, Indiana Rural News, Indiana Statewide Rural
Electric Cooperative, July 1979, p. 4.

Index

Adams, Henry, on energy, 173
Aggregation, political significance to environment
  of, 165-167, 169
Agriculture, effect of energy
  on, 60-61, 62, 63-66, 110,
  122, 140-143, 149, 240
Agriculture, government action
  concerning, 109, 117-119,
  142, 208, 243, 252, 256
Alternative energy sources,
  48-51, 53, 54, 64, 149,
  179, 206, 210, 212, 213,
  217, 239, 244, 248, 269
Animal power, problems of,
  61-62, 226
Aristotle, views on energy, 27
Artificial regimes, relation to
  nature of, 182-188, 193,
  197, 199, 201
Asimov, Isaac, science writer,
  25, 213
Atomic energy, problems of,
  50-51, 212, 223-224, 251,
  264
Arrow, Kenneth, economist, 28,
  214

Bateson, Gregory, anthropologist,
  196, 268
Barnett, Harold J., resource
  economist, 18, 210

Barraud, Jean, on leisure, 104,
  239
Beckman, Martin, location
  theorist, 111, 242
Beckerman, Wilfred, economist,
  186, 195-196, 200, 264,
  265, 268
Berry, Brian, demographer,
  101-103, 239, 241
"black cities", energy character
  of, 10-11
Borsodi, Ralph, agricultural
  planner, 52, 225
Brancato, Carolyn, energy
  economist, 51, 224
Bruneau, Leif, Swedish
  planner, 94, 236
Buchanan, Colin, traffic planner,
  79, 232
Buchanan, Scott, philosopher, 68

Calories, relation to energy of,
  9, 25, 28, 30, 64, 100, 155
Capital, alleged shortages of, 1,
  2, 55, 63, 75, 85, 105, 146,
  149, 187, 192-193, 195,
  199, 203, 231, 254, 267-268
Carey, Henry, American economist, 24, 27, 38, 40, 41,
  152, 153, 156, 212, 218,
  219, 255

Chabrol, Paul, historian, 158,
256
Chamberlain, John, journalist,
33-34, 215
China, energy history of, 19-20,
33, 211
Cheap energy, social demand for,
7, 20-21, 23, 29, 31-32,
33-34, 40, 41, 43, 45, 50,
51, 58, 132, 160-161, 207,
214, 215, 221, 229, 238
Ciamician, Giacomo Luigi,
Italian coal specialist, 33
City and region, relationship of,
95-97, 98, 99, 101-103,
111, 161, 191, 231, 237,
241-242, 246-247
Clark, Eleanore, on modern Rome,
88-89, 90, 235
Clawson, Marion, land economist,
97, 120-121, 237, 244
Club of Rome, 239, 252, 261
criticism of, 184
and Aurelio Peccei, 191-192,
266
Coal, social significance of, 6,
10-11, 17, 21, 22, 26, 33,
40, 48, 51, 62, 155, 223,
233, 262, 268
Collective benefits and harms,
163-167
Colinvaux, Paul, ecologist,
172, 173, 249, 260, 269
Common property, environmental
impact of, 81-82, 104,
113, 121, 128, 162, 163,
194, 208
Commoner, Barry, biologist, 33,
47, 55, 64, 85, 185, 195,
203, 215, 222, 227, 234,
268
Conurbation, 11, 21, 69, 74, 232
Costs, role of environmental, 15,
16, 26, 32, 47, 53, 79, 85,
86, 88, 119, 125-126,
145, 149-150, 166-167,
184, 200-201, 270

Costs, segregation from benefits
of, 11-13, 40, 43, 50, 61,
67, 68-69, 76, 80, 83, 87,
88, 93, 103, 106, 126, 132,
145, 164, 175, 200
Costs, when public indifferent
to, 7, 8, 11-12, 31, 40,
43-44, 48, 82, 132, 208
Cottrell, Fred, political theorist
on energy, 29, 30-31, 35,
36, 214, 216, 217, 227
Cousteau, Jacques, oceanographer,
82, 133, 135, 136, 204,
233, 249, 250
Craig, Paul, economist, 160-161,
257
Crenson, Mathew, 164-165, 258

Davis, Peter, environmental
lawyer, 136, 250
Demand, as determiner of social
values, 4, 5, 6, 8, 14, 16,
20, 27, 28, 31-32, 36, 38,
45, 51, 82, 93, 134, 204,
246, 259, 260, 268
deJouvenel, Bertrand, on water,
153-154, 255
deSantillana, Giorgio, historian,
181, 190, 263, 266
Doxiadis, Constantinos A., 52,
84, 87, 97, 119, 148,
207, 225, 234, 235, 237,
238, 242, 244, 254, 266
Dubos, Rene, biologist, 187, 210,
265

Ecumenopolis, 70, 74, 87, 89,
119, 225, 244, 254
Ekistics, editorial comment of,
73-74, 230
Elites, impact of energy usage
on, 71, 73, 103, 229-230
Electricity, effect on urban
growth of, 22-23, 32, 62,
211, 218, 234
Elizabeth I, order concerning
London, 58-59

Energy, ancient opinion of, 27,
28, 29, 96, 213, 235
Energy, brittle modern
dependency on, 21, 25, 26,
33, 41, 45, 50, 55, 129,
149, 177
Energy, cultural differences
caused by availability of,
29-30, 32, 34, 39, 56-57,
92, 111, 122-123, 134,
146, 209
Energy, cycle of, 9, 25, 156
Energy, disaggregated character
of, 30, 38, 39, 42, 64,
211, 227, 258
Energy, loss of, 172-174, 197,
206, 220
Energy, modern history of,
17-20, 22, 23, 24, 27, 29,
36-37, 100, 178, 205,
207, 210, 222, 235, 238,
262, 270
Energy, movements between
stored and current sources
of, 26-27, 55, 122, 213
Energy and social organization,
21, 23, 24, 27-28, 29-30,
32, 34, 38, 44-46, 53,
88, 111, 122-123, 183-184,
190, 207, 209
Energy as equivalent of society,
25, 27-28, 32, 140,
155-156, 207
Energy budgets, unified or
fragmented, 9, 10, 16, 25,
30-31, 39, 40, 42-43,
54-55, 64, 67, 75, 81, 82,
88, 89, 123, 139, 169,
206, 220, 227, 258
Energy conversion, environmental impact of, 9-10,
14, 17, 26, 30, 31, 39,
45, 46, 48-49, 54, 65, 73,
92, 101, 125, 127, 130,
132, 140, 146, 156, 160,
162, 169, 177, 195, 200,
204, 215, 232, 233, 237,
246

Energy crises, recurrences of,
17, 22, 23, 24-25, 30-31,
36-37, 48, 178
Energy demand and social instability, 78, 82, 85, 98,
99, 113, 119, 123, 129, 175,
177, 185, 219
Energy, importance of government to, 35, 38, 40, 41,
46, 108, 111, 118, 178-179,
183-184, 191, 199, 214,
217, 220, 221, 223, 233,
243-244, 254, 267
Energy patterns, need to change,
10, 20, 21, 23, 33, 46-47,
55, 205, 209, 239
denial of need, 198
Energy, relation to GNP of,
19-20, 32, 92, 194, 211,
215, 221-222
Energy resources, imbalanced
concentration of, 36,
48-49, 118, 212, 222, 223,
244
Energy sources, federal ownership in United States of,
48-49, 118, 126
Energy usage, increasing the
efficiency of, 39, 41, 42,
44, 45, 47, 197, 206, 209,
214, 218, 219, 220, 222,
225, 231, 247, 248, 269
Energy use, difficulties predicting,
18, 20, 43, 55, 131, 198-199,
209, 210, 211, 212, 214,
217, 222, 224
Engels, Friedrich, on nature,
153, 255
Entropy, 172-174, 176, 197,
199, 209, 253, 255,
260
Environmental impact statements (EIS), 188-189,
235, 264
Experts, limitations of, 166,
167, 169, 177-178, 182,
184, 186-187, 189, 204,
266

Faraday, Michael, on electricity, 22, 38
Fisher, Irving, economist, 51
Flawn, Peter, geologist, 126
Fontaine, Andre, on urban highways, 104, 240
Ford, Henry, 74
Forests, vulnerability of, 157-160, 170-172, 227, 244, 256, 260
Fossil fuels, as preserved energy, 9, 26, 28, 32, 33, 162
Fossil fuels, importance of, 6, 17, 22, 23, 25, 31, 46-47, 212
Fourastie, Jean, economist, 175, 192-193, 261, 267
Fuller, Buckminster, energy theorist, 39, 40, 173, 174, 180, 197, 218, 260, 268
Fuller, Margaret, philosopher, 174, 260
Furnas, C.C., historian of technology, 33, 264

Gabor, Denis, physicist, 192, 266
General fund, employment of, 12, 92, 93, 103-106, 123
Gentrification, 67, 68, 228
Georgescu-Roegen, Nicholas, energy ideas of, 209, 236, 251, 253, 255, 256, 260
Giedion, Siegfried, city planner, 77, 231
Goethe, J.W. von, ideas concerning nature, 130
Gordon, Mitchell, on city sprawl, 70-71, 229, 230, 235
Government, contribution to urban sprawl of, 12, 60, 63, 75-76, 88-89, 92, 100, 103, 108-109, 111, 179, 183, 217, 226, 231, 236
Government, role as mediator, 35, 36, 38, 39, 40, 41, 46, 48-49, 83-84, 105, 165-167, 169, 179, 182-184, 191, 193-194, 199-200, 257

Government and growth management, 83, 86-87, 88-90, 104-106, 107, 114-117, 118-119, 121, 124, 189-192, 199-200, 206, 241-242, 243-244, 245, 246, 253, 256, 258, 263
Greber, Jacques-Henri-Auguste, planner, 68, 229
Growth, limits and costs of, 2, 3, 5, 6, 11, 14, 16, 27, 52, 54, 70, 71, 77, 83, 86, 90, 91, 131, 140-141, 145, 147, 186, 187, 199, 252, 260, 261

Harris, Marshall, agricultural economist, 142, 143, 252
Heisenberg, Werner, physicist, 130, 247
Henry II, ordinance of, 58, 59, 226
Highway programs, effects of, 38, 44-45, 55, 57, 66, 70-71, 74, 79, 92, 93-94, 97, 98, 104, 108, 112-127
Homeostasis, ultimate attainment of, 15
Homo faber, 6-7
House, Peter, environmental planner, 97-98, 238
Howard, Ebenezer, Garden City of, 57, 74
Hurst, Willard, legal historian, 145

Illich, Ivan, theologian, 56, 225
Industrial Revolution, impact on attitudes of, 3-4, 6, 8, 10-11, 13, 17, 61, 95
Internal combustion engine, social effects of, 6, 8, 11, 22, 39, 43-45, 47, 56, 70-71, 98, 112, 132, 218, 221, 222, 229, 230, 231, 237, 240, 242, 246

Jaures, Jean, French historian, 4
Johnson, Brian, environmental lawyer, 144

Johnson, Warren, on the future, 185, 264
Jones, Emrys, Welsh planner, 94, 237
Jordan, Virgil, social commentator, 32, 33
Junger, Peter, environmental lawyer, 26, 213, 215, 246, 261

Kahn, Herman, social planner, 32, 179, 180, 203, 215, 262, 265
Kames, Lord, Henry Homes, on city size, 60, 61, 226
Keats, John, social commentator, 94, 236
Keynes, Lord, paradox of the aggregate, 194
on the future, 198-199, 269
Kopp, Ernst, theorist on technology, 182

Lamm, Richard, governor of Colorado, 36, 99, 108, 216, 238, 240
Land banking, 113-115
Land costs, 92, 100-101, 104-105, 106, 110, 111-113, 114, 118, 120, 122, 124, 126, 153, 208, 209, 224, 230, 235, 236, 242, 244-245, 255
Landscape, human invention of, 76-77, 82, 89-90, 95, 109-111, 183
Leases, government use of, 114, 116, 117, 118-119, 121, 126
Leavis, F.R., critic, 180, 263
Leech, Harper, social commentator, 23, 32, 33, 212, 213, 215
Leman, Alexander, city planner, 69, 229
Lewis, Walter, on land banking, 114, 243
Liebhafsky, H.H., economist, 170, 259

Life-support systems, fragmentation of, 6, 8, 10, 11, 13, 15, 31, 42, 49-50, 79, 131, 138, 144-145, 176-177, 195, 246
Lipinsky, Andrew, futurist, 78
Location theory in land use, 111-113, 259
Lovins, Amory, energy specialist, 20, 55, 193, 207, 211, 213, 217, 224, 225, 231, 267, 269
Lowi, Theodore, on nature, 165

Mahoney, J.R., on training experts, 166, 251, 258, 259
Margalef, Ramon, ecologist, 173, 260
Market, relation of law and politics to, 1, 12, 15, 35, 38, 40, 43, 46-47, 67, 83-84, 92, 103, 116, 128, 136, 149, 216, 220, 234, 240, 258, 269
Marx, Karl, on nature, 153
McIntyre, John T., novelist, 94, 236
McNeil, William, historian, 178, 262
Mead, Margaret, on city core, 66
Mead, Walter, 41, 220, 237
Megalopolis, 11, 69, 70, 74, 77, 81, 89, 95, 98, 101, 229
Merton, Robert, sociologist, 193, 267
Mill, John Stuart, stationary state, 153, 194
Mishan, E.J., economist, 180, 233, 262-263
Monitoring, value of, 135-137, 138, 139-140, 163, 164, 166, 168, 169, 181-182, 187, 191, 201, 251, 259, 267
More, St. Thomas, Utopia of, 57, 89
Moses, Robert, urban planner, 62-63, 227
Moynihan, Daniel Patrick, U.S. Senator, 108

Natural systems, interrelatedness of, 13-16, 67, 81, 83, 86, 87, 89, 133-135, 138, 144-145, 146, 148-149, 160, 161-163, 174, 181, 195, 209, 247-248

Nature, inability to serve as free good, 5, 14, 16, 80, 81, 85, 87, 92, 106, 127, 138, 143, 144-145, 146, 153, 156

Negentropy, 173, 197, 199

Oceans, impact on, 82-83, 130, 133-136, 143, 144, 187, 199, 204, 247, 249, 250, 252-253, 256

Odum, Howard, ecologist, 27, 28, 214, 256

Open planning, 124-125, 164-165, 245

Open space, urban impact on, 13, 14, 44-45, 54, 57, 66, 68, 74, 75, 79, 89, 91, 94, 101, 103-104, 106, 110-111, 114, 119, 120-123, 127, 232, 240, 246

Ophelimity, definition of, 140, 192

Owen, Richard, on nature, 154

Ozbekhan, Hasan, information specialist, 189, 191, 266

Parkinson, C. Northcote, historian, 68, 228

Piel, Gerard, social theorist, 194, 267

Planning, relation of values to, 16, 35, 43, 52, 77-78, 87, 100, 103, 105, 107, 108-109, 111, 112-113, 119, 125, 129, 137, 140, 147-148, 157, 160, 188-192, 195, 198, 200, 201, 265-266

Plato, attributed views on deforestation, 27, 158, 213 on city population, 87

Pollard, Sidney, economist, 175, 261

Price, effect on nature of, 141-145, 149, 150, 152-153, 171, 177, 185, 193, 205, 248, 252, 259, 269

Price resistance, 1, 34, 41, 44, 112, 141

Price elasticity, 19, 45, 248

Private demand, social support of, 91-92, 100, 102, 110-111, 118-119, 128, 141, 164-165, 196, 200, 226

Psomopoulos, Panayiotis, city planner, 127, 219, 246

Pushkarov, Boris, city planner, 79, 232, 241, 242

Rationing, 44, 46-47, 222

Refinery capacity, 37, 38, 216-217

Regulation, cost of, 117, 121, 124, 125, 129, 132-133, 164, 190, 193, 195, 209, 234, 235, 243, 247, 250

Ricardo, David, definition of land, 152-154, 155, 157-158, 159, 160

Richter, Conrad, novelist, 171, 260

Ritchie-Calder, Lord, on Mediterranean, 133

Roberts, Marc, economist, 137, 250

Rutenberg, Charles, American builder, 101

Saint Marc, Phillippe, city planner, 105

Sax, Joseph, environmental lawyer, 48, 223

Schumpeter, Joseph, economic historian, 8, 205, 255

Siebert, Horst, journalist, 56

Siebert, Russell, horticulturist, 159, 257

Sierra Club, proposals of, 53-54, 225

Sieyes, Abbe E.J.C., 3-5, 203

Simmel, George, sociologist, 5

Slurb, 11, 45, 67, 74, 79, 98
Smil, Vaclav, energy economist, 19, 211
Smith, E. Peshine, economist, 154-156, 255
Snow, Lord, two cultures, 140-141, 252
Social experience, obsolescence of, 3-4, 8, 21, 27, 29, 66, 120, 134, 171-172, 184-188, 197, 208, 261, 269
Soddy, Frederick, British scientist and economist, 24, 25, 212
Stirn, Jose, on Adriatic, 134, 249
Syniolis, A., bio-engineer, 168, 169
Synthetic fuels, 48-51, 126, 146, 149-150, 162, 184, 193, 215, 217, 244, 254

Talmadge, Herman, and Aiken, George, views on environmental planning of, 157, 256
Tankers, environmental effects of, 7-8, 204-205
Technology, relation to nature of, 15, 23, 26, 47, 54
Technology, relation to social decisions, 36-37, 38, 39, 40, 44, 45-46, 50, 54-55, 78, 130, 154, 169, 175-177, 180-182, 184, 188, 189, 197, 198, 219, 265, 268
Thompson, William Irwin, historian, 184, 263
Toynbee, Arnold J., on nature, 185-186, 237, 264
Tunnard, Christopher, city planner, 70, 79, 229, 232, 241, 242

Unified budgeting, values of, 81, 82, 83-84, 85, 87, 107, 127, 157, 169-170, 184, 188, 196, 209
United States, energy history of, 20, 24, 37, 44, 47, 100, 205, 211-212, 214, 216, 217, 221, 222, 239

Urban density, relation to energy of, 59-60, 62, 66, 79-80, 91, 96, 101-103, 109-110, 148, 179, 191, 226, 229, 230, 231, 236, 240-242, 246-247
Urban government, exposure of, 13, 62, 67, 68, 69, 81, 84, 85, 86-87, 98, 110, 114, 116, 191, 207
Urban growth, basis for fear of, 57, 58-60, 61-62, 65, 74, 78, 82, 129
Urban growth, character of, 11, 12, 22-23, 44-45, 56, 61, 70, 75, 91, 95-96, 98, 101-103, 104, 191, 206, 228, 229, 230, 231, 236, 242, 246-247
Urban growth, impact on environment of, 10-11, 12, 16, 17, 56, 66, 70, 73, 77, 80, 81, 82, 86, 91, 96, 99, 103, 107, 112-113, 122, 127, 130, 159, 160, 205-206, 247, 270
Urban mode, 11, 13, 22-23, 57, 62, 63, 64, 70, 74, 77, 79, 94, 121-122, 191, 229
Urban segregation and energy, 67, 68-69, 76, 82, 85, 86, 99, 102, 119, 129, 229, 239

Vacco, Roberto, predictions of, 138, 251, 258
Victorians energy problems and solutions of, 23, 57
Voluntary compliance, inadequacy of, 110, 137, 188, 251
von Laue, Theodore, educator, 63, 227, 232, 234
von Thunen, Johann Heinrich, location theorist, 111-113

Waddington, C.H., biologist, 76, 231
Wagner, Philip, theorist on technology, 182, 183, 184, 263
Wager, Warren, historian, 176, 261
Ward, J. Harris, 43

Waste, usages concerning, 9, 10,
        14, 30, 32, 42, 49, 71, 91,
        106, 133, 135-136, 161,
        162, 183-184, 186, 187, 195,
        206, 208, 232, 248, 265
Water, effect of demand on, 49-50,
        54, 65, 82-83, 136-137,
        138, 153-154, 158, 159, 199,
        208, 209, 224, 233, 251,
        265
Watt, Kenneth E.F., ecologist,
        100-101, 231, 238-239,
        248, 262
Wells, H.G., prophesies of, 56, 57,
        98-99, 226, 238
Weissbourd, Bernard, land
        specialist, 124, 244-245
Wilder, Thornton, novelist, 160,
        257
Wunderlich, Gene, on zoning, 115

Zoning, 108, 115-116, 121, 207,
        243

About the Author

Earl Finbar Murphy (J.D. Indiana University, LL.M and J.S.D., Yale) is Professor of law at the College of Law and Professor at the School of Natural Resources, College of Agriculture, both at Ohio State University. He is a member of the American Bar Association Special Committee on Energy Law, and a former member of the Advisory Panel at the Office of Water Resources Research at the United States Department of the Interior. Dr. Murphy is the author of Water Purity, Governing Nature, and Nature Bureaucracy and the Rules of Property: Regulating the Renewing Environment.